JOURNAL OF A WEST INDIA PROPRIETOR

MATTHEW GREGORY LEWIS was born in London in 1775, the first of the four children of Frances Maria and Matthew Lewis. His father, a high-ranking official in the War Office, hoped for a career in diplomacy for his son, but Matthew, who had been 'scribbling' since he was 14, started a prolific career as a writer by composing *The Monk* in ten weeks, at the age of 19. On publication in 1796 it became an extremely popular—and vilified—work, and Lewis, thereafter a literary celebrity, became known as 'Monk' Lewis. In 1798, legal action threatened and he was forced to produce a censored version of the work.

Lewis wrote no more novels. The majority of his work between 1796 and 1812 consists of plays, mainly spectacular melodramas and comedies, many of which proved extremely successful. He also produced some volumes of poetry, and was well respected as a poet.

After his father's death in 1812, and his inheritance of a large fortune, Lewis produced no more plays. Instead he made two visits to the plantations in the West Indies that he had inherited, in order to improve the lot of the slaves, between visits touring the Continent, staying with Byron and the Shelleys. His time in Jamaica would give rise to his final work, *Journal of a West India Proprietor*.

Lewis is constantly referred to as a lovable man; 'a jewel of a man' even, though according to Byron, argumentative and 'a damned bore'. Likewise, Walter Scott musing on Lewis in 1825 wrote 'How few friends one has whose faults are only ridiculous'. In 1818, returning from the West Indies, Lewis died of yellow fever.

JUDITH TERRY is Senior Instructor in the English Department at the University of Victoria, British Columbia. She is the author of *Miss Abigail's Part, or Version and Diversion* (London: Jonathan Cape, 1986), a novel which tells the story of *Mansfield Park* from a servant's point of view. One of her articles on Jane Austen makes use of Lewis's *Journal* in a discussion of *Mansfield Park*.

OXFORD WORLD'S CLASSICS

*For almost 100 years Oxford World's Classics have brought
readers closer to the world's great literature. Now with over 700
titles—from the 4,000-year-old myths of Mesopotamia to the
twentieth century's greatest novels—the series makes available
lesser-known as well as celebrated writing.*

*The pocket-sized hardbacks of the early years contained
introductions by Virginia Woolf, T. S. Eliot, Graham Greene,
and other literary figures which enriched the experience of reading.
Today the series is recognized for its fine scholarship and
reliability in texts that span world literature, drama and poetry,
religion, philosophy and politics. Each edition includes perceptive
commentary and essential background information to meet the
changing needs of readers.*

OXFORD WORLD'S CLASSICS

MATTHEW LEWIS

Journal of a West India Proprietor

Kept during a Residence in the Island of Jamaica

Edited with an Introduction and Notes by
JUDITH TERRY

OXFORD
UNIVERSITY PRESS

Oxford University Press, Great Clarendon Street, Oxford OX2 6DP

Oxford New York

Athens Auckland Bangkok Bogotá Buenos Aires Calcutta
Cape Town Chennai Dar es Salaam Delhi Florence Hong Kong Istanbul
Karachi Kuala Lumpur Madrid Melbourne Mexico City Mumbai
Nairobi Paris São Paulo Singapore Taipei Tokyo Toronto Warsaw
and associated companies in Berlin Ibadan

Oxford is a registered trade mark of Oxford University Press

Published in the United States
by Oxford University Press Inc., New York

First published as an Oxford World's Classics paperback 1999

British Library Cataloguing in Publication Data

Data available

Library of Congress Cataloging in Publication Data
Lewis, M. G. (Matthew Gregory), 1775–1818.
Journal of a West India proprietor: kept during a residence in
the island of Jamaica / Matthew Lewis; edited with an introduction
and notes by Judith Terry.
(Oxford world's classics)
Includes bibliographical references.
1. Jamaica—Description and travel. 2. Slavery—Jamaica.
3. Plantation life—Jamaica—History—19th century. 4. Lewis, M. G.
(Matthew Gregory), 1775–1818. I. Terry, Judith. II. Title.
III. Series: Oxford world's classics (Oxford University Press)
F1871.L67 1999   917.29204´34—dc21   98–31282

ISBN 0–19–283261–1

1 3 5 7 9 10 8 6 4 2

Typeset by Best-set Typesetter Ltd., Hong Kong
Printed in Great Britain by
Cox & Wyman Ltd., Reading, Berkshire

CONTENTS

ACKNOWLEDGEMENTS

I AM grateful to a number of old friends, and to some new found during the hunt for answers to elusive queries, especially Kim Blank, Michael Booth, Jean and Tom Cleary, Fred Frank, Gordon Fulton, Barry Higman, Jack Kolb, Cheryl Lumley, Judith Payne, Chris Petter, Elena Rossi, Mary Shelton, Mark Turner, and Christopher Wright. I also thank Peter Smith and Domenico Pietropaolo for giving so freely of their time and expertise in locating and translating some of Lewis's quotations. It has been a pleasure to make contact with Lorne Macdonald, who has generously shared with me his superior knowledge of Matthew Lewis. My greatest debt, however, is to Roger Bishop, who introduced me to Lewis's *Journal* in the first place.

INTRODUCTION

MATTHEW GREGORY or 'Monk' Lewis is remembered for one book, his first. Most people have not heard of the *Journal of a West India Proprietor*, his last, nor of the many works in between which made Lewis the leading popular dramatist of his day. In 1796, when Lewis was still only 20, *The Monk* broke upon the literary scene with spectacular success. It was the ultimate Terrorist novel or Hobgoblin romance, as the Gothic novel was then also known.[1] The work of a young man 'horribly bit by the rage of writing',[2] who had loved *The Castle of Otranto*, *The Monk* piled horror upon horror with cheerful exuberance: a sexually rapacious abbot, a cross-dressing female demon, dank dungeons, ghosts, gore, rape, murder, incest, sorcery, and a bleeding nun. Accordingly, it very quickly came under attack, and in the debate which followed, although it did nothing to lower sales, Lewis acquired a reputation for lewdness and blasphemy which, in the increasingly decorous temper of the times, haunted him like one of his own ghosts.

Following *The Monk*, Lewis had a string of other successes, chiefly on the stage, which was always his favourite medium. In the musical melodrama, *The Castle Spectre* (1798), he reworked—not for the last time—the horror story. But he also wrote a blank verse tragedy, *Alfonso* (1801), which was many times revived, as well as short stories, poems, songs, and translations, numbers of which remained current late into the nineteenth century. Lewis is a prototype of the mass popular writer, one of whose talents is to capture and give form to some incipient, collective emotion, as he did in 'Crazy Jane'. A ballad written after a chance encounter with a mentally disturbed woman, 'Crazy Jane' was set to music and it became a hit. Subsequently it

---

[1] Quoted by E. J. Clery, *The Rise of Supernatural Fiction, 1762–1800* (Cambridge: Cambridge University Press, 1995), 148.

[2] Self-description in a letter. Louis F. Peck, *A Life of Matthew G. Lewis* (Cambridge, Mass.: Harvard University Press, 1961), 210. The final section of Peck's biography is 'Selected Letters', his more accurate transcription of Lewis's letters than those in the first biography by Margaret Baron-Wilson: *The Life and Correspondence of M. G. Lewis . . . with many pieces in prose and verse, never before published*, 2 vols. (London: Henry Colburn, 1839). Baron-Wilson, however, records some material unavailable to Peck.

was mounted as a ballet, chapbooks appeared telling the 'true story' of Crazy Jane, the *Gentleman's Magazine* printed a Latin paraphrase, and there was even a vogue for Crazy Jane hats.[3] C. A. Somerset's play *Crazy Jane* was running at the Surrey Theatre, Drury Lane, in 1827. Lewis also captivated popular taste with an equestrian spectacle, *Timour the Tartar, A Grand Romantic Melo-Drama*, first performed at Covent Garden in 1811, and countless times later in the century. It is most famously alluded to in *Nicholas Nickleby*, where Crummles's proud boast that every member of his family has been involved in the theatrical profession includes the claim that 'my chaise-pony goes on, in Timour the Tartar' (ch. 22). No doubt if Lewis were writing today, his latest show would be in its tenth year in London and on Broadway, and the book of the show on full display in the airport terminal.

In such a context, Lewis's final work, the *Journal of a West India Proprietor*, is a sport. Although John Gibson Lockhart's comment in the *Quarterly Review* that it was 'the best of all creatures of his pen' reflects the general opinion, and Coleridge (who had lambasted *The Monk*) considered that it would 'live and be popular',[4] it created no great stir. It was not published until 1834, nearly twenty years after Lewis's death, by John Murray, who had refused it in 1817, probably only because he thought the £2,000 Lewis was asking too high. After the 1834 edition, there was another, slightly abridged, in Murray's Home and Colonial Library (1845, reissued 1861), under a revised title, *Journal of a Residence among the Negroes in the West Indies*, and it has reappeared only once since, in 1929. The notoriety of *The Monk* dominated Lewis's reputation, as it has continued to do.[5]

A reader today may well be surprised that the *Journal* has not fared better. It belongs to a well-established tradition of travel and explor-

---

[3] Peck, *A Life of Matthew G. Lewis*, 47. The painter Richard Dadd, in the mid-nineteenth century, sketched an illustration of Crazy Jane; certainly by the time of W. B. Yeats's poem, 'Crazy Jane and the Bishop', she had become proverbial.

[4] *Quarterly Review*, 50 (1834), 374; Coleridge, *Table Talk*, 2 Mar. 1834.

[5] *The Monk* has an impressive publication record, and in 1972 was even made into a movie: *Le Moine*, directed by Ado Kyrou, with screenplay by Luis Buñuel and Jean-Claude Carrière, France, Italy, West Germany, Cinerama, 1972. It has also generated much commentary as a forerunner of modern horror fiction, despite continuing opprobrium heaped upon it for artistic as well as moral reasons. See Frederick S. Frank, 'M. G. Lewis's *The Monk* after Two Hundred Years, 1796–1996', *Bulletin of Bibliography*, 52: 3. 241–60.

ation literature, and also to a considerable subset of the genre: accounts of the British West Indies published after 1787 as a result of the agitation about slavery. The *Journal* records a colonial encounter, between slave-holder and slaves, in the 'contact zone',[6] at a significant historical moment. Lively, engaging, self-aware, the *Journal* has much more instant appeal than Lewis's rococo fictions. Everything goes in—descriptions of scenery he admires, anecdotes, reportage in the form of dialogues with slaves, notes on cookery and natural history, many poems. The tone is set by the initial comical account of a pig and Lewis being hauled aboard ship, turn by turn, in a broken bucket. Ready to poke fun at himself, observant and sensitive to the animal as well as human life around him, the character of the recorder is instantly likeable. And when he arrives at his destination, Jamaica, here is a man enjoying himself more than he expected, receptive, enthusiastic, rejoicing in the warmth of the place and the people. Moreover, he went back again: the *Journal* records two separate visits. Lewis's commitment to his humanitarian purpose needs no other proof. The limits of his conceptual framework were those of a man of his time, but he was generous, broad-minded, soft-hearted, and engagingly gullible. If he had not been so, indeed, he would probably never have undertaken the journeys at all. The artificer of high romance was stepping out of his disguise and embarking upon a venture of some risk because he had a well-developed sense of responsibility and a horror of slavery.

Upbringing and personality

Matthew Gregory Lewis was born in 1775 in London, where his father was a senior civil servant, and London, the imperial centre, remained his permanent base. A single critical event in his childhood would overshadow what was otherwise an uneventful life: his mother left his father for another man by whom she later had a child. Lewis, who was only 6 years old, with three even younger siblings, adored his mother. The scandal and its aftermath, including enforced

---

[6] 'The space of colonial encounters . . . in which peoples geographically and historically separated come into contact with each other and establish ongoing relations . . . often synonymous with "colonial frontier"', but, unlike the latter term, not 'grounded within a European expansionist perspective'. Mary Louise Pratt, *Imperial Eyes: Travel Writing and Transculturation* (London and New York: Routledge, 1992), 6.

separation from her, were devastating. Young as he was, he tried to
act as conciliator, and the conflict between his parents would be a
continuing source of misery and frustration. He loved and respected
his father, and accepted the conventional wisdom that his mother's
action rendered her unfit to have any contact with his two sisters.
Moral rightness did not immunize him against anguish, however.
A letter written to her while she was living briefly in France demonstrates how intensely he still suffered on her behalf, even though he
was by now 15:

I need not tell you how much how very much concerned I am for your
illness, and it affords me a fresh obligation to my Father. I shudder to think
at what would have been your situation had he refused my request.
Without money, without friends, sick, in a foreign country. Oh my mother!
The remembrance of your being in pain and sorrow often clouds the
pleasures I enjoy, and I hardly conceive myself justified in partaking
amusements, when you perhaps may be in want of common comforts. God
bless you, my dear Mother, and may you soon return to this Country,
where whatever happens, you may at least have those you love, and who
love you near to assist you.[7]

In regular letters he passed on not only family news but the latest
titbits from the musical and literary world, understanding with imaginative insight how much she needed to be distracted from the
indignities of her position. Later he even provided something of an
occupation, encouraging her to act as his literary agent with the
prospect of a share in the profits. He certainly provided her with
money whenever he could. They remained extremely close and she
eventually settled near London.

The outward circumstances of Lewis's life remained privileged
and comfortable. He attended Westminster School and Oxford, and
spent some time in Germany and in Holland, complying with his
father's wishes that he prepare for a diplomatic career; from 1796
to 1802 he was even a member of the House of Commons. He had,
however, since the age of 14, been 'scribbling Novels and Plays',[8] and
by 1802 had a sufficiently impressive list of successes to persuade his
father that his vocation was writing not politics. His father gave in
gracefully, promising a handsome allowance to supplement his

---

[7] Peck, *A Life of Matthew G. Lewis*, 183.
[8] Quoted ibid. 17.

earnings from writing. Only a year later, however, they had a bitter quarrel: Lewis senior had taken as his mistress the widow of a friend of long standing, and his son was outraged. The promised allowance was reduced to irregular handouts, and a reconciliation did not take place until 1812, just before the elder Lewis died.

It is not clear that Lewis's outrage was justified. He had become a curiously difficult man: irascible, quarrelsome, quick to take offence. The most promising friendships—as with Walter Scott, to whom he gave generous professional help—ended badly. A very small man, with bulging eyes and a shrill voice, he was fussy, snobbish, and immoderately vain. In memoirs and letters everyone paid tribute to his good nature and generosity, but usually only as a preliminary to saying that he was a terrible bore. He stayed too long and he talked too much. It is hard to find anyone amongst the host of his literary and aristocratic acquaintances who was not glad to see the back of him. Having said goodbye to Lewis just before he embarked for his first visit to Jamaica, Byron wrote: 'Poor fellow! He really is a good man—an excellent man—he left me his walking-stick and a pot of preserved ginger. I shall never eat the last without tears in my eyes. It is so *hot*.'[9] It is a neat joke. Few people would cry real tears over Lewis's absence (although, as the epigraph on the title-page indicates, Byron lived to regret his early death). The depths of feeling sounded in those youthful letters to his mother were never to find satisfaction in any later relationship. 'Little Lewis', 'the little Monk', was tolerated, not loved. 'He has left many to regret his oddities', commented his aunt after his death in 1818.[10] No warmer tributes were forthcoming. Celebrity that he was, his death caused hardly a ripple.

Jamaica, sugar, and slavery

The current promotion of the West Indies as an unspoilt tropical paradise has no basis in reality; indeed, it is something of an insult to the complex and troubled history of the region. Small in area as they are, in Lewis's time the British West Indies were of prime importance to the imperial economy: in the 1770s West Indian imports were triple

[9] *Byron's Letters & Journals*, ed. Leslie A. Marchand (London: John Murray, 1974), iv. 330.
[10] Peck, *A Life of Matthew G. Lewis*, 267.

the value of East Indian. Sugar was king. Those who needed to make or mend their fortunes went to the West Indies. Vast profits were to be made from growing sugar cane (as many a noble British family could attest). Beautiful as the islands were, however, they were not places anyone wished to visit, let alone to live, except from strict necessity: the climate bred disease, and the society was decadent.

Yellow fever, to which Lewis himself would succumb in 1818, was the deadliest scourge.[11] The companies of regular soldiers stationed in the British West Indies from 1730 onwards suffered appalling losses: of 19,676 men sent there in 1796, 17,173 died within five years. Two-thirds of a regiment were destroyed by it in 1819.[12] As for West Indian society, its disadvantages, as one commentator, describing Jamaica in 1823, pointed out, 'partly grow out of and are inseparably connected with a state of slavery, but more especially arise from the gross immorality which prevails among all ranks'.[13] It was one evil—and not the only one—attendant upon absentee land-lordism, which was rampant. In 1804, only three out of the eighty landholders in the upper districts of the colony were resident on their estates. The smell of the West Indies, far from being tropical blossoms on a warm wind, was rum and sugar, money and shame.

Both sides of Lewis's family had strong ties with Jamaica. His father and his mother's father had been born there, and the family properties adjoined. In the usual tradition, his father had been sent to England for his education, and had never returned, although the family benefited from the income of two plantations, one in the far west of the island, Cornwall, one in the far east, Hordley, both of which Lewis inherited on his father's death in 1812. It was this inheritance which would prompt the two visits recorded in the *Journal*. The Jamaica Almanac of the period records 307 slaves and 287 head of stock on Cornwall and 283 slaves and 130 stock on Hordley.[14]

[11] It was not brought under control until after 1900, when the US Army's Yellow Fever Commission established that it was carried by the *Aedes aegypti* mosquito, which bred in clean water, unlike the swamp-dwelling malaria mosquito. See Lady [Maria] Nugent, *Lady Nugent's Journal of her residence in Jamaica from 1801 to 1805*, ed. Philip Wright (Kingston, Jamaica: Institute of Jamaica, 1966), 16.

[12] Lowell Joseph Ragatz, *The Fall of the Planter Class in the British Caribbean, 1763–1833* (New York: Octagon Books, 1963 [1928]), 31–2; J. Stewart, *A View of the Past and Present State of the Island of Jamaica* (Edinburgh, 1823), 47.

[13] Stewart, *View of Jamaica*, 169.

[14] 'Jamaica Worthies', *Journal of the Institute of Jamaica*, 1: 2 (Feb. 1892), 69.

Suddenly, Lewis, who had not even been sure he would be his father's heir, had inherited the responsibility and guilt of being a slave-holder.

In Britain, mobilization of public opinion against slavery had begun in the 1780s. As a child, Lewis would have been aware of the stir and outrage, the pamphleteering and petitions. Branches of the Society for Effecting the Abolition of the Slave Trade, founded in 1787, had rapidly sprung up all over the country. 'Abolition' at that time, indeed, quickly came to denote abolition of the trade in slaves between Africa and the West Indies, rather than the abolition of slavery itself (although the founders of the movement undoubtedly had that in mind). In parliament, the abolitionists, of all political stripes, were led by William Wilberforce. The opposition, both outside and in parliament, was spearheaded by the Society of West India Planters and Merchants. Legislative change came slowly. It was not until 1807 that the Act to abolish the slave trade was passed, and such a profitable and flourishing enterprise enterprise was not stamped out overnight: in 1811, the passing of another bill which made slave-trading a felony indicated the failure of the Act of 1807 to achieve its object. As for full emancipation, it would take another spate of agitation in the 1820s before that was achieved in two stages in the 1830s: 'apprenticeship', when slaves were compelled to work for their former owners, was initiated in 1834; in 1838 full freedom at last came into effect in all British colonies.

Lewis's *Journal*, kept between 1815 and 1818, is thus situated between the two most significant moments in the eradication of slavery under British imperialism. Lewis had long been aware of, and sympathetic to, the parliamentary initiatives connected with abolition, notably through his friendship with Lord and Lady Holland, which has a particular relevance to the *Journal*. Lewis had known Henry Richard Fox, 3rd Baron Holland, at Oxford, and met his wife about the time *The Monk* was published. Lady Holland was the most celebrated hostess of the day, renowned for her wit and for the distinguished company she assembled to dine at Holland House. To be invited was to have arrived, and Lewis was delighted and gratified to be so honoured. Over a period of twenty years he was a frequent visitor and corresponded with both Hollands. They were, like him, abolitionists with a particular interest in Jamaica, where Lady Holland had been born, and where she also had inherited plantations, one of which, Friendship and Greenwich, was just to the east of Lewis's Cornwall. At one point the same agent, Parkinson, had managed both estates; Parkinson had no doubt been a disaster at Friendship and Greenwich as he had certainly been at Cornwall (pp. 74–5).

Lord Holland was a pillar of strength in the 'cause', as the shorthand for abolition had it. Indeed, Wilberforce wrote to him immediately the 1807 abolition bill had passed both houses, even before it had been given royal assent, to recruit him for the next step in the campaign: setting up the African Institution, 'a plan I have long had in View', which would work for emancipation amongst other goals.[15] Lord Holland did indeed become a founder member of the African Institution, and remained on the Board until the establishment of the Society for the Mitigation and Gradual Abolition of Slavery Throughout the British Dominions in January 1823 rendered it superfluous. Thus there is a specific personal element in Lewis's several references to the 'Reporter' of the African Institution (i.e. the compiler of the report, which was read aloud at the annual meeting and later printed). But Lewis was not an emancipationist, as his barbed remarks about Wilberforce and the Reporter demonstrate. When he records, more than once, that the slaves' greatest fear is of 'having no massa', it is salutary to recognize the validity of such a perspective, to acknowledge that there was good reason to suppose they would be worse off if no one at all were responsible for their welfare. It is certainly Lewis's own view, as his lucid and compelling statement at the end of the *Journal* makes plain:

Every man of humanity must wish that slavery, even in its best and most mitigated form, had never found a legal sanction, and must regret that its system is now so incorporated with the welfare of Great Britain as well as of Jamaica, as to make its extirpation an absolute impossibility, without the certainty of producing worse mischiefs than the one which we annihilate. (p. 249)

Lewis was undoubtedly encouraged and supported by the Hollands in his idea of visiting Jamaica. He would be inspecting their property as well as his own, and specifically asks for written instructions. This was just Lewis the fusspot: they had already jointly determined on strategies for improving conditions. Slaves on Friendship

---

[15] British Library Add. MS 51820: letter dated 3 Mar. 1807.

FIG. 1. Woodcut of anti-slavery motif

and Greenwich as well as Cornwall were granted additional Saturdays off. Even the ship Lewis sailed on indicates how closely the Hollands were involved in this venture: Sir Godfrey Webster was the name of Lady Holland's first husband and eldest son. Lewis was also taking the honey locust plants he mentions (p. 22) on Lord Holland's behalf, as his joking enquiry in a letter not long before he sailed makes plain: 'I should know, how they are to be managed; whether they love warmth or cold; what they drink & what they eat; wild Honey I take it for granted, but still I should chuse to be quite certain'.[16]

Reading the Journal

The anti-slavery movement's stirring motto, reproduced most notably by Josiah Wedgwood in an oval medallion in the black-on-white stoneware for which the company is famous (see Fig. 1), is more

---

[16] British Library Add. MS 51641: letter dated 21 Oct. 1815. Lewis's joke suggests that these were cuttings of the honey locust (*Gleditsia triacanthos*), a tall North American leguminous tree, which has very hard durable wood, as well as long twisted pods containing a sweet edible pulp and bean-like seeds. Since there is nothing about the species in more recent records, presumably the cuttings did not thrive. They should be distinguished from the native Jamaican locust tree (see Glossary).

than a slogan. In conjunction with the kneeling slave who clasps his hands upward in supplication, it is also a plea. From our perspective, it is clear that the egalitarian impulse is restrained by the claim of a familial bond: that the humble posture perpetuates the slave's inferior status and leaves the superiority of the white race intact. The abolition movement was, in other words, by no means immune from racism. But it remains a powerful and evocative image, the sort to touch Lewis to the heart. Its principles prompted his visits, underpinned his actions in Jamaica, and influenced his entries in the *Journal*.

Given Lewis's nature, the expeditions to Jamaica were actually rather daring. The *Journal* may fit into the category of travel literature, but its author was no intrepid explorer. He had never been an outdoors man, he did not fish or shoot, his nerves were bad, and he suffered from headaches. The experience of a brief coastal voyage when he returned to London after a visit to Lord Grey, had led him to the heartfelt conclusion that 'A voyage by Sea can never be quite a safe thing'.[17] Once arrived in Jamaica, indeed, he remained almost stationary, 'determined to give up my whole time to my negroes during my stay' (p. 87). It is this object which gives the *Journal* its distinctive spin, for its chief interest today, aside from its lively and accessible style, lies in its situation within the discourse of colonialism. How did Lewis perceive his slaves? What can we recover of slave experience from his account?

Not surprisingly, only a handful of contemporary texts were actually written by slaves, although they reached a wide public in abolition days. The best known, *The Interesting Narrative of the Life of Olaudah Equiano, or Gustavus Vassa, the African, written by himself* (1789), which recounts the experience of an Ibo who had been captured and transported to the West Indies, had gone into nine editions by 1794. Such a text should be read in conjunction with the *Journal* since it illuminates areas of overlap and difference. Equiano subscribes to European notions of cultural superiority and otherness, even while battling against slavery and uncomfortable with his dual identity.[18] But such notions had constructed Lewis's view of the world, and the *Journal* does not challenge them. Yet it can contribute

---

[17] Peck, *A Life of Matthew G. Lewis*, 250.
[18] Olaudah Equiano, *The Interesting Narrative and Other Writings*, ed. Vincent Carretta (Harmondsworth: Penguin, 1995).

much to our understanding, providing the reader questions and interrogates—reads the text, as Edward Said has suggested, 'not univocally but contrapuntally'.[19] The questions may be ones to which there are no ready answers, but the exercise sharpens perception as it demands alert participation, and it undoubtedly increases the range of our vision, creates spaces in the text through which slave experience begins to take on a shadowy, suggestive shape. And Lewis, though in many ways a typical representative of the imperial observer, brought to the *Journal* a distinctive sensibility as writer and man: he understood what it felt like to be an outsider, he responded to the warmth shown him by the slaves. And being so situated he is sometimes led to record facts in ways which suggest the possibilities of a different kind of discourse.

'The Isle of Devils'

In keeping with eighteenth-century paradigms of travel narrative Lewis begins the *Journal* with an account of the voyage. Only when he finally arrives in Jamaica does his whole-hearted relief at finding things 'much better than I expected' reveal how anxious he had felt about what awaited him. The long verse narrative, 'The Isle of Devils', suggests the dimensions of that anxiety. Although not copied into the *Journal* until the first homeward voyage, 'The Isle of Devils' had been composed when Lewis was outward bound, and it is impossible to read it without feeling that suppressed fears and guilt are surfacing in this Gothic nightmare with its island setting, its monstrous black demon ruler, and its images of rape, constraint, and murder.[20] In fact, it awakens the reader to connections between the *Journal* and Lewis's earlier work, with which it initially seems to have so little in common. It becomes clear that '[t]he Gothic imagination itself, with its recurrent fantasies of domination and revolt, was shaped by the debate over slavery and abolition'.[21]

---

[19] Edward W. Said, *Culture and Imperialism* (New York: Vintage, 1994), 51.

[20] 'The Isle of Devils' was published separately in Jamaica in 1827, before the publication of the *Journal*, and in London in 1912. See Peck, *A Life of Matthew G. Lewis*, 170.

[21] D. L. Macdonald, 'The Isle of Devils: The Jamaican Journal of M. G. Lewis', in Timothy Fulford and Peter Kitson (eds.), *Romanticism and Colonialism* (Cambridge: Cambridge University Press, 1998), 203. Macdonald's article explores fully the allegorical implications of 'The Isle of Devils'.

'The Isle of Devils' is prefaced with a quotation from *The Tempest*, to which there are further internal allusions in the shipwreck, the isolated survivor, the magic isle whose sole inhabitant is a monster, and in the 'Song of the Tempest-Fiend'.[22] Even the monster/demon's rape of the shipwrecked Irza suggests a fulfilment of Caliban's desire to violate Miranda. Lewis's 'master-fiend', however, is rescuer as well as rapist. Twice saving Irza from 'monstrous dwarfs', he approaches her humbly, withdrawing when he sees her terror, and invites her to his cave (as beautiful as the Beast's palace in *Beauty and the Beast*). There, although she is his prisoner, he is also her slave. Irza bears the monster two children, in circumstances which also recall fairy-tale. First, as in early versions of *Sleeping Beauty*, both births are conceived during rapes while she is unconscious. Second, one child is beautiful, the other hideous. Such oppositions are common in fairy-tale, of course, but here the pairing also inevitably suggests a terror of miscegenation. When Irza is at last rescued from the island, she is obliged against her will to abandon the beautiful child, with whom the monster tries to coax her to return. Failing, he kills both children and himself.

The monster's 'gigantic' size, his blackness, his 'rolling eyes' allude not only to Caliban but also to the stereotype of the African workers on Lewis's plantation whom he had not yet seen. The response of the narrative voice to the monster is full of ambivalence, mingling dislike with admiration, pity, and guilt. The 'moan' announcing his presence is 'full . . . sad . . . strange'. Monarch of the island as he is, the monster is not only without language, as Caliban had been, but even without name. The moan, heard before he sets eyes on Irza, is a powerful trope conveying misery and subjugation: he has his own story predating Irza's, and it is obviously unhappy. His crude assertion of power through physical violation and, at the last, murder of his own children and suicide, is all that is available to him (as bloody rebellion was to the slaves). He has no words to tell his story, although in ten lines which he 'seem'd to say', Irza is reproved for her lack of feeling: 'My love, my service only wrought disdain'. Aside from reminding us that Irza, unlike Beauty, was not to be won by devotion, the monster has constantly sought a roman-

[22] For an exploration of the colonial implications of *The Tempest*, which has much relevance in this context, see Peter Hulme, *Colonial Encounters: Europe and the Native Caribbean, 1492–1797* (London and New York: Methuen, 1986), ch. 3.

tic union (suggestive of harmonious cultural parity), but has been utterly rejected. Abhorrent crimes result. Annihilation of the black monster and the two children of a union unwanted by the white mistress is all that the narrative can accomplish. Such closure indicates the true source of power and is an interesting amalgam of the racial stereotype with the sexual. There is no territorial imperative, however. After Irza's rescue, the island is abandoned.

The conclusion of the poem reflects upon Irza becoming a nun. Her choice of such a vocation, it suggests, may be the result of guilt for the sexual connection, for being the demon's 'wife', but the choice may also have spared her worse: the 'pangs from wilful guilt which flow, | The only serious ills that man can know'. The question of intentionality in the 'crime' of slave-holding was, of course, very much to the point in the case of those who acquired West Indian estates through inheritance. Then, although Irza is forced to leave the island, the presence of another 'crime' hovers also: the abandonment of children, with its implications of the precedence of racial ties over maternal. Whatever interpretation one may give 'The Isle of Devils', however—and such a fantasy tempts speculation—the central moral ambivalence is plain. Lewis's statement when he began to copy 'The Isle of Devils' into the *Journal* acknowledges that: 'I earnestly request that no person who may read these verses will ask me "who the hero really was?"' (p. 159).

Lewis in Jamaica (1 January–31 March 1816; 23 January–2 May 1818)

On landing, Lewis's sudden relief was blissful, and somewhat precipitate. New Year's celebrations were in progress at Black River, and as he compared the holiday crowd with its counterpart at fairs and races in England, Lewis found it, as those looking through imperialist eyes characteristically did, superior to the home variety: less concerned with commerce, better behaved, much happier (p. 40). Travelling on to Cornwall, his 1,600-acre estate in the west of the island, he was further reassured: 'the negroes seem happy and contented.'

During the first weeks of his stay the euphoria persisted. The affection shown him by the slaves when he arrived at Cornwall touched him deeply. 'All this may be palaver; but certainly they at

least play their parts with such an air of truth, and warmth and
enthusiasm, that, after the cold hearts and repulsive manners of
England, the contrast is infinitely agreeable . . . my own heart . . .
seems to expand itself again in the sunshine of the kind looks and
words which meet me at every turn' (p. 59). Lewis's store of happiness was enlarged in Jamaica. Whatever there was of vexation and
anxiety, the people and the place assuaged his deep loneliness. Moreover, despite the headaches caused by the noise of the slaves' party-
ing till all hours, he felt fit and healthy. There were times of irritation
and disillusion, but his enthusiasm abated little: judging from his
Aunt Blake's comment, between visits he would weary friends and
relations in England with it: 'Matt Lewis is *in Jamaica* again. It
appears to be His heaven!'[23]

Lewis's intention was to devote himself to improving conditions
for the slaves, establishing trust through close personal contact
and thus acquainting himself with what most needed attention.
Although he does not say so, it is clear that he had decided, as a
means of acknowledging the individuality of his slaves, to record
them by name, and, as a corollary, to avoid naming white employees.
Typically novel and idiosyncratic, it of course skews the record, but
then system and order are not characteristic of Lewis (and perhaps
if they were we would not enjoy the *Journal* so much). The greater
proportion of those named—about fifty out of the two hundred and
fifty slaves on the estate—are those with whom Lewis would naturally have had close contact, i.e. his own domestic servants (frequently the offspring of white fathers), and members of the black
élite, such as the blackslave driver(s) who supervised the field hands
(the positions termed in the *Journal* 'governor' and 'chief governor'),
the coopers, the carpenters, the supervisors of the boiling-house, etc.
Anecdotes about slaves also greatly outnumber any others, although
no slave narrative predating Jamaican experience is recorded, even
though it is clear that a number of Lewis's slaves were African rather
than creole (i.e. born in the Caribbean). There is often more than
one anecdote about the same individual, although these are usually
widely separated and without signposts. (Lewis died before he could
undertake any revision.) Piecing them together to achieve a sense of
ongoing story is a task readers themselves must undertake.

---

[23] Peck, *A Life of Matthew G. Lewis*, 265.

In cross-questioning the *Journal* it is necessary to be alert to what its format entails. The narration is sometimes as much as two removes from the subject, being not only in indirect speech, but also obtained from another source. Who were Lewis's unnamed informants? The superficial absence of whites from the text can be misleading. Whites ran Cornwall, after all. The trustee, or attorney, was directly responsible to the owner, and might own a plantation or two himself, as well as managing a number of others. Day-to-day management was the responsibility of the agent or overseer, who lived on site. Below him would be two or more bookkeepers, whose task it was to keep the stores and ensure that the slaves performed their tasks. There was often also a white physician. Some of these white employees were certainly in positions of influence over Lewis's text. Thus, although neither trustee nor agent at Cornwall are named, Lewis refers quite often to both, and they must of necessity have been his main informants when he uses a passive, or similarly suppressive grammatical structure such as 'It seems that' or 'I am told'. Lewis himself was present for only four months on each of two visits, both at the same time of year. Much of what he reports about people and events over a long period on the plantation—what often imparts a tone of authority to the *Journal*—had, then, been obtained from white employees who by no means always shared his convictions about the way things ought to be done. Lewis himself was adamantly opposed to the use of the cart-whip, but 'every morning my agent regales me with some fresh instance of insubordination: he says nothing plainly, but shakes his head, and evidently gives me to understand, that the estate cannot be governed properly without the cartwhip' (p. 87). Lewis's written code of laws and the measures for monitoring he set in place at the end of his first visit indicate that he maintained this opposition. Yet on his second visit (p. 214), he discovers that the whip has indeed been used (only in extreme cases, he is careful to point out). In other words, in his absence, the whites continued to run things much as they always had. The effectiveness of Lewis's reforms, often taken for granted, is actually very much in question. By his own admission, pleasant though Cornwall was by the time he visited it, it had been so only for a very short time: even during the three years since he inherited it, a former attorney (Parkinson), had so lied and mismanaged that 'The property was nearly ruined, and absolutely in a state of rebellion' (p. 75). As to

Lewis's reforms being instrumental in ensuring the continued prosperity of Cornwall after emancipation, when other plantations
had fallen into ruin, that is highly unlikely. Cornwall's survival, like
Hordley's, was probably the simple result of its excellent situation in
flood plain land.[24]

Lewis's 'system of management' (p. 239) was not based upon a
methodical assessment of plantation conditions. The imbalance in
the _Journal_ between the descriptions of the slaves at work and on
holiday makes that plain. No reader can finish the _Journal_ without a
strong sense of carnival, of the rhythm of the gumby drums and the
kitty-katties, and the night-long singing and dancing of the slaves.
But descriptions of their daily labour, which consumed so many
more hours, are fewer and less convincing. Field hands, who did
the toughest jobs, worked from sunrise to eight or nine o'clock, had
thirty to forty-five minutes for breakfast, worked till noon, had two
hours rest, and worked again until sunset, for a total of about thirteen hours, with ten hours physical labour.[25] Lewis's landscape with
figures (p. 56) is evocative and charming, but how much did those
bundles of ripe canes and trash actually weigh? Lewis did not get out
there to see; he merely took the usual tour of the works. Even on that
occasion, he was easily diverted from people to process. When he
writes of molasses 'being carried into the distillery' (p. 57), for
instance, the porters, who moved 'hogsheads of sugar weighing up
to a ton and puncheons of rum and molasses containing up to 120
gallons from the boiling house to the curing house, or the distillery
to the rum store'[26] are effectively erased. Nor did Lewis record the
level of danger in the tasks. Boiling the juice sometimes entailed
a heat so extreme that water had to be sprayed on the roof of the
boiling house to prevent the shingles catching fire; the repetitiveness
of some jobs over many hours entailed considerable risk. Most surprisingly, because it is a minor point almost universally noted, Lewis
makes no reference to the overpowering stench and heat of the
boiling house. What else might he have omitted?

Lewis tried to introduce improvements, but they generally did not
turn out well. He fell back on the usual solution to holing the canes

[24] Barry Higman: private e-mail, 29 Oct. 97.
[25] Quoted in Ragatz, _Fall of the Planter Class_, 26.
[26] B. W. Higman, _Slave Populations of the British Caribbean 1807–1834_ (Baltimore and
London: Johns Hopkins University Press, 1984), 166.

(the most arduous task): hiring jobbing gangs of slaves to do the work instead of his own.[27] He also tried unsuccessfully to introduce a better breed of oxen and the use of the plough.[28] Lewis's claims to success in his endeavours should be treated with caution. Probably the appointment of a good agent at Cornwall (and that, considering his wild misjudgement of the agent at Hordley, must have been as much by luck as judgement) was his greatest contribution to the slaves' comfort. Although Lewis is not to be classed with those who underestimated maltreatment or overwork from the profit motive, most slave-holders needed to justify their position. Given his temperament, none could have been more in need of believing that conditions were satisfactory, of being able to reassure himself that he was 'not guilty' in the crime of slave-holding, than Lewis.

The insidious corrupting influence of dealing face to face with slavery also becomes evident. It is most obvious in Lewis's references to child-bearing and child-rearing among the slaves. As part of the welcome at Cornwall which so touches him, one woman holds up her child for him to see: 'Look, Massa, look here! him nice lilly neger for Massa!' (p. 42). Lewis reports this without comment, and his continuing anxiety about the viability of the plantation if the slaves do not bear children leads him to speak of them as he would of breeding livestock. His practical improvements, including the building of a new hospital, were beneficial, but the unsavoury rewards system of medals and money for successful mothering indicates the moral erosion involved. Attributing much fond feeling to the slave mothers, he never considers that they may have any practical wisdom. And the man who upon his first arrival was so distressed at the word 'slave' that he resolved never to use it, can say, on discovering the number of deaths at Cornwall when he returns the second time 'I have lost several negroes' and 'I have lost several infants' (pp. 202–3) without any apparent awareness of slipping into an even more offensive verbal habit. Was it not the families who lost? Was it not the mothers?

[27] Around 1832, 6% of slaves in Jamaica belonged to 'jobbers' who did not themselves own land, and hired out their slaves in gangs. Inevitably such gangs were subject to the heaviest physical labour. See Higman. *Slave Populations of the British Caribbean*, 54, 164.

[28] The plough was never much used anywhere in the West Indies, the exception being Antigua. See Higman, *Slave Populations of the British Caribbean*, 162; also Ragatz, *Fall of the Planter Class*, 66.

Only rarely does Lewis seem on the point of breaking through the framework of imperialist discourse. At one point, he complains about a slave who has run away and taken his wife with him: 'In England, a man only runs away with another person's wife: but to run away with his own—what depravity!—' (p. 128). Suddenly two realities intersect, and to terrifying effect. Did Lewis recognize that? Did framing the remark as a joke enable him to evade the implications?

African-Caribbean society: Lewis as recorder

Lewis certainly had no conception (nor did any other European) of slave society as the complex organism it was. The developing African-Caribbean society naturally retained features of those from which its members had been riven, which were West African (in the case of Cornwall, mostly Ibo). Language, religion, and social practices of separate tribal groups amalgamated, adapted, and shifted during the African exodus, in ways that we are unlikely ever fully to understand. But the strength and continuity of African influence can be deduced from proverbs, songs, dances, stories, funeral rituals, etc. still extant in the West Indies for which exact African parallels have been found.

Lewis was increasingly fascinated by the creole language, which was based upon English but with an enlarged vocabulary and changes in structure and intonation as a result of African influences. Only three weeks after his arrival, he is employing it in a poem (p. 76), and he takes pleasure in recording and explaining some of its attractive expressions. He is also fascinated by the 'nancy-stories' and the figure of the story-teller, a pipe-smoking old woman of much authority described in Appendix I. The 'nancy' stories were the 'anansesem', the stories that belonged to Anansi, the African sky god, who was often personified as a spider (Anansi is the Ashanti word for spider), and has much in common with trickster gods of other cultures. The Anansi stories in the *Journal* have, as might be expected, many motifs in common with European fairy-tale: indeed, the loss of clothes while swimming (p. 191) is reminiscent of 'Puss-in-Boots'. By the time Lewis was recording them, of course, the identification of any Anansi story as specifically African in origin would be highly problematic; story exchange in pre-literate cultures is lightning-rapid.

The fine distinction made by the slaves between 'nancy-story' and 'neger-trick' (p. 194) is interesting as an exact parallel with that still made between the fairy-tale and its subset the 'droll'.

Deprived of priests and the right to hold meetings, transplanted Africans must often have been obliged to reconstruct traditional religious beliefs and practices. It is hardly surprising that Lewis can discover no 'external forms of worship' or 'any priests' (p. 216), except those who practised Obeah. It might well have been dangerous for his informants to reveal what they knew: reluctance and evasiveness can be read into a number of responses. Like most observers, Lewis deals chiefly with the two aspects of African religious belief, ancestor worship and Obeah, which were overt and often disruptive elements in plantation life. Ancestor worship was a daily matter since spirits of the dead, 'duppies', were believed to be active and influential; Obeah (Obi) was a version of practices recorded in the fairy-tales of every culture, a this-world magic or witchcraft, invoked for some personal benefit, such as curing sickness, winning a lover or wealth, obtaining revenge. Obeah had defied all efforts at suppression, and its practitioners, who provided charms, amulets, herbal remedies, and interpretation of dreams, wielded much power. Unlike most Europeans, Lewis does not—unless feeling particularly crotchety—deny that slaves have any religion at all. On the contrary, he argues that the concept of 'duppies' and the conduct of funeral rites prove that they do (p. 64).

Christianizing the slaves, the obvious antidote to Obeah, was not necessarily welcomed by the plantocracy. Christian marriage strengthens family ties and would compromise the easy sale of slaves. Worse, Christianity had a tendency to promote insubordination and encourage thoughts of emancipation. The Church of England, partly because it was the church of the plantocracy, had certainly never exerted itself: the *Jamaica Almanac* of 1812 shows only twelve Church of England clergymen listed at a time when there were approximately 310,000 slaves. The dissenting religions were far more active, beginning with the Moravians, who had established the ministry Lewis mentions, on Mesopotamia estate, not far from Cornwall, in 1754. By the time of Lewis's arrival, the Anglican Church was beginning to promote slave instruction, and greater tolerance for missionary work was acknowledged in the new slave code passed by the Jamaica Assembly in 1816—presumably the matter

Lewis refers to as being 'in agitation' (p. 100). Prospective missionaries of all denominations were instructed by their societies at home
to avoid politics at all costs. In practice, this meant emphasizing those
aspects of the Bible which enjoined obedience and promised heavenly rewards for faithful and devoted servants, thereby promoting
docility among the workers. Many missionaries ignored this instruction and suffered cruelly for promoting the slaves' interests. Lewis
believes that what is needed is not 'an importation of missionaries,
but of schoolmasters' (p. 89).

As always, everything depended on the character of the individual planter. Thus Lewis is benignly protective of his slaves' freedom to choose whether to be Christianized or not, and was without
prejudice as to sect, excepting always the Methodists, for reasons he
sets out (p. 108). He himself undertook baptism and a little religious instruction, feeling a mild dose of Christianity to be beneficial,
even if only to 'expel black Obeah by white' (p. 85). If a slave
agreed to be baptized, it might well have been for strategic political
reasons, as Lewis recognizes (p. 233); and certainly, if slaves refused
baptism, it was a sign of allegiance to their own culture, whether
or not they themselves would have thought of it that way. Voicing
such allegiance openly would, in any case, have been out of the
question. Most dialogues Lewis records show the black respondent
trying to comply with whatever the white seems to expect. The
waterman (pp. 102–3.) gained enough confidence at the last to tell
Lewis that 'blacks must not be treated now, massa, as they used to
be; they can think, and hear, and see, as well as white people: blacks
are wiser, massa, than they were, and will soon be still wiser'.
Lewis approved the waterman. He looks for reciprocity, unable to
acknowledge that the absolute power he embodies must almost
always prevent it.

Slave resistance and rebellion

Lewis blamed the failure of the ploughs he had sent out between his
two visits on the 'awkwardness, and still more the obstinacy' (p. 205)
of the slaves. He thus avoids by a hair the stereotype of the stupid slave, but stops short of recognizing a deliberate refusal to co-
operate. For the breaking of the ploughs and the spoiling of the oxen
were also an instinctive expression of non-violent resistance, even

while the superficial motivation might also have been the expression of preference for traditional African hoe culture.

Malingering, going slow, playing dumb, were unfailingly interpreted as stupidity and laziness. That such behaviour, or misdemeanours such as lying and stealing, might be strategies of resistance in a system where neither pay nor bargaining existed was certainly beyond imagining—although 'Massa's horse, massa's grass', a common Jamaican saying, demonstrates with sly wit slaves' acute awareness of the ironies of their situation: how could one of 'massa's' articles be guilty of 'stealing' another?[29] Absenteeism was the most obvious and frequent form of resistance, as the *Journal* makes clear. Lewis responded indulgently to running away, treating it like truancy from school. The offenders were lively children playing 'monkey-tricks' (p. 86). Such infantilizing was the norm, of course, but, in the case of a slave-holder, surrounded and totally outnumbered by those he held in subjection, it was also a discursive strategy essential for survival. Lewis's stubborn incomprehension of any possible strategies of resistance was certainly exploited by his slaves. Cubina's antics with the cats and the pigeon loft, and Nicholas's construction of the wrong-sized boxes (pp. 244 ff.), may well have been elaborate practical jokes, which they knew full well that Lewis would never suspect. Such jokes would provide a form of retaliation that carried no penalty, as well as opportunities for a refreshing conspiracy of laughter. Obliquely confirming such game-playing is the jolly, knowing burst of song 'All the stories them telling you are lies, oh!' (p. 119). There are a number of light-hearted moments to be cherished in the *Journal*.

Piecing together the fragments of the longest slave narrative in the *Journal*, that of Adam, demonstrates the continual undercurrent of resistance on a plantation. Adam is first mentioned by another slave, Edward, in an extended personal interview reported by Lewis (pp. 85 ff.). Edward, though denying it, seems himself to be an Obeah man, and he and his wife, Whaunica (who leads a strike over carrying the 'trash') are both clearly resisters. Edward is trying to shift blame for his actions to Adam for wanting him to Obeah 'a book-keeper whose conduct had been obnoxious'. Lewis explains that

[29] Michael Craton, *Testing the Chains: Resistance to Slavery in the British West Indies* (Ithaca, NY, and London: Cornell University Press, 1982), 53.

Adam 'has been long and strongly suspected of having connections with Obeah men', and later characterizes him as 'a most dangerous fellow, and the terror of all his companions' (p. 92), suspected of poisoning twelve slaves, as well as the former attorney, who had removed him as principal governor. Adam is 'unfortunately, clever and plausible'. Plainly, if a slave cannot be reassuringly infantilized, he is extremely threatening: there is no place for him in the dominant value system except as child or criminal. Adam is a creole, with 'creditable and praiseworthy' (p. 92) sisters, both of whom have obtained their freedom, and to one of whom Lewis feels indebted for saving 'poor Richard's life, when the tyranny of the overseer had brought him almost to the brink of the grave' (p. 92). (Lewis typically provides no details of either the obnoxious behaviour of the bookkeeper, or the tyranny of the overseer, but the latter is evidently an episode during the mismanagement referred to on pp. 74 ff.) Lewis cannot get rid of Adam because no one would buy him, or even accept him as a gift, and a slave may not be shipped off the island unless convicted of a felony. Abruptly, no more of Adam until Lewis's departure, when he hardly seems like the same man. On this festive occasion, no one could seem more docile: he is requesting that his little daughter be taught needlework, and is one of those christened (p. 145).

On Lewis's return twenty-one months later, however, 'the whole estate' is 'in an uproar about Adam' (p. 220). Adam had been claiming that Lewis's leniency towards him was proof of his own power and that he would get back his old job as chief governor. He had been fighting, quarrelling, attempting murder, and poisoning. Was this behaviour personally or politically motivated? That Adam was a potential leader is not in doubt. The chief governor (chief blackslave driver) was a powerful position: at the interface of black and white, he functioned as both policeman and mediator, but, as a slave himself, was always potentially a rebel. Adam had already been dismissed from this post. Why? Had he been fomenting resistance or contributing to the 'state of rebellion' under that incompetent attorney? At last, the discovery in his house of Obeah items, and also of musket, powder, and ball (were any of these items planted?) provides enough evidence to indict him. He is put on trial, and eventually sentenced to transportation. Upon hearing his sentence, Adam 'only said very coolly, "Well! I ca'n't help it!" turned himself round, and walked out of court'. To this final anecdote, Lewis appends some telling details: Adam's nickname among the slaves was 'Buonaparte, and he always appeared to exult in the appellation'; he was 'fine-looking', of 'great bodily strength', and with a countenance which 'equally expresses intelligence and malignity' (p. 224). The choice of detail and phrasing, not to speak of Lewis's concern to ensure that Adam's sentence is transportation rather than hanging, indicates Lewis's ambivalence. Adam's narrative is that of a dissident and thwarted leader, and Lewis's sympathy, reluctant, unacknowledged, may be gauged by his last words on Adam, the most recalcitrant slave on Cornwall.

No sugar island was without its slave uprisings. Resistance and rebellion had been continuous throughout Jamaica's colonial history from the time the British took over in 1655.[30] Permanent runaways who banded together and sustained themselves in the fastnesses of the hills—and there were many remote and inaccessible places in the mountainous interior of Jamaica—were known as maroons.[31] So successful had been their guerrilla tactics in 1739 that they had won concessions regarding land and status. Four maroon settlements, designated 'Negro-towns', show on a map of Jamaica of 1820. Earlier there had been more. The danger of revolt was ever present: Lewis himself was in residence when a planned uprising involving more than one thousand people on a neighbouring estate was discovered. The self-protective discursive strategies he employs are interesting: 'It is only to be wished, that the negroes would content themselves with . . . fashionable peccadilloes; but, unluckily, there are some palates among them which require higher seasoned vices . . . a plan has just been discovered . . . for giving themselves a grand fête by murdering all the whites in the island' (p. 137). It is, of course, a swagger of bravado to employ a vocabulary which belittles the opponent or the danger, but if we are to recover something of those silenced voices then the planned insurrection must be understood for what it really was: a serious attempt to mobilize the black population and overthrow a tyrannous regime. Similarly, when Lewis asserts that the overseer of this same estate 'is an old man of the mildest character, and the negroes had always been treated with peculiar

---

[30] For a full account of the wars and resistance in Jamaica, see Craton, *Testing the Chains*.

[31] In Spanish *cimarrón*, in French *marron*.

indulgence', the reader must recognize that he is employing a basic strategy of imperialist discourse in representing an act of rebellion by a subject people as ingratitude. Nevertheless, when the two leaders of the rebellion are put on trial, Lewis records them as 'cool and unconcerned'. The 'King of the Eboes', who was hanged, 'died, declaring that he left enough of his countrymen to prosecute the design in hand, and revenge his death upon the whites' (p. 143), and the other, sentenced to transportation, burned down the door of the prison and escaped, although he was later recaptured. The bravery, ingenuity, and fortitude of these leaders is not directly celebrated, but, as in the case of Adam, Lewis provides enough detail for us to be able to deduce them.

Lewis then, when at any point challenged or uncomfortable, retreats into a typical imperialist posture. At the same time, his recording and placement of details about potential or actual revolutionaries reveal aspects of the subject people he cannot openly acknowledge, even to himself, and indicate the presence of a sympathetic impulse running parallel to, but quite unlike, the paternal benevolence and charitable determination with which he tried to improve the conditions of the slaves. That the slaves themselves viewed Lewis as sympathetic is demonstrated by the inclusion of his name in the 'Song of the King of the Eboes', the revolutionary song produced as evidence in the trial of the leaders of the rebellion.

The *Journal* is almost exclusively concerned with Cornwall. But Lewis had two estates. The second, Hordley, as far east on the island as Cornwall was far west, he owned jointly with a man named Scott.[32] Scott had refused to sell, and he and Lewis were totally at odds over the management of the plantation, especially regarding treatment of the slaves. By the end of October 1817, however, the sale had taken place, and, during Lewis's second stay in Jamaica, he visited Hordley with the intent of ensuring that it operated with the same safeguards for the slaves' welfare as Cornwall. He was there only five days. Hordley proved to be the antithesis of Cornwall: Lewis 'expected to find a perfect paradise, and found a perfect hell'. The trustee—the man whom Lewis had met at Kingston two years earlier and judged

---

[32] John Scott of Moro, which was part of Hordley estate, is mentioned in *Lady Nugent's Journal*, not very complimentarily. He died in 1814, and it must have been his son, or whoever inherited the estate, with whom Lewis was negotiating. See *Lady Nugent's Journal*, 69–70; 315.

'most humane and intelligent' (p. 101)—had allowed the slaves 'to be maltreated . . . with absolute impunity'. Lewis dismissed one book-keeper for 'atrocious brutality'; another ran away. He demoted the chief black governor and sought out a neighbouring gentleman who agreed to hear the slaves' complaints in future. And then he showed a clean pair of heels. The account of Hordley (pp. 228 ff.) is com-pressed into a mere five pages of the original 408, and although examples of vicious treatment of slaves are detailed elsewhere in the *Journal*, here nothing is elaborated. Face to face with the reality of the nightmare he had long dreamt, Lewis could only condense, contract, retreat.

Not long afterwards he left Jamaica for the last time. The letter he wrote just before he sailed, to his neighbour Hill, often mentioned in the *Journal*, the final letter he would write, is entirely concerned with matters on the plantation.[33] It contains careful instructions about one of his bookkeepers who is in poor health, and two post-scripts follow his signature, the first a footnote to one of the ongoing stories in the *Journal*:

I told Cubina to desire Plummer to order that Catalina (the Madwoman) should be maintained by the Estate, and that her Husband should have nothing to do with her; and also Cubina is to repay Sully a Dollar, which I borrowed of him—will you be kind enough to remind Cubina of the one, and tell Plummer of the other, if the Negro should have forgotten his instructions?

The second note reads:

Pray, remind Plummer '[*sic*] not to forget to put up the paradosical piece of Deal Board in the Mill, which is to cost nothing, and prevent the Feeders from falling forwad, [*sic*]—This is serious, observe, *and really so*. I want the Board put up, and the sooner the better.

Probably only in such small ways did Lewis's good intentions make any real difference. He was dead twelve days later, and the great engine of change rolled on, no one greatly affected by his efforts. Between visits to Jamaica he had written a codicil to his will, where-by any subsequent owner would be obliged to visit the plantations for at least three months every third year, or forfeit the estate. The wording was by no means watertight, but he tried. And, as we know

[33] Peck, *A Life of Matthew G. Lewis*, 171.

all too well, when slavery was at last demolished, when the winds of freedom, fresh and welcome as they were, had blown it clean away, the social and economic structures needed to replace it were not erected. Those with grander schemes than Lewis's did not carry through. It is fitting that the final point of Lewis's last letter should show him insisting vehemently upon the fitting of a small device to improve the safety of 'feeders' in the cane factory and protect the slaves against injury.

NOTE ON THE TEXT

The *Journal of a West India Proprietor* was not published until 1834, nearly twenty years after Lewis's death. After the 1834 edition, there was another, slightly abridged, in Murray's Home and Colonial Library (1845, reissued 1861), under a revised title, *Journal of a Residence among the Negroes in the West Indies*. It has reappeared only once since, in 1929. 'The Isle of Devils' (pp. 160 ff.) was also published separately, in Jamaica in 1827, and in London in 1912.

This text of the *Journal* is that of the first edition (London: John Murray, 1834), with obvious errors silently corrected.

SELECT BIBLIOGRAPHY

Biography

[Baron-Wilson, Margaret], *The Life and Correspondence of M. G. Lewis . . . with many pieces in prose and verse, never before published*, 2 vols. (London: Henry Colburn, 1839). The first biography, full of interest, also many inaccuracies.

Peck, Louis F., *A Life of Matthew G. Lewis* (Cambridge, Mass.: Harvard University Press, 1961). A meticulous scholarly account, including a section 'Selected Letters'.

Criticism

Macdonald, D. L., 'The Isle of Devils: The Jamaican Journal of M. G. Lewis', in Timothy Fulford and Peter Kitson (eds.), *Romanticism and Colonialism* (Cambridge: Cambridge University Press, 1998), 189–205. This is the one substantial article on the *Journal*, as, although noticed by historians, the *Journal* has received very little critical attention from literary scholars.

Related Texts

Equiano, Olaudah, *The Interesting Narrative and Other Writings*, ed. with an introduction and notes by Vincent Carretta (Harmondsworth: Penguin, 1995).

Nugent, Lady [Maria], *Lady Nugent's Journal of her residence in Jamaica from 1801 to 1805*, ed. Philip Wright (Kingston, Jamaica: Institute of Jamaica, 1966).

Prince, Mary, *The History of Mary Prince, a West Indian Slave, related by herself*, ed. with an introduction by Moira Ferguson (Ann Arbor, Mich.: University of Michigan Press, 1993).

Related Critical Commentary

Hulme, Peter, *Colonial Encounters: Europe and the Native Caribbean, 1492–1797* (London and New York: Methuen, 1986).

Pratt, Mary Louise, *Imperial Eyes: Travel Writing and Transculturation* (London and New York: Routledge, 1992).

Said, Edward W., *Culture and Imperialism* (New York: Vintage, 1994).

Historical Background

Anstey, Roger, *The Atlantic Slave Trade and British Abolition 1760–1810* (London: Macmillan, 1975).

Bush, Barbara, *Slave Women in Caribbean Society, 1650–1838* (Kingston, Jamaica: Heinemann; Bloomington, Ind.: Indiana University Press; London: James Currey, 1990).

Craton, Michael, *Testing the Chains: Resistance to Slavery in the British West Indies* (Ithaca, NY, and London: Cornell University Press, 1982).

—— and Walvin, James, *A Jamaican Plantation: The History of Worthy Park 1670–1970* (London and New York: W. H. Allen, 1970).

Drescher, Seymour, *Capitalism and Antislavery: British Mobilization in Comparative Perspective* (New York and Oxford: Oxford University Press, 1987).

Duffy, Michael, *Soldiers, Sugar, and Seapower: The British Expeditions to the West Indies and the War against Revolutionary France* (Oxford and New York: Oxford University Press, 1987).

Higman, B. W., *Slave Population and Economy in Jamaica 1807–1834* (Cambridge: Cambridge University Press, 1976).

—— *Slave Populations of the British Caribbean 1807–1834* (Baltimore and London: Johns Hopkins University Press, 1984).

Ragatz, Lowell Joseph, *The Fall of the Planter Class in the British Caribbean, 1763–1833* (New York: Octagon Books, 1963 [1928]). Racist, but full of information.

Turner, Mary, *Slaves and Missionaries: The Disintegration of Jamaican Slave Society, 1787–1834* (Urbana, Ill.: University of Illinois Press, 1982).

Further Reading in Oxford World's Classics

Behn, Aphra, *Oroonoko and Other Writings*, ed. Paul Salzman.

Crèvecœur, J., Hector St Jean de, *Letters from an American Farmer*, ed. Susan Manning.

Empire Writing: An Anthology of Colonial Literature, 1870–1918, ed. Elleke Boehmer.

Lewis, Matthew, *The Monk*, ed. Emma McEvoy.

Stowe, Harriet Beecher, *Uncle Tom's Cabin*, ed. Jean Fagan Yellin.

Washington, Booker T., *Up from Slavery*, ed. William L. Andrews.

A CHRONOLOGY OF MATTHEW LEWIS

1775   9 July, born in London, first child of Matthew and Frances Maria Lewis.

1776   Quakers in England and Pennsylvania require their members to free their slaves or face expulsion from the Society of Friends.

1781   Mrs Lewis leaves her husband.

1782   12 April, Jamaica saved from capture by Admiral Rodney's victory over the French fleet at the Battle of the Saints.

1783–9   Lewis attends Westminster School.

1787   Founding of the *Society for Effecting the Abolition of the Slave Trade*.

1789   Beginning of the French Revolution with the storming of the Bastille.

1790–4   Lewis attends Christ Church, Oxford.

1791   Spends summer in Paris.
        Slave revolution breaks out in St Domingue (St Domingo).

1792   Lewis spends last half of year in Weimar in order to learn German; meets Goethe.

1793   Louis XVI beheaded and reign of terror begins. Conservative backlash in the rest of Europe and beyond puts at risk all movement towards liberalization and change.

1794   After receiving his bachelor's degree, Lewis arrives at The Hague on 15 May, to take a position as attaché in the British Embassy to Holland, where he remains until December. *The Monk* completed at The Hague, by 23 September.

1795–6   July–March. Second Maroon war in Trelawny and St James's parishes, Jamaica.

1796   Lewis takes his seat as Member of Parliament for Hindon, Wiltshire, a pocket borough (i.e. one controlled by a patron or sold to the highest bidder).
        The Monk: A Romance.
        Village Virtues: A Dramatic Satire. In Two Parts.

1797   Coleridge's attack on *The Monk* in the *Quarterly Review* begins a lengthy public debate, and Lewis gains a reputation for indecency and immorality.
        The Minister: A Tragedy, in Five Acts.

1798   *The Castle Spectre: A Drama in Five Acts* (performed at Drury Lane, 14 December 1797). Fourth edition of *The Monk* appears, Lewis having carefully excised all passages which might give offence. Meets Walter Scott.

1799   *The Love of Gain: A Poem.*
The Twins; or, Is It He, or His Brother? A Farce in Two Acts, unpublished (performed at Drury Lane, 8 April).
Rolla; or, the Peruvian Hero. A Tragedy in Five Acts.

1800   *The East Indian: A Comedy, in Five Acts* (performed at Drury Lane, 22 April 1799).

1801   *Tales of Wonder.*
Adelmorn, the Outlaw: A Romantic Drama, in Three Acts, 1801 (performed at Drury Lane, 4 May).
Alfonso, King of Castile: A Tragedy in Five Acts (performed at Covent Garden, 15 January 1802).

1802   Lewis resigns his seat in Parliament.

1803   *The Captive: A Scene in a Private Mad-House*, not separately published (performed at Covent Garden, 22 March).
The Harper's Daughter; or, Love and Ambition. A Tragedy in Five Acts (performed at Covent Garden, 4 May).

1805   *The Bravo of Venice: A Romance.*
Rugantino; or, The Bravo of Venice. A Grand Romantic Melo-Drama, in Two Acts (performed at Covent Garden, 18 October).

1806   *Adelgitha; or, The Fruits of a Single Error. A Tragedy, in Five Acts* (performed at Drury Lane, 30 April 1807).
Feudal Tyrants; or, the Counts of Carlsheim and Sargans. A Romance.

1807   Parliament passes legislation to abolish the slave trade.
The Wood Daemon; or, The Clock has Struck. A Grand Romantic Melo-Drama, in Two Acts, unpublished (performed at Drury Lane, 1 April).

1808   *He Loves and He Rides Away: A Favourite Ballad.*
Twelve Ballads, the Words and Music by M. G. Lewis.
Romantic Tales.

1809   *Venoni; or, The Novice of St Mark's. A Drama in Three Acts* (performed at Drury Lane, 1 December 1808).
Monody on the Death of Sir John Moore (recited at Drury Lane, 14 February 1809).

[Temper, or] The Domestic Tyrant: A Farce, in Two Acts, unpublished (performed at the Lyceum by Drury Lane Company, 1 May).

1811   Slave-trading is made a felony in Britain.
        Timour the Tartar: A Grand Romantic Melo-Drama in Two Acts (performed at Covent Garden, 29 April).
        One O'Clock! or, The Knight and the Wood Daemon, A Grand Musical Romance, in Three Acts (performed at the Lyceum, 1 August).

1812   Lewis's father dies 17 May. Lewis inherits two plantations, and a sizeable fortune.
        Rich and Poor: A Comic Opera, in Three Acts (performed at the Lyceum, 22 July).
        Poems.

1813   Meets Byron.

1815   Sails for Jamaica 11 November.

1816   Lands at Black River, Jamaica, 1 January. Departs for England on 1 April. Lands at Gravesend, 5 June. Remains in England only a few weeks. Begins eighteen-month tour of the Continent, spending most time in Italy. In Geneva, 20 August, a codicil to his will, designed to protect his slaves after his death, is witnessed by Byron, Shelley, and Polidori.

1817   Returns to England September–October, to stay only briefly. Embarks for Jamaica 5 November.

1818   Lands at Savannah-la-Mar, Jamaica, 24 January. Sails for England 4 May; dies on 16 May; buried at sea.

1834   Slavery is changed into 'apprenticeship' as the first stage of emancipation.
        Journal of a West India Proprietor.

1838   Full emancipation is instituted in all British colonies.

NB Lewis's principal works are here included as they are listed by Peck, *A Life of Matthew G. Lewis*, 275–6.

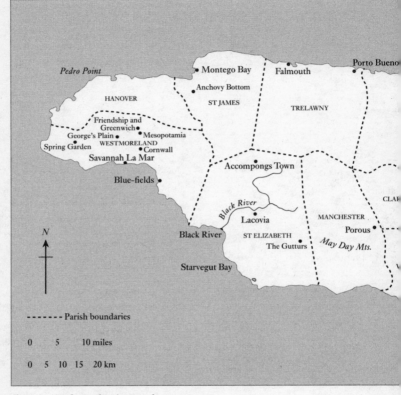

Jamaica in the early nineteenth century

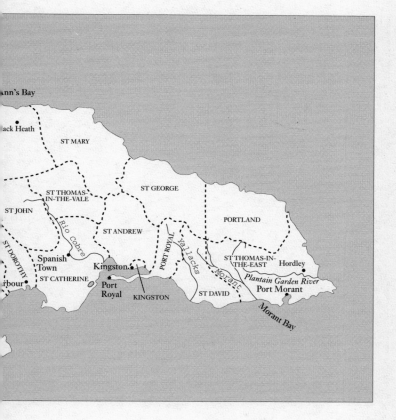

ann's Bay

lack Heath

ST MARY

ST GEORGE

ST THOMAS-
IN-THE-VALE

ST JOHN

PORTLAND

Rio Cobre

ST ANDREW

ST DOROTHY

PORT ROYAL

Yallacks

ST THOMAS-IN-
THE-EAST

Hordley

Spanish
Town

Kingston

Morant

Plantain Garden River

ST CATHERINE

rbour

Port
Royal

Port Morant

KINGSTON

ST DAVID

Morant Bay

JOURNAL OF
A WEST INDIA
PROPRIETOR,

KEPT DURING A RESIDENCE
IN THE ISLAND OF
JAMAICA

I would give many a sugar cane,
Mat. Lewis were alive again!

Byron*

ADVERTISEMENT

The following Journals of two residences in Jamaica, in 1815–16, and in 1817, are now printed from the MS of Mr Lewis; who died at sea, on the voyage homewards from the West Indies, in the year 1818.

JOURNAL OF
A WEST INDIA PROPRIETOR

Nunc alio patriam quæro sub sole jacentem

Virgil*

1815 November 8 (Wednesday)

I left London, and reached Gravesend at nine in the morning, having been taught to expect our sailing in a few hours. But although the vessel left the Docks on Saturday, she did not reach this place till three o'clock on Thursday, the 9th. The captain now tells me, that we may expect to sail certainly in the afternoon of to-morrow, the 10th. I expect the ship's cabin to gain greatly by my two days' residence at the '***** ****', which nothing can exceed for noise, dirt, and dulness. Eloisa would never have established 'black melancholy'* at the Paraclete as its favourite residence, if she had happened to pass three days at an inn at Gravesend: nowhere else did I ever see the sky look so dingy, and the river so dirty; to be sure, the place has all the advantages of an English November to assist it in those particulars. Just now, too, a carriage passed my windows, conveying on board a cargo of passengers, who seemed sincerely afflicted at the thoughts of leaving their dear native land! The pigs squeaked, the ducks quacked, and the fowls screamed; and all so dolefully, as clearly to prove, that *theirs* was no dissembled sorrow? And after them (more affecting than all) came a wheelbarrow, with a solitary porker tied in a basket, with his head hanging over on one side, and his legs sticking out on the other, who neither grunted nor moved, nor gave any signs of life, but seemed to be of quite the same opinion with Hannah More's heroine,

Grief is for *little* wrongs; despair for mine!

As Miss O'Neil* is to play 'Elwina'* for the first time to-morrow, it is a thousand pities that she had not the previous advantage of seeing the speechless despondency of this poor pig; it might have furnished her with some valuable hints, and enabled her to convey more perfectly to the audience the 'expressive silence' of irremediable distress.

November 10

At four o'clock in the afternoon, I embarked on board the 'Sir Godfrey Webster', Captain Boyes. On approaching the vessel, we heard the loudest of all possible shrieks proceeding from a boat lying near her: and who should prove to be the complainant, but my former acquaintance, the despairing pig. He had recovered his voice to protest against entering the ship: I had already declared against climbing up the accommodation ladder; the pig had precisely the very same objection. So a *soi-disant* chair, being a broken bucket, was let down for us, and the pig and myself entered the vessel by the same conveyance; only pig had the precedence, and was hoisted up first. The ship proceeded three miles, and then the darkness obliged us to come to an anchor. There are only two other cabin passengers, a Mr J—— and a Mr S——; the latter is a planter in the 'May-Day Mountains', Jamaica: he wonders, considering how much benefit Great Britain derives from the West Indies, that government is not careful to build more churches in them, and is of opinion, that 'hedicating the negroes is the only way to make them appy; indeed, in his umble hopinion, hedication his hall in hall!'

November 11

We sailed at six o'clock, passed through 'Nob's Hole', the 'Girdler's Hole', and 'the Pan' (all very dangerous sands, and particularly the last, where at times we had only one foot water below us), by half past four, and at five came to an anchor in the Queen's Channel. Never having seen any thing of the kind before, I was wonderfully pleased with the manœuvring of several large ships, which passed through the sands at the same time with us: their motions seemed to be effected with as much ease and dexterity as if they had been crane-necked carriages;* and the effect as they pursued each other's track and windings was perfectly beautiful.

November 12 (Sunday)

The wind was contrary, and we had to beat up the whole way; we did not reach the Downs till past four o'clock, and, as there were above sixty vessels arrived before us, we had some difficulty in finding a safe berth. At length we anchored in the Lower Roads, about four miles off Deal. We can see very clearly the double lights in the vessel moored off the Goodwin sands: it is constantly inhabited by two families, who reside there alternately every fortnight, except when the weather delays the exchange. The 'Sir Godfrey Webster' is a vessel of 600 tons, and was formerly in the East India service. I have a very clean cabin, a place for my books, and every thing is much more comfortable than I expected; the wind, however, is completely west, the worst that we could have, and we must not even expect a change till the full moon. The captain pointed out a man to me to-day, who had been with him in a violent storm off the Bermudas. For six hours together, the flashes of lightning were so unintermitting, that the eye could not sustain them: at one time, the ship seemed to be completely in a blaze; and the man in question (who was then standing at the wheel, near the captain) suddenly cried out, 'I don't know what has happened to me, but I can neither see nor stand'; and he fell down upon the deck. He was taken up and carried below; and it appeared that the lightning had affected his eyes and legs, in a degree to make him both blind and lame, though the captain, who was standing by his side, had received no injury: in three or four days, the man was quite well again. In this storm, no less than thirteen vessels were dismasted, or otherwise shattered by the lightning.

Sea Terms.—*Windward, from* whence the wind blows; *leeward, to* which it blows; *starboard*, the *right* of the stern; *larboard*, the *left*; *starboard helm*, when you go to the left; but when to the right, instead of larboard helm, *helm a-port*; *luff you may*, go nearer to the wind; *theis* (*thus*) you are near enough; *luff no near*, you are too near the wind; the *tiller*, the handle of the rudder; the *capstan*, the weigher of the anchor; the *buntlines*, the ropes which move the body of the sail, the *bunt* being the body; the *bowlines*, those which spread out the sails, and make them swell.

November 13

At six this morning, came on a tremendous gale of wind; the captain says, that he never experienced a heavier. However, we rode it out with great success, although, at one time, it was bawled out that we were driving; and, at another, a brig* which lay near us broke from her moorings, and came bearing down close upon us. The danger, indeed, from the difference of size, was all upon the side of the brig; but, luckily, the vessels cleared each other. This evening she has thought it as well to remove further from so dangerous a neighbourhood. There is a little cabin boy on board, and Mr J—— has brought with him a black terrier; and these two at first sight swore to each other an eternal friendship, in the true German style.* It is the boy's first voyage, and he is excessively sea-sick; so he has been obliged to creep into his hammock, and his friend, the little black terrier, has crept into the hammock with him. A boat came from the shore this evening, and reported that several vessels have been dismasted, lost their anchors, and injured in various ways. A brig, which was obliged to make for Ramsgate, missed the pier, and was dashed to pieces completely; the crew, however, were saved, all except the pilot; who, although he was brought on shore alive, what between bruises, drowning, and fright, had suffered so much, that he died two hours afterwards. The weather has now again become calm; but it is still full west.

November 14 (Tuesday)

THE HOURS

Ne'er were the zephyrs known disclosing
    More sweets, than when in Tempe's shades
They waved the lilies, where, reposing,
    Sat four and twenty lovely maids.

Those lovely maids were called 'the Hours,'
    The charge of Virtue's flock they kept;
And each in turn employ'd her powers
    To guard it, while her sisters slept.

False Love, how simple souls thou cheatest!
    In myrtle bower, that traitor near
Long watch'd an Hour, the softest, sweetest!
    The *evening* Hour, to shepherds dear.[1]

In tones so bland he praised her beauty,
    Such melting airs his pipe could play,
The thoughtless Hour forgot her duty,
    And fled in Love's embrace away.

Meanwhile the fold was left unguarded—
    The wolf broke in—the lambs were slain:

---

[1] L'heure du berger.

And now from Virtue's train discarded,
With tears her sisters speak their pain.

Time flies, and still they weep; for never
The fugitive can time restore:
An Hour once fled, has fled for ever,
And all the rest shall smile no more!

November 15

The wind altered sufficiently to allow us to escape from the Downs; and at dusk we were off Beachy Head. This morning, the steward left the trap-door of the store-hole open; of course, I immediately contrived to step into it, and was on the point of being precipitated to the bottom, among innumerable boxes of grocery, bags of biscuit, and porter barrels;—where a broken limb was the *least* that I could expect. Luckily, I fell across the corner of the trap, and managed to support myself, till I could effect my escape with a bruised knee, and the loss of a few inches of skin from my left arm.

November 16

Off the Isle of Wight.

November 17

Off the St Alban's Head. Sick to death! My temples throbbing, my head burning, my limbs freezing, my mouth all fever, my stomach all nausea, my mind all disgust.

November 18

Off the Lizard, the last point of England.

November 19 (Sunday)

At one this morning, a violent gust of wind came on; and, at the rate of ten miles an hour, carried us through the Chops of the Channel,* formed by the Scilly Rocks and the Isle of Ushant. But I thought, that the advance was dearly purchased by the terrible night which the storm made us pass. The wind roaring, the waves dashing against the stern, till at last they beat in the quarter gallery; the ship, too, rolling from side to side, as if every moment she were going to roll over and over! Mr J—— was heaved off one of the sofas, and rolled along, till he was stopped by the table. He then took his seat upon the floor, as the more secure position; and, half an hour afterwards, another heave chucked him back again upon the sofa. The captain snuffed out one of the candles, and both being tied to the table, could not relight it with the other: so the steward came to do it; when a sudden heel of the ship made him extinguish the second candle, tumbled him upon the sofa on which I was lying, and made the candle which he had brought with him fly out of the candlestick, through a cabin window at his elbow; and thus we were all left in the dark. Then the intolerable noise! the cracking of bulkheads! the sawing of ropes! the screeching of the tiller! the trampling of the sailors! the clattering of the crockery! Every thing above deck and below deck, all in motion at once! Chairs, writing-desks, books, boxes, bundles, fire-irons and fenders, flying to one end of the room; and the next moment (as if they had made a mistake) flying back again to the other with the same hurry and confusion! 'Confusion worse confounded!'* Of all the inconveniences attached to a vessel, the incessant noise appears to me the most insupportable! As to our live stock, they seem to have made up their minds on the subject, and say with one of Ariosto's knights (when he was cloven from the head to the chine), '*or convien morire*'.* Our fowls and ducks are screaming and quacking their last by dozens; and by Tuesday morning, it is supposed that we shall not have an animal alive in the ship, except the black terrier—and my friend the squeaking pig, whose vocal powers are still audible, maugre the storm and the sailors, and who (I verily believe) only continues to survive out of spite, because he can join in the general chorus, and help to increase the number of abominable sounds.

We are now tossing about in the Bay of Biscay: I shall remember it as long as I live. The 'beef-eater's front' could never have 'beamed more terrible' upon Don Ferolo Whiskerandos,* 'in Biscay's Bay, when he took him prisoner', than Biscay's Bay itself will appear to *me* the next time that I approach it.

November 20

Our live stock has received an increase; our fowls and ducks are dead to be sure, but a lark flew on board this morning, blown (as is supposed) from the coast of France. In five minutes it appeared to be quite at home, eat very readily whatever was given it, and hopped about the deck without fear of the sailors, or the more formidable black terrier, with all the ease and assurance imaginable.

I dare say, it *was* blown from the coast of France!

November 21

The weather continues intolerable. Boisterous waves running mountains high, with no wind, or a foul one. Dead calms by day, which prevent our making any progress; and violent storms by night, which prevent our getting any sleep.

Every thing is in a state of perpetual motion. '*Nulla quies intus* (nor *outus* indeed for the matter of that), *nullâque silentia parte*.'* We drink our tea exactly as Tantalus* did in the infernal regions; we keep bobbing at the basin for half an hour together without being able to get a drop; and certainly nobody on ship-board can doubt the truth of the proverb, 'Many things fall out between the cup and the lip.'

November 23

PANDORA'S BOX   (*Iliad* Λ.)

Prometheus once (in Tooke* the tale you'll see)
    In one vast box enclosed all human evils;
But curious Woman needs the inside would see,
    And out came twenty thousand million devils.

The story's spoil'd, and Tooke should well be chid;
    The fact, sir, happen'd thus, and I've no doubt of it:
'Twas not that Woman raised the coffer's lid,
    But when the lid *was* raised, Woman popp'd out of it.

'But Hope remain'd'—true, sir, she did; but still
    All saw of what Miss Hope gave intimation;
Her right hand grasp'd an undertaker's bill,
    Her left conceal'd a deed of separation.

N.B. I was most horribly sea-sick when I took this view of the subject. Besides, grapes on shipboard, in general, are remarkably sour.

November 24

Manibus date lilia plenis;
Purpureos spargam flores!*

The squeaking pig was killed this morning.

November 25

Letters were sent to England by a small vessel bound for Plymouth, and laden with oranges from St Michael's, one of the Azores.

November 26

A complete and most violent storm, from twelve at night till seven the next morning. The fore-top-sail, though only put up for the first time yesterday, was rent from top to bottom; and several of the other sails are torn to pieces. The perpetual tempestuous weather which we have experienced has so shaken the planks of the vessel, that the sea enters at all quarters. About one o'clock in the morning I was saluted by a stream of water, which poured down exactly upon my face, and obliged me to shift my lodgings. The carpenter had been made aware that there was a leak in my cabin, and ordered to caulk the seams; but, I suppose, he thought that during only a two months' voyage, the rain might very possibly never find out the hole, and that it would be quite time enough to apply the remedy when I should have felt the inconvenience. The best is, that the carpenter happening to be at work in the next cabin when the water came down upon me, I desired him to call my servant, in order that I might get up, on account of the leak; on which he told me 'that the leak could not be helped'; grumbled a good deal at calling up the servant; and seemed to think me not a little unreasonable for not lying quietly, and suffering myself to be pumped upon by this shower-bath of his own providing.

But if the water gets *into* the ship, on the other hand, last night the poor old steward was very near getting out of it. In the thick of the storm he was carrying some grog to the mate, when a gun, which drove against him, threw him off his balance, and he was just passing through one of the port-holes, when, luckily, he caught hold of a rope, and saved himself. A screech-owl flew on board this morning: I am sure we have no need of birds of ill omen; I could supply the place of a whole aviary of them myself.

November 28

Reading Don Quixote this morning, I was greatly pleased with an instance of the hero's politeness, which had never struck me before. The Princess Micomicona having fallen into a most egregious blunder, he never so much as hints a suspicion of her not having acted precisely as she has stated, but only begs to know her reasons for taking a step so extraordinary. 'But pray, madam,' says he, 'why *did* your ladyship land at Ossuna, seeing that it is not a seaport town?'

I was also much charmed with an instance of conjugal affection, in the same work. Sancho being just returned home, after a long absence, the first thing which his wife, Teresa, asks about, is the welfare of the ass. 'I have brought him back,' answers Sancho, 'and in much better health and condition than I am in myself.' 'The Lord be praised,' said Teresa, 'for this his great mercy to me!'

November 29

The wind continues contrary, and the weather is as disagreeable and perverse as it can well be; indeed, I understand that in these latitudes nothing can be expected but heavy gales or dead calms, which makes them particularly pleasant for sailing, especially as the calms are by far the most disagreeable of the two: the wind steadies the ship; but when she creeps as slowly as she does at present (scarcely going a mile in four hours), she feels the whole effect of the sea breaking against her, and rolls backwards and forwards with every billow as it rises and falls. In the mean while, every thing seems to be in a state of the most active motion, except the ship; while we are carrying a spoonful of soup to our mouths, the remainder takes the 'glorious golden opportunity' to empty itself into our laps, and the glasses and salt-cellars carry on a perpetual domestic warfare during the whole time of dinner, like the Guelphs and the Ghibellines.* Nothing is so common as to see a roast goose suddenly jump out of its dish in the middle of dinner, and make a frisk from one end of the table to the other; and we are quite in the habit of laying wagers which of the two boiled fowls will arrive at the bottom first.

N.B. To-day the fowl without the liver wing was the favourite, but the knowing ones were taken in; the uncarved one carried it hollow.

November 30

'Do those I love e'er think on me?'
    How oft that painful doubt will start,
To blight the roseate smile of glee,
    And cloud the brow, and sink the heart!

No more can I, estranged from home,
    Their pleasures share, nor soothe their moans;
To them I'm dead as were the foam
    Now breaking o'er my whitening bones.

And doubtless now with newer friends,
    The tide of life content they stem;
Nor on the sailor think, who bends
    Full many an anxious thought on them.

Should that reflection cause me pain?
    No ease for mine their grief could bring;
Enough if, when we meet again,
    Their answering hearts to greet me spring.

Enough, if no dull joyless eye
    Give signs of kindness quite forgot;
Nor heartless question, cold reply,
    Speak—'all is past; I love you not.'

Too much has heav'n ordain'd of woe,
    Too much of groans on earth abounds,
For me to wish one tear to flow
    Which brings no balm for sorrow's wounds.

Love's moisten'd lid and Friendship's sigh,
    I could not see, I could not hear!
To think 'they weep!' more fills mine eye,
    And smarts the more each tender tear.

Then, if there be one heart so kind,
    It mourns each hour the loss of me;
Shrinks, when it hears some gust of wind,
    And sighs—'Perhaps a storm at sea!'

Oh! if there be an heart *indeed*,
    Which beats for me, so sad, so true,
Swift to its aid, Oblivion, speed,
    And bathe it with thy poppy's dew;

My form in vapours to conceal,
    From Pleasure's wreath rich odours shake;
Nor let that heart one moment feel
    Such pangs as force my own to ache.

Demon of Memory, cherish'd grief!
    Oh, could I break thy wand in twain!
Oh, could I close thy magic leaf,
    Till those I love are mine again!

December 1 (Friday)

The captain to-day pointed out to me a sailor-boy, who, about three years ago, was shaken from the mast-head, and fell through the scuttle into the hold: the distance was above eighty feet, yet the boy was taken up with only a few bruises.

December 3 (Sunday)

The wind during the last two days has been more favourable; and at nine this morning we were in the latitude of Madeira.

December 5

Sea Terms.—*Ratlines*, the rope ladders by which the sailors climb the shrouds; the *companion*, the cabin-head; *reefs*, the divisions by which the sails are contracted; *stunsails*, additional sails, spread for the purpose of catching all the wind possible; the *fore-mast*, *main-mast*, *mizen-mast*; *fore*, the head; *aft*, the stern; *being pooped* (the very sound of which tells one, that it must be something very terrible), having the stern beat in by the sea; *to belay a rope*, to fasten it.

December 6

I had no idea of the expense of building and preserving a ship: that in which I am at present cost 30,000*l.* at its outset. Last year the repairs amounted to 14,000*l.*; and in a voyage to the East Indies they were more than 20,000*l.* In its return last year from Jamaica it was on the very brink of shipwreck. A storm had driven it into Bantry Bay, and there was no other refuge from the winds than Bear Haven, whose entrance was narrow and difficult; however, a gentleman from Castletown came on board, and very obligingly offered to pilot the ship. He was one of the first people in the place, had been the owner of a vessel himself, was most thoroughly acquainted with every inch of the haven, etc. etc., and so on they went. There was but one sunken rock, and that about ten feet in diameter; the captain knew it, and warned his gentleman-pilot to keep a little more to the eastward. 'My dear friend,' answered the Irishman, 'now do just make yourself *asy*; I know well enough what we are about; we are as clear of the rock as if we were in the Red Sea, by Jasus;'—upon which the vessel struck upon the rock, and there she stuck. The captain fell to swearing and tearing his hair. 'God damn you, sir! didn't I tell you to keep to eastward? Dam'me, she's on the rock!' 'Oh! well, my dear, she's now *on* the rock, and, in a few minutes, you know, why she'll be *off* the rock: to be sure, I'd have taken my oath that the rock was two hundred and fifty feet on the other side of her, but——'—'Two hundred and fifty feet! why, the channel is not two hundred and fifty feet wide itself! and as to getting her off, bumping against this rock, it can only be with a great hole in her side.'—'Poh! now, bother, my dear! why sure——'—'Leave the ship, sir; dam'me, sir, get out of my ship this moment!' Instead of which, with the most smiling and obliging air in the world, the Irishman turned to console the female passengers. 'Make yourselves *asy*, ladies, pray make yourselves perfectly *asy*; but, upon my soul, I believe your captain's mad; no danger in life! only make yourselves *asy*, I say; for the ship lies on the rock as safe and as quiet, by Jasus, as if she were lying on a mud bank!' Luckily the weather was so perfectly calm, that the ship having once touched the rock with her keel bumped no more. It was low water; she wanted but five inches to float her, and when the tide rose she drifted off, and with but little harm done. The gentleman-pilot then thought proper to return on shore, took a very polite leave of the lady-passengers, and departed with all the urbanity possible; only thinking the captain the strangest person that he had ever met with; and wondering that any man of common sense could be put out of temper by such a trifle.

December 7

Yesterday we had the satisfaction of falling in with the trade wind, and now we are proceeding both rapidly and steadily. The change of climate is very perceptible; and the deep and beautiful blue which colours the sea is a certain intimation of our approach to the tropic. A few flying fish have made their appearance; and the spears are getting in order for the reception of their constant attendant, the dolphin. These spears have ropes affixed to them, and at one end of the pole are five barbs, at the other a heavy ball of lead: then, when the fish is speared, the striker lets the staff fall, on which down goes the lead into the sea, and up goes the dolphin into the air, who is in the utmost astonishment to find itself all of a sudden turned into a flying fish; so determines to cultivate the art of flying for the future, and promises itself a great many pleasant airings. The dolphin and the flying fish are beautifully coloured, and both are very good food, particularly the latter, which move in shoals like the herring, and are about the size of that fish. They are supposed to feed on spawn and sea animalculæ, and will not take the bait; but on the shores of Barbadoes, which they frequent in great multitudes, they are caught in wide nets, spread upon the surface of the sea; then, upon beating the waters around, the fish rise in clouds, and fly till, their fins getting dry, they fall down into the nets which have been spread to receive them. The dolphin is seldom above three feet long; the immense strength which he exerts in his struggles for liberty occasions the necessity of catching him in the way before described.

December 8

At three o'clock this afternoon we entered the tropic of Cancer; and if our wind continues tolerably favourable, we may expect to see Antigua on Sunday se'nnight. On crossing the line, it was formerly usual for ships to receive a visit from an old gentleman and his wife, Mr and Mrs Cancer: the husband was, by profession, a barber; and, probably, the scullion, who insisted so peremptorily on shaving Sancho, at the duke's castle, had served an apprenticeship to Mr Cancer, for their mode of proceeding was much alike, and, indeed, very peculiar: the old gentleman always made a point of using a rusty iron hoop instead of a razor, tar for soap, and an empty beef-barrel was, in his opinion, the very best possible substitute for a basin; in consequence of which, instead of paying him for shaving them, people of taste were disposed to pay for not being shaved; and as Mrs Cancer happened to be particularly partial to gin (when good), the gift of a few bottles was generally successful in rescuing the donor's chin from the hands of her husband; however, to-day this venerable pair 'peradventure were sleeping, or on a journey',* for we neither saw nor heard any thing about them.

December 9

When, after his victory of the 1st of June, Lord Howe* again put to sea from Portsmouth, the number of women who were turned on shore out of the ships (wives, sisters, etc.) amounted to above thirty thousand!

December 10 (Sunday)

What triumph moves on the billows so blue?
In his car of pellucid pearl I view,
With glorious pomp, on the dancing tide,
The tropic Genius proudly ride.

The flying fish, who trail his car,
Dazzle the eye, as they shine from afar;
Twinkling their fins in the sun, and show
All the hues which adorn the showery bow.

Of dark sea-blue is the mantle he wears;
For a sceptre a plantain branch he bears;
Pearls his sable arms surround,
And his locks of wool with coral are crown'd.

Perpetual sunbeams round him stream;
His bronzed limbs shine with golden gleam;
The spicy spray from his wheels that showers,
Makes the sense ache with its odorous powers.

Myriads of monsters, who people the caves
Of ocean, attendant plough the waves;
Sharks and crocodiles bask in his blaze,
And whales spout the waters which dance in his rays.

And as onward floats that triumph gay,
The light sea-breezes around it play;

While at his royal feet lie bound
The Ouragans,* hush'd in sleep profound.

Dark Genius, hear a stranger's prayer,
Nor suffer those winds to ravage and tear
Jamaica's savannas, and loose to fly,
Mingling the earth, and the sea, and the sky.

From thy locks on my harvest of sweets diffuse,
To swell my canes, refreshing dews;
And kindly breathe, with cooling powers,
Through my coffee walks and shaddock bowers.

Let not thy strange diseases prey
On my life; but scare from my couch away
The yellow Plague's imps; and safe let me rest
From that dread black demon, who racks the breast:

Nor force my throbbing temples to know
Thy sunbeam's sudden and maddening blow;
Nor bid thy day-flood blaze too bright
On nerves so fragile, and brain so light:

And let me, returning in safety, view
Thy triumph again on the ocean blue;
And in Britain I'll oft with flowers entwine
The Tropic Sovereign's ebony shrine!

Was it but fancy? did He not frown,
And in anger shake his coral crown?
Gorgeous and slow the pomp moves on!
Low sinks the sun—and all is gone!

'And pray now do you mean to say that you really saw all this fine show?' Oh, yes, really, 'in my mind's eye, Horatio',* as Shakspeare says; or, if you like it better in Greek—

Οσσομενος Πατερ' εσθλον ενι φρησιν!*
Odyssey, A.

December 11

A dead centipes was found on the deck, supposed to have made its way on board, during the last voyage, among the logwood. This is not the only species of disagreeable passengers, who are in the habit of introducing themselves into homeward bound vessels without leave. While sleeping on deck last year, the Captain felt something run across his face; and, supposing it to be a cock-roach, he brushed off a scorpion; but not without its first biting him upon the cheek: the pain for about four hours was excessive; but although he did no more than wash the wound with spirits, he was perfectly well again in a couple of days.

December 12

Since we entered the tropic, the rains have been incessant, and most violent; but the wind was brisk and favourable, and we proceeded rapidly. Now we have lost the trade-wind, and move so slowly, that it might almost be called standing still. On the other hand, the weather is now perfectly delicious; the ship makes but little way, but she moves steadily: the sun is brilliant; the sky cloudless; the sea calm, and so smooth that it looks like one extended sheet of blue glass; an awning is stretched over the deck; although there is not wind enough to fill the canvass, there is sufficient to keep the air cool, and thus, even during the day, the weather is very pleasant; but the nights are quite heavenly, and so bright, that at ten o'clock yesterday evening little Jem Parsons (the cabin boy), and his friend the black terrier, came on deck, and sat themselves down on a gun-carriage, to read by the light of the moon. I looked at the boy's book, (the terrier, I suppose, read over the other's shoulder,) and found that it was 'The Sorrows of Werter'.* I asked who had lent him such a book, and whether it amused him? He said that it had been made a present to him, and so he had read it almost through, for he had got to Werter's dying; though, to be sure, he did not understand it all, nor like very much what he understood; for he thought the man a great fool for killing himself *for love*. I told him I thought every man a great fool who killed himself for love or for any thing else: but had he no books but 'The Sorrows of Werter'?—Oh dear, yes, he said, he had a great many more; he had got 'The Adventures of a Louse',* which was a very curious book, indeed; and he had got besides 'The Recess',* and 'Valentine and Orson',* and 'Roslin Castle',* and a book of Prayers, just like the Bible; but he could not but say that he liked 'The Adventures of a Louse' the best of any of them.

December 13

We caught a dolphin, but not with the spear: he gorged a line which was fastened to the stern, and baited with salt pork; but being a very large and strong fish, his efforts to escape were so powerful, that it was feared that he would break the line, and a *grainse* (as the dolphin-spear is technically termed) was thrown at him: he was struck, and three of the prongs were buried in his side; yet, with a violent effort, he forced them out again, and threw the lance up into the air. I am not much used to take pleasure in the sight of animal suffering; but if Pythagoras himself had been present, and 'of opinion that the soul of his grandam might haply inhabit'* this dolphin, I think he must still have admired the force and agility displayed in his endeavours to escape. Imagination can picture nothing more beautiful than the colours of this fish: while covered by the waves he was entirely green; and as the water gave him a case of transparent crystal, he really looked like one solid piece of living emerald; when he sprang into the air, or swam fatigued upon the surface, his fins alone preserved their green, and the rest of his body appeared to be of the brightest yellow, his scales shining like gold wherever they caught the sun; while the blood which, as long as he remained in the sea, continued to spout in great quantities, forced its way upwards through the water, like a wreath of crimson smoke, and then dispersed itself in separate globules among the spray. From the great loss of blood, his colours soon became paler; but when he was at length safely landed on deck, and beating himself to death against the flooring, agony renewed all the lustre of his tints: his fins were still green and his body golden, except his back, which was olive, shot with bright deep blue; his head and belly became silvery, and the spots with which the latter was mottled changed, with incessant rapidity, from deep olive to the most beautiful azure. Gradually his brilliant tints disappeared: they were succeeded by one uniform shade of slate-colour; and when he was quite dead, he exhibited nothing but dirty brown and dull dead white. As soon as all was over with him, the first thing done was to convert one of his fins into the resemblance of a flying fish, for the purpose of decoying other dolphins; and the second, to order some of the present gentleman to be got ready for dinner. He measured above four feet and a half.

December 14

At noon to-day, we found ourselves in the latitude of Jamaica. We were promised the sight of Antigua on Sunday next, but that is now quite out of the question. We made but eight miles in the whole of yesterday; and as Jamaica is still at the distance of eighteen hundred miles, at this rate of proceeding we may expect to reach it about eight months hence. The sky this evening presented us with quite a new phenomenon, a rose-coloured moon: she is to be at her full to-morrow; and this afternoon, about half-past four, she rose like a disk of silver, perfectly white and colourless; but, as she was exactly opposite to the sun at the time of his setting, the reflection of his rays spread a kind of pale blush over her orb, which produced an effect as beautiful as singular. Indeed, the size and inconceivable brilliance of the sun, the clearness of the atmosphere, which had assumed a faint greenish hue, and was entirely without a cloud, the smoothness of the ocean, and the aforesaid rose-coloured moon, altogether rendered this sunset the most magical in effect that I ever beheld; and it was with great reluctance that I was called away from admiring it, to ascertain whether the merits of our new acquaintance, the dolphin, extended any further than his skin. Part of him, which was boiled for yesterday's dinner, was rather coarse and dry, and might have been mistaken for indifferent haddock. But his having been steeped in brine, and then broiled with a good deal of pepper and salt, had improved him wonderfully; and to-day I thought him as good as any other fish.

December 15

Our wind is like Lady Townley's* separate allowance: 'that little has been made less'; or, rather, it has dwindled away to nothing. We are now so absolutely becalmed, that I begin seriously to suspect all the crew of being Phæacians*; and that at this identical moment Neptune is amusing himself by making the ship take root in the ocean; a trick which he played once before to a vessel (they say) in the days of Ulysses. I have got some locust plants on board in pots: if we continue to sail as slowly as we have done for the last week, before we reach Jamaica my plants will be forest trees, little Jem, the cabin-boy, will have been obliged to shave, and the black terrier will have died of old age long ago. Great numbers of porpoises were playing about to-day, and tumbling under the ship's very nose. When in their gambols they allow themselves to be seen above the surface, they are of a dirty blackish brown, and as ugly as heart can wish; but in the waves they acquire a fine sea-green cast, and their spouting up water in the sunbeams is extremely ornamental.

THE HELMSMAN

Hark! the bell! it sounds midnight!—all hail, thou new heav'n!
    How soft sleep the stars on their bosom of night!
While o'er the full moon, as they gently are driven,
    Slowly floating the clouds bathe their fleeces in light.

The warm feeble breeze scarcely ripples the ocean,
    And all seems so hush'd, all so happy to feel!
So smooth glides the bark, I perceive not her motion,
    While low sings the sailor who watches the wheel.

That sailor I've noted—his cheek, fresh and blooming
    With health, scarcely yet twenty springs can have seen;
His looks they are lofty, but never presuming,
    His limbs strong, but light, and undaunted his mien.

Frank and clear is his brow, yet a thoughtful expression,
    Half tender, half mournful, oft shadows his eye;
And murmurs escape him, which make the confession,
    If not check'd by a hem, they had swell'd to a sigh.

His song is not pour'd to beguile the lone hour,
    When mid-watch on deck 'tis his duty to keep;
Nor of painful reflection to weaken the power,
    Nor chase from his eyelids the pinions of sleep.

'Tis so sad . . . 'tis so sweet . . . and some tones come so swelling,
    So right from the heart, and so pure to the ear;—
That sure at this moment his thoughts must be dwelling
    On one who is absent, most kind and most dear.

Perhaps on a mother his mind loves to linger,
    Whose wants to relieve, the rough seas hath he cross'd;
Who kiss'd him at parting, and vow'd he could bring her
    No jewel so dear as the one she then lost!

No, no! 'tis a sweetheart, his soul's cherish'd treasure,
    Those full melting notes . . . hark! he breathes them again!
So mournful, and yet they're prolong'd with such pleasure . . .
    Oh, nothing but love could have prompted the strain.

Yet, whate'er be the cause of thy sadness, young seaman,
  That the weight be soon lighten'd, I send up my vow;
From the stings of remorse, I'll be sworn, thou'rt a freeman,
  No guilt ever ruffled the smooth of that brow!

That sigh which you breath'd sprang from pensive affection;
  That song, though so plaintive, sheds balm on the heart;
And the pain which you feel at each fond recollection,
  Is worth all the pleasures that vice could impart.

Oh, still may the scenes of your life, like the present,
  Shine bright to the eye, and speak calm to the breast;
May each wave flow as gentle, each breeze play as pleasant,
  And warm as the clime prove the friends you love best!

And may she, who now dictates that ballad so tender,
  Diffuse o'er your days the heart's solace and ease,
As yon lovely moon, with a gleam of mild splendour,
  Pure, tranquil, and bright, over-silvers the seas!

December 16

What little wind there is blows so perversely, that we have been obliged to alter our course; and instead of Antigua, we are now told that the Summer Islands (Shakspeare's 'still vexed Bermoothes')* are the first land that we must expect to see.

I am greatly disappointed at finding such a scarcity of monsters; I had flattered myself, that as soon as we should enter the Atlantic Ocean, or at least the tropic, we should have seen whole shoals of sharks, whales, and dolphins wandering about as plenty as sheep upon the South Downs: instead of which, a brace of dolphins, and a few flying fish and porpoises, are the only inhabitants of the ocean who have as yet taken the trouble of paying us the common civility of a visit. However, I am promised, that as soon as we approach the islands, I shall have as many sharks as heart can wish.

As I am particularly fond of proofs of conjugal attachment between animals (in the human species they are so universal that I set no store by them), an instance of that kind which the captain related to me this morning gave me great pleasure. While lying in Black River harbour, Jamaica, two sharks were frequently seen playing about the ship; at length the female was killed, and the desolation of the male was excessive:—

Che faro senz' Eurydice?*

What he did *without* her remains a secret, but what he did *with* her was clear enough; for scarce was the breath out of his Eurydice's body, when he stuck his teeth in her, and began to eat her up with all possible expedition. Even the sailors felt their sensibility excited by so peculiar a mark of posthumous attachment; and to enable him to perform this melancholy duty the more easily, they offered to be his carvers, lowered their boat, and proceeded to chop his better half in pieces with their hatchets; while the widower opened his jaws as wide as possible, and gulped down pounds upon pounds of the dear departed as fast as they were thrown to him, with the greatest delight and all the avidity imaginable. I make no doubt that all the while he was eating, he was thoroughly persuaded that every morsel which went into his stomach would make its way to his heart directly! 'She was perfectly consistent,' he said to himself; 'she was excellent through life, and really she's extremely good now she's dead!' and then, 'unable to conceal his pain',

> He sigh'd and swallow'd, and sigh'd and swallow'd,
> And sigh'd and swallow'd again.*

I doubt, whether the annals of Hymen can produce a similar instance of post-obitual affection. Certainly Calderon's '*Amor despues de la Muerte*'* has nothing that is worthy to be compared to it; nor do I recollect in history any fact at all resembling it, except perhaps a circumstance which is recorded respecting Cambletes, King of Lydia, a monarch equally remarkable for his voracity and uxoriousness; and who, being one night completely overpowered by sleep, and at the same time violently tormented by hunger, eat up his queen without being conscious of it, and was mightily astonished, the next morning, to wake with her hand in his mouth, the only bit that was left of her. But then, Cambletes was quite unconscious what he was doing; whereas, the shark's mark of attachment was evidently intentional. It may, however, be doubted, from the voracity with which he eat, whether his conduct on this occasion was not as much influenced by the sentiment of hunger as of love; and if he were absolutely on the point of starving, Tasso might have applied to this couple, with equal truth, although with somewhat a different meaning, what he says of his 'Amanti e Sposi';—

——————Pende
D'un fato sol e l'una e l'altra vita:*

for if Madam Shark had not died first, Monsieur must have died himself for want of a dinner.

December 17 (Sunday)

On this day, from a sense of propriety no doubt, as well as from having nothing else to do, all the crew in the morning betook themselves to their studies. The carpenter was very seriously spelling a comedy; Edward* was engaged with 'The Six Princesses of Babylon';* a third was amusing himself with a tract 'On the Management of Bees'; another had borrowed the cabin-boy's 'Sorrows of Werter', and was reading it aloud to a large circle—some whistling—and others yawning; and Werter's abrupt transitions, and exclamations, and raptures, and refinements, read in the same loud monotonous tone, and without the slightest respect paid to stops, had the oddest effect possible. 'She did not look at me; I thought my heart would burst; the coach drove off; she looked out of the window; was that look meant for me? yes it was; perhaps it might be; do not tell me that it was not meant for me. Oh, my friend, my friend, am I not a fool, a madman?' (This part is rather stupid, or so, you see, but no matter for that; where was I? oh!) 'I am now sure, Charlotte loves me: I prest my hand on my heart; I said "Klopstock"; yes, Charlotte loves me; what! does Charlotte love me? oh, rapturous thought! my brain turns round:—Immortal powers!—how!—what!—oh, my friend, my friend,' etc. etc. etc. I was surprised to find that (except Edward's Fairy Tale) none of them were reading works that were at all likely to amuse them (Smollett or Fielding, for instance), or any which might interest them as relating to their profession, such as voyages and travels; much less any which had the slightest reference to the particular day. However, as most of them were reading what they could not possibly understand, they might mistake them for books of devotion, for any thing they knew to the contrary; or, perhaps, they might have so much reverence for all books in print, as to think that, provided they did but read something, it was doing a good work, and it did not much matter what. So one of Congreve's fine ladies swears Mrs Mincing, the waiting maid, to secrecy, 'upon an odd volume of Messalina's Poems'.* Sir Dudley North, too, informs us, (or is it his brother Roger? but I mean the Turkey merchant:)*—that at Constantinople the respect for printed books is so great, that when people are sick, they fancy that they can be *read* into health again; and if the Koran should not be in the way, they will make a shift with a few verses of the Bible, or a chapter or two of the Talmud, or of any other book that comes first to hand, rather than not read something. I think Sir Dudley says, that he himself cured an old Turk of the toothache, by administering a few pages of 'Ovid's Metamorphoses'; and in an old receipt-book, we are directed for the cure of a double tertian fever, 'to drink plentifully of cock-broth, and sleep with the Second Book of the Iliad under the pillow'. If, instead of sleeping with it under the pillow, the doctor had desired us to read the Second Book of the Iliad in order that we *might* sleep, I should have had some faith in his prescription myself.

December 19

During these last two days nothing very extraordinary, or of sufficient importance to deserve its being handed down to the latest posterity, has occurred; except that this morning a swinging rope knocked my hat into the sea, and away it sailed upon a voyage of discovery, like poor La Perouse,* to return no more, I suppose; unless, indeed,—like Polycrates, the fortunate tyrant of Samos, who threw his favourite ring into the ocean, and found it again in the stomach of the first fish that was served up at his table,—I should have the good luck (but I by no means reckon upon it) to catch a dolphin with my hat upon his head: as to a porpoise, he never could squeeze his great numskull into it; but our dolphin of last week was much about my own size, and I dare say such another would find my hat fit him to a miracle, and look very well in it.

December 20

The weather is so excessively close and sultry, that it would be allowed to be too hot to be pleasant, even by that perfect model for all future lords of the bedchamber, who was never known to speak a word, except in praise, of any thing living or dead, through the whole course of his life: but, at last, one day he met with an accident—

he happened to die; and the next day he met with another accident—
he happened to be damned: and immediately upon his arrival in the
infernal regions, the Devil (who was determined to be as well bred
as the other could be for his ears,) came to pay his compliments to
the new-comer, and very obligingly expressed his concern that his
lordship was not likely to feel satisfied with his new abode; for that
he must certainly find hell very hot and disagreeable. 'Oh, dear, no!'
exclaimed the Lord of the Bedchamber, 'not at all disagreeable, by
any manner of means, Mr Devil, upon my word and honour! Rather
warm, to be sure.' In point of heat there is no difference between the
days and the nights; or if there is any, it is that the nights are rather
the hottest of the two. The lightning is incessant, and it does not
show itself forked or in flashes, but in wide sheets of mild blue light,
which spread themselves at once over the sky and sea; and, for the
moment which they last, make all the objects around as distinct as
in daylight. The moon now does not rise till near ten o'clock, and
during her absence the size and brilliancy of the stars are admirable.
In England they always seemed to me (to borrow a phrase of Shakspeare's, which, in truth, is not worth borrowing,) to 'peep through
the blanket of the dark';* but here the heavens appear to be studded
with them on the outside, as if they were chased with so many jewels:
it is really Milton's 'firmament of living sapphires';* and what with
the lightning, the stars, and the quantity of floating lights which just
gleamed round the ship every moment, and then were gone again,
to-night the sky had an effect so beautiful, that when at length the
moon thought proper to show her great red drunken face, I thought
that we did much better without her.

The above-mentioned floating lights are a kind of sea-meteors,
which, as I am told, are produced by the concussion of the waves,
while eddying in whirlpools round the rudder; but still I saw them
rise sometimes at so great a distance from the ship, and there
appeared to be something so like *Will* in the direction of their
course,—sometimes hurrying on, sometimes gliding along quite
slowly; now stopping and remaining motionless for a minute or two,
and then hurrying on again,—that I could not be convinced of their
not being Medusæ, or some species or other of phosphoric animal:
but whatever be the cause of this appearance, the effect is singularly
beautiful. As to air, we have not enough to bless ourselves with. I had

been led to believe, that when once we should have fallen in with the trade winds, from that moment we should sail into our destined port as rapidly and as directly as Truffaldino travels in Gozzi's farce;* when, having occasion to go from Asia to Europe, and being very much pressed for time, he persuades a conjuror of his acquaintance to lend him a devil, with a great pair of bellows, the nozzle of which being directed right against his stern, away goes the traveller before the stream of wind, with the devil after him, and the infernal bellows never cease from working till they have blown him out of one quarter of the globe into another: but our trade winds must 'hide their diminished heads'* before Truffaldino's bellows. It seems that like the Moors, 'in Africa the torrid', they are 'of temper somewhat mulish';* for, although, to be sure, when they *do* blow, they will only blow in one certain direction, yet very often they will not blow at all; which has been our case for the last week: indeed, they seem to be but a queerish kind of a concern at best. About three years ago a fleet of merchantmen was becalmed near St Vincent's: in a few days after their arrival, there happened a violent eruption of a volcano in that island, nor was it long before a favourable breeze sprang up. Unluckily, one of the ships had anchored rather nearer to the shore than the others, and was at the distance of about one hundred and fifty yards from the stream of the trade wind; nor could any possible efforts of the crew, by tacking, by towing, or otherwise, ever enable the vessel to conquer that one hundred and fifty yards: there she remained, as completely becalmed as if there were not such a thing as a breath of wind in the universe; and on the one hand she had the mortification to see the rest of the merchantmen, with their convoy (for it was in the very heat of the war), sail away with all their canvass spread and swelling; while, on the other hand, the sailors had the comfortable possibility of being suffocated every moment by the clouds of ashes which continued to fall on their deck every moment, from the burning volcano, although they were not nearer to St Vincent's than eight or nine miles; indeed that distance went for nothing, as ashes fell upon vessels that were out at sea at least five hundred miles; and Barbadoes being to windward of the volcano, such immense quantities of its contents were carried to that island as almost covered the fields; and destroying vegetation completely wherever they fell, did inconceivable damage, while that which St Vincent's itself experienced was but trifling in proportion.

Our captain is quite out of patience with the tortoise pace of our progress; for my part I care very little about it. Whether we have sailed slowly or rapidly, when a day is once over, I am just as much nearer advanced towards April, the time fixed for my return to England; and, what is of much more consequence, whether we have sailed slowly or rapidly, when a day is once over, I am just as much nearer advanced towards 'that bourne',* to reach which, peaceably and harmlessly, is the only business of life, and towards which the whole of our existence forms but one continued journey.

December 21

We succeeded in catching another dolphin to-day; but he had not a hat on; however, I just asked him whether he happened to have seen mine, but to little purpose; for I found that he could tell me nothing at all about it; so, instead of bothering the poor animal with any more questions, we eat him.

December 22

About three years ago the Captain had the ill luck to be captured by a French frigate. As she had already made prizes* of two other merchant-men, it was determined to sink his ship; which, after removing the crew and every thing in her that was valuable, was effected by firing her own guns down the hatchways. It was near three hours before she filled, then down she went with a single plunge, head foremost, with all her sails set and colours flying. This display of the ship's magnificence in her last moments reminded me of Mary Queen of Scots, arraying herself in her richest robes that she might go to the scaffold. If Yorick had fallen in with this anecdote in the course of his journey, the situation of the Captain, standing on the enemy's deck, and seeing his 'brave vessel' in full and gallant trim, possessing all the abilities for a long existence, yet abandoned by every one, and sinking from the effect of her own shot, might have furnished him with a companion for his old commercial Marquis, lamenting over the rust of his newly recovered sword.*

December 23

THE DOLPHIN

Does then the insatiate sea relent?
And hath he back those treasures sent,
    His stormy rage devoured?
All starred with gems the billows bound,
And emeralds, jacinths, sapphires round
    The bark in spray are showered.

No, no! 't is there the Dolphin plays;
His scales, enriched with sunny rays,
    Celestial tints unfold;
And as he darts, the waters blue
Are streaked with gleams of many a hue,
    Green, orange, purple, gold!

And brighter still will shine your skin,
Poor fish, more dazzling play each fin,
    On deck when dying cast;
Like good men, who, expiring, bless
The Power that calls them, all confess
    Your brightest hour your last.

And now the Spearman watchful stands!
The five-pronged *grainse*, which arms his hands,
    Your scales is doomed to gore;
The lead will sink, and soon on high,
Borne from the deep, perforce you'll fly,
    Nor e'er regain it more.

Weep, Beauty, weep! those vivid dyes,
Those splendours, but the harpooner's eyes
    To strike his victim call!
Ambition, mark the Dolphin's close—
To dangerous heights he only rose
    To find the heavier fall!

Mark, too, ye witty, rich, and gay,
How quick those sportive fins could play,
    How gay, how rich was he!
He moves no more—he's cold to touch—
He's dull—dark—dead! The Dolphin's such,
    And such we all must be!

There is a technical fault in the above lines: the grainse, or dolphin-spear, has five barbs; but the *harpooner* never uses a lance with more than a single point. However, the word was so agreeable to my ear, that I could not find in my heart to leave it out.

December 24 (Sunday)

At length we have crawled into the Caribbean Sea. I was told that we were not to expect to see land to-day; but on shipboard our not seeing a thing *to-day* by no means implies that we shall not see it before *to-morrow*; for the nautical day is supposed to conclude at noon, when the solar observation is taken; and, therefore, the making land *to-day*, or not, very often depends upon our making it before twelve o'clock, or after it. This was the case in the present instance; for noon was scarcely passed when we saw Deseada* (a small island totally unprovided with water, and whose only produce consists in a little cotton), Guadaloupe, and Marie Galante, though the latter was at so great a distance as to be scarcely visible. At sunset Antigua was in sight.

December 25

The sun rose upon Montserrat and Nevis, with the *Rodondo* rock between them, 'apricis natio gratissima mergis,—'* for it is perpetually covered with innumerable flocks of gulls, boobies, pelicans, and other sea birds. Then came St Christopher's and St Eustatia;* and in the course of the afternoon we passed over the *Aves* bank, a collection of sand, rock, and mud, extending about two hundred miles, and terminated at each end by a small island: one of them inhabited by a few fishermen, the other only by sea birds. Of all the Atlantic isles the soil of St Christopher's is by some supposed to be the richest, the land frequently producing three hogsheads an acre. I rather think that this was the first island discovered by Columbus,* and that it took its name from his patron-saint. Montserrat is so rocky, and the roads so steep and difficult, that the sugar is obliged to be brought down in bags upon the backs of mules, and not put into casks, till its arrival on the sea shore.

The weather is now quite delicious; there is just wind enough to send us forward and keep the air cool: the sun is brilliant without being overpowering; the swell of the waves is scarcely perceptible;

and the ship moves along so steadily, that the deck affords almost as firm footing as if we were walking on land. One would think that Belinda had been smiling on the Caribbean Sea, as she once before did on the Thames, and had 'made all the world look gay'.* During the night we passed Santa Cruz, an island which, from the perfection to which its cultivation has been carried, is called 'the Garden of the West Indies'.

December 28

Having left Porto Rico behind us, at noon to-day we passed the insulated rock of Alcavella, lying about six miles from St Domingo, which is now in sight. As this part of the Caribbean Sea is much infested by pirates from the Caraccas,* all our muskets have been put in repair, and to-day the guns were loaded, of which we mount eight; but as one of them, during the last voyage, went overboard in a gale of wind, its place has been supplied by a *Quaker*, i.e. a sham gun of wood, so called, I suppose, because it would not fight if it were called upon. These pirate-vessels are small schooners, armed with a single twenty-four pounder, which moves upon a swivel, and their crew is composed of negroes and outlaws of all nations, their numbers generally running from one hundred to one hundred and fifty men. To-day, for the first time, I saw some flying fish: we have also been visited by several men-of-war birds and tropic birds; the latter is a species of gull, perfectly white, and distinguished by a single very long feather in its tail: its nautical name is 'the boatswain'.

As we sail along, the air is absolutely loaded with 'Sabean odours from the spicy shores'* of St Domingo, which we were still coasting at sunset.

December 30

At day-break Jamaica was in sight, or rather it would have been in sight, only that we could not see it. The weather was so gloomy, and the wind and rain were so violent, that we might have said to the Captain, as one of the two Punches who went into the ark is reported to have said to the patriarch, during the deluge, 'Hazy weather, Master Noah.'—I remember my good friend, Walter Scott, asserts, that at the death of a poet the groans and tears of his heroes and heroines swell the blast and increase the river; perhaps something of the same kind takes place at the arrival of a West India proprietor from Europe, and all this rain and wind proceed from the eyes and lungs of my agents and overseers, who, for the last twenty years, have been reigning in my dominions with despotic authority; but now

> Whose groans in roaring winds complain,
> Whose tears of rage impel the rain;*

because, on the approach of the sovereign himself, they must evacuate the palace, and resign the deputed sceptre. 'Hinc illæ lachrymæ!'* this is the cause of our being soaked to the skin this morning. However, about noon the weather cleared up, and allowed us to verify, with our own eyes, that we had reached 'the Land of Springs', without having been invited by any Piccaroon* vessel to 'walk the plank' instead of the deck; which is a compliment very generally paid by those gentry, after they have taken the trouble of laying a plank over the side of a captured ship, in order that the passengers and the crew may walk overboard without any inconvenience.

We arrived at the east end of the island, passed Pedro Point and Starvegut Bay, and arrived before Black River Bay (our destined harbour) soon after two o'clock; but here we were obliged to come to a stand still: the channel is very dangerous, extremely narrow, and full of sunken rocks; so that it can only be entered by a vessel drawing so much water as ours with a particular wind, and when there is not any apprehension of a sudden squall. We were, therefore, obliged to drop anchor, and are now riding within a couple of miles of the shore, but with as utter an incapability of reaching it as if we were still at Gravesend. The north side of the island is said to be extremely beautiful and romantic; but the south, which we coasted to-day, is low, barren, and without any recommendation whatever. As yet I can only look at Jamaica as one does on a man who comes to pay money, and whom we are extremely well pleased to see, however little the fellow's appearance may be in his favour.

December 31 (Sunday)

We passed the whole of the day in vain endeavours to work ourselves into the bay. At one time, indeed, we got very near the shore, but the consequence was, that we were within an ace of striking upon a rock, and very much obliged to a sudden gust of wind, which, blowing right off shore, blew us out of the channel, and left us at night in a much more perilous situation than we had occupied the evening before, though even that had been by no means secure. At three o'clock, the other passengers went on shore in the jolly-boat, and proceeded to their destination; but as I was still more than thirty miles distant from my estate, I preferred waiting on board till the Captain should have moored his vessel in safety, and be at liberty to take me in his pinnace* to Savannah la Mar, when I should find myself within a few miles of my own house.

In the course of the afternoon, one of the sailors took up a fish of a very singular shape and most brilliant colours, as it floated along upon the water. It seemed to be gasping, and lay with its belly upwards; it was supposed to have eaten something poisonous, as whenever it was touched it appeared to be full of life, and squirted the water in our faces with great spirit and dexterity. But no sooner was he suffered to remain quiet in the tub, than he turned upon his back and again was gasping. He had a large round transparent globule, intersected with red veins, under the belly, which some imagined to proceed from a rupture, and to be the occasion of his disease. But I could not discover any vestige of a wound; and the globule was quite solid to the touch; neither did the fish appear to be sensible when it was pressed upon. No one on board had ever seen this kind of fish till then; its name is the 'Doctor Fish'.

A black pilot came on board yesterday, in a canoe hollowed out of the cotton-tree; and when it returned for him this morning, it brought us a water-melon. I never met with a worse article in my life; the pulp is of a faint greenish yellow, stained here and there with spots of moist red, so that it looks exactly as if the servant in slicing it had cut his finger, and suffered it to bleed over the fruit. Then the seeds, being of a dark purple, present the happiest imitation of drops of clotted gore; and altogether (prejudiced as I was by its appearance), when I had put a single bit into my mouth, it had such a kind of Shylocky taste of raw flesh about it (not that I recollect having ever eaten a bit of raw flesh itself), that I sent away my plate, and was perfectly satisfied as to the merits of the fruit.

1816—January 1

At length the ship has squeezed herself into this champagne bottle of a bay! Perhaps, the satisfaction attendant upon our having overcome the difficulty, added something to the illusion of its effect; but the beauty of the atmosphere, the dark purple mountains, the shores covered with mangroves of the liveliest green down to the very edge of the water, and the light-coloured houses with their lattices and piazzas completely embowered in trees, altogether made the scenery of the Bay wear a very picturesque appearance. And, to complete the charm, the sudden sounds of the drum and banjee, called our attention to a procession of the *John-Canoe*,* which was proceeding to celebrate the opening of the new year at the town of Black River. The John-Canoe is a Merry-Andrew dressed in a striped doublet, and bearing upon his head a kind of pasteboard house-boat, filled with puppets, representing, some sailors, others soldiers, others again slaves at work on a plantation, etc. The negroes are allowed three days for holidays at Christmas, and also New-year's day, which being the last is always reckoned by them as the festival of the greatest importance. It is for this day that they reserve their finest dresses, and lay their schemes for displaying their show and expense to the greatest advantage; and it is then that the John-Canoe is considered not merely as a person of material consequence, but one whose presence is absolutely indispensable. Nothing could look more gay than the procession which we now saw with its train of attendants, all dressed in white, and marching two by two (except when the file was broken here and there by a single horseman), and its band of negro music, and its scarlet flags fluttering about in the breeze, now disappearing behind a projecting clump of mangrove trees, and then again emerging into an open part of the road, as it wound along the shore towards the town of Black River.

> ——Magno telluris amore
> Egressi optatâ Tröes potiuntur arenâ.*

I had determined not to go on shore, till I should land for good and all at Savannah la Mar. But although I could resist the 'telluris amor', there was no resisting John-Canoe; so, in defiance of a broiling afternoon's sun, about four o'clock we left the vessel for the town.

It was, as I understand, formerly one of some magnitude; but it now consists only of a few houses, owing to a spark from a tobacco-pipe or a candle having lodged upon a mosquito-net during dry weather; and although the conflagration took place at mid-day, the whole town was reduced to ashes. The few streets—(I believe there were not above two, but those were wide and regular, and the houses looked very neat)—were now crowded with people, and it seemed to be allowed, upon all hands, that New-year's day had never been celebrated there with more expense and festivity.

It seems that, many years ago, an Admiral of the Red was super-seded on the Jamaica station by an Admiral of the Blue;* and both of them gave balls at Kingston to the '*Brown Girls*';* for the fair sex elsewhere are called the 'Brown Girls' in Jamaica. In consequence of these balls, all Kingston was divided into parties: from thence the division spread into other districts: and ever since, the whole island, at Christmas, is separated into the rival factions of the Blues and the Reds (the Red representing also the English, the Blue the Scotch), who contend for setting forth their processions with the greatest taste and magnificence. This year, several gentlemen in the neigh-bourhood of Black River had subscribed very largely towards the expenses of the show; and certainly it produced the gayest and most amusing scene that I ever witnessed, to which the mutual jealousy and pique of the two parties against each other contributed in no slight degree. The champions of the rival Roses,—the Guelphs and the Ghibellines,—none of them could exceed the scornful animosity and spirit of depreciation with which the Blues and the Reds of Black River examined the efforts at display of each other. The Blues had the advantage beyond a doubt; this a Red girl told us that she could not deny; but still, 'though the Reds were beaten, she would not be a Blue girl for the whole universe!' On the other hand, Miss Edwards (the mistress of the hotel from whose window we saw the show), was rank Blue to the very tips of her fingers, and had, indeed, contributed one of her female slaves to sustain a very impor-tant character in the show; for when the Blue procession was ready to set forward, there was evidently a hitch, something was wanting; and there seemed to be no possibility of getting on without it— when suddenly we saw a tall woman dressed in mourning (being Miss Edwards herself) rush out of our hotel, dragging along by the hand a strange uncouth kind of a glittering tawdry figure, all feathers, and pitchfork, and painted pasteboard, who moved most reluctantly, and turned out to be no less a personage than Britannia herself, with a pasteboard shield covered with the arms of Great Britain, a trident in her hand, and a helmet made of pale blue silk and silver. The poor girl, it seems, was bashful at appearing in this conspicuous manner before so many spectators, and hung back when it came to the point. But her mistress had seized hold of her, and placed her by main force in her destined position. The music struck up; Miss Edwards gave the Goddess a great push forwards; the drumsticks and the elbows of the fiddlers attacked her in the rear; and on went Britannia willy-nilly!

The Blue girls called themselves 'the Blue girls of Waterloo'. Their motto was the more patriotic; that of the Red was the more gallant:—'Britannia rules the day!' streamed upon the Blue flag; 'Red girls for ever!' floated upon the Red. But, in point of taste and invention, the former carried it hollow. First marched Britannia; then came a band of music; then the flag; then the Blue King and Queen— the Queen splendidly dressed in white and silver (in scorn of the opposite party, her train was borne by a little girl in red); his Majesty wore a full British Admiral's uniform, with a white satin sash, and a huge cocked hat with a gilt paper crown upon the top of it. These were immediately followed by 'Nelson's car', being a kind of canoe decorated with blue and silver drapery, and with 'Trafalgar' written on the front of it; and the procession was closed by a long train of Blue grandees (the women dressed in uniforms of white, with robes of blue muslin), all Princes and Princesses, Dukes and Duchesses, every mother's child of them.

The Red girls were also dressed very gaily and prettily, but they had nothing in point of invention that could vie with Nelson's Car and Britannia; and when the Red throne made its appearance, language cannot express the contempt with which our landlady eyed it. 'It was neither one thing nor t'other,' Miss Edwards was of opinion. 'Merely a few yards of calico stretched over some planks— and look, look, only look at it behind! you may see the bare boards! By way of a throne, indeed! Well, to be sure, Miss Edwards never saw a poorer thing in her life, that she must say!' And then she told me, that somebody had just snatched at a medal which Britannia wore round her neck, and had endeavoured to force it away. I asked her who had done so? 'Oh, one of the Red party, *of course*!' The Red party was evidently Miss Edwards's Mrs Grundy. John-Canoe made no part of the procession; but he and his rival, John-Crayfish (a personage of whom I heard, but could not obtain a sight), seemed to act upon quite an independent interest, and go about from house to house, tumbling and playing antics to pick up money for themselves.

A play was now proposed to us, and, of course, accepted. Three men and a girl accordingly made their appearance; the men dressed like the tumblers at Astley's,* the lady very tastefully in white and silver, and all with their faces concealed by masks of thin blue silk; and they proceeded to perform the quarrel between Douglas and Glenalvon,* and the fourth act of 'The Fair Penitent'.* They were all quite perfect, and had no need of a prompter. As to Lothario, he was by far the most comical dog that I ever saw in my life, and his dying scene exceeded all description; Mr Coates* himself might have taken hints from him! As soon as Lothario was fairly dead, and Calista had made her exit in distraction, they all began dancing reels like so many mad people, till they were obliged to make way for the Waterloo procession, who came to collect money for the next year's festival; one of them singing, another dancing to the tune, while she presented her money-box to the spectators, and the rest of the Blue girls filling up the chorus. I cannot say much in praise of the black Catalani;* but nothing could be more light, and playful, and graceful, than the extempore movements of the dancing girl. Indeed, through the whole day, I had been struck with the precision of their march, the ease and grace of their action, the elasticity of their step, and the lofty air with which they carried their heads—all, indeed, except poor Britannia, who hung down hers in the most ungoddess-like manner imaginable. The first song was the old Scotch air of 'Logie of Buchan', of which the girl sang one single stanza forty times over. But the second was in praise of the Hero of Heroes; so I gave the songstress a dollar to teach it to me, and drink the Duke's health. It was not easy to make out what she said, but as well as I could understand them, the words ran as follows:—

> Come, rise up, our gentry,
> And hear about Waterloo;
> Ladies, take your spy-glass,
> And attend to what we do;

For one and one makes two,
But one alone must be.
Then singee, singee Waterloo,
None so brave as he!

—and then there came something about green and white flowers, and
a Duchess, and a lily-white Pig, and going on board of a dashing man
of war; but what they all had to do with the Duke, or with each other,
I could not make even a guess. I was going to ask for an explanation,
but suddenly half of them gave a shout loud enough 'to fright the
realms of Chaos and old Night',* and away they flew, singers, dancers,
and all. The cause of this was the sudden illumination of the
town with quantities of large chandeliers and bushes, the branches of
which were stuck all over with great blazing torches: the effect was
really beautiful, and the excessive rapture of the black multitude at
the spectacle was as well worth the witnessing as the sight itself.

I never saw so many people who appeared to be so unaffectedly
happy. In England, at fairs and races, half the visiters at least seem
to have been only brought there for the sake of traffic, and to be too
busy to be amused; but here nothing was thought of but real pleasure; and that pleasure seemed to consist in singing, dancing, and
laughing, in seeing and being seen, in showing their own fine clothes,
or in admiring those of others. There were no people selling or
buying; no servants and landladies bustling and passing about; and
at eight o'clock, as we passed through the market-place, where was
the greatest illumination, and which, of course, was most thronged,
I did not see a single person drunk, nor had I observed a single
quarrel through the course of the day; except, indeed, when some
thoughtless fellow crossed the line of the procession, and received
by the way a good box of the ear from the Queen or one of her attendant Duchesses. Every body made the same remark to me; 'Well, sir,
what do you think Mr Wilberforce* would think of the state of the
negroes, if he could see this scene?' and certainly, to judge by this
one specimen, of all beings that I have yet seen, these were the happiest. As we were passing to our boat, through the market-place,
suddenly we saw Miss Edwards dart out of the crowd, and seize
the Captain's arm—'Captain! Captain!' cried she, 'for the love of
Heaven, only look at the *Red* lights! Old iron hoops, nothing but old
iron hoops, I declare! Well! for my part!' and then, with a contemptuous toss of her head, away frisked Miss Edwards triumphantly.

January 2

The St Elizabeth, which sailed from England at the same time with our vessel, was attacked by a pirate from Carthagena, near the rocks of Alcavella, who attempted three times to board her, though he was at length beaten off; so that our Piccaroon preparations were by no means taken without foundation.

At four o'clock this morning I embarked in the cutter for Savannah la Mar, lighted by the most beautiful of all possible morning stars: certainly, if this star be really Lucifer, that 'Son of the Morning',* the Devil must be 'an extremely pretty fellow'. But in spite of the fineness of the morning, our passage was a most disagreeable concern: there was a violent swell in the sea; and a strong north wind, though it carried us forward with great rapidity, overwhelmed us with whole sheets of foam so incessantly, that I expected, as soon as the sun should have evaporated the moisture, to see the boat's crew covered with salt, and looking like so many Lot's wives* after her metamorphosis.

The distance was about thirty miles, and soon after nine o'clock we reached Savannah la Mar, where I found my trustee, and a whole cavalcade, waiting to conduct me to my own estate; for he had brought with him a curricle and pair for myself, a gig* for my servant, two black boys upon mules, and a cart with eight oxen to convey my baggage. The road was excellent, and we had not above five miles to travel; and as soon as the carriage entered my gates, the uproar and confusion which ensued sets all description at defiance. The works were instantly all abandoned; every thing that had life came flocking to the house from all quarters; and not only the men, and the women, and the children, but, 'by a bland assimilation', the hogs, and the dogs, and the geese, and the fowls, and the turkeys, all came hurrying along by instinct, to see what could possibly be the matter, and seemed to be afraid of arriving too late. Whether the pleasure of the negroes was sincere may be doubted; but certainly it was the loudest that I ever witnessed: they all talked together, sang, danced, shouted, and, in the violence of their gesticulations, tumbled over each other, and rolled about upon the ground. Twenty voices at once enquired after uncles, and aunts, and grandfathers, and great-grandmothers of mine, who had been buried long before I was in existence, and whom, I verily believe, most of them only knew by tradition. One woman held up her little naked black child to me, grinning from ear to ear;—'Look, Massa, look here! him nice lilly neger for Massa!' Another complained,—'So long since none come see we, Massa; good Massa, come at last.' As for the old people, they were all in one and the same story: now they had lived once to see Massa, they were ready for dying to-morrow, 'them no care'.

The shouts, the gaiety, the wild laughter, their strange and sudden bursts of singing and dancing, and several old women, wrapped up in large cloaks, their heads bound round with different-coloured handkerchiefs, leaning on a staff, and standing motionless in the middle of the hubbub, with their eyes fixed upon the portico which I occupied, formed an exact counterpart of the festivity of the witches in Macbeth. Nothing could be more odd or more novel than the whole scene; and yet there was something in it by which I could not help being affected; perhaps it was the consciousness that all these human beings were my *slaves*;—to be sure, I never saw people look more happy in my life; and I believe their condition to be much more comfortable than that of the labourers of Great Britain; and, after all, slavery, in *their* case, is but another name for servitude, now that no more negroes can be forcibly carried away from Africa, and subjected to the horrors of the voyage, and of the seasoning after their arrival: but still I had already experienced, in the morning, that Juliet was wrong in saying 'What's in a name?'* For soon after my reaching the lodging-house at Savannah la Mar, a remarkably clean-looking negro lad presented himself with some water and a towel: I concluded him to belong to the inn; and, on my returning the towel, as he found that I took no notice of him, he at length ventured to introduce himself, by saying,—'Massa not know me; *me your slave!*'—and really the sound made me feel a pang at the heart. The lad appeared all gaiety and good humour, and his whole countenance expressed anxiety to recommend himself to my notice; but the word 'slave' seemed to imply, that, although he did feel pleasure then in serving me, if he had detested me he must have served me still. I really felt quite humiliated at the moment, and was tempted to tell him,—'Do not say that again; say that you are my negro, but do not call yourself my slave.'

Altogether, they shouted and sang me into a violent headach. It is now one in the morning, and I hear them still shouting and singing. I gave them a holiday for Saturday next, and told them that I had brought them all presents from England; and so, I believe, we parted very good friends.

January 3

I have reached Jamaica in the best season for seeing my property in a favourable point of view; it is crop time,* when all the laborious work is over, and the negroes are the most healthy and merry. This morning I went to visit the hospital, and found there only eight patients out of three hundred negroes, and not one of them a serious case. Yesterday I had observed a remarkably handsome Creole* girl, called Psyche, and she really deserved the name. This morning a little brown girl made her appearance at breakfast, with an orange bough, to flap away the flies, and, on enquiry, she proved to be an emanation of the aforesaid Psyche. It is evident, therefore, that Psyche has already visited the palace of Cupid; I heartily hope that she is not now upon her road to the infernal regions: but, as the ancients had two Cupids, one divine and the other sensual, so am I in possession of two Psyches; and on visiting the hospital, *there* was poor Psyche the second. Probably this was the Psyche of the sensual Cupid.

I passed the morning in driving about the estate: my house is frightful to look at, but very clean and comfortable on the inside; some of the scenery is very picturesque, from the lively green of the trees and shrubs, and the hermitage-like appearance of the negro buildings, all situated in little gardens, and embosomed in sweet-smelling shrubberies. Indeed, every thing appears much better than I expected; the negroes seem healthy and contented, and so perfectly at their ease, that our English squires would be mightily astonished at being accosted so familiarly by their farmers. This delightful north wind keeps the air temperate and agreeable. I live upon shaddocks and pine-apples. The dreaded mosquitoes are not worse than gnats, nor as bad as the Sussex harvest-bugs; and, as yet, I never felt myself in more perfect health. There was a man once, who fell from the top of a steeple; and, perceiving no inconvenience in his passage through the air,—'Come,' said he to himself, while in the act of falling, 'really this is well enough yet if it would but last.' Cubina, my young Savannah la Mar acquaintance, is appointed my black attendant; and as I had desired him to bring me any native flowers of Jamaica, this evening he brought me a very pretty one; the negroes, he said, called it 'John-to-Heal', but in white language it was *hoccoco-pickang*; it proved to be the wild Ipecacuanha.

January 4

There were three things against which I was particularly cautioned, and which three things I was determined *not* to do: to take exercise after ten in the day; to be exposed to the dews* after sun-down; and to sleep at a Jamaica lodging-house. So, yesterday, I set off for Montego Bay at eight o'clock in the morning, and travelled till three; walked home from a ball after midnight; and that home was a lodging-house at Montego Bay; but the lodging-house was such a cool clean lodging-house, and the landlady was such an obliging smiling landlady, with the whitest of all possible teeth, and the blackest of all possible eyes, that no harm could happen to me from occupying an apartment which had been prepared by *her*. She was called out of her bed to make my room ready for me; yet she did every thing with so much good-will and cordiality; no quick answers, no mutterings: inns would be bowers of Paradise, if they were all rented by mulatto landladies, like Judy James.

I was much pleased with the scenery of Montego Bay, and with the neatness and cleanliness of the town; indeed, what with the sea washing it, and the picturesque aspect of the piazzas and verandas, it is impossible for a West Indian town so situated, and in such a climate, not to present an agreeable appearance. But the first part of the road exceeds in beauty all that I have ever seen: it wound through mountain lands of my own, their summits of the boldest, and at the same time of the most beautiful shapes; their sides ornamented with bright green woods of bamboo, logwood, prickly-yellow, broad-leaf, and trumpet trees; and so completely covered with the most lively verdure, that once, when we found a piece of barren rock, Cubina pointed it out to me as a curiosity;—'Look, massa, rock quite naked!' The cotton-tree presented itself on all sides; but as this is the season for its shedding its leaves, its wide-spreading bare white arms contributed nothing to the beauty of the scene, except where the wild fig and various creeping plants had completely mantled the stems and branches; and then its gigantic height, and the fantastic wreathings of its limbs, from which numberless green withes and strings of wild flowers were streaming, rendered it exactly the very tree for which a landscape-painter would have wished. The air, too, was delicious; the fragrance of the Sweet-wood, and of several other scented trees, but above all, of the delicious Logwood (of which most of the fences in Westmoreland are made) composed an atmosphere, such, that if Satan, after promising them 'a buxom air, embalmed with odours',* had transported Sin and Death thither, the charming couple must have acknowledged their papa's promises fulfilled.

We travelled these first ten miles (Montego Bay being about thirty from my estate of Cornwall) without seeing a human creature, nor, indeed, any thing that had life in it, except a black snake basking in the sunshine, and a few John Crows—a species of vulture, whose utility is so great that its destruction is prohibited by law under a heavy penalty. In a country where putrefaction is so rapid, it is of infinite consequence to preserve an animal which, if a bullock or horse falls dead in the field, immediately flies to the carcass before it has time to corrupt, and gobbles it up before you can say 'John Crow', much less Jack Robinson. The bite of the black snake is slightly venomous, but that is all; as to the great yellow one, it is perfectly innoxious, and so timid that it always runs away from you. The only dangerous species of serpent is the Whip-snake, so called from its exactly resembling the lash of a whip, in length, thinness, pliability, and whiteness; but even the bite of this is not mortal, except from very great neglect. The most beautiful tree, or, rather, group of trees, all to nothing, is the Bamboo, both from its verdure and from its elegance of form: as to the Cotton tree, it answers no purpose, either of ornament or utility; or, rather, it is not suffered to answer any, since it is forbidden by law to export its down, lest it should hurt the fur trade in the manufacture of hats: its only present use is to furnish the negroes with canoes, which are hollowed out of its immense trunks. I am as yet so much enchanted with the country, that it would require no very strong additional inducements to make me establish myself here altogether; and in that case my first care would be to build for myself a cottage among these mountains, in which I might pass the sultry months,

E bruna-si; ma il bruno il bel non toglie.*

January 5

As I was returning this morning from Montego Bay, about a mile from my own estate, a figure presented itself before me, I really think the most picturesque that I ever beheld: it was a mulatto girl, born upon Cornwall, but whom the overseer of a neighbouring estate had obtained my permission to exchange for another slave, as well as two little children, whom she had borne to him; but, as yet, he has been unable to procure a substitute, owing to the difficulty of purchasing single negroes, and Mary Wiggins is still my slave. However, as she is considered as being manumitted, she had not dared to present herself at Cornwall on my arrival, lest she should have been considered as an intruder; but she now threw herself in my way to tell me how glad she was to see me, for that she had always thought till now (which is the general complaint) that '*she had no massa*'; and also to obtain a regular invitation to my negro festival to-morrow. By this universal complaint, it appears that, while Mr Wilberforce is lamenting their hard fate in being subject to a master, *their* greatest fear is the not having a master whom they know; and that to be told by the negroes of another estate that 'they belong to no massa', is one of the most contemptuous reproaches that can be cast upon them. Poor creatures, when they happened to hear on Wednesday evening that my carriage was ordered for Montego Bay the next morning, they fancied that I was going away for good and all, and came up to the house in such a hubbub, that my agent was obliged to speak to them, and pacify them with the assurance that I should come back on Friday without fail.

But to return to Mary Wiggins: she was much too pretty not to obtain her invitation to Cornwall; on the contrary, I *insisted* upon her coming, and bade her tell her *husband* that I admired his taste very much for having chosen her. I really think that her form and features were the most *statue-like* that I ever met with: her complexion had no yellow in it, and yet was not brown enough to be dark—it was more of an ash-dove colour than any thing else; her teeth were admirable, both for colour and shape; her eyes equally mild and bright; and her face merely broad enough to give it all possible softness and grandness of contour: her air and countenance would have suited Yarico;* but she reminded me most of Grassini in 'La Vergine del Sole',* only that Mary Wiggins was a thousand times more beautiful, and that, instead of a white robe, she wore a mixed dress of brown, white, and dead yellow, which harmonised excellently well with her complexion; while one of her beautiful arms was thrown across her brow to shade her eyes, and a profusion of rings on her fingers glittered in the sunbeams. Mary Wiggins and an old Cotton-tree are the most picturesque objects that I have seen for these twenty years.

On my arrival at home, my agent made me a very elegant little present of a scorpion and a couple of centipedes: the first was given to him, but the large centipede he had shaken out of a book last night, and having immediately covered her up in a phial of rum, he found this morning that she had produced a young one, which was lying drowned by her side.

I find that my negroes were called away from their attention to the works yesterday evening (for the crop is now making with the greatest activity), and kept up all night by a fire at a neighbouring estate. On these occasions a fire-shell* is blown, and all the negroes of the adjoining plantations hasten to give their assistance. On this occasion the fire was extinguished with the loss of only five negro houses; but this is a heavy concern to the poor negro proprietors, who have lost in it their whole stock of clothes, and furniture, and finery, which they had been accumulating for years, and to which their attachment is excessive.

LANDING

When first I gain'd the Atlantic shore,
And bade farewell to ocean's roar,
What gracious power my bosom eased,
My senses soothed, my fancy pleased,
And bade me feel, in whispers bland,
No Stranger in a Stranger-land?
'Twas not at length my goal to reach,
And tread Jamaica's burning beach:
'Twas not from Neptune's chains discharged,
To move, think, feel with powers enlarged:
Nor that no more my bed the wave,
Ere morning dawn'd, might prove my grave:—
A livelier chord was struck: a spell,
While heav'd my heart with gentle swell,
Crept o'er my soul with magic sweet,
And made each pulse responsive beat.
    No Sheep-bell e'er to Pilgrim's ear,
Wandering in woods unknown and drear,

No midnight lay to Spanish maid,
Conscious by whom the lute was played;
Not on the breeze the sounding wings
Of him who nurture homeward brings
To mother-bird, whose callow brood
Pain her fond heart with chirps for food,—
E'er seem'd more charming than to me,
(When two long months had past at sea,
During whose course my thirsty ear
No softer voice, no strain could hear
Nearer allied to love and pity,
Than the strong bass of seaman's ditty,)
Seem'd by the sea-gale round me flung,
Approaching sounds of female tongue!
    No, Venus, no! Small right hast thou
To claim for this my grateful vow;
Nor on thine altar now bestows
My hand the gift of one poor rose!
No eager glance, no heighten'd dye
Blush'd on my cheek, nor fired mine eye;
I heard, nor felt, at each soft note,
Flutter my heart, and swell my throat.
Those sounds but spoke of bosom-balm,
Of pity prompt and kindness calm;
Of tender care, of anxious zeal;
For here were breasts whose hearts could feel!
'Twas as to guest in stranger halls
If voice of friend a welcome calls:
Such pleasure soothes the starting maid,
Who finds some jewel long mislaid;
Pleasure, which blessed dew supplies,
To ease the heart, and float the eyes;
As when in pain attentions prove
A mother's care, a sister's love.
To Woman, Life its value owes!
Robb'd of her love, its dawn and close
Would find nor aid, nor soothing care;
Its middle course no joys would share.
Childhood in vain would thirst and cry,
And Age, unheeded, moan and die;
And Manhood frown to see the hours
Weave scentless wreaths unblest with flowers.
    It beam'd on cheek of sable dye;

No matter, since 'twas *woman*'s eye!
Each phrase the tortured language broke;
Enough for me—'twas *woman* spoke!
   Once raven locks my temples wore;
Time has pluck'd many, sorrow more:
Through forty springs (thank God they 're run!)
These weary eyes have seen the sun;
And in that space full room is found
For flowers to fade, and thorns to wound.
But now, (all fancy's freaks supprest,
Each thread-bare sneer and wanton jest,)
With hand on heart in serious tone,
With thanks, with truth, I needs must own,
Wide as I've roam'd the world around,
Roam where I would, I ever found,
The worst of Women still possest
More virtues than of Men the best.
And, oh! if shipwreck proves my lot,
Guide me, kind Heav'n, to some lone cot
Where *woman* dwells! Her hand she'll stretch
In pity to the stranger-wretch;
If virtuous want mine eye surveys,
Nor mine the power his head to raise,
I'll pour the tale in *woman*'s ear,
She'll aid, and, aiding, drop a tear.
And when my life-blood sickness drains,
And racks my nerves, and fires my brains,
What kinder juice, what livelier power,
Than mineral yields, or opiate flower,
Can make me e'en in pain rejoice?—
A few sweet words in that sweet voice!

January 6

This was the day given to my negroes as a festival on my arrival. A couple of heifers were slaughtered for them: they were allowed as much rum, and sugar, and noise, and dancing as they chose; and as to the two latter, certainly they profited by the permission. About two o'clock they began to assemble round the house, all drest in their holiday clothes, which, both for men and women, were chiefly white; only that the women were decked out with a profusion of beads and corals, and gold ornaments of all descriptions; and that while the blacks wore jackets, the mulattoes generally wore cloth coats; and inasmuch as they were all plainly clean instead of being shabbily fashionable, and affected to be nothing except that which they really were, they looked twenty times more like gentlemen than nine tenths of the bankers' clerks who swagger up and down Bond Street. It is a custom as to the mulatto children, that the males born on an estate should never be employed as field negroes, but as tradesmen; the females are brought up as domestics about the house. I had particularly invited '*Mr* John-Canoe' (which I found to be the polite manner in which the negroes spoke of him), and there arrived a couple of very gay and gaudy ones. I enquired whether one of them was 'John-Crayfish'; but I was told that John-Crayfish was John-Canoe's rival and enemy, and might belong to the factions of 'the Blues and the Reds'; but on Cornwall they were all friends, and therefore there were only the father and the son—Mr John-Canoe, senior, and Mr John-Canoe, junior.

The person who gave me this information was a young mulatto carpenter, called Nicholas, whom I had noticed in the crowd, on my first arrival, for his clean appearance and intelligent countenance; and he now begged me to notice the smaller of the two John-Canoe machines. 'To be sure,' he said, 'it was not so large nor so showy as the other, but then it was much better *proportioned* (his own word), and altogether much prettier'; and he said so much in praise of it, that I asked him whether he knew the maker? and then out came the motive: 'Oh, yes! it was made by John Fuller, who lived in the next house to him, and worked in the same shop, and indeed they were just like brothers.' So I desired to see his *fidus Achates*,* and he brought me as smart and intelligent a little fellow as eye ever beheld, who came grinning from ear to ear to tell me that he had made every bit of the canoe with his own hands, and had set to work upon it the moment that he knew of massa's coming to Jamaica. And indeed it was as fine as paint, pasteboard, gilt paper, and looking-glass could make it! Unluckily, the breeze being very strong blew off a fine glittering umbrella, surmounted with a plume of John Crow feathers, which crowned the top; and a little wag of a negro boy whipped it up, clapped it upon his head, and performed the part of an impromptu Mr John-Canoe with so much fun and grotesqueness, that he fairly beat the original performers out of the pit, and carried off all the applause of the spectators, and a couple of my dollars. The John-Canoes are fitted out at the expense of the rich negroes, who afterwards share the money collected from the spectators during their performance, allotting one share to the representator himself; and it is usual for the master of the estate to give them a couple of guineas apiece.

This Nicholas, whom I mentioned, is a very interesting person, both from his good looks and gentle manners, and from his story. He is the son of a white man, who on his death-bed charged his nephew and heir to purchase the freedom of this natural child. The nephew had promised to do so; I had consented; nothing was necessary but to find the substitute (which now is no easy matter); when about six months ago the nephew broke his neck, and the property went to a distant relation. Application in behalf of poor Nicholas has been made to the heir, and I heartily hope that he will enable me to release him. I felt strongly tempted to set him at liberty at once; but if I were to begin in that way, there would be no stopping; and it would be doing a kindness to an individual at the expense of all my other negroes—others would expect the same; and then I must either contrive to cultivate my estate with fewer hands—or must cease to cultivate it altogether—and, from inability to maintain them, send my negroes to seek bread for themselves—which, as two thirds of them have been born upon the estate, and many of them are lame, dropsical, and of a great age, would, of all misfortunes that could happen to them, be the most cruel. Even when Nicholas was speaking to me about his liberty, he said, 'It is not that I wish to go away, sir; it is only for the name and honour of being free: but I would always stay here and be your servant; and I had rather be an under-workman on Cornwall, than a head carpenter any where else.' Possibly, this was all palaver (in which the negroes are great dealers), but at least he *seemed* to be sincere; and I was heartily grieved that I could not allow myself to say more to him than that I sincerely wished him to get his liberty, and would receive the very lowest exchange for him that common prudence would authorize. And even for those few kind words, the poor fellow seemed to think it impossible to find means strong enough to express his gratitude.

Nor is this the only instance in which Nicholas has been unlucky. It seems that he was the first lover of the beautiful Psyche, whom I had noticed on my arrival. This evening, after the performance of the John-Canoes, I desired to see some of the girls dance; and by general acclamation Psyche was brought forward to exhibit, she being avowedly the best dancer on the estate; and certainly nothing could be more light, graceful, easy, and spirited, than her performance. She perfectly answered the description of Sallust's Sempronia, who was said—'Saltare elegantius, quam necesse est probæ, et cui cariora semper omnia, quam decus et pudicitia fuit.'* When her dance was over, I called her to me, and gave her a handful of silver. 'Ah, Psyche,' said Nicholas, who was standing at my elbow, 'Massa no give you all that if massa know you so bad girl! she run away from me, massa!' Psyche gave him a kind of pouting look, half kind, and half reproachful, and turned away. And then he told me that Psyche had been his wife (*one* of his wives he should have said); that he had had a child by her, and then she had left him for one of my 'white people' (as they call the book-keepers), because he had a good salary, and could afford to give her more presents than a slave could. 'Was there not another reason for your quarrelling?' said my agent. 'Was there not a shade of colour too much?'—'Oh, massa!' answered Nicholas, 'the child is not my own, that is certain; it is a black man's child. But still I will always take care of the child because it have no friends, and me wish make it good neger for massa—and *she* take good care of it too,' he added, throwing his arm round the waist of a sickly-looking woman rather [advanced] in years; 'she my wife, too, massa, long ago; old now and sick, but always good to me, so I still live with her, and will never leave her, never, massa; she Polly's mother, sir.' Polly is a pretty, delicate-looking girl, nursing a young child; she belongs to the mansion-house, and seems to think it as necessary a part of her duty to nurse *me* as the child. To be sure she has not as yet insisted upon suckling me; but if I open a *jalousie* in the evening, Polly walks in and shuts it without saying a word. 'Oh, don't shut the window, Polly.'—'Night-air not good for massa'; and she shuts the casement without mercy. I am drinking orangeade, or some such liquid; Polly walks up to the table, and seizes it; 'Leave that jug, Polly, I am dying with thirst.'—'More hurt, massa'; and away go Polly and the orangeade. So that I begin to fancy myself Sancho in Barataria, and that Polly is the Señor Doctor Pedro in petticoats.*

The difference of colour, which had offended Nicholas so much in Psyche's child, is a fault which no mulatto will pardon; nor can the separation of castes in India be more rigidly observed, than that of complexional shades among the Creoles. My black page, Cubina, is married: I told him that I hoped he had married a pretty woman;

why had he not married Mary Wiggins? He seemed quite shocked at the very idea. 'Oh, massa, me black, Mary Wiggins sambo; that not allowed.'

The dances performed to-night seldom admitted more than three persons at a time: to me they appeared to be movements entirely dictated by the caprice of the moment; but I am told that there is a regular figure, and that the least mistake, or a single false step, is immediately noticed by the rest. I could indeed sometimes fancy, that one story represented an old duenna guarding a girl from a lover; and another, the pursuit of a young woman by two suitors, the one young and the other old; but this might be only fancy. However, I am told, that they have dances which not only represent courtship and marriage, but being brought to bed. Their music consisted of nothing but Gambys (Eboe drums), Shaky-shekies, and Kitty-katties: the latter is nothing but any flat piece of board beat upon with two sticks, and the former is a bladder with a parcel of pebbles in it. But the principal part of the music to which they dance is vocal; one girl generally singing two lines by herself, and being answered by a chorus. To make out either the rhyme of the air, or meaning of the words, was out of the question. But one very long song was about the Duke of Wellington, every stanza being chorussed with,

> Ay! hey-day! Waterloo!
> Waterloo! ho! ho! ho!

I too had a great deal to do in the business, for every third word was 'massa'; though how I came there, I have no more idea than the Duke.

The singing began about six o'clock, and lasted without a moment's pause till two in the morning; and such a noise never did I hear till then. The whole of the floor which was not taken up by the dancers was, through every part of the house except the bedrooms, occupied by men, women, and children, fast asleep. But although they were allowed rum and sugar by whole pailfuls, and were most of them *merry* in consequence, there was not one of them drunk; except indeed, one person, and that was an old woman, who sang, and shouted, and tossed herself about in an elbow chair, till she tumbled it over, and rolled about the room in a manner which shocked the delicacy of even the least prudish part of the company. At twelve, my agent wanted to dismiss them; but I would not suffer them to be interrupted on the first holiday that I had given them; so they continued to dance and shout till two; when human nature could bear no more, and they left me to my bed, and a violent headache.

January 7 (Sunday)

In spite of their exertions of last night, the negroes were again with me by two o'clock in the day, with their drums and their chorusses. However, they found themselves unable to keep it up as they had done on the former night, and were content to withdraw to their own houses by ten in the evening. But first they requested to have to-morrow to themselves, in order that they might go to the mountains for provisions. For although their cottages are always surrounded with trees and shrubs, their provision grounds are kept quite distinct, and are at a distance among the mountains. Of course, I made no difficulty of acceding to their request, but upon condition, that they should ask for no more holidays till the crop should be completed. For the purpose of cultivating their provision-grounds, they are allowed every Saturday; but on the occasion of my arrival, they obtained permission to have the Saturday to themselves, and to fetch their week's provisions from the mountains on the following Monday. All the slaves maintain themselves in this manner by their own labour; even the domestic attendants are not exempted, but are expected to feed themselves, except stated allowances of salt fish, salt pork, etc.

January 8

I really believe that the negresses can produce children at pleasure; and where they are barren, it is just as hens will frequently not lay eggs on shipboard, because they do not like their situation. Cubina's wife is in a family way, and I told him that if the child should live, I would christen it for him, if he wished it. 'Tank you, kind massa, me like it very much: much oblige if massa do that for *me*, too.' So I promised to baptize the father and the baby on the same day, and said that I would be godfather to any children that might be born on the estate during my residence in Jamaica. This was soon spread about, and although I have not yet been here a week, two women are in the straw* already, Jug Betty and Minerva: the first is wife to my head driver, the Duke of Sully; but my sense of propriety was much gratified at finding that Minerva's husband was called Captain. I think nobody will be able to accuse me of neglecting the religious education of my negroes: for I have not only promised to baptize all the infants, but, meeting a little black boy this morning, who said that his name was Moses, I gave him a piece of silver, and told him that it was for the sake of Aaron; which, I flatter myself, was planting in his young mind the rudiments of Christianity.

In my evening's drive I met the negroes, returning from the mountains, with baskets of provisions sufficient to last them for the week. By law they are only allowed every other Saturday for the purpose of cultivating their own grounds, which, indeed, is sufficient; but by giving them every alternate Saturday into the bargain, it enables them to perform their task with so much ease as almost converts it into an amusement; and the frequent visiting their grounds makes them grow habitually as much attached to them as they are to their houses and gardens. It is also adviseable for them to bring home only a week's provisions at a time, rather than a fortnight's; for they are so thoughtless and improvident, that, when they find themselves in possession of a larger supply than is requisite for their immediate occasions, they will sell half to the wandering higglers,* or at Savanna la Mar, in exchange for spirits; and then, at the end of the week, they find themselves entirely unprovided with food, and come to beg a supply from the master's storehouse.

January 9

The sensitive plant is a great nuisance in Jamaica: it over-runs the pastures, and, being armed with very strong sharp prickles, it wounds the mouths of the cattle, and, in some places, makes it quite impossible for them to feed. Various endeavours have been made to eradicate this inconvenient weed, but none as yet have proved effectual.

January 10

The houses here are generally built and arranged according to one and the same model. My own is of wood, partly raised upon pillars; it consists of a single floor: a long gallery, called a piazza, terminated at each end by a square room, runs the whole length of the house. On each side of the piazza is a range of bed-rooms, and the porticoes of the two fronts form two more rooms, with balustrades, and flights of steps descending to the lawn. The whole house is viran-doed with shifting Venetian blinds to admit air; except that one of the end rooms has sash-windows on account of the rains, which, when they arrive, are so heavy, and shift with the wind so suddenly from the one side to the other, that all the blinds are obliged to be kept closed; consequently the whole house is in total darkness during their continuance, except the single sash-windowed room. There is nothing underneath except a few store-rooms and a kind of waiting-hall; but none of the domestic negroes sleep in the house, all going home at night to their respective cottages and families.

Cornwall House itself stands on a dead flat, and the works are built in its immediate neighbourhood, for the convenience of their being the more under the agent's personal inspection (a point of material consequence with them all, but more particularly for the hospital). This dead flat is only ornamented with a few scattered bread-fruit and cotton trees, a grove of mangoes, and the branch of a small river, which turns the mill. Several of these buildings are ugly enough; but the shops of the cooper, carpenter, and blacksmith, some of the trees in their vicinity, and the negro-huts, embowered in shrubberies, and groves of oranges, plantains, cocoas, and pepper-trees, would be reckoned picturesque in the most ornamented grounds. A large spreading tamarind fronts me at this moment, and overshadows the stables, which are formed of open wickerwork; and an orange-tree, loaded with fruit, grows against the window at which I am writing.

On three sides of the landscape the prospect is bounded by lofty purple mountains; and the variety of occupations going on all around me, and at the same time, give an inconceivable air of life and animation to the whole scene, especially as all those occupations look clean,—even those which in England look dirty. All the trades-people are dressed either in white jackets and trousers, or with stripes of red and sky-blue. One band of negroes are carrying the ripe canes on their heads to the mill; another set are conveying away the *trash*, after the juice has been extracted; flocks of turkeys are sheltering from the heat under the trees; the river is filled with ducks and geese; the coopers and carpenters are employed about the puncheons; carts drawn some by six, others by eight, oxen, are bringing loads of Indian corn from the fields; the black children are employed in gathering it into the granary, and in quarrelling with pigs as black as themselves, who are equally busy in stealing the corn whenever the children are looking another way: in short, a plantation possesses all the movement and interest of a farm, without its dung, and its stench, and its dirty accompaniments.

January 11

I saw the whole process of sugar-making this morning. The ripe canes are brought in bundles to the mill, where the cleanest of the women are appointed, one to put them into the machine for grinding them, and another to draw them out after the juice has been extracted, when she throws them into an opening in the floor close to her; another band of negroes collects them below, when, under the name of *trash*, they are carried away to serve for fuel. The juice, which is itself at first of a pale ash-colour, gushes out in great streams, quite white with foam, and passes through a wooden gutter into the boiling-house, where it is received into the siphon or 'cock copper', where fire is applied to it, and it is slaked with lime, in order to make it granulate. The feculent parts of it rise to the top, while the purer and more fluid flow through another gutter into the second copper. When little but the impure scum on the surface remains to be drawn off, the first gutter communicating with the copper is stopped, and the grosser parts are obliged to find a new course through another gutter, which conveys them to the distillery, where, being mixed with the molasses, or treacle, they are manufactured into rum. From the second copper they are transmitted into the first, and thence into two others, and in these four latter basins the scum is removed with skimmers pierced with holes, till it becomes sufficiently free from impurities to be *skipped* off, that is, to be again ladled out of the coppers and spread into the coolers, where it is left to granulate. The sugar is then formed, and is removed into the *curing-house*, where it is put into hogsheads, and left to settle for a certain time, during which those parts which are too poor and too liquid to granulate, drip from the casks into vessels placed beneath them: these drippings are the molasses, which, being carried into the distillery, and mixed with the coarser scum formerly mentioned, form that mixture from which the spirituous liquor of sugar is afterwards produced by fermentation: when but once distilled, it is called 'low wine'; and it is not till after it has gone through a second distillation, that it acquires the name of rum. The 'trash' used for fuel consists of the empty canes, that which is employed for fodder and for thatching is furnished by the superabundant cane-tops; after so many have been set apart as are required for planting. After these original plants have been cut, their roots throw up suckers, which, in time, become canes, and are called *ratoons*: they are far inferior in juice to the planted canes; but then, on the other hand, they require much less weeding, and spare the negroes the only laborious part of the business of sugar-making, the digging holes for the plants; therefore, although an acre of ratoons will produce but one hogshead of sugar, while an acre of plants will produce two, the superiority of the ratooned piece is very great, inasmuch as the saving of time and labour will enable the proprietor to cultivate five acres of ratoons in the same time with one of plants. Unluckily, after three crops, or five at the utmost, in general the ratoons are totally exhausted, and you are obliged to have recourse to fresh plants.

Last night a poor man, named Charles, who had been coachman to my uncle ages ago, was brought into the hospital, having missed a step in the boiling-house, and plunged his foot into the siphon: fortunately, the fire had not long been kindled, and though the liquor was hot enough to scald him, it was not sufficiently so to do him any material injury. The old man had presented himself to me on Saturday's holiday (or *play-day*, in the negro dialect), and had shown me, with great exultation, the coat and waistcoat which had been the last present of his old massa. Charles is now my chief mason, and, as one of the principal persons on the estate, was entitled, by old custom, to the compliment of a *distinguishing* dollar *on* my arrival; but at the same time that I gave him the dollar, to which his situation entitled him, I gave him another for himself, as a keepsake: he put it into the pocket of 'his old massa's' waistcoat, and assured me that they should never again be separated. On hearing of his accident, I went over to the hospital to see that he was well taken care of; and immediately the poor fellow began talking to me about my grandfather, and his young massa, and the young missies, his sisters, and while I suffered him to chatter away for an hour, he totally forgot the pain of his burnt leg.

It was particularly agreeable to me to observe, on Saturday, as a proof of the good treatment which they had experienced, so many old servants of the family, many of whom had been born on the estate, and who, though turned of sixty and seventy, were still strong, healthy, and cheerful. Many manumitted negroes, also, came from other parts of the country to this festival, on hearing of my arrival, because, as they said,—'if they did not come to see massa, they were afraid that it would look ungrateful, and as if they cared no longer about him and Cornwall, now that they were free.' So they stayed two or three days on the estate, coming up to the house for their dinners, and going to sleep at night among their friends in their own former habitations, the negro huts; and when they went away, they assured me, that nothing should prevent their coming back to bid me farewell, before I left the island. All this may be palaver; but certainly they at least play their parts with such an air of truth, and warmth, and enthusiasm, that, after the cold hearts and repulsive manners of England, the contrast is infinitely agreeable.

Je ne vois que des yeux toujours prêts à sourire.*

I find it quite impossible to resist the fascination of the conscious pleasure of pleasing; and my own heart, which I have so long been obliged to keep closed, seems to expand itself again in the sunshine of the kind looks and words which meet me at every turn, and seem to wait for mine as anxiously as if they were so many diamonds.

January 12

In the year '80, this parish of Westmoreland was kept in a perpetual state of alarm by a runaway negro called *Plato*, who had established himself among the Moreland Mountains, and collected a troop of banditti, of which he was himself the chief. He robbed very often, and murdered occasionally; but gallantry was his every day occupation. Indeed, being a remarkably tall athletic young fellow, among the beauties of his own complexion he found but few Lucretias;* and his retreat in the mountains was as well furnished as the haram of Constantinople. Every handsome negress who had the slightest cause of complaint against her master, took the first opportunity of eloping to join *Plato*, where she found freedom, protection, and unbounded generosity; for he spared no pains to secure their affections by gratifying their vanity. Indeed, no Creole lady could venture out on a visit, without running the risk of having her bandbox run away with by Plato for the decoration of his sultanas; and if the maid who carried the bandbox happened to be well-looking, he ran away with the maid as well as the bandbox. Every endeavour to seize this desperado was long in vain: a large reward was put upon his head, but no negro dared to approach him; for, besides his acknowledged courage, he was a professor of Obi, and had threatened that whoever dared to lay a finger upon him should suffer spiritual torments, as well as be physically shot through the head.

Unluckily for Plato, rum was an article with him of the first necessity; the look-out, which was kept for him, was too vigilant to admit of his purchasing spirituous liquors for himself; and once, when for that purpose he had ventured into the neighbourhood of Montego Bay, he was recognised by a slave, who immediately gave the alarm. Unfortunately for this poor fellow, whose name was Taffy, at that moment all his companions happened to be out of hearing; and, after the first moment's alarm, finding that no one approached, the exasperated robber rushed upon him, and lifted the bill-hook, with which he was armed, for the purpose of cleaving his skull. Taffy fled for it; but Plato was the younger, the stronger, and the swifter of the two, and gained upon him every moment. Taffy, however, on the other hand, possessed that one quality by which, according to the fable, the cat was enabled to save herself from the hounds, when the fox, with his thousand tricks, was caught by them. He was an admirable climber, an art in which Plato possessed no skill; and a bread-nut tree, which is remarkably difficult of ascent, presenting itself before him, in a few moments Taffy was bawling for help from the very top of it. To reach him was impossible for his enemy; but still his destruction was hard at hand; for Plato began to hack the tree with his bill, and it was evident that a very short space of time would be sufficient to level it with the ground. In this dilemma, Taffy had nothing for it but to break off the branches near him; and he contrived to pelt these so dexterously at the head of his assailant, that he fairly kept him at bay till his cries at length reached the ears of his companions, and their approach compelled the banditti-captain once more to seek safety among the mountains.

After this Plato no longer dared to approach Montego town; but still spirits must be had:—how was he to obtain them? There was an old watchman on the outskirts of the estate of Canaan, with whom he had contracted an acquaintance, and frequently had passed the night in his hut; the old man having been equally induced by his

presents and by dread of his corporeal strength and supposed supernatural power, to profess the warmest attachment to the interests of
his terrible friend. To this man Plato at length resolved to entrust
himself: he gave him money to purchase spirits, and appointed a
particular day when he would come to receive them. The reward
placed upon the robber's head was more than either gratitude or
terror could counterbalance; and on the same day when the watchman set out to purchase the rum, he apprised two of his friends at
Canaan, for whose use it was intended, and advised *them* to take the
opportunity of obtaining the reward.

The two negroes posted themselves in proper time near the watchman's hut. Most unwisely, instead of sending down some of his
gang, they saw Plato, in his full confidence in the friendship of his
confidant, arrive himself and enter the cabin; but so great was their
alarm at seeing this dreadful personage, that they remained in their
concealment, nor dared to make an attempt at seizing him. The
spirits were delivered to the robber: he might have retired with them
unmolested; but, in his rashness and his eagerness to taste the liquor,
of which he had so long been deprived, he opened the flagon, and
swallowed draught after draught, till he sunk upon the ground in a
state of complete insensibility. The watchman then summoned the
two negroes from their concealment, who bound his arms, and conveyed him to Montego Bay, where he was immediately sentenced to
execution. He died most heroically; kept up the terrors of his impos-
ture to his last moment; told the magistrates, who condemned him,
that his death should be revenged by a storm, which would lay waste
the whole island, that year; and, when his negro gaoler was binding
him to the stake at which he was destined to suffer, he assured him
that he should not live long to triumph in his death, for that he had
taken good care to Obeah him before his quitting the prison. It certainly did happen, strangely enough, that, before the year was over,
the most violent storm took place ever known in Jamaica; and as
to the gaoler, his imagination was so forcibly struck by the threats of
the dying man, that, although every care was taken of him, the power
of medicine exhausted, and even a voyage to America undertaken,
in hopes that a change of scene might change the course of his ideas,
still, from the moment of Plato's death, he gradually pined and
withered away, and finally expired before the completion of the
twelvemonth.

The belief in Obeah is now greatly weakened, but still exists in some degree. Not above ten months ago, my agent was informed that a negro of very suspicious manners and appearance was harboured by some of my people on the mountain lands. He found means to have him surprised, and on examination there was found upon him a bag containing a great variety of strange materials for incantations; such as thunder-stones, cat's ears, the feet of various animals, human hair, fish bones, the teeth of alligators, etc.: he was conveyed to Montego Bay; and no sooner was it understood that this old African was in prison, than depositions were poured in from all quarters from negroes who deposed to having seen him exercise his magical arts, and, in particular, to his having sold such and such slaves medicines and charms to deliver them from their enemies; being, in plain English, nothing else than rank poisons. He was convicted of Obeah upon the most indubitable evidence. The good old practice of burning has fallen into disrepute; so he was sentenced to be transported, and was shipped off the island, to the great satisfaction of persons of all colours—white, black, and yellow.

January 13

Throughout the island many estates, formerly very flourishing and productive, have been thrown up for want of hands to cultivate them, and are now suffered to lie waste: four are in this situation in my own immediate neighbourhood. Finding their complement of negroes decrease, and having no means of recruiting them, proprietors of two estates have in numerous instances found themselves obliged to give up one of them, and draw off the negroes for the purpose of properly cultivating the other.

I have just had an instance strikingly convincing of the extreme nicety required in rearing negro children. Two have been born since my arrival. My housekeeper was hardly ever out of the lying-in apartment; I always visited it myself once a day, and sometimes twice, in order that I might be certain of the women being well taken care of; not a day passed without the inspection of a physician; nothing of indulgence, that was proper for them, was denied; and, besides their ordinary food, the mothers received every day the most nourishing and palatable dish that was brought to my own table. Add to this, that the women themselves were kind-hearted creatures, and particularly anxious to rear these children, because I had promised to be their godfather myself. Yet, in spite of all this attention and indulgence, one of the mothers, during the nurse's absence for ten minutes, grew alarmed at her infant's apparent sleepiness. To rouse it, she began dancing and shaking it till it was in a strong perspiration, and then she stood with it for some minutes at an open window, while a strong north wind was blowing. In consequence, it caught cold, and the next morning symptoms of a locked jaw showed itself. The poor woman was the image of grief itself: she sat on her bed, looking at the child which lay by her side with its little hands clasped, its teeth clenched, and its eyes fixed, writhing in the agony of the spasm, while she was herself quite motionless and speechless, although the tears trickled down her cheeks incessantly. All assistance was fruitless: her thoughtlessness for five minutes had killed the infant, and, at noon to-day it expired.*

This woman was a tender mother, had borne ten children, and yet has now but one alive: another, at present in the hospital, has borne seven, and but one has lived to puberty; and the instances of those who have had four, five, six children, without succeeding in bringing up one, in spite of the utmost attention and indulgence, are very numerous; so heedless and inattentive are the best-intentioned mothers, and so subject in this climate are infants to dangerous complaints. The locked jaw is the common and most fatal one; so fatal, indeed, that the midwife (the *graundee* is her negro appellation) told me, the other day, 'Oh, massa, till nine days over,* we *no hope* of them.' Certainly care and kindness are not adequate to save the children, for the son of a sovereign could not have been more anxiously well treated than was the poor little negro who died this morning.

The negroes are always buried in their own gardens, and many strange and fantastical ceremonies are observed on the occasion. If the corpse be that of a grown person, they consult it as to which way it pleases to be carried; and they make attempts upon various roads without success, before they can hit upon the right one. Till that is accomplished, they stagger under the weight of the coffin, struggle against its force, which draws them in a different direction from that in which they had settled to go; and sometimes in the contest the corpse and the coffin jump off the shoulders of the bearers. But if, as is frequently the case, any person is suspected of having hastened the catastrophe, the corpse will then refuse to go any road but the one which passes by the habitation of the suspected person, and as soon as it approaches his house, no human power is equal to persuading it to pass. As the negroes are extremely superstitious, and very much afraid of ghosts (whom they call the *duppy*), I rather wonder at their choosing to have their dead buried in their gardens; but I understand their argument to be, that they need only fear the duppies of their enemies, but have nothing to apprehend from those after death, who loved them in their lifetime; but the duppies of their adversaries are very alarming beings, equally powerful by day as by night, and who not only are spiritually terrific, but who can give very hard substantial knocks on the pate, whenever they see fit occasion, and can find a good opportunity.

Last Saturday a negro was brought into the hospital, having fallen into epileptic fits, with which till then he had never been troubled. As the faintings had seized him at the slaughter-house, and the fellow was an African, it was at first supposed by his companions, that the sight and smell of the meat had affected him; for many of the Africans cannot endure animal food of any kind, and most of the Eboes in particular are made ill by eating turtle, even although they can use any other food without injury. However, upon enquiry among his shipmates, it appeared that he had frequently eaten beef without the slightest inconvenience. For my own part, the symptoms of his complaint were such as to make me suspect him of having tasted something poisonous, especially as, just before his first fit, he had been observed in the small grove of mangoes near the house; but I was assured by the negroes, one and all, that nothing could possibly have induced him to eat an herb or fruit from that grove, as it had been used as a burying-ground for 'the white people'. But although my idea of the poison was scouted, still the mention of the burying-ground suggested another cause for his illness to the negroes, and they had no sort of doubt, that in passing through the burying-ground he had been struck down by the duppy of a white person not long deceased, whom he had formerly offended, and that these repeated fainting fits were the consequence of that ghostly blow. The negroes have in various publications been accused of a total want of religion, but this appears to me quite incompatible with the ideas of spirits existing after dissolution of the body, which necessarily implies a belief in a future state; and although (as far as I can make out) they have no outward forms of religion, the most devout

Christian cannot have 'God bless you' oftener on his lips than the negro; nor, on the other hand, appear to feel the wish for their enemy's damnation more sincerely when he utters it.

The Africans (as is well known) generally believe, that there is a life beyond this world, and that they shall enjoy it by returning to their own country; and this idea used frequently to induce them, soon after their landing in the colonies, to commit suicide; but this was never known to take place except among fresh negroes, and since the execrable slave-trade has been abolished, such an illusion is unheard of. As to those who had once got over the dreadful period of 'seasoning',* they were generally soon sensible enough of the amelioration of their condition, to make the idea of returning to Africa the most painful that could be presented to them. But, to be sure, poor creatures! what with the terrors and sufferings of the voyage, and the unavoidable hardships of the seasoning, those advantages were purchased more dearly than any in this life can possibly be worth. God be thanked, all that is now at an end; and certainly, as far as I can as yet judge, if I were now standing on the banks of Virgil's Lethe,* with a goblet of the waters of oblivion in my hand, and asked whether I chose to enter life anew as an English labourer or a Jamaica negro, I should have no hesitation in preferring the latter. For myself, it appears to me almost worth surrendering the luxuries and pleasures of Great Britain, for the single pleasure of being surrounded with beings who are always laughing and singing, and who seem to perform their work with so much *nonchalance*, taking up their baskets as if it were perfectly optional whether they took them up or left them there; sauntering along with their hands dangling; stopping to chat with every one they meet; or if they meet no one, standing still to look round, and examine whether there is nothing to be seen that can amuse them, so that I can hardly persuade myself that it is really *work* that they are about. The negro might well say, on his arrival in England—'Massa, in England every thing work!' for here nobody appears to work at all.

I am told that there is one part of their business very laborious, the digging holes for receiving the cane-plants, and which I have not as yet seen; but this does not occupy above a month (I believe) at the utmost, at two periods of the year; and on my estate this service is chiefly performed by extra negroes, hired for the purpose; which, although equally hard on the hired negroes (called a jobbing gang), at least relieves my own, and after all, puts even the former on much the same footing with English day-labourers.

But if I could be contented to *live* in Jamaica, I am still more certain, that it is the only agreeable place for me to die in; for I have got a family mausoleum, which looks for all the world like the theatrical representation of the 'tomb of all the Capulets'. Its outside is most plentifully decorated 'with sculptured stones',—

Arms, angels, epitaphs, and bones.

Within is a tomb of the purest white marble, raised on a platform of ebony; the building, which is surmounted by a statue of Time, with his scythe and hour-glass, stands in the very heart of an orange grove, now in full bearing; and the whole scene this morning looked so cool, so tranquil, and so gay, and is so perfectly divested of all vestiges of dissolution, that the sight of it quite gave me an appetite for being buried. It is a matter of perfect indifference to me what becomes of this little ugly husk of mine, when once I shall have 'shuffled off this mortal coil';* or else I should certainly follow my grandfather's example, and, die where I might, order my body to be sent over for burial to Cornwall; for I never yet saw a place where one could lie down more comfortably to listen for the last trumpet.

January 14 (Sunday)

I gave a dinner to my 'white people', as the book-keepers, etc. are called here, and who have a separate house and establishment for themselves; and certainly a man must be destitute of every spark of hospitality, and have had 'Caucasus horrens'* for his great-grandmother, if he can resist giving dinners in a country where Nature seems to have set up a superior kind of 'London Tavern'* of her own. They who are possessed by the 'Ciborum ambitiosa fames, et lautæ gloria mensæ',* ought to ship themselves off for Jamaica out of hand; and even the lord mayor himself need not blush to give his aldermen such a dinner as is placed on my table, even when I dine alone. Land and sea turtle, quails, snipes, plovers, and pigeons and doves of all descriptions—of which the ring-tail has been allowed to rank with the most exquisite of the winged species, by epicures of such distinction, that their opinion, in matters of this nature, almost carries with it the weight of a law,—excellent pork, barbicued pigs, pepperpots, with numberless other excellent dishes, form the ordinary fare; while the poultry is so large and fine, that if the Dragon of Wantley* found 'houses and churches to be geese and turkies' in England, he would mistake the geese and turkies for houses and churches here. Then our tarts are made of pine-apples, and pine-apples make the best tarts that I ever tasted; there is no end of the variety of fruits, of which the shaddock is 'in itself an host'; but the most singular and exquisite flavour, perhaps, is to be found in the granadillo, a fruit which grows upon a species of vine, and, in fact, appears to be a kind of cucumber. It must be suffered to hang till it is dead ripe, when it is scarcely any thing except juice and seeds, which can only be eaten with a spoon. It requires sugar, but the acid is truly delicious, and like no other separate flavour that I ever met with; what it most resembles is a *mace-doine*, as it unites the different tastes of almost all other fruits, and has, at the same time, a very strong flavour of wine.

As to fish, Savannah la Mar is reckoned the best place in the island, both for variety and *safety*; for, in many parts, the fish feed upon copperas banks, and cannot be used without much precaution: here, none is necessary, and it is only to be wished that their names equalled their flesh in taste; for it must be owned, that nothing can be less tempting than the sounds of Jew-fish, hog-fish, mud-fish, snappers, god-dammies, groupas, and grunts! Of the Sea Fish which I have hitherto met with, the Deep-water Silk appears to me the best; and of rivers, the Mountain-Mullet: but, indeed, the fish is generally so excellent, and in such profusion, that I never sit down to table without wishing for the company of Queen Atygatis of Scythia,* who was so particularly fond of fish, that she prohibited all her subjects from eating it on pain of death, through fear that there might not be enough left for her majesty.

This fondness for fish seems to be a sort of royal passion: more than one of our English sovereigns died of eating too many lampreys;* though, to own the truth, it was suspected that the monks, in an instance or two, improved the same by the addition of a little ratsbane; and Mirabeau assures us, that Frederick the Second of Prussia might have prolonged his existence, if he could but have resisted the fascination of an eel-pye; but the charm was too strong for him, and, like his great-grandmother of all, he ate and died— 'All for eel-pye, or this world well lost!'* And now, which had to resist the most difficult temptation, Frederic or Eve? *She* longed to experience pleasures yet untasted, and which she fancied to be exquisite: *he*, like Sigismunda,* pined after known pleasures, and which he knew to be good; *she* was the dupe of imagination; *he* fell a victim to established habit. Which was the most deserving pardon? There is a question for the bishops: those clergymen who reside constantly on their livings (as all clergymen ought to do, or they ought not to be clergymen), I shall, in charity, believe to have something better to do with their time than to solve it.

The provision-grounds of the negroes furnish them with plantains, bananas, cocoa-nuts, and yams: of the latter there is a regular harvest once a year, and they remain in great perfection for many months, provided they are dug up carefully, but the slightest wound with the spade is sufficient to rot them. Calalue (a species of spinach) is a principal article in their pepper-pots: but in this parish their most valuable and regular supply of food arises from the cocoa-finger, or coccos, a species of the yam, but which lasts all the year round. These vegetables form the basis of negro sustenance; but the slaves also receive from their owners a regular weekly allowance of red herrings and salt meat, which serves to relish their vegetable diet; and, indeed, they are so passionately fond of salted provisions, that, instead of giving them fresh beef (as at their festival of Saturday last), I have been advised to provide some hogsheads of salt fish, as likely to afford them more gratification, at such future additional holidays as I may find it possible to allow them in this busy season of crop.

January 15

The offspring of a white man and black woman is a *mulatto*; the mulatto and black produce a *sambo*; from the mulatto and white comes the *quadroon*; from the quadroon and white the *mustee*; the child of a mustee by a white man is called a *musteefino*;* while the children of a musteefino are free by law, and rank as white persons to all intents and purposes. I think it is Long who asserts,* that two mulattoes will never have children; but, as far as the most positive assurances can go, since my arrival in Jamaica, I have reason to believe the contrary, and that mulattoes breed together just as well as blacks and whites; but they are almost universally weak and effeminate persons, and thus their children are very difficult to rear. On a sugar estate one black is considered as more than equal to two mulattoes. Beautiful as are their forms in general, and easy and graceful as are their movements (which, indeed, appear to me so striking, that they cannot fail to excite the admiration of any one who has ever looked with delight on statues), still the women of colour are deficient in one of the most requisite points of female beauty. When Oromases was employed in the formation of woman, and said,—'Let her enchanting bosom resemble the celestial spheres', he must certainly have suffered the negress to slip out of his mind. Young or old, I have not yet seen such a thing as a *bosom*.

January 16

I never witnessed on the stage a scene so picturesque as a negro village. I walked through my own to-day, and visited the houses of the drivers, and other principal persons; and if I were to decide according to my own taste, I should infinitely have preferred their habitations to my own. Each house is surrounded by a separate garden, and the whole village is intersected by lanes, bordered with all kinds of sweet-smelling and flowering plants; but not such gardens as those belonging to our English cottages, where a few cabbages and carrots just peep up and grovel upon the earth between hedges, in square narrow beds, and where the tallest tree is a gooseberry bush: the vegetables of the negroes are all cultivated in their provision-grounds; these form their *kitchen*-gardens, and these are all for ornament or luxury, and are filled with a profusion of oranges, shaddocks, cocoa-nuts, and peppers of all descriptions: in particular I was shown the abba, or palm-tree, resembling the cocoa-tree, but much more beautiful, as its leaves are larger and more numerous, and, feathering to the ground as they grow old, they form a kind of natural arbour. It bears a large fruit, or rather vegetable, towards the top of the tree, in shape like the cone of the pine, but formed of seeds, some scarlet and bright as coral, others of a brownish-red or purple. The abba requires a length of years to arrive at maturity: a very fine one, which was shown me this morning, was supposed to be upwards of an hundred years old; and one of a very moderate size had been planted at the least twenty years, and had only borne fruit once.

It appears to me a strong proof of the good treatment which the negroes on Cornwall have been accustomed to receive, that there are many very old people upon it; I saw to-day a woman near a hundred years of age; and I am told that there are several of sixty, seventy, and eighty. I was glad, also, to find, that several negroes who have obtained their freedom, and possess little properties of their own in the mountains, and at Savannah la Mar, look upon my estate so little as the scene of their former sufferings while slaves, that they frequently come down to pass a few days in their ancient habitations with their former companions, by way of relaxation. One woman in particular expressed her hopes, that I should not be offended at her still coming to Cornwall now and then, although she belonged to it no longer; and begged me to give directions before my return to England, that her visits should not be hindered on the grounds of her having no business there.

My visit to Jamaica has at least produced one advantage to myself. Several runaways, who had disappeared for some time (some even for several months), have again made their appearance in the field, and I have desired that no questions should be asked. On the other hand, after enjoying herself during the Saturday and Sunday, which were allowed for holidays on my arrival, one of my ladies chose to *pull foot*, and did not return from her hiding-place in the mountains till this morning. Her name is Marcia; but so unlike is she to Addison's Marcia, that she is not only as black as Juba, (instead of being 'fair, oh! how divinely fair!')* but,—whereas Sempronius complains, that 'Marcia, the lovely Marcia, is left behind', the complaint against my heroine is, that 'Marcia, the lovely Marcia' is always running away. In excuse for her disappearance she alleged, that so far was her husband from thinking that 'she towered above her sex', that he had called her 'a very bad woman', which had provoked her so much, that she could not bear to stay with him; and she assured me, that he was himself 'a very bad man'; which, if true, was certainly enough to justify any lady, black or white, in making a little incognito excursion for a week or so; therefore, as it appeared to be nothing more than a conjugal quarrel, and as Marcia engaged never to run away any more (at the same time allowing that she had suffered her resentment to carry her too far, when it had carried her all the way to the mountains), I desired that an act of oblivion might be passed in favour of Cato's daughter, and away she went, quite happy, to pick hog's meat.

The negro houses are composed of wattles on the outside, with rafters of sweet-wood, and are well plastered within and whitewashed; they consist of two chambers, one for cooking and the other for sleeping, and are, in general, well furnished with chairs, tables, etc., and I saw none without a four-post bedstead and plenty of bed-clothes; for, in spite of the warmth of the climate, when the sun is not above the horizon the negro always feels very chilly. I am assured that many of my slaves are very rich (and their property is inviolable), and that they are never without salt provisions, porter, and even wine, to entertain their friends and their visiters from the bay or the mountains. As I passed through their grounds, many little requests were preferred to me: one wanted an additional supply of lime for the whitewashing his house; another was building a new house for a superannuated wife (for they have all so much decency as to call their sexual attachments by a conjugal name), and wanted a little assistance towards the finishing it; a third requested a new axe to work with; and several entreated me to negotiate the purchase of some relation or friend belonging to another estate, and with whom they were anxious to be reunited: but all their requests were for additional indulgences; not one complained of ill-treatment, hunger, or over-work.

Poor Nicholas gave me a fresh instance of his being one of those whom Fortune pitches upon to show her spite: he has had four children, none of whom are alive; and the eldest of them, a fine little girl of four years old, fell into the mill-stream, and was drowned before any one was aware of her danger. His wife told me that she had had fifteen children, had taken the utmost care of them, and yet had now but two alive: she said, indeed, fifteen at the first, but she afterwards corrected herself, and explained that she had had 'twelve whole children and three half ones'; by which she meant miscarriages.

Besides the profits arising from their superabundance of provisions, which the better sort of negroes are enabled to sell regularly once a week at Savannah la Mar to a considerable amount, they keep a large stock of poultry, and pigs without number; which latter cost their owners but little, though they cost me a great deal; for they generally make their way into the cane-pieces,* and sometimes eat me up an hogshead of sugar in the course of the morning: but the most expensive of the planter's enemies are the rats, whose numbers are incredible, and are so destructive that a reward is given for killing them. During the last six months my agent has paid for three thousand rats killed upon Cornwall. Nor is the sugar which they consume the worst damage which they commit; the worst mischief is, that if, through the carelessness of those whose business it is to supply the mill, one cane which has been gnawed by the rats is allowed admittance, that single damaged piece is sufficient to produce acidity enough to spoil the whole sugar.

January 17

In this country there is scarcely any twilight, and all nature seems to wake at the same moment. About six o'clock the darkness disperses, the sun rises, and instantly every thing is in motion: the negroes are going to the field, the cattle are driving to pasture, the pigs and the poultry are pouring out from their hutches, the old women are preparing food on the lawn for the *pickaninnies* (the very small children), whom they keep feeding at all hours of the day; and all seem to be going to their employments, none to their work, the men and the women just as quietly and leisurely as the pigs and the poultry. The sight is really quite gay and amusing, and I am generally out of bed in time to enjoy it, especially as the continuance of the cool north breezes renders the weather still delicious, though the pleasure is rather an expensive one. Not a drop of rain has fallen since the 16th of November; the young canes are burning; and the drying quality of these norths is still more detrimental than the want of rain, so that these winds may be said to blow my pockets inside out; and as every draught of air, which I inhale with so much pleasure, is estimated to cost me a guinea, I feel, while breathing it, like Miss Burney's Citizen at Vauxhall, who kept muttering to himself, with every bit of ham that he put into his mouth, 'There goes sixpence, and there goes a shilling!'

January 18

A Galli-wasp, which was killed in the neighbouring morass, has just been brought to me. This is the Alligator in miniature, and is even more dreaded by the negroes than its great relation: it is only to be found in swamps and morasses: that which was brought to me was about eighteen inches in length, and I understand that it is seldom longer, although, as it grows in years, its thickness and the size of its jaws and head become greatly increased. It runs away on being encountered, and conceals itself; and it is only dangerous if tram-pled upon by accident, or if attacked; but then its bite is a dreadful one, not only from its tongue being armed with a sting (the venom of which is very powerful, although not mortal), but from its teeth being so brittle that they generally break in the wound, and as it is hardly possible to extract the pieces entirely, the wound corrupts, and becomes an incurable sore of the most offensive nature. Luckily, these reptiles are very scarce, but nothing can exceed the terror and aversion in which they are held by the negroes. This dead one had been lying in the room for several hours, yet, on my servant's acci-dentally stirring the board on which the galli-wasp was stretched for my inspection, my little negro servant George darted out of the room in terror, and was at the bottom of the staircase in a moment. The skin of this animal appeared to be like shagreen* in looks and strength, and was almost entirely composed of layers of very small scales; the colours were brownish-yellow and olive-green, the teeth numerous and piercing, and the claws of the feet very long and sharp: altogether it is a hideous and disgusting creature. As to the alligator of Jamaica, it is a timid animal, which never was known to attack the human species, though it frequently takes the liberty of running away with a dog or two, which appears to be their venison and turtle. There is no river on my estate large enough for their inhabiting; but, in Paradise River, which is not above four miles off, I understand that they are common.

January 19

A young mulatto carpenter, belonging to Horace Beckford's* estate of Shrewsbury, came to beg my intercession with his overseer. He had been absent two days without leave, and on these occasions it is customary for the slaves to apply to some neighbouring gentleman for a note in their behalf, which, as I am told, never fails to obtain the pardon required, as the managers of estates are in general but too happy to find an excuse for passing over without punishment any offences which are not very heinous; indeed, what with the excellent laws already enacted for the protection of the slaves, and which every year are still further ameliorated, and what with the difficulty of procuring more negroes—(which can now only be done by pur-chasing them from other estates),—which makes it absolutely necessary for the managers to preserve the slaves, if they mean to preserve their own situations,—I am fully persuaded that instances of tyranny to negroes are now very rare, at least in this island. But I must still acknowledge, from my own sad experience, since my arrival, that unless a West-Indian proprietor occasionally visit his estates himself, it is utterly impossible for him to be *certain* that his deputed authority is not abused, however good may be his intentions, and however vigilant his anxiety.

My father was one of the most humane and generous persons that ever existed; there was no indulgence which he ever denied his negroes, and his letters were filled with the most absolute injunctions for their good treatment. When his estates became mine, the one upon which I am now residing was managed by an attorney, considerably advanced in years, who had been long in our employment, and who bore the highest character for probity and humanity. He was both attorney and overseer; and it was a particular recommendation to me that he lived in my own house, and therefore had my slaves so immediately under his eye, that it was impossible for any subaltern to misuse them without his knowledge. His letters to me expressed the greatest anxiety and attention respecting the welfare and comfort of the slaves;—so much so, indeed, that when I detailed his mode of management to Lord Holland,* he observed, 'that if he did all that was mentioned in his letters, he did as much as could possibly be expected or wished from an attorney'; and on parting with his own, Lord Holland was induced to take mine to manage his estates, which are in the immediate neighbourhood of Cornwall. This man died about two years ago, and since my arrival, I happened to hear, that during his management a remarkably fine young penn-keeper, named Richard (the brother of my intelligent carpenter, John Fuller), had run away several times to the mountains. I had taken occasion to let the brothers know, between jest and earnest, that I was aware of Richard's misconduct; and at length, one morning, John, while he blamed his brother's running away, let fall, that he had some excuse in the extreme ill-usage which he had received from one of the book-keepers, who 'had had a spite against him'. The hint alarmed me; I followed it, and nothing could equal my anger and surprise at learning the whole truth.

It seems, that while I fancied my attorney to be resident on Cornwall, he was, in fact, generally attending to a property of his own, or looking after estates of which also he had the management in distant parts of the island. During his absence, an overseer of his own appointing, without my knowledge, was left in absolute possession of his power, which he abused to such a degree, that almost every slave of respectability on the estate was compelled to become a runaway. The property was nearly ruined, and absolutely in a state of rebellion; and at length he committed an act of such severity, that the negroes, one and all, fled to Savannah la Mar, and threw themselves upon the protection of the magistrates, who immediately came over to Cornwall, investigated the complaint, and *now*, at length, the attorney, who had known frequent instances of the overseer's tyranny, had frequently rebuked him for them, and had redressed the sufferers, but who still had dared to abuse my confidence so grossly as to continue him in his situation, upon this public exposure thought proper to dismiss him. Yet, while all this was going on—while my negroes were groaning under the iron rod of this petty tyrant—and while the public magistrature was obliged to interfere to protect them from his cruelty—my attorney had the insolence and falsehood to write me letters, filled with assurances of his perpetual vigilance for their welfare—of their perfect good treatment and satisfaction; nor, if I had not come myself to Jamaica, in all probability should I ever have had the most distant idea how abominably the poor creatures had been misused.

I have made it my business to mix as much as possible among the negroes, and have given them every encouragement to repose confidence in me; and I have uniformly found all those, upon whom any reliance can be placed, unite in praising the humanity of their present superintendant. Instantly on his arrival, he took the whole power of punishment into his own hands: he forbade the slightest interference in this respect of any person whatever on the estate, white or black; nor have I been able to find as yet any one negro who has any charge of harsh treatment to bring against him. However, having been already so grossly deceived, I will never again place implicit confidence in any person whatever in a matter of such importance. Before my departure, I shall take every possible measure that may prevent any misconduct taking place without my being apprised of it as soon as possible; and I have already exhorted my negroes to apply to the magistrates on the very first instance of ill-usage, should any occur during my absence.

I am indeed assured by every one about me, that to manage a West-

Indian estate without the occasional use of the cart-whip, however rarely, is impossible; and they insist upon it, that it is absurd in me to call my slaves ill-treated, because, when they act grossly wrong, they are treated like English soldiers and sailors. All this may be very true; but there is something to me so shocking in the idea of this execrable cart-whip, that I have positively forbidden the use of it on Cornwall; and if the estate must go to rack and ruin without its use, to rack and ruin the estate must go. Probably, I should care less about this punishment, if I had not been living among those on whom it may be inflicted; but now, when I am accustomed to see every face that looks upon me, grinning from ear to ear with pleasure at my notice, and hear every voice cry 'God bless you, massa', as I pass, one must be an absolute brute not to feel unwilling to leave them subject to the lash; besides, they are excellent cajolers, and lay it on with a trowel. Nicholas and John Fuller came to me this morning to beg a favour, 'and beg massa hard, quite hard!' It was, that when massa went away, he would leave his picture for the negroes; 'that they might talk to it, all just as they did to massa.' Shakspeare says—

A little flattery does well sometimes!*

But, although the mode of expressing it may be artifice, the sentiment of good-will may be shown. A dog grows attached to the person who feeds and makes much of him; and as they have never experienced as yet any but kind treatment from me personally, it would be against common sense and nature to suppose that my negroes do not feel kindly towards me.

January 20

THE RUNAWAY

Peter, Peter was a black boy;
　　Peter, him pull foot one day:
Buckra* girl, him[1] Peter's joy;
　　Lilly white girl entice him away.
Fye, Missy Sally, fye on you!
Poor Blacky Peter why undo?

[1] The negroes never distinguish between 'him' and 'her' in their conversation.

Oh! Peter, Peter was a bad boy;
Peter was a runaway.

Peter, him Massa thief—Oh! fye!
    Missy Sally, him say him do so.
Him money spent, Sally bid him bye,
    And from Peter away him go;
Fye, Missy Sally, fye on you!
Poor Blacky Peter what him do?
Oh! Peter, Peter was a sad boy;
Peter was a runaway!

Peter, him go to him Massa back;
    There him humbly own him crime:
'Massa, forgib one poor young Black!
    Oh! Massa, good Massa, forgib dis time!'—
Then in come him Missy so fine, so gay,
And to him Peter thus him say:
'Oh! Missy, good Missy, you for me pray!
Beg Massa forgib poor runaway!'

'Missy, you cheeks so red, so white;
    Missy, you eyes like diamond shine!
Missy, you Massa's sole delight,
    And Lilly Sally, him was mine!
Him say—"Come, Peter, mid me go!"—
Could me refuse him? Could me say "no?"—
Poor Peter—"no" him could no say!
So Peter, Peter ran away!'—

Him Missy him pray; him Massa so kind
    Was moved by him prayer, and to Peter him say:
'Well, boy, for this once I forgive you!—but mind!
    With the buckra girls you no more go away!
Though fair without, they're foul within;
Their heart is black, though white their skin.
Then Peter, Peter with me stay;
Peter no more run away!'—

January 21 (Sunday)

The hospital has been crowded, since my arrival, with patients who have nothing the matter with them. On Wednesday there were about thirty invalids, of whom only four were cases at all serious; the rest had 'a lilly pain here, Massa', or 'a bad pain me know nowhere,

Massa', and evidently only came to the hospital in order to sit idle, and chat away the time with their friends. Four of them the doctor ordered into the field peremptorily; the next day there came into the sick-house six others; upon this I resolved to try my own hand at curing them; and I directed the head-driver to announce, that the presents which I had brought from England should be distributed to-day, that the new-born children should be christened, and that the negroes might take possession of my house, and amuse themselves till twelve at night. The effect of my prescription was magical; two thirds of the sick were hale and hearty, at work in the field on Saturday morning, and to-day not a soul remained in the hospital except the four serious cases.

The christening took place about four o'clock. Sully's infant, which had been destined to perform a part on this occasion, had died in the hospital; but this morning the father came to complain of his disappointment, and to beg leave to substitute a child by *another* wife, which had been born about two months before my arrival; and as the father is a very serviceable fellow, and the mother, besides having brought up three children of her own, had the additional merit of having reared an infant whose own mother had died in child-bed, I broke through the rule of only christening those myself who should be born since my coming to Jamaica, and granted his request. By good luck, the first child to be named was the offspring of Minerva and Captain; so I told the parents that as it would be highly proper to call the boy after the greatest Captain that the world could produce, he should be named Wellington; and that I hoped that he would grow up to serve *me* in Jamaica as well as the Duke of Wellington had served his massa, the King of England, in Europe. The Duke of Sully's child I wanted to call Navarre; but the father had brought over a free negro from Savannah la Mar to stand god-father, who was his *fidus Achates*, by the name of John Davies, and I found that he had set his heart upon calling the boy John Lewis, after his friend and myself; so John Lewis he was.

There ought to have been a third child, born at seven months, whom the *graundee* had reared with great difficulty, and dismissed, quite strong, from the hospital; the mother had taken great care of it till the tenth day, when she was entitled to an allowance of clothes, provisions, etc.; but no sooner had she received her reward, than on that very night she suffered the child to remain so long without food, while she went herself to dance on a neighbouring estate, that it was brought, in an exhausted state, back to the hospital; and, in spite of every care, it expired within four and twenty hours after its return.

The ceremony was performed with perfect gravity and propriety by all parties; I thought it as well to cut the reading part of it very short; but I read a couple of prayers, marked the foreheads of the children with the sign of the cross, and, instead of the concluding prayer, I substituted a wish, 'that God would bless the children, and make them live to be as good servants to me, as I prayed him to make me a kind massa to them'; upon which all present very gravely made me their lowest bows and courtesies, and then gave me a loud huzza; so unusual a mode of approbation at a christening that it had nearly overturned my seriousness; and I made haste to serve out Madeira to the parents and assistants, that they might drink the healths of the new Christians and of each other. The mothers and the *graundee* were then called up to the table, and the ladies in a family way were arranged behind them.

Their title in Jamaica is rather coarse, but very expressive. I asked Cubina one day 'who was that woman with a basket on her head?' 'Massa,' he answered, 'that one belly-woman going to sell provisions at the Bay.' As she was going to sell *provisions*, I supposed that *belly*-woman was the name of her trade; but it afterwards appeared that she was one of those females who had given in their names as being then labouring under

The pleasing punishment which women bear;*

and who, in consequence, were discharged from all severe labour. I then gave the *graundee* and the mothers a dollar each, and told them, that for the future they might claim the same sum, in addition to their usual allowance of clothes and provisions, for every infant which should be brought to the overseer alive and well on the fourteenth day; and I also gave each mother a present of a scarlet girdle with a silver medal in the centre, telling her always to wear it on feasts and holidays, when it should entitle her to marks of peculiar respect and attention, such as being one of the first served, and receiving a larger portion than the rest; that the *first* fault which she might commit, should be forgiven on the production of this girdle; and that when she should have any favour to ask, she should always put it round her waist, and be assured, that on seeing it, the overseer would allow the wearer to be entitled to particular indulgence. On every additional child an additional medal is to be affixed to the belt, and precedence is to follow the greater number of medals. I expected that this notion of an order of honour would have been treated as completely fanciful and romantic; but to my great surprise, my manager told me, that 'he never knew a dollar better bestowed than the one which formed the medal of the girdle, and that he thought the institution likely to have a very good effect'.*

Immediately after the christening the Eboe drums were produced, and in defiance of Sunday the negroes had the irreverence to be gay and happy, while the presents were getting in order for distribution. All the men got jackets, the women seven yards of stuff each for petticoats, etc., and the children as much printed cotton as would make a couple of frocks. The Creoles were delighted beyond measure when some of the African male negroes exclaimed, 'Tank, massa', and made a low courtesy in the confusion of their gratitude. As they were all called to receive their presents alphabetically in pairs, some of the combinations were very amusing. We had Punch and Plato, Priam and Pam, Hemp and Hercules, and Minerva and Moll come together. By twelve they dispersed, and I went to bed, as usual on these occasions, with a violent headach.

January 22

While I was at dinner, a violent uproar was heard below stairs. On enquiry, it proved to be Cubina, quarrelling with his niece Phillis (a good-looking black girl employed about the house), about a broken pitcher; and as her explanation did not appear satisfactory to him, he had thought proper to give her a few boxes on the ear. Upon hearing this, I read him such a lecture upon the baseness of a man's striking a woman, and told him with so much severity that his heart must be a bad one to commit such an offence, that poor Cubina, having never heard a harsh word from me before, scarcely knew whether he stood upon his head or his heels. When he afterwards brought my coffee, he expressed his sorrow for having offended me, and begged my pardon in the most humble manner. I told him, that to obtain mine, he must first obtain that of Phillis, and he immediately declared himself ready to make her any apology that I might dictate. So the girl was called in;

and her uncle going up to her, 'I am very sorry, Phillis,' said he, 'that I gave way to high passion, and called you hard names, and struck you: which I ought not to have done while massa was in the house'; (here I was going to interrupt him, but he was too clever not to perceive his blunder, and made haste to add) 'nor if he had *not* been here, nor at all; so I hope you will have the kindness to forgive me this once, and I never will strike you again, and so I beg your pardon.' And he then put out his hand to her in the most frank and hearty manner imaginable; and on her accepting it, made her three or four of his very lowest and most graceful bows. I furnished him with a piece of money to give her as a peace-offering; they left the room thoroughly reconciled, and in five minutes after they and the rest of the servants were all chattering, laughing, and singing together, in the most perfect harmony and good-humour. I suppose, if I had desired an upper servant in England to make the same submission, he would have preferred quitting my service to doing what he would have called 'humbling himself to an inferior'; or, if he had found himself compelled to give way, he would have been sulky with the girl, and found fault with every thing that she did in the house for a twelvemonth after.

On the other hand, there are some choice ungrateful scoundrels among the negroes: on the night of their first dance, a couple of sheep disappeared from the pen, although they could not have been taken from want of food, as on that very morning there had been an ample distribution of fresh beef; and last night another sheep and a quantity of poultry followed them. Yesterday, too, a young rascal of a boy called 'massa Jackey', who is in the frequent habit of running away for months at a time, and whom I had distinguished from the cleverness of his countenance and buffoonery of his manners, came to beg my permission to go and purchase food with some money which I had just given him, 'because he was almost starving; his parents were dead, he had no provision-grounds, no allowance, and nobody ever gave him anything.' Upon this I sent Cubina with the boy to the store-keeper, when it appeared that he had always received a regular allowance of provisions twice a week, which he generally sold, as well as his clothes, at the Bay, for spirits; had received an additional portion only last Friday; and, into the bargain, during the whole of that week had been fed from the house. What he could propose to himself by telling a lie which must be so soon detected,

I cannot conceive; but I am assured, that unless a negro has an interest in telling the truth, he always lies—in order to keep his tongue in practice.

One species of flattery (or of *Congo-saw*, as we call it here) amused me much this morning: an old woman who is in the hospital wanted to express her gratitude for some stewed fish which I had sent her for supper, and, instead of calling me 'massa', she always said—'Tank him, *my husband*.'*

January 24

This was a day of perpetual occupation. I rose at six o'clock, and went down to the Bay to settle some business; on my return I visited the hospital while breakfast was getting ready; and as soon as it was over, I went down to the negro-houses to hear the whole body of Eboes lodge a complaint against one of the book-keepers, and appoint a day for their being heard in his presence. On my return to the house, I found two women belonging to a neighbouring estate, who came to complain of cruel treatment from their overseer, and to request me to inform their trustee how ill they had been used, and see their injuries redressed. They said, that having been ill in the hospital, and ordered to the field while they were still too weak to work, they had been flogged with much severity (though not beyond the limits of the law); and my head driver, who was less scrupulously delicate than myself as to ocular inspection of Juliet's person (which Juliet, to do her justice, was perfectly ready to submit to in proof of her assertions), told me, that the woman had certainly suffered greatly; the other, whose name was Delia, was but just recovering from a miscarriage, and declared openly that the overseer's conduct had been such, that nothing should have prevented her running away long ago if she could but have had the heart to abandon a child which she had on the estate. Both were poor feeble-looking creatures, and seemed very unfit subjects for any severe correction. I promised to write to their trustee; and, as they were afraid of being punished on their return home for having thrown themselves on my protection, I wrote a note to the overseer, requesting that the women might remain quite unmolested till the trustee's arrival, which was daily expected; and, with this note and a present of cocoa-fingers and salt fish, Delia and Juliet departed, apparently much comforted.

They were succeeded by no less a personage than *Venus* herself—a poor, little, sickly, timid soul, who had purchased her freedom from my father by substituting in her place a fine stout black wench, who, being Venus's *locum tenens*, was, by courtesy, called Venus, too, though her right name was 'Big Joan'; but, by some neglect of the then attorney, Venus had never received any title, and she now came to beg 'massa so good as give paper'; otherwise she was still, to all intents and purposes, my slave, and I might still have compelled her to work, although, at the same time, her substitute was on the estate. Of course, I promised the paper required, and engaged to act the part of a second Vulcan* by releasing Venus from my chains: but the paper was not the only thing that Venus wanted; she also wanted a petticoat! She told me, that when the presents were distributed on Sunday, the petticoat, which she would otherwise have had, was, of course, 'given to the *other* Venus'; and though, to be sure, she was free now, yet, 'when she belonged to massa, she had always worked for him well', and 'she was quite as glad to see massa as the other Venus', and, therefore, 'ought to have quite as much petticoat.' I tried to convince her, that for Venus to wear a petticoat of blue durant,* or, indeed, any petticoat at all, would be quite unclassical: the goddess of beauty stuck to her point, and finally carried off the petticoat.

Venus had scarcely evacuated the premises, when her place was occupied by the minister of Savannah la Mar,* with proposals for instructing the negroes in religion; and the minister, in his turn, was replaced by one of the Sunday-night thieves, who had been caught while in the actual possession of one of my sheep and a great turkey-cock; and, to make the matter worse, the depredator's name was Hercules! Hercules, whom Virgil states to have exercised so much severity on Cacus,* when his own oxen were stolen, was taken up himself for stealing my sheep in Jamaica! The demi-god had nothing to say in his excuse: he had just received a large allowance of beef:—therefore, hunger had no share in his transgression; and the committing the offence during the very time that I was giving the negroes a festival, rendered his ingratitude the more flagrant.

I perfectly well understood that the man was sent to me by my agent, in order to show the absolute necessity of sometimes employing the cart-whip, and to see whether I would suffer the fellow to escape unpunished. But, as this was the first offender who had been brought before me, I took that for a pretext to absolve him: so I lectured him for half an hour with great severity, swore that on the very next offence I would order him to be sold; and that if he would not do his fair proportion of work without being lashed, he should be sent to work somewhere else; for I would suffer no such worthless fellows on my estate, and would not be at the expense of a cartwhip to correct him. He promised most earnestly to behave better in future, and Hercules was suffered to depart: but I am told that no good can be expected of him; that he is perpetually running away; and that he had been absent for five weeks together before my arrival, and only returned home upon hearing that there was a distribution of beef, rum, and jackets going forward; in return for all which, he stole my sheep and my poor great turkey-cock.

But now came the most puzzling business of the day. About four years ago, two Eboes, called Pickle and Edward, were rivals, after being intimate friends: Pickle (who is an excellent faithful negro, but not very wise) was the successful candidate; and, of course, the friendship was interrupted, till Edward married the sister of the disputed fair one. From this time the brothers-in-law lived in perfect harmony together; but, during the first festival given on my arrival, Pickle's house was broken open, and robbed of all his clothes, etc. The thief was sought for, but in vain. On Monday last I found Pickle in the hospital, complaining of a pain in his side; and the blood, which had been taken from him, gave reason to apprehend a pleurisy arising from cold; but, as the disorder had been taken in its earliest stage, nothing dangerous was expected. The fever abated; the medicines performed their offices properly; still the man's spirits and strength appeared to decline, and he persisted in saying that he was not better, and should never do well. At length, to-day, he got out of his sick bed, came to the house, attended by the whole body of drivers, and accused his brother-in-law of having been the stealer of his goods. I asked, 'Had Edward been seen near his house? Had any of his effects been seen in Edward's possession? Did Edward refuse to suffer his hut to be searched?' No. Edward, who was present, pressed for the most strict scrutiny, and asserted his perfect ignorance; nor could the accuser advance any grounds for the charge, except his belief of Edward's guilt. 'Why did he think so?' After much beating about the bush, at length out came the real *causa doloris**—'Edward had *Obeahed* him!' He had accused Edward of breaking open his house, and had begged him to help him to his goods again; and 'Edward had gone at midnight into the bush' (i.e. the wood), and 'had gathered the plant whangra, which he had boiled in an iron pot, by a fire of leaves, over which he went puff, puffie!' and said the sautee-sautee; and then had cut the whangra root into four pieces, three to bury at the plantation gates, and one to burn; and to each of these three pieces he gave the name of a Christian, one of which was Daniel; and Edward had said, that this would help him to find his goods; but instead of that, he had immediately felt this pain in his side, and therefore he was sure that, instead of using Obeah to find his goods, Edward had used it to kill himself. 'And were these all his reasons?' I enquired. 'No; when he married, Edward was very angry at the loss of his mistress, and had said that they never would live well and happily together; and they never *had* lived happily and well together.'

This last argument quite got the better of my gravity. By parity of reasoning, I thought that almost every married couple in Great Britain must be under the influence of Obeah! I endeavoured to convince the fellow of his folly and injustice, especially as the person accused was the identical man who had detected the Obeah priest harboured in one of my negro huts last year, had seized him with his own hands, and delivered him up to my agent, who had prosecuted and transported him. It was, therefore, improbable in the highest degree, that he should be an Obeah man himself; and all the bystanders, black and white, joined me in ridiculing Pickle for complaints so improbable and childish. But anger, argument, and irony were all ineffectual. I offered to christen him, and expel black Obeah by white, but in vain; the fellow persisted in saying, that 'he had a pain in his side, and, *therefore*, Edward must have given it to him'; and he went back to his hospital, shaking his head all the way, sullen and unconvinced. He is a young strong negro, perfectly well disposed, and doing his due portion of work willingly; and it will be truly provoking to lose him by the influence of this foolish prejudice.

January 25

I sent for Edward, had him alone with me for above two hours, and pressed him most earnestly to confide in me. I gave him a dollar to convince him of my good-will towards him; assured him that whatever he might tell me should remain a secret between us; said, that

I was certain of his not having used any poison, or done any thing really mischievous; but as I suspected him of having played some monkey-tricks or other, which, however harmless in themselves, had evidently operated dangerously upon Pickle's imagination, I begged him to tell me precisely what had passed, in order that I might counteract its baleful effects. In reply, Edward swore to me most solemnly, 'by the great God Almighty, who lives above the clouds', that he never had used any such practices: that he had never gone into the wood to gather whangra; and that he had considered Pickle, from the moment of his own marriage, as his brother, and had always, till then, loved him as such. His eyes filled with tears while he protested that he should be as sorry for Pickle's death as if it were himself; and he complained bitterly of having the ill name of an Obeah man given to him, which made him feared and shunned by his companions, and entirely without cause. But he said that he was certain that Pickle would never have suspected him of such a crime, if a third person had not put it into his head. There is a negro on my estate called Adam, who has been long and strongly suspected of having connections with Obeah men. When Edward was quite young, he was under this fellow's superintendence, and he now assured me, that Adam had not only endeavoured to draw him into similar practices, but had even pressed him very earnestly to lay a magical egg under the door of a book-keeper whose conduct had been obnoxious. Edward had positively refused: from that moment his superintendent, from being his protector, had become his enemy, had shown him spite upon every occasion; and he it was, he had no doubt, who, for the purpose of injuring him, had put this foolish notion into Pickle's head.

Upon enquiry it appeared, that on the very morning succeeding Pickle's entering the hospital, this suspected man had gone there also, on pretence of sickness, and had remained there to watch the invalid; although it was so evident that nothing was the matter with him, that the doctor had frequently ordered him to the field, but the man had always found means for evading the order. The first thing that we now did was to turn him out of the sick-house, neck and heels; I then took Edward with me to Pickle's bedside, where the former told his brother-in-law, that if he had ever done any thing to offend him, he heartily begged his pardon; that he swore by the Almighty God that he had never been in the bush to hurt him, nor any where else; on the contrary, that he had always loved him, and wished him well; and that he now begged him to be friends with him again, to forget and forgive all former quarrels, and to accept the hand which he offered him in all sincerity. The sick man also confessed, that he had always loved Edward as his brother, had 'eaten and drunk with him for many years with perfect good-will', and that it was his ingratitude for such affection which vexed him more than any thing. On this I told him, that I insisted upon their being good friends for the future, and that I should never hear the word Obeah, or any such nonsense, mentioned on my estate, on pain of my extreme displeasure. I promised that, as soon as Pickle should be quite recovered, I would buy for him exactly a set of such things as had been stolen from him; that Edward should bring them to his house, to show that he had rather give him things than take them away; and I then desired to see them shake hands. They did so, with much apparent cordiality; Edward then went back to his work; and this evening, when I sent him a dish from my table, Pickle desired the servant to tell me, that he had hardly any fever, and felt '*quite so so*', which, in the negro dialect, means 'a great deal better'. I begin, therefore, to hope that we shall save the foolish fellow's life at last, which, at one time, appeared to be in great jeopardy.

There was a great dinner and ball for the whole county given to-day at Montego Bay, to which I was invited; but I begged leave to decline this and all other invitations, being determined to give up my whole time to my negroes during my stay in Jamaica.

January 26

Every morning my agent regales me with some fresh instance of insubordination: he says nothing plainly, but shakes his head, and evidently gives me to understand, that the estate cannot be governed properly without the cart-whip. It seems that this morning, the women, one and all, refused to carry away the *trash* (which is one of the easiest tasks that can be set), and that without the slightest pretence: in consequence, the mill was obliged to be stopped; and when the driver on that station insisted on their doing their duty, a little fierce young devil of a Miss Whaunica* flew at his throat, and endeavoured to strangle him: the agent was obliged to be called in, and, at length, this petticoat rebellion was subdued, and every thing went on as usual. I have, in consequence, assured the women, that since they will not be managed by fair treatment, I must have recourse to other measures; and that, if any similar instance of misconduct should take place, I was determined, on my return from Kingston, to sell the most refractory, ship myself immediately for England, and never return to them and Jamaica more. This threat, at the time, seemed to produce a great effect; all hands were clasped, and all voices were raised, imploring me not to leave them, and assuring me, that in future they would do their work quietly and willingly. But whether the impression will last beyond the immediate moment is a point greatly to be doubted.

January 27

Another morning, with the mill stopped, no liquor in the boiling-house, and no work done. The driver brought the most obstinate and insolent of the women to be lectured by me; and I bounced and stormed for half an hour with all my might and main, especially at Whaunica, whose ingratitude was peculiar; as she is the wife of Edward, the Eboe, whom I had been protecting against the charge of theft and Obeahism, and had shown him more than usual kindness. They, at last, appeared to be very penitent and ashamed of themselves, and engaged never to behave ill again, if I would but forgive them this present fault; Whaunica, in particular, assuring me very earnestly, that I never should have cause to accuse her of 'bad manners' again; for, in negro dialect, ingratitude is always called 'bad manners'. My agent declares, that they never conducted themselves so ill before; that they worked cheerfully and properly till my arrival; but now they think that I shall protect them against all punishment, and have made regularly ten hogsheads of sugar a week less than they did before my coming upon the estate. This is the more provoking, as, by delaying the conclusion of the crop, the latter part of it may be driven into the rainy season, and then the labour is infinitely more severe both for the slaves and the cattle, and more detrimental to their health.

The minister of Savannah la Mar has shown me a plan for the religious instruction of the negroes, which was sent to him by the ecclesiastical commissaries at Kingston. It consisted but of two points: against the first (which recommended the slaves being *ordered* to go to church on a Sunday) I positively declared myself. Sunday is now the absolute property of the negroes for their relaxation, as Saturday is for the cultivation of their grounds; and I will not suffer a single hour of it to be taken from them for any purpose whatever. If my slaves choose to go to church on Sundays, so much the better; but not one of them shall be *ordered* to do one earthly thing on Sundays, but that which he chooses himself. The second article recommended occasional pastoral visits of the minister to the different estates; and in this respect I promised to give him every facility— although I greatly doubt any good effect being produced by a few short visits, at considerable intervals, on the minds of ignorant creatures, to whom no palpable and immediate benefit is offered. It appears, indeed, to me, that the only means of giving the negroes morality and religion must be through the medium of education, and their being induced to read such books in the minister's absence as may recall to their thoughts what they have heard from him; otherwise, he may talk for an hour, and they will have understood but little—and remember nothing. There is not a single negro among my whole three hundred who can read a line; and what I suppose to be wanted on West-Indian estates is not an importation of missionaries, but of schoolmasters on Dr Bell's plan,* if it could by any means be introduced here with effect. However, in the mean while I told the minister, that I was perfectly well inclined to have every measure tried that might enlighten the minds of the negroes, provided it did not interfere with their own hours of leisure, and were not compulsory. I mentioned to him a plan for commencing his instructions under the most favourable auspices, of which he seemed to approve; and he has promised to make occasional visits on my estate during my absence, which may do good and can do no harm; and, even should it fail to make the negroes religious, will, at least, add another humane inspector to my list. Soon after the minister's departure, John Fuller came to repair one of the windows. Now John is in great disgrace with me in one respect. Instead of having a wife on the estate, he keeps one at the Bay, so that his children will not belong to me. Phillis, too, who formerly lived with John, says, that she parted with him, because he threw away all his money upon the Bay girls; though John asserts that the cause of separation was his catching the false Phillis coming out of one of the book-keepers' bedrooms.

However, it is certain, that now his connections are all at the Bay; and I have assured him, that if he does not provide himself with a

wife at Cornwall, before my return from Kingston, I will put him up
to auction, and call the girls together to bid for him, one offering half
a dozen yams, and another a bit of salt fish; and the highest bidder
shall carry him off as her property. But to-day, as he came into the
room just as the minister left it, I told him that Dr Pope was coming
to give the negroes some instruction; and that he had left part of a
catechism for him, which he was to get by heart against his next visit.
John promised to study it diligently, and went off to get it read to
him by one of the book-keepers. Several of his companions came to
hear it from curiosity, and the book-keeper read aloud:—

> John Fuller is gone to the Bay, boys,
>   On the girls to spend his cash;
> And when John Fuller comes home, boys,
>   John Fuller deserves the lash.

So John went away shaking his head, and saying, 'Massa had told
him, that the minister had left that paper to make him a better Christian. But he was certain that the minister had nothing to do with that,
and that massa had made it all himself about the Bay girls.'

January 28 (Sunday)

I shall have enough to do in Jamaica if I accept all the offices that are
pressed upon me. A large body of negroes, from a neighbouring
estate, came over to Cornwall this morning, to complain of hard
treatment, in various ways, from their overseer and drivers, and
requesting me to represent their injuries to their trustee here, and
their proprietor in England. The charges were so strong, that I am
certain that they must be fictitious; however, I listened to their story
with patience; promised that the trustee (whom I was to see in a few
days) should know their complaint;—and they went away apparently
satisfied. Then came a runaway negro, who wanted to return home,
and requested me to write a few lines to his master, to save him from
the lash. He was succeeded by a poor creature named Bessie, who,
although still a young woman, is dispensed with from labour, on
account of her being afflicted with the *cocoa-bay*,* one of the most
horrible of negro diseases. It shows itself in large blotches and
swellings, and which generally, by degrees, moulder away the joints

of the toes and fingers, till they rot and drop off; sometimes as much as half a foot will go at once. As the disease is communicable by contact, the person so afflicted is necessarily shunned by society; and this poor woman, who is married to John Fuller, one of the best young men on the estate, and by whom she has had four children (although they are all dead), has for some time been obliged to live separated from him, lest he should be destroyed by contracting the same complaint. She now came to tell me, that she wanted a blanket, 'for that the cold killed her of nights'; cold being that which negroes dislike most, and from which most of their illnesses arise. Of course she got her blanket; then she said, that she wanted medicine for her complaint. 'Had not the doctor seen her?' 'Oh, yes! Dr Goodwin; but the white doctor could do her no good. She wanted to go to a black doctor,* named Ormond, who belonged to a neighbouring gentleman.' I told her, that if this black doctor understood her particular disease better than others, certainly she should go to him; but that if he pretended to cure her by charms or spells, or any thing but medicine, I should desire his master to cure the black doctor by giving him the punishment proper for such an impostor. Upon this Bessie burst into tears, and said 'that Ormond was not an Obeah man, and that she had suffered too much by Obeah men to wish to have any more to do with them. She had made Adam her enemy by betraying him, when he had attempted to poison the former attorney; he had then cursed her, and wished that she might never be hearty again: and from that very time her complaint had declared itself; and her poor pickaninies had all died away, one after another; and she was sure that it was Adam who had done all this mischief by Obeah.' Upon this, I put myself in a great rage, and asked her 'how she could believe that God would suffer a low wicked fellow like Adam to make good people die, merely because he wished them dead?' 'She did not know; she knew nothing about God; had never heard of any such Being, nor of any other world.' I told her, that God was a great personage, 'who lived up yonder above the blue, in a place full of pleasures and free from pains, where Adam and wicked people could not come; that her pickaninies were not dead for ever, but were only gone up to live with God, who was good, and would take care of them for her; and that if she were good, when she died, she too would go up to God above the blue, and see all her four pickaninies again.' The idea seemed so new and so agreeable to the poor creature, that she clapped her hands together, and began laughing for joy; so I said to her every thing that I could imagine likely to remove her prejudice; told her that I should make it a crime even so much as to mention the word Obeah on the estate; and that, if any negro from that time forward should be proved to have accused another of Obeahing him, or of telling another that he had been Obeahed, he should forfeit his share of the next present of salt-fish, which I meant soon to distribute among the slaves, and should never receive any favour from me in future; so I gave Bessie a piece of money, and she seemed to go away in better spirits than she came.

This Adam, of whom she complained, is a most dangerous fellow, and the terror of all his companions, with whom he lives in a constant state of warfare. He is a creole, born on my own property, and has several sisters, who have obtained their freedom, and are in every respect creditable and praiseworthy; and to one of whom I consider myself as particularly indebted, as she was the means of saving poor Richard's life, when the tyranny of the overseer had brought him almost to the brink of the grave. But this brother is in every thing the very reverse of his sisters: there is no doubt of his having (as Bessie stated) infused poison into the water-jars through spite against the late superintendent. It was this same fellow whom Edward suspected of having put into his brother-in-law's head the idea of his having been bewitched; and it was also in his hut that the old Obeah man was found concealed, whom my attorney seized and transported last year. He is, unfortunately, clever and plausible; and I am told that the mischief which he has already done, by working upon the folly and superstition of his fellows, is incalculable; yet I cannot get rid of him: the law will not suffer any negro to be shipped off the island, until he shall have been convicted of felony at the sessions; I cannot sell him, for nobody would buy him, nor even accept him, if I would offer them so dangerous a present; if he were to go away, the law would seize him, and bring him back to me, and I should be obliged to pay heavily for his re-taking and his maintenance in the workhouse. In short, I know not what I can do with him, except indeed make a Christian of him! This might induce the negroes to believe, that he had lost his infernal power by the superior virtue of the holy water; but, perhaps he may refuse to be christened. However, I will at least ask him the question; and if he consents, I will send him—

and a couple of dollars—to the clergyman—for he shall not have so great a distinction as baptism from massa's own hand—and see what effect 'white Obeah' will have in removing the terrors of this professor of the black.

As to my sick Obeah patient, Pickle, from the moment of his reconciliation with his brother-in-law he began to mend, and has recovered with wonderful rapidity: the fellow seems *really* grateful for the pains which I have taken about him; and our difficulty now is to prevent his fancying himself too soon able to quit the hospital, so eager is he to return 'to work for massa'.

There are certainly many excellent qualities in the negro character; their worst faults appear to be, this prejudice respecting Obeah, and the facility with which they are frequently induced to poison to the right hand and to the left. A neighbouring gentleman, as I hear, has now three negroes in prison, all domestics, and one of them grown grey in his service, for poisoning him with corrosive sublimate;* his brother was actually killed by similar means; yet I am assured that both of them were reckoned men of great humanity. Another agent, who appears to be in high favour with the negroes whom he now governs, was obliged to quit an estate, from the frequent attempts to poison him; and a person against whom there is no sort of charge alleged for tyranny, after being brought to the doors of death by a cup of coffee, only escaped a second time by his civility, in giving the beverage, prepared for himself, to two young bookkeepers, to both of whom it proved fatal. It, indeed, came out, afterwards, that this crime was also effected by the abominable belief in Obeah: the woman, who mixed the draught, had no idea of its being poison; but she had received the deleterious ingredients from an Obeah man, as 'a charm to make her massa good to her'; by which the negroes mean, the compelling a person to give another every thing for which that other may ask him.

Next to this vile trick of poisoning people (arising, doubtless, in a great measure, from their total want of religion, and their ignorance of a future state, which makes them dread no punishment hereafter for themselves, and look with but little respect on human life in others), the greatest drawback upon one's comfort in a Jamaica existence seems to me to be the being obliged to live perpetually in public. Certainly, if a man was desirous of leading a life of vice *here*, he must have set himself totally above shame, for he may depend upon every thing done by him being seen and known. The houses are absolutely transparent; the walls are nothing but windows—and all the doors stand wide open. No servants are in waiting to announce arrivals: visiters, negroes, dogs, cats, poultry, all walk in and out, and up and down your living-rooms, without the slightest ceremony.

Even the Temple of Cloacina (which, by the bye, is here very elegantly spoken of generally as '*The* Temple') is as much latticed and as pervious to the eye as any other part of my premises; and many a time has my delicacy been put to the blush by the ill-timed civility of some old woman or other, who, wandering that way, and happening to cast her eye to the left, has stopped her course to curtsy very gravely, and pay me the passing compliment of an 'Ah, massa! bless you, massa! how day?'

January 29

I find that Bessie's black doctor is really nothing more than a professor of medicine as to this particular disease; and I have ordered her to be sent to him in the mountains immediately. Several gentlemen of the county dined with me to-day, and when they left me, one of the carriages contrived to get overturned, and the right shoulder of one of the gentlemen was dislocated. Luckily, it happened close to the house; and as the physician who attends my estate had dined with me also, a boy, on a mule, was despatched after him with all haste. He was soon with us, the bone was replaced with perfect ease, and this morning the patient left me with every prospect of finding no bad effects whatever from his accident.

We had at dinner a land tortoise and a barbecued pig, two of the best and richest dishes that I ever tasted;—the latter, in particular— which was dressed in the true maroon fashion, being placed on a barbecue (a frame of wicker-work, through whose interstices the steam can ascend), filled with peppers and spices of the highest flavour, wrapt in plantain leaves, and then buried in a hole filled with hot stones, by whose vapour it is baked, no particle of the juice being thus suffered to evaporate. I have eaten several other good Jamaica dishes, but none so excellent as this, a large portion of which was transferred to the most infirm patients in the hospital. Perhaps an English physician would have felt every hair of his wig bristle upon his head with astonishment, at hearing me ask, this morning, a woman in a fever, how her bark and her barbecued pig had agreed with her. But, with negroes, I find that feeding the sick upon stewed fish and pork, highly seasoned, produces the very best effects possible.

Some of the fruits here are excellent, such as shaddocks, oranges, granadelloes, forbidden fruit; and one between an orange and a lemon, called 'the grape or cluster fruit', appears to me quite delicious. For the vegetables, I cannot say so much, yams, plantains, cocoa poyers, yam-poys, bananas, etc. look and taste all so much alike, that I scarcely know one from the other: they are all something between bread and potatoes, not so good as either, and I am quite tired of them all. The Lima Bean is said to be more like a pea than a bean, but whatever it be like, it appeared to me very indifferent. As to peas themselves, nothing can be worse. The achie fruit is a kind of vegetable, which generally is fried in butter; many people, I am told, are fond of it, but I could find no merit in it. The palm-tree (or abba, as it is called here) produces a long scarlet or reddish brown cone, which separates into beads, each of which contains a roasting nut surrounded by a kind of stringy husk—which, being boiled in salt and water, upon being chewn has a taste of artichoke, but the consistence is very disagreeable. The only native vegetable, which I like much, is the ochra, which tastes like asparagus, though not with quite so delicate a flavour.

As to fish, the variety is endless; but I think it rather consists in variety of names than of flavour. From this, however, I must except the Silk-Fish and Mud-Fish, and above all, the Mountain-Mullet, which is almost the best fish that I ever tasted. All the shell-fish, that I have met with as yet, have been excellent; the oysters have not come in my way, but I am told that they are not only poor and insipid, but frequently are so poisonous that I had better not venture upon them; and so ends this chapter of the 'Almanach des Gourmands'* for Jamaica.

January 30

There were above twenty ladies literally at my feet this morning. I went down to the negro-village to speak to Bessie about going to her black doctor; and all the refractory females of last week heard of my being there, and came in a body to promise better conduct for the future, and implore me not to go away. The sight of my carriage getting ready to take me to Kingston, and the arrival of post-horses, had alarmed them with the idea that I was really going to put my threats into execution of leaving them for ever. They had artfully enough prevailed on the wife of Clifford (the driver whom Whaunica had collared) to be their spokes-woman; and they begged, and lifted up their folded hands, and cried, and fell on the ground, and kissed my feet—and, in short, acted their part so well, that they almost made me act mine to perfection, and fall to blubbering. I told them, that I certainly should go to Kingston on Thursday; but if I had good accounts of them during my absence, I should return in a few days;—if, on the contrary, the idle negroes continued to refuse to work without compulsion, then, in justice to the good ones (who last week were obliged to do more than their share), those punishments, which I had stopped, must be resumed;—but that, as Cornwall would be unsupportable to me, if I could not live there without hearing the crack of the abominable cart-whip all day long, I would not return to it, but ship myself off for England, and never visit them or Jamaica any more. And then I talked very sternly and positively about 'punishments' and 'making bad negroes do their work properly', and every third word was the cart-whip, till I almost fancied myself the princess in the 'Fairy Tale', who never opened her mouth, but out came two toads and three couple of serpents.* However, to sweeten my oration a little at the end, I told them, that, 'having enquired closely into the characters of the present book-keepers, I had found no charge against any of them except one, who was accused of having occasionally struck a negro, of using bad language to them, and of being a hasty passionate man, though in other respects very serviceable to the estate. But although these faults were but trifling, and some of them not proved, so determined was I to show that I would suffer no white person on the estate who maltreated the negroes, either by word or deed, that I had determined to make an example of him for the warning of the rest; and accordingly had dismissed him this morning.'

The man in question (by his own account) had made himself obnoxious to them; and on hearing of his discharge, they, one and all, sprawled upon the ground in such a rapture of joy and gratitude, that now I may safely say with Sir Andrew Aguecheek, 'I was adored once!'*

The book-keeper had denied positively the charge of striking the negroes, and ascribed it to the revenge of the Eboe Edward, whom he had detected in cutting out part of a boiling-house window, in order that he might pass out stolen sugar unperceived; for, to do the negroes justice, it is a doubt whether they are the greatest thieves or liars, and the quantity of sugar which they purloin during the crop, and dispose of at the Bay for a mere trifle, is enormous. However, whether the charge of striking were true or not, it was sufficiently proved that this book-keeper was a passionate man, and he said himself, 'that the negroes had conceived a spite against him', which alone were reasons enough for removing him. Indeed, I had the less scruple from the slight nature of his offence making it easy for him to find another situation; and I have besides desired him to stay out his quarter on the estate, and then receive a double salary on going away, which will free him from any charge of having been dismissed disgracefully.

January 31

I went to enquire after my petitioners Juliet and Delia, and had the satisfaction to find that the trustee had enquired into their complaint; and, as it appeared not to be entirely unfounded, he had done every thing that was right and necessary. Aberdeen, too, the runaway cooper, who had applied to me to obtain his pardon, had been suffered to return to his work unpunished; and as it had been found that his flight had in a great measure been occasioned by his being in a bad state of health, which rendered him apprehensive of being put to labour beyond his strength, he had been permitted to select his own occupation, which, of course, was the easiest one in his trade. But I found it a more difficult matter to ascertain the truth or falsehood of the charges brought to me on Sunday last: the books positively contradicted them, but the register might have been falsely kept; and as the negroes persisted most positively in their complaint against the overseer (particularly as to his having curtailed them of the legal allowance of time for their meals, and the cultivation of their own grounds) with the concurrence of the trustee, I wrote to the magistrates of the county, desiring that they would summon the negroes in question before a council of protection, and examine into the injuries of which they had complained to me.

February 1 (Thursday)

I left Cornwall for Spanish Town at six in the morning, accompanied by a young naval officer, the son of my next neighbour, Mr Hill of Amity, who not only was good enough to lend me a kittereen,* with a canopy, to perform my journey, but his son to be my *cicerone* on my tour. The road wound through mountain passes, or else on a shelf of rock so narrow—though without the slightest danger—that one of the wheels was frequently in the sea, while my other side was fenced by a line of bold broken cliffs, clothed with trees completely from their brows down to the very edge of the water. Between eight and nine we reached a solitary tavern, called Blue-fields, where the horses rested for a couple of hours. It had a very pretty garden on the sea-shore, which contained a picturesque cottage, exactly resembling an ornamental Hermitage; and leaning against one of the pillars of its porch we found a young girl, who exactly answered George Colman's description of Yarico,* 'quite brown, but extremely genteel, like a Wedgewood teapot'. She told us that she was a Spanish creole, who had fled with her mother from the disputes between the royalists and independents in the island of Old Providence;* and the owner of the tavern being a relation of her mother, he had permitted the fugitives to establish themselves in his garden-cottage, till the troubles of their own country should be over. She talked perfectly good English, for she said that there were many of that nation established in Providence. Her name was Antonietta. Her figure was light and elegant; her black eyes mild and bright; her countenance intelligent and good-humoured; and her teeth beautiful to perfection: altogether, Antonietta was by far the handsomest creole that I have ever seen.

From Blue-fields we proceeded at once to Lakovia (a small village), a stage of thirty miles. Here we found a relay of horses, which conveyed us by seven o'clock to 'the Gutturs'; a house belonging to the proprietor of the post-horses, and which is situated at the very foot of the tremendous May-day Mountains. The house is an excellent one, and we found good beds, eatables, and, in short, every thing that travellers could wish. The distance from Lakovia to 'the Gutturs' is sixteen miles.

February 2

Yesterday the only very striking point of view (although the whole of the road was picturesque) was 'the Cove', situated between Blue-fields and Lakovia, and which resembled the most beautiful of the views of coves to be found in 'Cook's Voyages'; but our journey to-day was a succession of beautiful scenes, from beginning to end. Instantly on leaving 'the Gutturs', we began to ascend the May-day Mountains, and it was not till after travelling for five and twenty miles, that we found ourselves at the foot of them on the other side, at a place called Williamsfield, about twelve miles from the toll-house, where we rested for the night. To be sure, the road was so rough, that it was enough to make one envy the Mahometan women, who, having no souls at all, could not possibly have them jolted out of their bodies; but the beauty of the scenery amply rewarded us for our bruised sides and battered backs. The road was, for the most part, bounded by lofty rocks on one side, and a deep precipice on the other, and bordered with a profusion of noble trees and flowering shrubs in great variety. In particular, I was struck with the picturesque appearance of some wild fig-trees of singular size and beauty. Although there were only two of us, besides servants, we found it necessary to employ seven horses and a couple of mules; and, as our cavalcade wound along through the mountains, the Spanish look of our sumpter-mules, and of our kittereens (which are precisely the vehicle in which Gil Blas* is always represented when travelling with Scipio towards Lirias) gave us quite the appearance of a caravan; nor should I have been greatly surprised to see a trap-door open in the middle of the road, and Captain Rolando's whiskers make their appearance. Every one spoke to me with contempt of this south road, in respect of beauty, when compared with the north; however, it certainly seemed to me more beautiful than any road which I have ever travelled as yet.

February 3

A stage of twenty miles brought us to Old Harbour, and, passing through the Dry River, twelve more landed us at Spanish Town, otherwise called St Jago de la Vega, and the seat of government in Jamaica, although Kingston is much larger and more populous, and must be considered as the principal town. We found very clean and comfortable lodgings at Miss Cole's. Spanish Town has no recommendations whatever; the houses are mostly built of wood: the streets are very irregular and narrow; every alternate building is in a ruinous state, and the whole place wears an air of gloom and melancholy. The government house is a large clumsy-looking brick building, with a portico the stucco of which has suffered by the weather, and it can advance no pretensions to architectural beauty. On one side of the square in which it stands there is a small temple protecting a statue of Lord Rodney, executed by Bacon:* some of the bas-reliefs on the pedestal appeared to me very good; but the old admiral is most absurdly dressed in the habit of a Roman General, and furnished out with buskins and a truncheon. The temple itself is quite in opposition to good taste, with very low arches, surmounted by heavy bas reliefs out of all proportion.

February 4 (Sunday)

We breakfasted with the Chief Justice,* who is my relation, and of my own name, and then went to the church, which is a very handsome one; the walls lined with fine mahogany, and ornamented with many monuments of white marble, in memory of the former governors and other principal inhabitants. It seems that my ancestors, on both sides, have always had a taste for being well lodged after their decease; for, on admiring one of these tombs, it proved to be that of my maternal grandfather; but still this was not to be compared for a moment with my mausoleum at Cornwall. After church I went home with the Rector, who is one of the ecclesiastical commissaries, and had a long conversation with him respecting a plan which is in agitation for giving the negroes something of a religious education. We afterwards dined with the member for Westmoreland; and as every body in Jamaica is on foot by six in the morning, at ten in the evening we were quite ready to go to bed.

February 5

The Chief Justice went with me to Kingston, where I had appointed the agent for my other estate in St Thomas's-in-the-East to meet me. The short time allotted for my stay in the island makes it impossible to attend properly both to this estate and to Cornwall at this first visit, and therefore I determined to confine my attention to the negroes on the latter estate till my return to Jamaica. I now contented myself by impressing on the mind of my agent (whom I am certain of being a most humane and intelligent man) my extreme anxiety for the abolition of the cart-whip; and I had the satisfaction of hearing from him, that for a long time it had never been used more than perhaps twice in the year, and then only very slightly, and for some offence so flagrant that it was impossible to pass it over; and he assured me, that whenever I visit Hordley, I may depend upon its not being employed at all. On the other hand, I am told that a gentleman of the parish of Vere, who came over to Jamaica for the sole purpose of ameliorating the condition of his negroes, after abolishing the cart-whip, has at length been constrained to resume the occasional use of it, because he found it utterly impossible to keep them in any sort of subordination without it.

There is not that air of melancholy about Kingston which pervades Spanish Town; but it has no pretensions to beauty; and if any person will imagine a large town entirely composed of booths at a race-course, and the streets merely roads, without any sort of paving, he will have a perfect idea of Kingston.

February 6

The Jamaica canoes are hollowed cotton-trees. We embarked in one of them at six in the morning, and visited the ruins of Port Royal, which, last year, was destroyed by fire: some of the houses were rebuilding; but it was a melancholy sight, not only from the look of the half-burnt buildings, but the dejected countenances of the ruined inhabitants. I returned to breakfast at the rectory, with two other ecclesiastical commissaries; had more conversation about their proposed plan; and became still more convinced of the difficulty of doing any thing effectual without danger to the island and to the negroes themselves, and of the extreme delicacy requisite in whatever may be attempted. We afterwards visited the school of the children of the poor, who are educating upon Dr Bell's system; and then saw the church, a very large and handsome one on the inside, but mean enough as to its exterior. I was shown the tombstone of Admiral Benbow,* who was killed in a naval engagement, and whose ship afterwards

Bore down to Port Royal, where the people flocked very much
To see brave Admiral Benbow laid in Kingston Town Church,

as the admiral's Homer informs us.

The church is a large one, but it is going to be still further extended; the negroes in Kingston and its neighbourhood being (as the rector assured me) so anxious to obtain religious instruction, that on Sundays not only the church but the churchyard is so completely thronged with them, as to make it difficult to traverse the crowd; and those who are fortunate enough to obtain seats for the morning service, through fear of being excluded from that of the evening, never stir out of the church during the whole day. They also flock to be baptized in great numbers, and many have lately come to be married; and their burials and christenings are performed with great pomp and solemnity.

One of the most intelligent of the negroes with whom I have yet conversed, was the coxswain of my Port Royal canoe. I asked him whether he had been christened? He answered, no; he did not yet think himself good enough, but he hoped to be so in time. Nor was he married; for he was still young, and afraid that he could not break off his bad habits, and be contented to live with no other woman than his wife; and so he thought it better not to become a Christian till he could feel certain of performing the duties of it. However, he said, he had at least cured himself of one bad custom, and never worked upon Sundays, except on some very urgent necessity. I asked what he did on Sundays instead: did he go to church?—No. Or employ himself in learning to read?—Oh, no; though he thought being able to read *was a great virtue*; (which was his constant expression for any thing right, pleasant, or profitable;) but he had no leisure to learn on week days, and as he had heard the parson say that Sunday ought to be a day of rest, he made a point of doing nothing at all on that day. He praised his former master, of whose son he was now the property, and said that neither of them had ever occasion to lay a finger on him. He worked as a waterman, and paid his master ten shillings a week, the rest of his earnings being his own profit; and when he owed wages for three months, if he brought two his master would always give him time for the remainder, and that in so kind a manner, that he always fretted himself to think that so kind a master should wait for his rights, and worked twice as hard till the debt was discharged. He said that kindness was the only way to make good negroes, and that, if *that* failed, flogging would never succeed; and he advised me, when I found my negro worthless, 'to sell him at once, and not stay to flog him, and so, by spoiling his appearance, make him sell for less; for blacks must not be treated now, massa, as they used to be; they can think, and hear, and see, as well as white people: blacks are wiser, massa, than they were, and will soon be still wiser.' I thought the fellow himself was a good proof of his assertion.

I left Kingston at two o'clock, in defiance of a broiling sun; reached Spanish Town in time to dine with the Attorney-General;* and went afterwards to the play, where I found my acquaintance Mr Hill* of Covent Garden theatre performing Lord William in 'The Haunted Tower',* and Don Juan in the pantomime which followed. The theatre is neat enough,* but, I am told, very inferior in splendour to that in Kingston. As to the performance, it was about equal to any provincial theatricals that I ever saw in England; although the pieces represented were by no means well selected, being entirely musical, and the orchestra consisting of nothing more than a couple of fiddles. My stay in Spanish Town has been too short to admit of my inspecting the antiquities of it, which must be reserved for a future visit, although I never intend to make a longer than the present. The difference of climate was very sensible, both at Spanish Town and Kingston; and the suffocating closeness made me long to breathe again in the country.

The governor* happened to be absent on a tour in the north; but I had an opportunity of seeing many of the principal persons of the island during my residence here; and the civilities which I received from all of them were not only more than I expected, but such as I should be unreasonable if I had desired more, and very ungrateful if I could ever forget them.

February 7

We were to return by the North Road, and set out at six in the morning. The first stage was to the West Tavern, nineteen miles; and nothing can be imagined at once more sublime and more beautiful than the scenery. Our road lay along the banks of the Rio Cobre, which runs up to Spanish Town, where its floods frequently commit dreadful ravages. Large masses of rock intercept its current at small intervals, which, as well as its shallowness, render it unnavigable. The cliffs and trees are of the most gigantic size, and the road goes so near the brink of a tremendous precipice, that we were obliged always to send a servant forwards to warn any other carriage of our approach, in order that it might stay in some broader part while we passed it. A bridge had been attempted to be built over the river, but a storm had demolished it before its completion, and nothing was now left standing but a single enormous arch. In like manner, 'the Dry River' sets all bridges at defiance: when we crossed it between Old Harbour and Spanish Town, it was nothing but a waste of sand; but its floods frequently pour down with irresistible strength and rapidity, and sometimes render it impassable for weeks together. I was extremely delighted with the first ten miles of this stage: unluckily, a mist then arose, so thick, that it was utterly impossible even to guess at the surrounding scenery; and the morning was so cold, that I was very glad to wrap myself up in my cloak as closely as if I had been travelling in an English December.

By the time of our leaving the West Tavern the mist had dispersed, and I was able to admire the extraordinary beauty of Mount Diavolo, which we were then crossing. Though we had left the river, the road was still a narrow shelf of rock running along the edge of ravines of great depth, and filled with broken masses of stone and trees of wonderful magnitude; only that at intervals we emerged for a time into places resembling ornamental parks in England, the lawns being of the liveliest verdure, the ground rising and falling with an endless variety of surface, and enriched with a profusion of trees majestic in stature and picturesque in their shapes, many of them entirely covered with the beautiful flowers of 'hogsmeat', and other creeping plants. The logwood, too, is now perfectly golden with its full bloom, and perfumes all the air; and nothing can be more gay than the quantity of wild flowers which catch the eye on all sides, particularly the wild pine, and the wild ipecacuanha. We travelled for sixteen miles, which brought us to our harbour for the night,—a solitary tavern called Blackheath, situated in the heart of the mountains of St Anne.

February 8

The road soon brought us down to the very brink of the sea, which we continued to skirt during the whole of the stage. It then brought us to St Anne's Bay, where we found an excellent breakfast, at an inn quite in the English fashion,—for the landlady had been long resident in Great Britain. Every thing was clean and comfortable, and the windows looked full upon the sea. This stage was sixteen miles: the next was said to be twenty-five; but from the time which we took to travel it, I can scarcely believe it to be so much. Our road still lay by the sea-side, till we began to ascend the mountain of Rio Bueno; from which we at length perceived the river itself running into the sea. It was at Porto Bueno that Columbus is said to have made his first landing on the island. Rio Bueno is a small town with a fort, situated close to the sea. Here also we found a very good inn, kept by a Scotchman.

The present landlady (her father being from home) was a very pretty brown girl, by name Eliza Thompson. She told me that she was only residing with her parents during her *husband's* absence; for she was (it seems) the *soi-disant* wife of an English merchant in Kingston, and had a house on Tachy's Bridge. This kind of establishment is the highest object of the *brown* females of Jamaica; they seldom marry men of their own colour, but lay themselves out to captivate some white person, who takes them for mistresses, under the appellation of housekeepers.

Soon after my arrival at Cornwall, I asked my attorney whether a clever-looking brown woman, who seemed to have great authority in the house, belonged to me?—No; she was a free woman.—Was she in my service, then?—No; she was not in my service. I began to grow impatient.—'But what *does* she do at Cornwall? Of what use is she in the house?'—'Why sir, as to use . . . of no great use, sir'; and then, after a pause, he added in a lower voice, 'It is the custom, sir, in this country, for unmarried men to have housekeepers, and Nancy is mine.' But he was unjust in saying that Nancy is of no use on the estate; for she is perpetually in the hospital, nurses the children, can bleed, and mix up medicines, and (as I am assured) she is of more service to the sick than all the doctors. These brown housekeepers generally attach themselves so sincerely to the interests of their protectors, and make themselves so useful, that they in common retain their situation; and their children (if slaves) are always honoured by their fellows with the title of Miss. My mulatto housemaid is always called 'Miss Polly', by her fellow-servant Phillis. This kind of connection is considered by a brown girl in the same light as marriage. They will tell you, with an air of vanity, 'I am Mr Such-a-one's *Love!*' and always speak of him as being her *husband*; and I am told, that, except on these terms, it is extremely difficult to obtain the favours of a woman of colour. To gain the situation of housekeeper to a white man, the mulatto girl

> directs her aim;
> This makes her happiness, and this her fame.*

February 9

The sea-view from a bridge near Falmouth was remarkably pleasing; a stage of eighteen miles brought us to the town itself, which I understand to be in size the second in the island.

However various are the characters which actors sustain, I find their own to be the same every where. Although the Jamaica company* did not consist of more than twenty persons, their green-room squabbles had divided it, and we found one half performing at Falmouth. We did not wait for the play, but proceeded for twenty-two miles to Montego Bay, where I once more found myself under the protecting roof of Miss Judy James.

On our return from dinner at Mr Dewer's, we discovered a ball of brown ladies and gentlemen opposite to the inn. No whites nor blacks were permitted to attend this assembly; but as our landlady had two nieces there, under her auspices we were allowed to be spectators. The females chiefly consisted of the natural daughters of attorneys and overseers, and the young men were mostly clerks and book-keepers. I saw nothing at all to be compared, either for form or feature, to many of the humbler people of colour, much less to the beautiful Spaniard at Blue-fields. Long, or Bryan Edwards, asserts that mulattos never breed* except with a separate black or white; but at this ball two girls were pointed out to me, the daughters of mulatto parents; and I have been assured that the assertion was a mistake, arising from such a connection being very rarely formed; the females generally preferring to live with white men, and the brown men having thus no other resource than black women. As to the above girls, the fact is certain; and the different shades of colour are distinguished by too plain a line to allow any suspicion of infidelity on the part of their parents.

February 10

We passed the day at Mr Plummer's estate, Anchovy Bottom.

When Lord Bolingbroke was resident in America, large flocks of turkeys used to ravage his corn-fields; but, from their extreme wildness, he never could make any of them prisoners. He had a barn lighted by a large sash window, and into this he laid a train of corn, hiding some servants with guns behind the large doors, which were folded back. The turkeys picked up the corn, and gradually were enticed to enter the barn. But as soon as a dozen had passed in, the servants clapped the doors to with all possible expedition. Now they reckoned themselves secure of their game; but to their utter consternation, the turkeys in a body darted towards the light, dashed against the glass, forced out the wood-work, and away went turkeys, glass, wood-work, and all.

February 11 (Sunday)

I reached Cornwall about three o'clock, after an excursion the most amusing and agreeable that I ever made in my life. Almost every step of the road presented some new and striking scene; and although we travelled at all hours, and with as little circumspection as if we had been in England, I never felt a headach except for one half hour. On my arrival, I found the satisfactory intelligence usually communicated to West Indian proprietors. My estate in the west is burnt up for want of moisture; and my estate in the east has been so completely flooded, that I have lost a whole third of my crop. At Cornwall, not a drop of rain has fallen since the 16th of November. Not a vestige of verdure is to be seen; and we begin to apprehend a famine among the negroes in consequence of the drought destroying their provision grounds. This alone is wanting to complete the dangerous state of the island; where the higher classes are all in the utmost alarm at rumours of Wilberforce's intentions to set the negroes entirely at freedom; the next step to which would be, in all probability, a general massacre of the whites, and a second part of the horrors of St Domingo:* while, on the other hand, the negroes are impatient at the delay; and such disturbances arose in St Thomas's in the East, last Christmas, as required the interposition of the magistrates. They say that the negroes of that parish had taken it into their heads that *The Regent and Wilberforce* had actually determined upon setting them all at liberty at once on the first day of the present year, but that the interference of the island had defeated the plan. Their discontent was most carefully and artfully fomented by some brown Methodists, who held secret and nightly meetings on the different estates, and did their best to mislead and bewilder these poor creatures with their fantastic and absurd preaching. These fellows harp upon sin, and the devil, and hell-fire incessantly, and describe the Almighty and the Saviour as beings so terrible, that many of their proselytes cannot hear the name of Christ without shuddering. One poor negro, on one of my own estates, told the overseer that he knew himself to be so great a sinner that nothing could save him from the devil's clutches, even for a few hours, except singing hymns; and he kept singing so incessantly day and night, that at length terror and want of sleep turned his brain, and the wretch died raving mad.

February 12

A Sir Charles Price,* who had an estate in this island infested by rats, imported, with much trouble, a very large and strong species for the purpose of extirpating the others. The new-comers answered his purpose to a miracle; they attacked the native rats with such spirit, that in a short time they had the whole property to themselves; but no sooner had they done their duty upon the rats, than they extended their exertions to the cats, of whom their strength and size at length enabled them completely to get the better; and since that last victory, Sir Charles Price's rats, as they are called, have increased so prodigiously, that (like the man in Scripture, who got rid of one devil, and was taken possession of by seven others) this single species is now a greater nuisance to the island than all the others before them were together. The best mode of destroying rats here is with terriers; but those imported from England soon grow useless, being blinded by the sun, while their puppies, born in Jamaica, are provided by nature with a protecting film over their eyes, which effectually secures them against incurring that calamity.

February 12

Poor Philippa, the woman who used always to call me her 'husband', and whom I left sick in the hospital, during my absence has gone out of her senses; and there cannot well happen any thing more distressing, as there is no separate place for her confinement, and her ravings disturb the other invalids. There is, indeed, no kind of bedlam in the whole island of Jamaica: whether this proceeds from people being so very sedate and sensible, that they never go mad, or from their all being so mad, that no one person has a right to shut up another for being out of his senses, is a point which I will not pretend to decide. One of my domestic negroes, a boy of sixteen, named Prince, was abandoned by his worthless mother in infancy, and reared by this Philippa; and since her illness he passes every moment of his leisure in her sick-room. On the other hand, there is a woman named Christian, attending two fevered children in the hospital; one her own, and the other an adopted infant, whom she reared upon the death of its mother in child-birth; and there she sits, throwing her eyes from one to the other with such unceasing solicitude, that no one could discover which was her own child and which the orphan.

February 13

Two Jamaica nightingales have established themselves on the orange tree which grows against my window, and their song is most beautiful. This bird is also called 'the mocking-bird', from its facility of imitating, not only the notes of every other animal, but—I am told—of catching every tune that may be played or sung two or three times in the house near which it resides, after which it will go through the air with the greatest taste and precision, throwing in cadences and ornaments that Catalani herself might envy.

But by far the most curious animal that I have yet seen in Jamaica is 'the soldier', a species of crab, which inhabits a shell like a snail's, so small in proportion to its limbs, that nothing can be more curious or admirable than the machinery by which it is enabled to fold them up instantly on the slightest alarm. They inhabit the mountains, but regularly once a year travel in large troops down to the seaside to spawn and change their shells. If I recollect right, Goldsmith* gives a very full and entertaining account of this animal, by the name of 'the soldier crab'. They are seldom used in Jamaica except for soups, which are reckoned delicious: that which was brought to me was a very small one, the shell being no bigger than a large snail's, although the animal itself, when marching with his house on his back, appears to be above thrice the size; but I am told that they are frequently as large as a man's fist. Mine was found alone in the public road: how it came to be in so solitary a state, I know not, for in general they move in armies, and march towards the sea in a straight line; I am afraid, by his being found alone, that my soldier must have been a deserter.

February 14

To-day there was a shower of rain for the first time since my arrival; indeed, not a drop has fallen since the 16th of November; and in consequence my present crop has suffered terribly, and our expectations for next season are still worse.

February 18 (Sunday)

The rain has brought forth the fire-flies, and in the evening the hedges are all brilliant with their numbers. In the day they seem to be torpid beetles of a dull reddish colour, but at night they become of a shining purple. The fire proceeds from two small spots in the back part of the head. It is yellow in the light, and requires motion to throw out its radiance in perfection; but as soon as it is touched, the fly struggles violently, and bends itself together with a clicking noise like the snap of a spring; and I understand that this effort is necessary to set it in motion. It is sufficiently strong to turn itself upwards with a single movement, if lying on its back: some people say that it is always obliged to throw itself upon its back in order to take wing; but this I have, again, heard others contradict. When confined in a glass, the light seems almost extinguished; nothing can be discerned but two pale yellow spots; but on being pressed by the hand it becomes more brilliant than any emerald, and when on the wing it seems entirely composed of the most beautifully coloured fire.

February 20

I attended the Slave Court, where a negro was tried for sheep-stealing, and a black servant girl for attempting to poison her master. The former was sentenced to be transported. The latter was a girl of fifteen, called Minetta: she acknowledged the having infused corrosive sublimate in some brandy and water; but asserted that she had taken it from the medicine chest without knowing it to be poison, and had given it to her master at her grandmother's desire. This account was evidently a fabrication: there was no doubt of the grandmother's innocence, although some suspicion attached to the mother's influence; but as to the girl herself, nothing could be more hardened than her conduct through the whole transaction. She stood by the bed to see her master drink the poison; witnessed his agonies without one expression of surprise or pity; and when she was ordered to leave the room, she pretended to be fast asleep, and not to hear what was said to her. Even since her imprisonment, she could never be prevailed upon to say that she was sorry for her master's having been poisoned; and she told the people in the gaol, that 'they could do nothing to her, for she had turned king's evidence against her grandmother'. She was condemned to die on Thursday next, the day after to-morrow: she heard the sentence pronounced without the least emotion; and I am told, that when she went down the steps of the court-house, she was seen to laugh.

The trial appeared to be conducted with all possible justice and propriety; the jury consisted of nine respectable persons; the bench of three magistrates, and a senior one to preside. There were no lawyers employed on either side; consequently no appeals to the passions, no false lights thrown out, no traps, no flaws, no quibbles, no artful cross-examinings, and no brow-beating of witnesses; and I cannot say that the trial appeared to me to go on at all the worse. Nobody appeared to be either for or against the prisoner; the only object of all present was evidently to come at the truth, and I sincerely believe that they obtained their object. The only part of the trial of which I disapproved was the ordering the culprit to such immediate execution, that sufficient time was not allowed for the exercise of the royal prerogative, should the governor have been disposed to commute the punishment for that of transportation.

February 21

During my excursion to Spanish Town, the complaining negroes of Friendship, who had applied to me for relief, were summoned to Savannah la Mar, before the Council of Protection, and the business thoroughly investigated. Their examination has been sent to me, and they appear to have had a very fair hearing. The journals of the estate were produced;—the book-keepers examined upon oath; and in order to make out a case at all, the chief complainant contradicted himself so grossly, as left no doubt that the whole was a fabrication. They were, therefore, dismissed without relief, but also without punishment, in spite of their gross falsehoods and calumnies; and although they did not gain their object, I make no doubt that they will go on more contentedly for having had attention paid to their complaints. It was indeed evident, that Nelly (the chief complainant) was actuated more by wounded pride than any real feeling of hardship; for what she laid the most stress upon was, the overseer's turning his back upon her, when she stated herself to be injured, and walking away without giving her any answer.

There are so many pleasing and amusing parts of the character of negroes, that it seems to me scarcely possible not to like them. But when they are once disposed to evil, they seem to set no bounds to the indulgence of their bad passions. A poor girl came into the hospital to-day, who had had some trifling dispute with two of her companions; on which the two friends seized her together, and each fixing her teeth on one of the girl's hands, bit her so severely, that we greatly fear her losing the use of both of them. I happened also to ask, this morning, to whom a skull had belonged, which I had observed fixed on a pole by the roadside, when returning last from Montego Bay. I was told, that about five years ago a Mr Dunbar had given some discontent to his negroes in the article of clothing them, although, in other respects, he was by no means a severe master. However, this was sufficient to induce his head driver, who had been brought up in his own house from infancy, to form a plot among his slaves to assassinate him; and he was assisted in this laudable design by two young men from a neighbouring property, who barely knew Mr Dunbar by sight, had no enmity against him whatever, and only joined in the conspiracy in compliment to their worthy friend the driver. During several months a variety of attempts were made for effecting their purpose; but accident defeated them; till at length they were made certain of his intention to dine out at some distance, and of his being absolutely obliged to return in the evening. An ambuscade was therefore laid to intercept him; and on his passing a clump of trees, the assassins sprang upon him, the driver knocked him from his horse, and in a few moments their clubs despatched him. No one suspected the driver; but in the course of enquiry, his house as well as the other was searched, and not only Mr Dunbar's watch was found concealed there, but with it one of his ears, which the villain had carried away, from a negro belief that, as long as the murderer possesses one of the ears of his victim, he will never be haunted by his spectre. The stranger-youths, two of Dunbar's negroes, and the driver, were tried, confessed the crime, and were all executed; the head of the latter being fixed upon a pole *in terrorem*. But while the offenders were still in prison, the overseer upon a neighbouring property had occasion to find fault in the field with a woman belonging to a gang hired to perform some particular work; upon which she flew upon him with the greatest fury, grasped him by the throat, cried to her fellows— 'Come here! come here! Let us Dunbar him!' and through her strength and the suddenness of her attack had nearly accomplished her purpose, before his own slaves could come to his assistance. This woman was also executed.

This happened about five years ago, when the mountains were in a very rebellious state. Every thing there is at present quiet. But only last year a book-keeper belonging to the next estate to me was found with his skull fractured in one of my own cane-pieces; nor have any enquiries been able to discover the murderer.

February 22

During many years the Moravians have been established upon the neighbouring estate of Mesopotamia. As the ecclesiastical commissaries had said so much to me respecting the great appetite of the negroes for religious instruction, I was desirous of learning what progress had been made in this quarter, and this morning I went over to see one of the teachers. He told me, that he and his wife had jointly used their best efforts to produce a sense of religion in the minds of the slaves; that they were all permitted to attend his morning and evening lectures, if they chose it; but that he could not say that they showed any great avidity on the subject. It seems that there are at least three hundred negroes on the estate; the number of believers has rather increased than diminished, to be sure, but still in a very small proportion. When this gentleman arrived, there were not more than forty baptised persons: he has been here upwards of five years, and still the number of persons 'belonging to his church' (as he expressed it) does not exceed fifty. Of these, seldom more than ten or a dozen attend his lectures at a time. As to the remaining two hundred and fifty, they take no more notice of his lectures or his exhortations, than if there were no such person on the property, are only very civil to him when they see him, and go on in their own old way, without suffering him to interfere in any shape. By the overseer of Greenwich's express desire, the Moravian has, however, agreed to give up an hour every day for the religious instruction of the negro children on that property: and I should certainly request him to extend his labours to Cornwall, if I did not think it right to give the Church of England clergymen full room for a trial of their intended periodical visitations; which would not be the case, if the negroes were to be interfered with by the professors of any other communion: otherwise I am myself ready to give free ingress and egress upon my several estates to the teachers of any Christian sect whatever, the Methodists always excepted, and 'Miss Peg, who faints at the sound of an organ'.*

For my own part, I have no hope of any material benefit arising from these religious visitations made at quarterly intervals. It seems to me as nugatory as if a man were to sow a field with horse-hair, and expect a crop of colts.

February 23

This morning my picture was drawn by a self-taught genius, a negro Apelles,* belonging to Dr Pope, the minister; and the picture was exactly such as a self-taught genius might be expected to produce. It was a straight hard outline, without shade or perspective; the hair was a large black patch, and the face covered with an uniform layer of flesh-colour, with a red spot in the centre of each cheek. As to likeness, there was not even an attempt to take any. But still, such as they were, there were eyes, nose, and mouth, to be sure. A long red nose supplied the place of my own snub; an enormous pair of whiskers stretched themselves to the very corner of my mouth; and in place of three hairs and a half, the painter, in the super-abundance of his generosity, bestowed upon me a pair of eye-brows more bushy than Dr Johnson's, and which, being formed in an exact semicircle, made the eyes beneath them stare with an expression of the utmost astonishment. The negroes, however, are in the highest admiration of the painter's skill, and consider the portrait as a striking resemblance; for there is a very blue coat with very yellow buttons, and white gaiters and trowsers, and an eye-glass so big and so blue, that it looks as if I had hung a pewter plate about my neck; and a bunch of watch-seals larger than those with which Pope has decorated Belinda's great great grand-sire.* John Fuller (to whom, jointly with Nicholas, the charge of this inestimable treasure is to be entrusted) could not find words to express his satisfaction at the performance. 'Dere massa coat! and dere him chair him sit in! and dere massa seals, all just de very same ting! just all as one! And oh! ki! dere massa pye-glass!' In the midst of his raptures he dropped the picture, and fractured the frame-glass. His despair now equalled his former joy;—'Oh, now what for him do? Such a pity! Just to break it after it was all done so well! All so pretty!' However, we stuck the broken glass together with wafers,* and he carried it off, assuring me, 'that when massa gone, he should talk to it every morning, all one as if massa still here'. Indeed, this 'talking to massa' is a favourite amusement among the negroes, and extremely inconvenient: they come to me perpetually with complaints so frivolous, and requests so unreason-able, that I am persuaded they invent them only to have an excuse for 'talk to massa'; and when I have given them a plump refusal, they go away perfectly satisfied, and 'tank massa for dis here great indulgence of talk'.

There is an Eboe carpenter named Strap, who was lately sick and in great danger, and whom I nursed with particular care. The poor fellow thinks that he never can express his gratitude sufficiently; and whenever he meets me in the public road, or in the streets of Savan-nah la Mar, he rushes towards the carriage, roars out to the postilion to stop, and if the boy does not obey instantly, he abuses him with all his power; 'for why him no stop when him want talk to massa?'—'But look, Strap, your beast is getting away!'—'Oh! damn beast, massa.'—'But you should go to your mountain, or you will get no vittle.'—'Oh, damn vittle, and damn mountain! me to want vittle, me want talk wid massa'; and then, all that he has got to say is, 'Oh massa, massa! God bless you, massa! me quite, *quite* glad to see you come back, my own massa!' And then he bursts into a roar of laughter so wild and so loud, that the passers-by cannot help stopping to stare and laugh too.

February 24

On the Sunday after my first arrival, the whole body of Eboe negroes came to me to complain of the attorney, and more particularly of one of the book-keepers. I listened to them, if not with unwearied patience, at least with unsubdued fortitude, for above an hour and a half; and finding some grounds for their complaint against the latter, in a few days I went down to their quarter of the village, told them that to please them I had discharged the book-keeper, named a day for examining their other grievances, and listened to them for an hour more. When the day of trial came, they sent me word that they were perfectly satisfied, and had no complaint to make. I was, therefore, much surprised to receive a visit from Edward, the Eboe, yesterday evening, who informed me, that during my absence his fellows had formed a plan of making a complaint *en masse* to a neighbouring magistrate; and that, not only against the attorney, but against myself 'for not listening to them when they were injured'; and Edward claimed great merit with me for having prevented their taking this step, and convinced them, that while I was on the estate myself, there could be no occasion for applying to a third person. Now, having made me aware of my great obligations to him, here Edward meant the matter to rest; but being a good deal incensed at their ingratitude, I instantly sent for the Eboes, and enquired into the matter; when it appeared, that Edward (who is a clever fellow, and has great influence over the rest) had first goaded them into a resolution of complaining to a magistrate, had then stopped them from putting their plan into execution, and that the whole was a plot of Edward's, in order to make a merit with me for himself at the expense of his countrymen. However, as they confessed their having had the intention of applying to Mr Hill as a magistrate, I insisted upon their executing their intention. I told them, that as Mr Hill was the person whom they had selected for their protector, to Mr Hill they should go; that they should either make their complaint to him against me, or confess that they had been telling lies, and had no complaint to make; and that, as the next day was to be a play-day given them by me, instead of passing it at home in singing and dancing, they should pass it at the Bay in stating their grievances.

This threw them into terrible confusion; they cried out that they wanted to make no complaint whatever, and that it was all Edward's fault, who had misled them. Three of them, one after the other, gave him the lie to his face; and each and all (Edward as well as the rest) declared that go to the Bay they absolutely would *not*. The next morning they were all at the door waiting for my coming out: they positively refused to go to Mr Hill, and begged and prayed, and humbled themselves; now scraping and bowing to me, and then blackguarding Edward with all their might and main; and when I ordered the driver to take charge of them, and carry them to Mr Hill, some of them fairly took to their heels, and ran away. However, the rest soon brought them back again, for they swore that if one went, all should go; and away they were marched, in a string of about twenty, with the driver at their head. When they got to the Bay, they told Mr Hill that, as to their massa, they had no complaint to make against him, except that he had compelled them to make one; and what they said against the attorney was so trifling, that the magistrate bade the driver take them all back again. Upon which they slunk away to their houses, while the Creoles cried out 'Shame! shame!' as they passed along.

Indeed, the Creoles could not have received a greater pleasure than the mortification of the Eboes; for the two bodies hate each other as cordially as the Guelphs and Ghibellines; and after their departure for the Bay, I heard the head cook haranguing a large audience, and declaring it to be her fixed opinion, 'that massa ought to sell all the Eboes, and buy Creoles instead'. Probably, Mrs Cook was not the less loud in her exclamations against the ingratitude of the Eboes, from her own loyalty having lately been questioned. She had found fault one day in the hospital with some women who feigned sickness in order to remain idle. 'You no work willing for massa,' said Mrs Cook, 'and him so vex, him say him go to Kingston to-morrow, and him wish him neber come back again!'—'What!' cried Philippa, the mad woman, 'you wish massa neber come back from Kingston?' So she gave Mrs Cook a box on the ear with all her might; upon which Mrs Cook snatched up a stick and broke the mad woman's pate with it. But though she could beat a hole in her head, she never could beat out of it her having said that she wished massa might never come back. And although Philippa has recovered her senses, in her belief of Mrs Cook's disloyalty she continues firm; and they never meet without renewing the dispute.

To-day being a play-day, the gaiety of the negroes was promoted by a distribution of an additional quantity of salt-fish (which forms a most acceptable ingredient in their pepper-pots), and as much rum and sugar as they chose to drink. But there was also a dinner prepared at the house where the 'white people' reside, expressly for none but the *piccaninny-mothers*; that is, for the women who had children living. I had taken care, when this play-day was announced by the head driver, to make him inform the negroes that they were indebted for it entirely to these mothers; and to show them the more respect, I went to them after dinner myself, and drank their healths. The most respectable blacks on the estate were also assembled in the room; and I then told them that clothes would wear out, and money would be spent, and that I wished to give them something more lasting than clothes or money. The law only allows them, as a matter of right, every alternate Saturday for themselves, and holidays for three days at Christmas, which, with all Sundays, forms their whole legal time of relaxation. I therefore granted them as a matter of right, and of which no person should deprive them on any account whatever, *every* Saturday to cultivate their grounds; and in addition to their holidays at Christmas, I gave them for play-days Good-Friday, the second Friday in October, and the second Friday in July. By which means, they will in future have the same number of holidays four times a year, which hitherto they have been allowed only once, *i.e.* at Christmas. The first is to be called 'the royal play-day', in honour of that excellent Princess, the Duchess of York;* and the negroes are directed to give three cheers upon the head driver's announcing 'The health of our good lady, HRH the Duchess of York.' And I told them, that before my leaving the island, I should hear them drink this health, and should not fail to let Her Royal Highness know, that the negroes of Cornwall drank her health every year. This evidently touched the right chord of their vanity, and they all bowed and courtesied down to the very ground, and said, that would do them much high honour. The ninth being my own birthday, the July play-day is to be called 'the massa's'; and that in October is to be in honour of the piccaninny-mothers, from whom it is to take its name.

The poor creatures overflowed with gratitude; and the prospective indulgences which had just been announced, gave them such an increase of spirits, that on returning to my own residence, they fell to singing and dancing again with as much violence as if they had been a pack of French furies at the Opera. The favourite song of the night was,

> Since massa come, we very well off;

which words they repeated in chorus, without intermission (dancing all the time), for hours together; till, at half-past three, neither my eyes nor my brain could endure it any longer, and I was obliged to send them word that I wanted to go to bed, and could not sleep till the noise should cease. The idea of my going to bed seemed never to have occurred to them till that moment. Fortunately, like Johnson's definition of wit, 'the idea, although novel, was immediately acknowledged to be just'. So instantly the drums and gumbies left off beating; the children left off singing; the women and men left off dancing; and they all with one accord fell to kicking, and pulling, and thumping about two dozen of their companions, who were lying fast asleep upon the floor. Some were roused, some resisted, some began fighting, some got up and lay down again; but at length, by dint of their leading some, carrying others, and rolling the remainder down the steps, I got my house clear of my black guests about four in the morning.

Another of their popular songs this evening was—

All the stories them telling you are lies, oh!

which was meant as a satire upon the Eboes. My friend Strap being an Eboe, and one who had hitherto generally taken a leading part in all the discontents and squabbles of his countrymen, I was not without apprehensions of his having been concerned in the late complaint. I was, therefore, much pleased to find that he had positively refused to take any share in the business, and had been to the full as violent as any of the Creoles in reprobating the ingratitude of the Eboes. To-day he came up to the house dressed in his best clothes, to show me his seven children; and he marched at their head in all the dignity of paternal pride. He begged me particularly to notice two fine little girls, who were twins. I told him that I had seen them already. 'Iss! iss!' he said; 'massa see um; but massa no *admire* um enough yet.' Upon which I fell to admiring them, tooth and nail, and the father went away quite proud and satisfied.

February 25

Yesterday it was observed at George's Plain, an estate about four miles off, that the water-mill did not work properly, and it was concluded that the grating was clogged up with rubbish. To clear it away, a negro immediately jumped down into the trench upon a log of wood; when he felt the log move under him, and of course jumped out again with all possible expedition. It was then discovered that the impediment in question proceeded from a large alligator which had wandered from the morass, and, in the hope of finding his way to the river, had swam up the mill-trench till he found himself stopped by the grating; and the banks being too high for him to gain them by leaping upwards, and the place of his confinement too narrow to admit of his turning round to go back again, his escape was impossible, and a ball, lodged near his eye, soon put an end to him. I went over to see him this morning; but I was not contented with merely seeing him, so I begged to have a steak cut off for me, brought it home, and ordered it to be broiled for dinner. One of the negroes happened to see it in the kitchen; the news spread through the estate like wildfire; and I had immediately half a dozen different deputations, all hoping that massa would not think of eating the alligator, for it was poisonous. However, I was obstinate, and found the taste of the flesh, when broiled with pepper and salt, and assisted by an onion sauce, by no means to be despised; but the consistence of the meat was disagreeable, being as tough as a piece of eel-skin. Perhaps any body who wishes to eat alligator steaks in perfection, ought to keep them for two or three days before dressing them; or the animal's age might be in fault, for the fellow was so old that he had scarcely a tooth in his head; I therefore contented myself with two or three morsels; but a person who was dining with me ate a whole steak, and pronounced the dish to be a very good one. The eggs are said to be very palatable; nor have the negroes who live near morasses, the same objection with those of Cornwall to eating the flesh; it is, however, true that the gall of the alligator, if not extracted carefully, will render the whole animal unfit for food; and when this gall is reduced to powder, it forms a poison of the most dangerous nature, as the negroes know but too well.

February 26

I had given the most positive orders that no person whatever should presume to strike a negro, or give him abusive language, or, however great the offence might be, should inflict any punishment, except by the sole direction of the trustee himself. Yet, although I had already discharged one book-keeper on this account, this evening another of them had a dispute in the boiling-house with an African named Frank, because a pool of water was not removed fast enough; upon which he called him a rascal, sluiced him with the dirty water, and finally knocked him down with the broom. The African came to me instantly; four eye-witnesses, who were examined separately, proved the truth of his ill-usage; and I immediately discharged the book-keeper, who had contented himself with simply denying the blow having been given by him: but I told him that I could not possibly allow his single unsupported denial to outweigh five concordant witnesses to the assertion; and that, if he grounded his claim to being believed merely upon his having a white skin, he would find that, on Cornwall estate at least, that claim would not be admitted. The fact was established as evident as the sun; and nothing should induce me to retain him on my property, except his finding some means of appeasing the injured negro, and prevailing on him to intercede in his behalf. This was an humiliation to which he could not bring himself to stoop; and, accordingly, the man has left the estate. Probably, indeed, the attempt at reconciliation would have been unsuccessful; for when one of his companions asked Frank whether, if Mr Barker would make him a present, he had not better take it, and beg massa to let him stay, he exclaimed, in the true spirit of a Zanga,*— 'No, no, no! me no want present! me no want noting! Me no beg for Mr Barker! him go away!'—I was kept awake the greatest part of the night by the songs and rejoicings of the negroes, at their triumph over the offending book-keeper.

February 27

The only horned cattle said to be fit for Jamaica work, are those which have a great deal of black in them. The white are terribly tormented by the insects, and they are weak and sluggish in proportion to their quantity of white.* On the contrary I am told that such a thing as a black horse is not to be found in the island; those which may be imported black soon change their colour into a bay; and colts are said to have been dropped perfectly black, which afterwards grew lighter and lighter till they arrived at being perfectly white.

February 28

Hearing that a manati (the sea-cow) had been taken at the mouth of the Cabrita River, and was kept alive at the Hope Wharf, I got a sailing-boat, and went about eight miles to see the animal. It was suffered to live in the sea, a rope being fastened round it, by which it could be landed at pleasure. It was a male, and a very young one, not exceeding nine feet in length, whereas they have frequently been found on the outside of eighteen. The females yield a quart of milk at a time: a gentleman told me that he had tasted it, and could not have distinguished it from the sweetest cow's milk. Unlike the seal, it never comes on shore, although it ventures up rivers in the night, to feed on the grass of their banks; but during the day it constantly inhabits the ocean, where its chief enemy is the shark, whose attacks it beats off with its tail, the strength of which is prodigious. It was killed this morning, and the gentleman to whom it belonged was obliging enough to send me part of it; we roasted it for dinner, and, except that its consistence was rather firmer, I should not have known it from veal.

February 29

The wife of an old negro on the neighbouring estate of Anchovy had lately forsaken him for a younger lover. One night, when she happened to be alone, the incensed husband entered her hut unexpectedly, abused her with all the rage of jealousy, and demanded the clothes to be restored, which he had formerly given her. On her refusal he drew a knife, and threatened to cut them off her back; nor could she persuade him to depart, till she had received a severe beating. He had but just left the hut, when he encountered his successful rival, who was returning home: a quarrel instantly ensued; and the husband, having the knife still unsheathed in his hand, plunged it into the neck of his antagonist. It pierced the jugular vein; of course the man fell dead on the spot; and the murderer has been sent to Montego Bay, to take his trial.

March 1 (Friday)

One of my house-boys, named Prince, is son to the Duke of Sully; and to-day his Grace came to beg that, when I should leave Jamaica, I would direct the boy to be made a tradesman, instead of being sent back to be a common field-negro: but my own shops are not only full at present, but loaded with future engagements. Sully then requested that I would send his son to learn some other trade (a tailor's, for instance) at Savannah la Mar, as had been frequently done in former times; but this, also, I was obliged to refuse. I told him, that formerly a master could pay for the apprenticeship of a clever negro boy, and, instead of employing him afterwards on the estate, could content himself with being repaid by a share of the profits; but that, since The Abolition had made it impossible for the proprietor of an estate to supply the place of one negro by the purchase of another, it would be unjust to his companions to suffer any one in particular to be withdrawn from service; as in that case two hundred and ninety-nine would have to do the work, which was now performed by three hundred; and, therefore, I could allow my negroes to apply themselves to no trades but such as related to the business of the property, such as carpenters, coopers, smiths, etc. 'All true, massa,' said Sully; 'all fair and just; and, to be sure, a tailor or a saddler would be of no great use towards your planting and getting in your crop; nor——' He hesitated for a moment, and then added, with a look of doubt, and in a lower voice,— 'Nor—nor a fiddler either, I suppose, massa?' I began to laugh. 'No, indeed, Sully; nor a fiddler either!' It seems the lad, who is about sixteen, very thoughtless, and *un tantino* stupid, has a passion for playing the fiddle, and, among other trades, had suggested this to his father, as one which would be extremely to his taste. We finally settled, that when the plough should be introduced on my estate (which I am very anxious to accomplish, and substitute the labour of oxen for that of negroes, wherever it can possibly be done), Prince should be instructed in farming business, and in the mean while should officiate as a pen-keeper to look after the cattle.

Just now Prince came to me with a request of his own. 'Massa, please, me want one little coat.'—'A little coat! For what?'—'Massa, please, for wear when me go down to the Bay.'—'And why should you wear a little coat when you go to the Bay?'—'Massa, please, make me look eerie (buckish) when me go abroad.' So I assured him that he looked quite *eerie* enough already; and that, as I was going away too soon to admit of my seeing him in his little coat, there could not be the slightest occasion for his being a bit *eerier* than he was. A master in England would probably have been not a little astonished at receiving such a request from one of his groom-boys; but here one gets quite accustomed to them; and when they are refused,

the petitioners frequently laugh themselves at their own un-
reasonableness.

March 2

Most of those negroes who are tolerably industrious, breed cattle on
my estate, which are their own peculiar property, and by the sale of
which they obtain considerable sums. The pasturage of a steer
would amount, in this country, to 12*l.* a year; but the negro cattle get
their grass from me without its costing them a farthing; and as they
were very desirous that I should be their general purchaser, I ordered
them to agree among themselves as to what the price should be.
It was, therefore, settled that I should take their whole stock,
good and bad indifferently, at the rate of 15*l.* a head for every three-
year-old beast; and they expressed themselves not only satisfied, but
very grateful for my acceptance of their proposal. John Fuller and
the beautiful Psyche had each a steer to sell (how Psyche came to be
so rich, I had too much discretion to enquire), and they were paid
down their 15*l.* a piece instantly, which they carried off with much
glee.

March 3 (Sunday)

In this country it may be truly said that 'it never rains but it pours.'
After a drought of three months, it began to rain on Thursday
morning, and has never stopped raining since, with thunder all the
day, and lightning all the night; one consequence of which incessant
showers is, that it has brought out all sorts of insects and reptiles in
crowds: the ground is covered with lizards; the air is filled with mosquitoes, and their bite is infinitely more envenomed than on my first
arrival. A centipes was found squeezed to death under the door
of my bed-room this morning. As to the cock-roaches, they are
absolutely in legions; every evening my negro boys are set to hunt
them, and they kill them by dozens on the chairs and sofas, in the
covers of my books, and among the leaves in my fruit-baskets. Yesterday I wanted to send away a note in a great hurry, snatched up a
wafer, and was on the point of putting it into my mouth, when I felt
it move, and found it to be a cock-roach, which had worked its way
into the wafer-box.

March 4 (Monday)

Since my arrival in Jamaica, I am not conscious of having omitted any means of satisfying my negroes, and rendering them happy and secure from oppression. I have suffered no person to be punished, except the two female demons who almost bit a girl's hands off (for which they received a slight switching), and the most worthless rascal on the estate, whom for manifold offences I was compelled, for the sake of discipline, to allow to pass two days in the bilboes.* I have never refused a favour that I could possibly grant. I have listened patiently to all complaints. I have increased the number of negro holidays, and have given away money and presents of all kinds incessantly. Now for my reward. On Saturday morning there were no fewer than forty-five persons (not including children) in the hospital; which makes nearly a fifth of my whole gang. Of these, the medical people assured me that not above seven had any thing whatever the matter with them; the rest were only feigning sickness out of mere idleness, and in order to sit doing nothing, while their companions were forced to perform their part of the estate-duty. And sure enough, on Sunday morning they all walked away from the hospital to amuse themselves, except about seven or eight: they will, perhaps, go to the field for a couple of days; and on Wednesday we may expect to have them all back again, complaining of pains, which (not existing) it is not possible to remove. Jenny (the girl whose hands were bitten) was told by the doctoress, that having been in the hospital all the week, she ought not, for very shame, to go out on Sunday. She answered, 'She wanted to go to the mountains, and go she would.' 'Then,' said the doctoress, 'you must not come back again on Monday at least.' 'Yes,' Jenny said, 'she *should* come back'; and back this morning Jenny came. But as her wounds were almost completely well, she had tied packthread round them so as to cut deep into the flesh, had rubbed dirt into them, and, in short, had played such tricks as nearly to produce a mortification in one of her fingers.

The most worthless fellow on the whole property is one Nato,— a thief, a liar, a runaway, and one who has never been two days together out of the hospital since my arrival, although he has nothing the matter with him; indeed, when the other negroes abused him for his laziness, and leaving them to do his work for him, he told them plainly that he did not mean to work, and that nobody should make him. The only real illness which brought him to the hospital, within my knowledge, was the consequence of a beating received from his own father, who had caught him in the act of robbing his house by the help of a false key. In the hospital he found his wife, Philippa, the mad woman, with whom he instantly quarrelled, and she cut his head open with a plate; and as she might have served one of the children in the same way, we were obliged to confine her. Her husband was thought to be the fittest person to guard her; and accordingly they were locked up together in a separate room from the other invalids, till a straight waistcoat could be made. The husband was then restored to freedom, and desired to go to work, which he declared to be impossible from illness; yet he disappeared the whole of the next day; and on his return on the following morning, he had the impudence to assert that he had never been out of the hospital for an hour. For this runaway offence, and for endeavouring to exasperate his wife's phrensy, he was put into the bilboes for two days: on the third he was released; when he came to me with tears in his eyes, implored me most earnestly to forgive what had past, and promised to behave better for the future, 'to so good a massa'. It appeared afterwards, that he had employed his absence in complaining to Mr Williams, a neighbouring magistrate, that, 'having a spite against them, although neither he nor his wife had committed any fault, I had punished them both by locking them up for several days in a solitary prison, under pretence of his wife's insanity, when, in fact, she was perfectly in her senses'. Unluckily, one of my physicians had told Mr Williams, that very morning, how much he had been alarmed at Cornwall, when, upon going into a mad woman's room, her husband had fastened the door, and he had found himself shut up between them; the woman really mad, and the man pretending to be so too. The moment that Nato mentioned the mad woman as his wife, 'What then,' said Mr Williams, 'you are the fellow who alarmed the doctor so much two days ago?' Upon which Nato had the impudence to burst into a fit of laughter,— 'Oh, ki, massa, doctor no need be fright; we no want to hurt him; only make lilly bit fun wid him, massa, that all.' On which he was ordered to get out of Mr Williams's house, slunk back into the Cornwall hospital, and in a few days came to me with such a long story of penitence, and 'so good massa', that he induced me to forgive him.

To sum up the whole, about three this morning an alarm was given that the pen-keeper had suffered the cattle to get among the canes, where they might do infinite mischief; the trustee was roused out of his bed; the drivers blew their shells to summon the negroes to their assistance; when it appeared, that there was not a single watchman at his post; the watch-fires had all been suffered to expire; not a single domestic was to be found, nor a horse to be procured; even the little servant boys, whom the trustee had locked up in his own house, and had left fast asleep when he went to bed, had got up again, and made their escape to pass the night in play and rioting; and although they were perfectly aware of the detriment which the cattle were doing to my interests, not a negro could be prevailed upon to rouse himself and help to drive them out, till at length Cubina (who had run down from his own house to mine on the first alarm) with difficulty collected about half a dozen to assist him: but long before this, one of my best cane-pieces was trampled to pieces, and the produce of this year's crop considerably diminished.—And so much for negro gratitude! However, they still continue their eternal song of 'Now massa come, we very well off'; but their satisfaction evidently begins and ends with themselves. They rejoice sincerely at being very well off, but think it unnecessary to make the slightest return to massa for making them so.

March 5

The worst of negro diseases is 'the cocoa-bay': it is both hereditary and contagious, and will lurk in the blood of persons apparently the most healthy and of regular habits, till a certain age; when it declares itself in the form of offensive sores, attended with extreme debility. No cure for it has yet been discovered: there are negro doctors, who understand how to prepare diet drinks from simples of the island, which moderate its virulence for a time; but the disease itself is never entirely subdued. On the contrary, 'the yaws',* although it defies the power of medicine, ultimately cures itself. This, also, is communicated by contact, and that of so slight a nature, that a fly, which has touched an ulcer produced by the yaws, has been known to convey the infection by merely alighting on the wound of a cut finger. It generally shows itself by a slight pimple, which is soon converted into a sore;

and this spreads itself gradually over the invalid's whole body, till having made its progress through the system completely, its virulence gradually abates, and at length the disease disappears all together. As 'the yaws' can only be taken once, inoculation has been tried upon the most hopeful subjects; but the disease showed itself with as much violence as when contracted in the natural way.

March 6

Nato has kept his promise as yet, and has actually past a whole week in the field; a thing which he was never known to do before within the memory of man. So I sent him a piece of money to encourage him; and told him, that I sent him a *maccarony** for behaving well, and wished to know whether any one had ever given him a maccarony for behaving ill. I hear that he was highly delighted at my thinking him worthy to receive a present from me, and sent me in return the most positive assurances of perseverance in good conduct. On the other hand, Mackaroo has not only run away himself, but has carried his wife away with him. This is improving upon the profligacy of British manners with a vengeance. In England, a man only runs away with another person's wife: but to run away with his own—what depravity!—As to my ungrateful demigod of a sheep-stealer, Hercules, the poor wretch has brought down upon himself a full punishment for all his misdeeds. By running away, and sleeping in the woods, exposed to all the fury of the late heavy rains, he has been struck by the palsy. Yesterday some of my negroes found him in the mountains, unable to raise himself from the ground, and brought him in a cart to the hospital; where he now lies, having quite lost the use of one side, and without any hopes of recovery. He is still a young man, and in every other respect strong and healthy; so that he may look forward to a long and miserable existence.

March 8

THE HUMMING BIRD

Deck'd with all that youth and beauty
E'er bestow'd on sable maid,
Gathering bloom her fragrant duty,
Down the lime-walk Zoè stray'd.

Many a logwood brake was ringing
    With the chicka-chinky's cry;
Many a mock-bird loudly singing
    Bless'd the groves with melody.

Fly-birds, on whose plumage showers
    Nature's hand her wealth profuse,
Humming round, from banks of flowers
    Suck'd the rich ambrosial juice.

There an orange-plant, perfuming
    All the air with blossoms white,
Near a bush of roses blooming,
    Charm'd at once the scent and sight.

Of that plant the loveliest daughter,
    One sweet bloom-bough all preferr'd;
When his glittering eye had caught her,
    Oh, how joy'd the Humming Bird!

Here the fairest blossoms thinking,
    Swift he flies, nor loads the stem;
Poised in air, and odour drinking,
    Fluttering hangs the feather'd Gem.

Sure, he deems, these cups untasted,
    Many a honied drop allow!
Soon he finds his labour wasted;
    Bees have robb'd that orange bough.

Wandering bees, at blush of morning,
    Drain'd of all their sweets the bells;
Then the rifled beauty scorning,
    How his angry throat he swells!

See his bill the blossoms rending;
    Round their leaves in wrath he throws;
Then, once more his wings extending,
    Flies to woo the opening rose.

'Mark, my Zoè,' said her mother,
    'Mark that bough, so lovely late!
Thou in bloom art such another—
    Such, perhaps, may be thy fate.

'Some wild youth may charm and cheat thee,
    Sip thy sweets, and break his vow;
Then the world will scorn and treat thee
    As the Fly-Bird did just now.'

British mothers thus impress on
  Virgin minds some maxim true;
Zoè heard and used the lesson
Just as British daughters do.

March 9

The shaddock contains generally thirty-two seeds, two of which only
will reproduce shaddocks; and these two it is impossible to distinguish: the rest will yield, some sweet oranges, others bitter ones,
others again forbidden fruit, and, in short, all the varieties of the
orange; but until the trees actually are in bearing, no one can guess
what the fruit is likely to prove; and even then, the seeds which
produce shaddocks, although taken from a tree remarkable for the
excellence of its fruit, will frequently yield only such as are scarcely
eatable. So also the varieties of the mango are infinite: the fruit of
no two trees resembling each other; and the seeds of the very finest
mango (although sown and cultivated with the utmost care) seldom
affording any thing at all like the parent stock. The two first mangoes
which I tasted were nothing but turpentine and sugar; the third was
very delicious; and yet I was told that it was by no means of a superior quality. The *sweet* cassava requires no preparation; the *bitter*
cassava, unless the juice is carefully pressed out of it, is a deadly
poison; there is a third kind, called the *sweet-and-bitter* cassava, which
is perfectly wholesome till a certain age, when it acquires its deleterious qualities. Many persons have been poisoned by mistaking
these various kinds of cassava for each other. As soon as the plantain
has done bearing, it is cut down; when four or five suckers spring
from each root, which become plants themselves in their turn.
Ratoons are suckers of the sugar-cane: they are far preferable to the
original plants, where the soil is rich enough to support them; but
they are much better adapted to some estates than to others. Thus,
on my estate in St Thomas's in the East, they can allow of ten ratoons
from the same plant, and only dig cane-holes every eleventh year;
while, at Cornwall, the strength of the cane is exhausted in the fourth
ratoon, or the fifth at furthest. The fresh plants are cane-tops; but
those canes which bear *flags* or feathers at their extremities will not
answer the purpose, as dry weather easily burns up the slight arrows
to which the flags adhere, and destroys them before they can acquire
sufficient vigour to resist the climate.

March 10 (Sunday)

I find that I have not done justice to the cotton tree, and, on the other hand, have given too much praise to the Jamaica kitchen. The first cotton trees which I saw, were either withered by age, or struck by lightning, or happened to be ill-shaped of their kind; but I have since met with others, than which nothing could be more noble or picturesque, from their gigantic height, the immense spread of their arms, the colour of their stems and leaves, and the wild fantastic wreathings of their roots and branches. As to the kitchen, nothing can be larger and finer in appearance than the poultry of all kinds, but nothing can be uniformly more tough and tasteless; and the same is the case with all butcher's meat, pork excepted, which is much better here than in Europe. The fault is in the climate, which prevents any animal food from being kept sufficiently long to become tender; so that when a man sits down to a Jamaica dinner, he might almost fancy himself a guest at Macbeth's Covent-Garden banquet, where the fowls, hams, and legs of mutton are all made of deal boards. I ordered a duck to be kept for two days; but it was so completely spoiled, that there was no bearing it upon the table. Then I tried the expedient of boiling a fowl till it absolutely fell to pieces; but even this violent process had not the power of rendering it tender. The only effect produced by it was, that instead of being helped to a wing of solid wood, I got a plateful of splinters. Perhaps, my having totally lost my appetite (probably from my not being able to take, in this climate, sufficient of my usual exercise) makes the meat appear to me less palatable than it may to others; but I have observed, that most people here prefer living upon soups, stews, and salted provisions. For my own part, I have for the last few weeks eaten nothing except black crabs, than which I never met with a more delicious article for the table. I have also tried the *soldier* soup, which is in great estimation in this island; but although it greatly resembled the very richest cray-fish soup, it seemed to be composed of cray-fish which had been kept too long. The *soldiers* themselves were perfectly fresh, for they were brought to the kitchen quite alive and merry; but I was told that this taste of staleness is their peculiar flavour, as well as their peculiar scent even when alive, and is precisely the quality which forms their recommendation. It was quite enough to fix my opinion of the soup: I ate two spoonfuls, and never mean to venture on a third.

March 12

The most general of negro infirmities appears to be that of lameness. It is chiefly occasioned by the *chiga*, a diminutive fly which works itself into the feet to lay its eggs, and, if it be not carefully extracted in time, the flesh around it corrupts, and a sore ensues not easily to be cured. No vigilance can prevent the attacks of the chiga; and not only soldiers, but the very cleanest persons of the highest rank in society, are obliged to have their feet examined regularly. The negroes are all provided with small knives for the purpose of extracting them: but as no pain is felt till the sore is produced, their extreme laziness* frequently makes them neglect that precaution, till all kinds of dirt getting into the wound, increases the difficulty of a cure; and sometimes the consequence is lameness for life.

There is another disease* which commits great ravages among them; for although in this climate its quality is far from virulent, and it is easy to be cured in its beginning, the negro will most carefully conceal his having such a complaint, till it has made so great a progress that its effects are perceived by others. Even then, they will never acknowledge the way in which they have contracted it; but men and women, whose noses almost shake while speaking to you, will still insist upon it that their illness arises from catching cold, or from a strain in lifting a weight, or, in short, from any cause except the true one. Yet why they act thus it is difficult to imagine; for certainly it does not arise from shame.

Indeed, it is one of their singular obstinacies, that, however ill they may be, they scarcely ever will confess to the physician what is really the matter with them on their first coming into the hospital, but will rather assign some other cause for their being unwell than the true one; and it is only by cross-questioning, that their superintendents are able to understand the true nature of their case. Perhaps this duplicity is occasioned by fear; for in any bodily pain it is not possible to be more cowardly than the negro; and I have heard strong young men, while the tears were running down their cheeks, scream and roar as if a limb was amputating, although the doctoress was only applying a poultice to a whitlow on the finger. I suppose, therefore, that dread of the pain of some unknown mode of treatment makes them conceal their real disease, and name some other, of which they know the cure to be unattended with bodily suffering or long restraint. In the disease I allude to, such a motive would operate with peculiar force, as one of their chief aversions is the necessarily being long confined to one certainly not fragrant room.

March 13

The Reporter of the African Institution* asserts, in a late pamphlet, that in the West Indies the breeding system is to this day discouraged, and that the planters are still indifferent to the preservation of their present stock of negroes, from their confidence of getting fresh supplies from Africa. Certainly the negroes in Jamaica are by no means of this Reporter's opinion, but are thoroughly sensible of their intrinsic value in the eyes of the proprietor. On my arrival, every woman who had a child held it up to show to me, exclaiming,—'See massa, see! here nice new neger me bring for work for massa'; and those who had more than one did not fail to boast of the number, and make it a claim to the greater merit with me. Last week, an old watchman was brought home from the mountains almost dead with fever; he would neither move, nor speak, nor notice any one, for several days. For two nights I sent him soup from my own table; but he could not even taste it, and always gave it to his daughter. On the third evening, there happened to be no soup at dinner, and I sent other food instead; but old Cudjoe had been accustomed to see the soup arrive, and the disappointment made him fancy himself hungry, and that he could have eaten the soup if it had been brought as usual: accordingly, when I visited him the next morning, he bade the doctoress tell me that massa had send him no soup the night before. This was the first notice that he had ever taken of me. I promised that some soup should be ordered for him on purpose that evening. Could he fancy any thing to eat *then?*—'Milk! milk!' So milk was sent to him, and he drank two full calabashes of it. I then tried him with an egg, which he also got down; and at night, by spoonfuls at a time, he finished the whole bason of soup; but when I next came to see him, and he wished to thank me, the words in which he thought he could comprise most gratitude were bidding the doctoress tell me he would do his best not to die yet; he promised to *fight hard* for it. He is now quite out of danger, and seems really to be grateful. When he was sometimes too weak to speak, on my leaving the room he would drag his hand to his mouth with difficulty, and kiss it three or four times to bid me farewell; and once, when the doctoress mentioned his having charged her to tell me that he owed his recovery to the good food that I had sent him, he added, 'And him kind words too, massa; kind words do neger much good, much as good food.' In my visits to the old man, I observed a young woman nursing him with an infant in her arms, which (as they told me) was her own, by Cudjoe. I therefore supposed her to be his wife: but I found that she belonged to a *brown* man in the mountains; and that Cudjoe hired her from her master, at the rate of thirty pounds a year!

I hope this fact will convince the African *Reporter*, that it is possible for some of this 'oppressed race of human beings'—'of these our most unfortunate fellow-creatures,'—to enjoy at least *some* of the luxuries of civilised society; and I doubt, whether even Mr Wilberforce himself, with all his benevolence, would not allow a negro to be quite rich enough, who can afford to pay thirty pounds a year for the hire of a kept mistress.

March 14

Poor Nato's stock of goodness is quite exhausted; and the day before yesterday he returned to the hospital with most piteous complaints of pains and aches, whose existence he could persuade no person to credit. His pulse was regular, his skin cool, his tongue red and moist, and the doctor declared nothing whatever to be the matter with him. However, on my arrival, he began to moan, and groan, and grunt, and all so lamentably, that every soul in the hospital, sick or well, burst into a fit of laughter. For my part, I told him that I really believed him to be very bad; and that, as he met with no sympathy in the hospital, I should remove him from such unfeeling companions. Accordingly I had a comfortable bed made for him in a separate house. Here he was plentifully supplied with provisions: but, in order that he might enjoy perfect repose during his illness, the doors were kept locked, and no person allowed to disturb him with their conversation; while, by the doctor's orders, he was obliged to take frequent doses of Bitter-Wood and Assafœtida.* Shame would not suffer him to get well all at once; so yesterday he still complained of a pain in his chest, and begged to be blooded. His request was granted; and the blood proved to be so pure and well-coloured, that every one exclaimed, that for a man who had such good blood to part with it so wantonly was a shame and a folly. The fellow was at length convinced that his tricks would serve no object; and this morning he begged me to suffer him to return to his duty, and promised that I should have no more cause to complain of him. So I consented to consider his cure as completed, and he set off for the field perfectly satisfied with his release.

March 15

On opening the Assize-court for the county of Cornwall on March 4, Mr Stewart, the Custos* of Trelawny, and Presiding Judge, said, in his charge to the jury, he wished to direct their attention in a peculiar manner to the infringement of slave-laws in the island, in consequence of charges having been brought forward in England of slave laws not being enforced in this country, and being in fact perfect dead letters. The charge was unfounded; but it became proper, in consequence, for the bench to call in a strong manner on the grand jury to be particularly vigilant and attentive to the discharge of this part of their duty. The bench at the same time adverted to another subject connected with the above. Many out of the country, and *some in it*, had thought proper to interfere with our system, and by their insidious practices and dangerous doctrines to call the peace of the island into question, and to promote disorder and confusion. The jury were therefore enjoined, in every such case, to investigate it thoroughly, and to bring the parties concerned before the country, and not to suffer the systems of the island, as established by the laws of the land, to be overset or endangered. It was their bounden duty to watch over and support the established laws, and to act against those who dared to infringe them; and that, otherwise, it was imperiously called for on the principle of self-preservation. Every country had its peculiar laws, on the due maintenance of which depended the public safety and welfare. I read all this with the most perfect unconsciousness; when, lo and behold! I have been assured, from a variety of quarters, that all this was levelled at myself! It is I (it seems) who am 'calling the peace of the island in question'; who am 'promoting disorder and confusion'; and who am 'infringing the established laws!' I should never have guessed it! By 'insidious practices' is meant (as I am told) my over-indulgence to my negroes; and my endeavouring to obtain either redress or pardon for those belonging to other estates, who occasionally appeal to me for protection: while 'dangerous doctrines' alludes to my being of opinion, that the evidence of negroes ought at least to be *heard** against white persons; the jury always making proportionable abatements of belief, from bearing in mind the bad habits of most negroes, their general want of probity and good faith in every respect, and their total ignorance of the nature of religious obligations. At the same time, these defects may be counterbalanced by the respectable character of the particular negro; by the strength of corroborating circumstances; and, finally, by the irresistible conviction which his evidence may leave upon the minds of the jury. They are not obliged to *believe* a negro witness, but I maintain that he ought to be *heard*, and then let the jury give their verdict according to their conscience. But this, in the opinion of the bench at Montego Bay, it seems, is 'dangerous doctrine'! At least, the venom of my doctrines is circumscribed within very narrow limits; for as I have made a point of never stirring off my own estate, nobody could possibly be corrupted by them, except those who were at the trouble of walking into my house for the express purpose of being corrupted.

At all events, if I *really* am the person to whom Mr Stewart alluded, I must consider his speech as the most flattering compliment that I ever received. If my presence in the island has made the bench of a whole country think it necessary to exact from the jury a more severe vigilance than usual in all causes relating to the protection of negroes, I cannot but own myself most richly rewarded for all my pains and expense in coming hither, for every risk of the voyage, and for every possible sacrifice of my pleasures. There is nothing earthly that is too much to give for the power of producing an effect so beneficial; and I would set off for Constantinople to-morrow, could I only be convinced that my arrival would make the Mufti redress the complaints of the lower orders of Turks with more scrupulous justice, and the Bashaws relax the fetters of their slaves as much as their safety would permit. But I cannot flatter myself with having done either the one or the other in Jamaica; and if Mr Stewart *really* alluded to me in his charge, I am certainly greatly obliged to him; but he has paid me much too high a compliment;—God grant that I may live to deserve it!

March 16

Hercules, the poor paralytic runaway, has neither moved nor spoken since his being brought into the hospital. For the two last days he refused all sustenance; blisters, rubbing with mustard, etc. were tried without producing the least sensation; and in the course of last night he expired without a groan.

Another offender, by name Charles Fox, is also under the doctor's hands, suffering under the effects of his own transgressions. Having been Pickle's shipmate, he professed the strongest attachment to him, and was perpetually at his house; till Pickle's wife made her husband aware that love for herself was the real object of his shipmate's visits. Finding her story disbelieved, she hid Pickle behind the bed, when he had an opportunity of hearing the solicitations of his perfidious Pylades;* and, rushing from his concealment, he gave Fox so complete a thrashing, that he was obliged to come to the hospital. Here is another proof that negroes, 'our unfortunate fellow-creatures', are not without some of the luxuries of civilised life; old men of sixty keeping mistresses, and young ones seducing their friends' wives; why, what would the Reporter of the African Institution have?

It is only to be wished, that the negroes would content themselves with these fashionable peccadilloes; but, unluckily, there are some palates among them which require higher seasoned vices; and besides their occasional amusements of poisoning, stabbing, thieving, etc., a plan has just been discovered in the adjoining parish of St Elizabeth's, for giving themselves a grand fête by murdering all the whites in the island. The focus of this meditated insurrection was on Martin's Penn, the property of Lord Balcarras,* where the overseer is an old man of the mildest character, and the negroes had always been treated with peculiar indulgence. Above a thousand persons were engaged in the plot, three hundred of whom had been regularly sworn to assist in it with all the usual accompanying ceremonies of drinking human blood, eating earth from graves, etc. Luckily, the plot was discovered time enough to prevent any mischief; and yesterday the ringleaders were to be tried at Black River.

March 17 (Sunday)

The Cornwall Chronicle informs us, that, at the Montego Bay assizes, a man was tried on the Monday, for assaulting, while drunk, an officer who had served with great distinction, and calling him a coward; for which offence he was sentenced to a month's imprisonment and fine of 100*l.*; and on the Tuesday the same man brought an action against another person for calling him a 'drunken liar', for which he was awarded 1,000*l.* for damages! A plain man would have supposed two such verdicts to be rather incompatible; but one lives to learn.

I remember to have read the case of a French nobleman, who was accused of impotence by his wife before the Parliament of Paris, and by a farmer's daughter for seduction and getting her with child before the Parliament of Rouen; he thought himself perfectly sure of gaining either the one cause or the other; but, however, he was condemned in both. Certainly the poor Frenchman had no luck in matters of justice.

To make the matter better, in the present instance, the man was a clergyman; and his cause of quarrel against the officer was the latter's refusal to give him a puncheon of rum to christen all his negroes in a lump.

March 22

Mr Plummer came over from St James's to-day, and told me, that the 'insidious practices and dangerous doctrines' in Mr Stewart's speech were intended for the Methodists, and that only the charge to the grand jury respecting 'additional vigilance' was in allusion to myself; but he added that it was the report at Montego Bay, that, in consequence of my over-indulgence to my negroes, a song had been made at Cornwall, declaring that I was come over to set them all free, and that this was now circulating through the neighbouring parishes. If there be any such song (which I do not believe), I certainly never heard it. However, my agent here says, that he has reason to believe that my negroes really have spread the report that I intend to set *them* free in a few years; and this merely out of vanity, in order to give themselves and their master the greater credit upon other estates. As to the truth of an assertion, that is a point which never enters into negro consideration.

The two ringleaders of the proposed rebellion have been condemned at Black River, the one to be hanged, the other to transportation. The plot was discovered by the overseer of Lyndhurst Penn (a Frenchman from St Domingo) observing an uncommon concourse of stranger negroes to a child's funeral, on which occasion a hog was roasted by the father. He stole softly down to the feasting hut, and listened behind a hedge to the conversation of the supposed mourners; when he heard the whole conspiracy detailed. It appears that above two hundred and fifty had been sworn in regularly, all of them Africans; not a Creole was among them. But there was a *black* ascertained to have stolen over into the island from St Domingo, and a *brown* Anabaptist missionary, both of whom had been very active in promoting the plot. They had elected a King of the Eboes, who had two Captains under him; and their intention was to effect a complete massacre of all the whites on the island; for which laudable design His Majesty thought Christmas the very fittest season in the year, but his Captains were more impatient, and were for striking the blow immediately. The next morning information was given against them: one of the Captains escaped to the woods; but the other, and the King of the Eboes, were seized and brought to justice. On their trial they were perfectly cool and unconcerned, and did not even profess to deny the facts with which they were charged. Indeed, proofs were too strong to admit of denial; among others, a copy of the following song was found upon the King, which the overseer had heard him sing at the funeral feast, while the other negroes joined in the chorus:—

SONG OF THE KING OF THE EBOES

Oh me good friend, Mr Wilberforce, make we free!
God Almighty thank ye! God Almighty thank ye!
   God Almighty, make we free!
Buckra in this country no make we free:
What Negro for to do? What Negro for to do?
   Take force by force! Take force by force!

CHORUS

To be sure! to be sure! to be sure!

The Eboe King said, that he certainly had made use of this song, and what harm was there in his doing so? He had sung no songs but such as his brown priest had assured him were approved of by John the Baptist. 'And who, then, was John the Baptist?' He did not very well know; only he had been told by his brown priest, that John the Baptist was a friend to the negroes, and had got his head in a pan!

As to the Captain, he only said in his defence, that if the court would forgive him this once, he would not do so again, 'as he found the whites did not like their plans'; which, it seems, till that moment they had never suspected! They had all along imagined, no doubt, that the whites would find as much amusement in having their throats cut, as the blacks would find in cutting them. I remember hearing a sportsman, who was defending the humanity of hunting, maintain, that it being as much the nature of a hare to run away as of a dog to run after her, consequently the hare must receive as much pleasure from being coursed, as the dog from coursing.

March 23

Two negroes upon Amity estate quarrelled the other day about some trifle, when the one bit the other's nose off completely. Soon after his accident, the overseer meeting the sufferer—'Why, Sambo,' he exclaimed, 'where's your nose?' 'I can't tell, massa,' answered Sambo; 'I looked every where about, but I could not find it.'

March 24 (Sunday)

Every Sunday since my return from Kingston I have read prayers to such of the negroes as chose to attend, preparatory to the intended visitations of the minister, Dr Pope. About twenty or thirty of the most respectable among them generally attended, and behaved with great attention and propriety. I read the Litany, and made them repeat the responses. I explained the Commandments and the Lord's Prayer to them, teaching them to say each sentence of the latter after me, as I read it slowly, in hopes of impressing it upon their memory. Then came 'the good Samaritan', or some such apologue; and, lastly, I related to them a portion of the life of Christ, and explained to them the object of his death and sufferings. The latter part of my service always seemed to interest them greatly; but, indeed, they behaved throughout with much attention. Unluckily, the head driver, who was one of the most zealous of my disciples, never could repeat the responses of the Litany without an appeal to myself, and always made a point of saying—'Good Lord, deliver us; yes, sir!' and made me a low bow: and one day when I was describing the wonderful precocity of Christ's under-standing, as evidenced by his interview with the doctors in the temple, while but a child, the head driver thought fit to interrupt me with—'Beg massa pardon, but want know one ting as puzzle me. Massa say "the child", and me want know, massa, one ting much; was Jesus Christ a boy or a girl?' Like my friend the Moravian, at Mesopotamia, I cannot boast of any increased audience; and if the negroes will not come to hear massa, I have little hope of their giving up their time to hear Dr Pope, who inspires them with no interest, and can exert no authority. Indeed, I am afraid that I am indebted for the chief part of my present auditory to my quality of massa rather than that of priest; and when I ask any of them why they did not come to prayers on the preceding Sunday, their excuse is always coupled with an assurance, that they wished very much to come, 'because they wish to do *any thing* to oblige massa'.

March 25

The negroes certainly are perverse beings. They had been praying for a sight of their master year after year; they were in raptures at my arrival; I have suffered no one to be punished, and shown them every possible indulgence during my residence amongst them; and one and all they declare themselves perfectly happy and well treated. Yet, previous to my arrival, they made thirty-three hogsheads a week; in a fortnight after my landing, their product dwindled to twenty-three; during this last week they have managed to make but thirteen. Still they are not ungrateful; they are only selfish: they love me very well, but they love themselves a great deal better; and, to do them justice, I verily believe that every negro on the estate is extremely anxious that all should do their full duty, except himself. My censure, although accompanied with the certainty of their not being punished, is by no means a matter of indifference. If I express myself to be displeased, the whole property is in an uproar; every body is finding fault with every body; nobody that does not represent the shame of neglecting my work, and the ingratitude of vexing me by their ill-conduct; and then each individual—having said so much, and said it so strongly, that he is convinced of its having its full effect in making the others do their duty—thinks himself quite safe and snug in skulking away from his own.

March 26

Young Hill was told at the Bay this morning, that I make a part of the Eboe King's song! According to this report, 'good King George and good Mr Wilberforce' are stated to have 'given me a paper' to set the negroes free (i.e. an order), but that the white people of Jamaica will not suffer me to show the paper, and I am now going home to say so, and 'to resume my chair, which I have left during my absence to be filled by the Regent'.

Since I heard the report of a rebellious song issuing from Cornwall, I have listened more attentively to the negro chaunts; but they seem, as far as I can make out, to relate entirely to their own private situation, and to have nothing to do with the negro state in general. Their favourite, 'We varry well off', is still screamed about the estate by the children; but among the grown people its nose has been put out of joint by the following stanzas, which were explained to me this morning. For several days past they had been dinned into my ears so incessantly, that at length I became quite curious to know their import, which I learned from Phillis, who is the family minstrel. It will be evident from this specimen, that the Cornwall bards are greatly inferior to those of Black River, who have actually advanced so far as to make an attempt at rhyme and metre.

NEGRO SONG AT CORNWALL

Hey-ho-day! me no care a dammee! (i.e. a damn,)
Me acquire a house, (i.e. I have a solid foundation to build on,)
Since massa come see we—oh!

Hey-ho-day! neger now quite eerie, (i.e. hearty,)
For once me see massa—hey-ho-day!
When massa go, me no care a dammee,
For how them usy we—hey-ho-day!

*

An Alligator, crossing the morass at Bellisle, an estate but a few miles distant from Cornwall, fell into a water-trench, from which he struggled in vain to extricate himself, and was taken alive; so that, according to the vulgar expression, he may literally be said to 'have put his foot in it'. Fontenelle says, that when Copernicus published his system, he foresaw the contradictions which he should have to undergo—'Et il se tira d'affaire très-habilement. Le jour qu'on lui présentoit le premier exemplaire, scavez-vous ce qu'il fit? Il mourut';* which was precisely the resource resorted to by the alligator. He died on the second morning of his captivity, and his proprietor, Mr Storer, was obliging enough to order the skin to be stuffed, and to make me a present of him. Neptune was despatched to bring him (or rather her, for nineteen eggs were found within her) over to Cornwall; and at dinner to-day we were alarmed with a general hubbub. It proved to be occasioned by Neptune's arrival (if Thames or Achelous* had been despatched on this errand, it would have been more appropriate) with the alligator on his head. In a few minutes every thing on the estate that was alive, without feathers, and with only two legs, flocked into the room, and requested to take a bird's-eye view of the monster; for as to coming near her, *that* they were much too cowardly to venture. It was in vain that I represented to them, that being dead it was utterly impossible that the animal could hurt them: they allowed the impossibility, but still kept at a respectful distance; and when at length I succeeded in persuading them to approach it, upon some one accidentally moving the alligator's tail, they all, with one accord, set up a loud scream, and men, women, and children tumbled out of the room over one another, to the irreparable ruin of some of my glasses and decanters, and the extreme trepidation of the whole side-board.

*

The negro-husband, who stabbed his rival in a fit of jealousy, has been tried at Montego Bay, and acquitted. On the other hand, the King of the Eboes has been hung at Black River, and died, declaring that he left enough of his countrymen to prosecute the design in hand, and revenge his death upon the whites. Such threats of a rescue were held out, that it was judged advisable to put the militia under arms, till the execution should have taken place; and also to remove the King's Captain to the gaol at Savannah la Mar, till means can be found for transporting him from the island.

March 27

The Eboe Captain has effected his escape by burning down the prison door. It is supposed that he has fled towards the fastnesses in the interior of the mountains, where I am assured that many settlements of run-away slaves have been formed, and with which the inhabited part of the island has no communication. However, the chief of the Accompong Maroons,* Captain Roe, is gone in pursuit of him, and has promised to bring him in, alive or dead. The latter is the only reasonable expectation, as the fugitive is represented as a complete desperado.

*

The negroes have at least given me one proof of their not being entirely selfish. When they heard that the boat was come to convey my baggage to the ship at Black River, they collected all their poultry, and brought it to my agent, desiring him to add it to my sea-stores. Of course I refused to let them be received, and they were evidently much disappointed, till I consented to accept the fowls and ducks, and then gave them back to them again, telling them to consider them as a present from my own hen-house, and to distinguish them by the name of 'massa's poultry'.

March 28

I have been positively assured, that an attempt was made to persuade the grand jury at Montego Bay, to present me for over-indulgence to my own negroes! It is a great pity that so reasonable an attempt should not have succeeded.—The rebel captain who broke out of prison, has been found concealed in the hut of a notorious Obeah-man, and has been lodged a second time in the gaol of Savannah la Mar.

March 29

About two months ago, a runaway cooper, belonging to Shrewsbury estate, by name Edward, applied to me to intercede for his not being punished on his return home. As soon as he got the paper requested, he gave up all idea of returning to the estate, and instead of it went about the country stealing every thing upon which he could lay his hands; and whenever his proceedings were enquired into by the magistrates, he stated himself to be on the road to his trustee, and produced my letter as a proof of it. At length some one had the curiosity to open the letter, and found that it had been written two months before.

March 30

This was the day appointed for the first 'Royal play-day', when I bade farewell to my negroes. I expected to be besieged with petitions and complaints, as they must either make them on this occasion or not at all. I was, therefore, most agreeably surprised to find, that although they had opportunities of addressing me from nine in the morning till twelve at night, the only favours asked me were by a poor old man, who wanted an iron cooking pot, and by Adam, who begged me to order a little daughter of his to be instructed in needle-work: and as to complaints, not a murmur of such a thing was heard; they all expressed themselves to be quite satisfied, and seemed to think that they could never say enough to mark their gratitude for my kindness, and their anxiety for my getting safe to England. We began our festival by the head driver's drinking the health of HRH the Duchess of York,* whom the negroes cheered with such a shout as might have 'rent hell's concave'.*

Then we had a christening of such persons as had been absent on the former occasion, one of whom was Adam, the reputed Obeah-man. In the number was a new-born child, whom we called Shakspeare, and whom Afra, the Eboe mother, had very earnestly begged me to make a Christian, as well as a daughter of hers, about four or five years old; at the same time that she declined being christened herself! In the same manner Cubina's wife, although her father and husband were both baptised on the former occasion, objected to going through the ceremony herself; and the reason which she gave was, that 'she did not like being christened while she was with child, as she did not know what change it might not produce upon herself and the infant'.

After the christening there was a general distribution of salt-fish by the trustee; and I also gave every man and woman half a dollar each, and every child a maccarony (fifteen pence) as a parting present, to show them that I parted with them in good-humour. While the money was distributing, young Hill arrived, and finding the house completely crowded, he enquired what was the matter. 'Oh, massa,' said an old woman, 'it is only *my son*, who is giving the negroes all something.'

I also read to them a new code of laws, which I had ordered to be put in force at Cornwall, for the better security of the negroes. The principal were, that 'a new hospital for the lying-in women, and for those who might be seriously ill, should be built, and made as comfortable as possible; while the present one should be reserved for those whom the physicians might declare to be very slightly indisposed, or not ill at all; the doors being kept constantly locked, and the sexes placed in separate chambers, to prevent its being made a place of amusement by the lazy and lying, as is the case at present.'—'A book register of punishments to be kept, in which the name, offence, and nature and quantity of punishment inflicted must be carefully put down; and also a note of the same given to the negro, in order that if he should think himself unjustly, or too severely punished, he may show his note to my other attorney on his next visit, or to myself on my return to Jamaica, and thus get redress if he has been wronged.'— 'No negro is to be struck, or punished in any way, without the trustee's express orders: the black driver so offending to be immediately degraded, and sent to work in the field; and the white person, for such a breach of my orders, to be discharged upon the spot.'— 'No negro is to be punished till twenty-four hours shall have elapsed between his committing the fault and suffering for it, in order that nothing should be done in the heat of passion, but that the trustee should have time to consider the matter coolly. But to prevent a guilty person from avoiding punishment by running away, he is to pass those twenty-four hours in such confinement as the trustee may think most fitting.'—'Any white person, who can be proved to have had an improper connection with a woman known publicly to be living as the wife of one of my negroes, is to be discharged immediately upon complaint being made.' I also gave the head driver a complete list of the allowances of clothing, food, etc. to which the negroes were entitled, in order that they might apply to it if they should have any doubts as to their having received their full proportion; and my new rules seemed to add greatly to the satisfaction of the negroes, who were profuse in their expressions of gratitude.

The festival concluded with a grander ball than usual, as I sent for music from Savanna la Mar to play country dances to them; and at twelve o'clock at night they left me apparently much pleased, only I heard some of them saying to each other, 'When shall we have such a day of pleasure again, since massa goes to-morrow?'

March 31 (Sunday)

With their usual levity, the negroes were laughing and talking as gaily as ever till the very moment of my departure; but when they saw my curricle actually at the door to convey me away, then their faces grew very long indeed. In particular, the women called me by every endearing name they could think of. 'My son! my love! my husband! my father!' 'You no my massa, you my tata!' said one old woman (upon which another wishing to go a step beyond her, added, 'Iss, massa, iss! It was you'); ******* and when I came down the steps to depart, they crowded about me, kissing my feet, and clasping my knees, so that it was with difficulty that I could get into the carriage. And this was done with such marks of truth and feeling, that I cannot believe the whole to be mere acting and mummery.

I dined with Mr Allwood at Shaftstone, his pen* near Blue-fields, and at half past seven found myself once more on board the Sir Godfrey Webster.

To fill up my list of Jamaica delicacies, I must not forget to mention, that I did my best to procure a Cane-piece Cat roasted in the true African fashion. The Creole negroes, however, greatly disapproved of my venturing upon this dish, which they positively denied having tasted themselves; and when, at length, the Cat was procured, last Saturday, instead of plainly boiling it with negro-pepper and salt, they made into a high seasoned stew, which rendered it impossible to judge of its real flavour. However, I tasted it, as did also several other people, and we were unanimous in opinion, that it might have been mistaken for a very good game-soup, and that, when properly dressed, a Cane-piece Cat must be excellent food.

One of the best vegetable productions of the island is esteemed to be the Avogada pear, sometimes called 'the vegetable marrow'. It was not the proper season for them, and with great difficulty I procured a couple, which were said to be by no means in a state of perfection. Such as they were, I could find no great merit in them; they were to be eaten cold with pepper and salt, and seemed to be an insipid kind of melon, with no other resemblance to marrow than their softness.

April 1 (Monday)

At eight this morning we weighed anchor on our return to England.

YARRA

Poor Yarra comes to bid farewell,
    But Yarra's lips can never say it!
Her swimming eyes—her bosom's swell—
    The debt she owes you, these must pay it.
She ne'er can speak, though tears can start,
    Her grief, that fate so soon removes you;
But One there is, who reads the heart,
    And well He knows how Yarra loves you!

See, massa, see this sable boy!
    When chill disease had nipp'd his flower,
You came and spoke the word of joy,
    And poured the juice of healing power.
To visit far Jamaica's shore
    Had no kind angel deign'd to move you,
These laughing eyes had laugh'd no more,
    Nor Yarra lived to thank and love you.

Then grieve not, massa, that to view
    Our isle you left your British pleasures:
One tear, which falls in grateful dew,
    Is worth the best of Britain's treasures.
And sure, the thought will bring relief,
    What e'er your fate, wherever rove you,
Your wealth's not given by pain and grief,
    But hands that know, and hearts that love you.

May He, who bade you cross the wave,
    Through care for Afric's sons and daughters;
When round your bark the billows rave,
    In safety guide you through the waters!
By all you love with smiles be met;
    Through life each good man's tongue approve you:
And though far distant, don't forget,
    While Yarra lives, she'll live to love you!

April 3

The trade-winds* which facilitate the passage to Jamaica, effectually prevent the return of vessels by the same road. The common passage is through the Gulf of Florida, but there is another between Cuba and St Domingo, which is at least 1,000 miles nearer. The first, however, affords almost a certainty of reaching Europe in a given time; while you may keep tacking in the attempt to make the windward passage (as it is called) for months together. Last night the wind was so favourable for this attempt, that the captain determined upon risking it. Accordingly he altered his course; and had not done so for more than a few hours, when the wind changed, and became as direct for the Gulf, as till then it had been contrary. The consequence was, that the Gulf passage was fixed once for all, and we are now steering towards it with all our might and main. Besides the distance saved, there was another reason for preferring the windward passage, if it could have been effected. The Gulf of Florida has for some time past been infested by a pirate called Captain Mitchell, who, by all accounts, seems to be of the very worst description. It is not long ago, since, in company with another vessel of his own stamp, he landed on the small settlement of St Andrews,* plundered it completely, and on his departure carried off the governor, whom he kept on board for more than fourteen days, and then hung him at the yard-arm out of mere wanton devilry; and indeed he is said to show no more mercy to any of his prisoners than he did to the poor governor. His companion has been captured and brought into Kingston, and the conquering vessel is gone in search of Captain Mitchell. If it does not fall in with him, and *we* do, I fear that we shall stand but a bad chance; for he has one hundred men on board according to report, while we have not above thirty. However, the captain has harangued them, represented the necessity of their fighting if attacked, as Captain Mitchell is known to spare no one, high or low, and has engaged to give every man five guineas apiece, if a gun should be fired. The sailors promise bravery; whether their promises will prove to be pie-crust,* we must leave to be decided by time and Captain Mitchell. In the mean while, every sail that appears on the horizon is concluded to be this terrible pirate, and every thing is immediately put in readiness for action.

April 4

This day we passed the Caymana islands; but owing to our having always either a contrary wind, or no wind at all, it was not till the 12th that Cuba was visible, nor till the 14th that we reached Cape Florida.

April 15

At noon this day we found ourselves once more sailing on the Atlantic, and bade farewell to the Gulf of Florida without having heard any news of the dreaded Commodore Mitchell. The narrow and dangerous part of this Gulf is about two hundred miles in length, and fifty in breadth, bordered on one side by the coast of Florida, and on the other, first by Cuba, and then by the Bahama Islands, of which the Manilla reef forms the extremity, and which reef also terminates the Gulf. But on both sides of these two hundred miles, at the distance of about four or five miles from the main land, there extends a reef which renders the navigation extremely dangerous. The reef is broken at intervals by large inlets; and the sudden and violent squalls of wind to which the Gulf is subject, so frequently drive vessels into these perilous openings, that it is worth the while of many of the poorer inhabitants of Florida to establish their habitations within the reef, and devote themselves and their small vessels entirely to the occupation of assisting vessels in distress. They are known by the general name of 'wreckers', and are allowed a certain salvage upon such ships as they may rescue. As a proof of the violence of the gales which are occasionally experienced in this Gulf, our captain, about nine years ago, saw the wind suddenly take a vessel (which had unwisely suffered her canvass to stand, while the rest of the ships under convoy had taken theirs down,) and turn her completely over, the sails in the water and the keel uppermost. It happened about four o'clock in the afternoon: the captain and the passengers were at dinner in the cabin; but as she went over very leisurely, they and the crew had time allowed them to escape out of the windows and port-holes, and sustain themselves upon the rigging, till boats from the ships near them could arrive to take them off. As she filled, she gradually sunk, and in a quarter of an hour she had disappeared totally.

April 17

THE FLYING FISH

Bright ocean-bird, alike who sharing
Both elements, could sport the air in,
Or swim the sea, your winged fins wearing
 The rainbow's hues,
Your fate this day full long shall bear in
 Her mind the muse.

In vain for you had nature blended
Two regions, and your powers extended;
Now high you rose, now low descended;
 But folly marred
Those gifts, the bounteous dame intended
 To prove your guard.

A flying fish, could bounds include her?
She winged the deep, if birds pursued her;
She swam the sky, if dolphins viewed her;
 But now what wish
Tempts you to watch yon bright deluder,
 Unthinking fish?

Alas!—a fly above you viewing,
Gay tints his gilded wings imbuing,
You mount; and ah! too far pursuing
 At fancy's call,
Heedless you strike the sails, where ruin
 Awaits your fall.

Your fins, too dry, no longer play you,
And soon those fins no more upstay you;
You drop; and now on deck survey you
 Jack, Tom, and Bill,
Who up may take, and down may lay you,
 As suits their will.

Oh! list my tale, fair maids of Britain!
This subject fain I'd try my wit on,
And show the rock you're apt to split on:
 Then cry not—'Pish!'—
You're all (I'm glad the thought I hit on)
 Just flying fish!

Beauty, does nature's hand bestow it?
It swells your pride, and plain you show it;
Though wealthy cit, and airy poet
    Your charms pursue,
Church—physic—law—you're fair, you know it,
    You'll none, not you!

Age looks too dry, and youth too blooming:
The scholar's face there's too much gloom in;
This man's too dull, *that* too presuming;
    His mouth's too wide!—
For mending, Lord! you think there's room in
    The best, when tried.

In each you find some fault to snarl at,
And wilful seek the sun by starlight;
Till some gay glittering rogue in scarlet,*
    Who lures the eye,
Dazzles poor miss, and then the varlet
    Pretends to fly.

His flight has piqued, his glitter caught her;
And soon her mammy's darling daughter,
Whose eyes have made such mighty slaughter,
    Charm'd by a fop,
Is fairly hit 'twixt wind and water,
    And, miss! you drop!

Then certain fate of fallen lasses,
When short-lived bliss more frail than glass is,
To eyes of all degrees and classes
    Exposed you stand,
And soon your beauty circling passes
    From hand to hand.

In vain your flattering charms display you;
From home and parents far away, you
See former friends with scorn survey you;
    While fools and brutes
May take you up, or down may lay you,
    As humour suits.

Oh! mark, dear girls, the moral story
Of one, who breathes but to adore ye!
Let no rash action mar your glory;
    But when you wish
To catch some coxcomb, place before ye
    The flying fish.

April 20

Two or three years ago, our captain, while his vessel was lying in Black River Bay, for the purpose of loading, was informed by his sailors, that their beef and other provisions frequently disappeared in a very unaccountable manner. However, by setting a strict watch during the night, he soon managed to clear up the mystery: and a negro, who had made his escape from the workhouse, and concealed himself on board among the bags of cotton, was found to be the thief. He was sent back to the workhouse, of which the chain was still about his neck. But another negro had better luck in a similar attempt on board of a different vessel. He contrived to secrete himself in the lower part of it, where the sugar hogsheads are stored, unknown to any one. As soon as the cargo was completed, the planks above it were caulked down, and raised no more till their ship reached Liverpool; when, to the universal astonishment, upon opening the hold, out walked Mungo, in a wretched condition to be sure, but still at least alive, and a freeman* in Great Britain. During his painful voyage, he had subsisted entirely upon sugar, of which he had consumed nearly an hogshead; how he managed for water I could not learn, nor can imagine.

April 23

The old steward, this morning, told one of the sailors, who complained of being ill, that he would get well as soon as he should reach England, and could have plenty of vegetables; 'for,' he said, 'the man had only got a *stomachick* complaint; nothing but just scurvy!'

April 24

Sea Terms.—The *sheets*, a term for various ropes; the *halyards*, ropes which extend the topsails; the *painter*, the rope which fastens the boat to the vessel; the *eight points of the compass*, south, south and by east, south-south east, south east and by east, south-east, east south and by east, east south east, east and by south east. The knowledge of these points is termed 'knowing how to box the compass'.

April 27

Many years ago, a new species of grass was imported into Jamaica, by Mr Vassal, (to whom an estate near my own then belonged), as he said 'for the purpose of feeding his pigs and his book-keepers'. Its seeds being soon scattered about by the birds, it has taken possession of the cane-pieces, whence to eradicate it is an utter impossibility, the roots being as strong as those of ginger, and insinuating themselves under ground to a great extent; so that the only means of preventing it from entirely choking up the canes, is plucking it out with the hand, which is obliged to be done frequently, and has increased the labour of the plantation at least one third. This nuisance, which is called 'Vassal's grass', from its original introducer, has now completely over-run the parish of Westmoreland, has begun to show itself in the neighbouring parishes, and probably in time will get a footing throughout the island. St Thomas's in the East has been inoculated with another self-inflicted plague, under the name of 'the rifle-ant', which was imported for the purpose of eating up the ants of the country; and so to be sure they did, but into the bargain they eat up every thing else which came in their way, a practice in which they persist to this hour; so that it may be doubted whether in Jamaica most execrations are bestowed in the course of the day upon Vassal's grass, the rifle-ants, Sir Charles Price's rats, or the Reporter of the African Society; only that the maledictions uttered against the three first are necessarily local, while the Reporter of the African Society comes in for curses from all quarters.

April 30 (Tuesday)

A whole calendar month has elapsed since our quitting Jamaica, during which the wind has been favourable for something less than four-and-twenty hours; either it has blown precisely from the point on which we wanted to sail, or has been so faint, that we scarcely made one knot an hour. However, on Tuesday last, finding ourselves in the latitude of the 'still-vexed Bermoothes', by way of variety, a sudden squall carried away both our lower stunsails in the morning; and at nine in the evening there came on a gale of wind truly tremendous. The ship pitched and rolled every minute, as if she had been on the point of overturning; the hen-coops floated about the deck, and many of the poultry were found drowned in them the next morning. Just as the last dead-light was putting up, the sea embraced the opportunity of the window being open, to whip itself through, and half filled the after-cabin with water; and in half an hour more a mountain of waves broke over the vessel, and pouring itself through the sky-light, paid the same compliment to the fore-cabin, with which it had already honoured the after one. About four in the morning the storm abated, and then we relapsed into our good old jog-trot pace of a knot an hour. Our passengers consist of a Mrs Walker with her two children, and a sick surgeon of the name of Ashman.

May 5 (Sunday)

We continue to proceed at such a tortoise-pace, that it has been thought advisable to put the crew upon an allowance of water.

May 7

A negro song.—'Me take my cutacoo (i.e. a basket made of matting) and follow him to Lucea, and all for love of my bonny man-O—My bonny man come home, come home! Doctor no do you good. When neger fall into neger hands, buckra doctor no do him good more. Come home, my gold ring, come home!' This is the song of a wife, whose husband had been Obeahed by another woman, in conse-quence of his rejecting her advances. A negro riddle: 'Pretty Miss Nancy was going to market, and she tore her fine yellow gown, and there was not a taylor in all the town who could mend it again.' This is a ripe plantain with a broken skin. The negroes are also very fond of what they call Nancy stories,* part of which is related, and part sung. The heroine of one of them is an old woman named Mamma Luna, who having left a pot boiling in her hut, found it robbed on her return. Her suspicions were divided between two children whom she found at play near her door, and some negroes who had passed that way to market. The children denied the theft positively. It was necessary for the negroes, in order to reach their own estate, to wade through a river at that time almost dry; and on their return, Mammy Luna (who it should seem, was not without some skill in witchcraft) warned them to take care in venturing across the stream, for that the water would infallibly rise and carry away the person who had stolen the contents of her pot; but if the thief would but confess the offence, she engaged that no harm should happen, as she only wanted to exculpate the innocent, and not to punish the guilty. One and all denied the charge, and several crossed the river without fear or danger; but upon the approach of a *belly-woman* to the bank, she was observed to hesitate. 'My neger, my neger,' said Mammy Luna, 'why you stop? me tink, you savee well, who thief me?' This accusation spirited up the woman, who instantly marched into the river, singing as she went (and the woman's part is always chanted frequently in chorus, which the negroes call, 'taking up the sing').

> If da me eat Mammy Luna's pease-O,
> Drowny me water, drowny, drowny!

'My neger, my neger,' cried the old woman, 'me sure now you the thief! me see the water wet you feet. Come back, my neger, come back.' Still on went the woman, and still continued her song of

> If da me eat Mammy Luna's pease, etc.

'My neger, my neger,' repeated Mammy Luna, 'me no want punish you; my pot smell good, and you belly-woman. Come back, my neger, come back; me see now water above your knee!' But the woman was obstinate; she continued to sing and to advance, till she reached the middle of the river's bed, when down came a tremendous flood, swept her away, and she never was heard of more; while Mammy Luna warned the other negroes never to take the property of another; always to tell the truth; and, at least, if they should be betrayed into telling a lie, not to persist in it, otherwise they must expect to perish like their companion. Observe, that a moral is always an indispensable part of a Nancy story. Another is as follows:—'Two sisters had always lived together on the best terms; but, on the death of one of them, the other treated very harshly a little niece, who had been left to her care, and made her a common drudge to herself and her daughter. One day the child having broken a water-jug, was turned out of the house, and ordered not to return till she could bring back as good a one. As she was going along, weeping, she came to a large cotton-tree, under which was sitting an old woman without a head. I suppose this unexpected sight made her gaze rather too earnestly, for the old woman immediately enquired—"Well, my pic-caniny, what you see?" "Oh, mammy," answered the girl, "me no see nothing." "Good child!" said again the old woman; "and good will come to you." Not far distant was a cocoa-tree; and here was another old woman, without any more head than the former one. The same question was asked her, and she failed not to give the same answer which had already met with so good a reception. Still she travelled forwards, and began to feel faint through want of food, when, under a mahogany tree, she not only saw a third old woman, but one who, to her great satisfaction, had got a head between her shoulders. She stopped, and made her best courtesy—"How day, grannie!" "How day, my piccaniny; what matter, you no look well?" "Grannie, me lilly hungry." "My piccaniny, you see that hut, there's rice in the pot, take it, and yam-yamme;* but if you see one black puss, mind you give him him share." The child hastened to profit by the permission; the "one black puss" failed not to make its appearance, and was served first to its portion of rice, after which it departed; and the child had but just finished her meal, when the mistress of the hut entered, and told her that she might help herself to three eggs out of the fowl-house, but that she must not take any of the *talking* ones: perhaps, too, she might find the black puss there, also; but if she did, she was to take no notice of her. Unluckily all the eggs seemed to be as fond of talking as if they had been so many old maids; and the moment that the child entered the fowl-house, there was a cry of "Take *me!* Take *me!*" from all quarters. However she was punctual in her obedience; and although the conversable eggs were remarkably fine and large, she searched about till at length she had collected three little dirty-looking eggs, that had not a word to say for themselves. The old woman now dismissed her guest, bidding her to return home without fear; but not to forget to break one of the eggs under each of the three trees near which she had seen an old woman that morning. The first egg produced a water-jug exactly similar to that which she had broken; out of the second came a whole large sugar estate; and out of the third a splendid equipage, in which she returned to her aunt, delivered up the jug, related that an old woman in a red docker (i.e. petticoat) had made her a great lady, and then departed in triumph to her sugar estate. Stung by envy, the aunt lost no time in sending her own daughter to search for the same good fortune which had befallen her cousin. She found the cotton-tree and the headless old woman, and had the same question addressed to her; but instead of returning the same answer—"What me see?" said she; "me see one old woman without him head!" Now this reply was doubly offensive; it was rude, because it reminded the old lady of what might certainly be considered as a personal defect; and it was dangerous, as, if such a circumstance were to come to the ears of the buckras, it might bring her into trouble, women being seldom known to walk and talk without their heads, indeed, if ever, except by the assistance of Obeah. "Bad child!" cried the old woman; "bad child! and bad will come to you!" Matters were no better managed near the cocoa-tree; and even when she reached the mahogany, although she saw that the old woman had not only got her head on, but had a red docker besides, she could not prevail on herself to say more than a short "How day?" without calling her "grannie". [Among negroes it is almost tantamount to an affront to address by the name, without affixing some term of relationship, such as 'grannie', or 'uncle', or 'cousin'. My Cornwall boy, George, told me one day, that 'Uncle Sully wanted to speak to massa.' 'Why, is Sully your uncle, George?' 'No, massa; me only call him so for honour.'] However, she received the permission to eat rice at the cottage, coupled with the injunction of giving a share to the black puss; an injunction, however, which she totally disregarded, although she scrupled not to assure her hostess that she had suffered puss to eat till she could eat no more. The old lady in the red petticoat seemed to swallow the lie very glibly, and despatched the girl to the fowl-house for three eggs, as she had before done her cousin; but having been cautioned against taking the talking eggs, she conceived that these must needs be the most valuable; and, therefore, made a point of selecting those three which seemed to be the greatest gossips of the whole poultry yard. Then, lest their chattering should betray her disobedience, she thought it best not to return into the hut, and, accordingly, set forward on her return home; but she had not yet reached the mahogany tree, when curiosity induced her to break one of the eggs. To her infinite disappointment it proved to be empty; and she soon found cause to wish that the second had been empty too; for, on her dashing it against the ground, out came an enormous yellow snake, which flew at her with dreadful hissings. Away ran the girl; a fallen bamboo lay in her path; she stumbled over it, and fell. In her fall the third egg was broken; and the old woman without the head immediately popping out of it, told her, that if she had treated her as civilly, and had adhered as closely to the truth as her cousin had done, she would have obtained the same good fortune; but that as she had shown her nothing but rudeness, and told her nothing but lies, she must be contented to carry nothing home but the empty egg-shells. The old woman then jumped upon the yellow snake, galloped away with incredible speed, and never showed her red docker in that part of the island any more.'

May 8*

At breakfast the captain was explaining to me the dangerous consequences of breaking the wheel-rope: two hours afterwards the wheel-rope broke, and round swung the vessel. However, as the accident fortunately took place in the day time, and when the sea was perfectly calm, it was speedily remedied: but this was 'talking of the devil and his imps' with a vengeance.

May 10

During the early part of my outward-bound voyage I was extremely afflicted with sea-sickness; and between eight o'clock on a Monday morning, and twelve on the following Thursday, I actually brought up almost a thousand lines, with rhymes at the end of them. Having nothing better to do at present, I may as well copy them into this book. Composed with such speed, and under such circumstances, I take it for granted that the verses cannot be very good; but let them be ever so bad, I defy any one to be more sick while reading them than the author himself was while writing them. This strange story was found by me in an old Italian book, called 'Il Palagio degli Incanti', in which it was related as a fact, and stated to be taken from the 'Annals of Portugal', an historical work. I will not vouch for the truth of it myself; and, at all events, I earnestly request that no person who may read these verses will ask me 'who the hero really was?' If he does, I shall only return the same answer which the lady gave her husband when, being on the point of shipwreck, he requested her to tell him whether she had really ever wronged his bed? 'My dear,' said she, 'sink or swim, that secret shall go to the grave with me.'

THE ISLE OF DEVILS*
A METRICAL TALE

Should I report this now, would they believe me?
If I should say, I saw such islanders,
Who, though they were of monstrous shape, yet, note,
Their manners were more gentle-kind, than of
Our human generation you shall find
Many; nay, almost any!—

Tempest, Act 3*

I

Speed, Halcyon,* speed, and here construct thy nest:
Brood on these waves, and charm the winds to rest!
No wave should dare to rage, no wind to roar,
Till lands you blooming maid on Lisbon's shore.
That maid, as Venus fair and chaste is she,
When first to dazzled sky and glorying sea
The bursting conch Love's new-born queen exposed,
The fairest pearl that ever shell inclosed.
  While love's fantastic hand had joyed to braid
Her locks with weeds and shells like some sea-maid,
High seated at the stern was Irza seen,
And seemed to rule the tide, as ocean's queen.
Smooth sailed the bark; the sun shone clear and bright;
The glittering billows danced along in light;
While Irza, free from fear, from sorrow free,
Bright as the sun, and buoyant as the sea,
Bade o'er the lute her flying fingers move,
And sang a Spanish lay of Moorish love.

ZAYDE AND ZAYDA
(*From Las Guerras Civiles de Granada*)*

Lo! beneath yon haughty towers,
    Where the young and gallant Zayde
Fondly chides the lingering hours,
    Till they bring his lovely maid.

Evening shades are gathering round him;
    Doubting fear his heart alarms;
But nor doubt nor fear can wound him,
    If he views his lady's charms.

Hark! the window softly telling,
    Zayda comes to bless his sight;
Bright as sun-beams clouds dispelling,
    Mild as Cynthia's* trembling light.

'Dearest, say, to what I'm fated!'
    Cried the Moor, as near he drew:
'Is the tale my page related,
    Loveliest lady, is it true?

'To an ancient lord thy beauty
    Does thy tyrant father doom?
Must my love, the slave of duty,
    Waste in age's arms her bloom?

'If my lot be still to languish,
    Thine, another's bride to be,
Let thy lips pronounce my anguish;
    'Twill be bliss to die by thee!'

Rising sighs her grief discover;
    Fast her tears, while speaking, pour—
'Zayde, my Zayde, our loves are over!
    Zayde, my Zayde, we meet no more!

'Allah knows, I cherished dearly,
    Fondest hopes of being thine!
Allah knows, I grieve sincerely,
    When I those fond hopes resign!

'May some lady, happier, fairer,
    Blest with every charm and grace,
Whose kind friends would grieve to tear her
    From all comfort, fill my place:

'May all pleasures greet your bridal;
    May she give you heart for heart!
Never be she from her idol
    Forced, as I am now, to part!'

'Rumour did not then deceive me!'
    Wild the Moor in anguish cries:
'Then 'tis true! for wealth you leave me!
    Wealth has charms for Zayda's eyes!

'Blind to beauty, cold to pleasure,
    Ozmyn shall my hopes destroy!
Yes; though worthless such a treasure,
    He shall Zayda's charms enjoy!

'Fare thee well! so soon to sever
   Little thought I, when you said,
"Thine it is, and thine for ever
   Shall be Zayda's heart, my Zayde!"'

II

Scarce moved the zephyr's wings, while breathed the song,
And waves in silence bore the bark along.
'Twas Irza sang! Rosalvo at her side
Gazed on his cherub-love, his destined bride,
Felt at each look his soul in softness melt,
Nor wished to feel more bliss than then he felt.
'Gainst the high mast, intent on book and beads,
A reverend abbot leans, and prays, and reads:
Yet oft with secret glance the pair surveys,
Marks how *she* looks, and listens what *he* says.
An idle task! The terms which speak their love
Had served for prayer, and passed unblamed above.
He finds each tender phrase so free from harm,
So pure each thought, each look so chaste though warm,
Still to his book and beads he turns again,
Pleased to have found his guardian care so vain;
While oft a blush of shame his pale cheek wears,
To find his thoughts so much less pure than theirs.
   Oh! they *were* pure! pure as the moon, whose ray
Loves on the shrines of virgin-saints to play;
Pure as the falling snow, ere yet its shower
Bends with its weight its own pale fragile flower.
Not fourteen years were Irza's; nay, 'tis true,
Most maids at twelve know more than Irza knew:
And scarce two more had spread with silken down
Her youthful cousin's cheek of glowing brown.
His tutor sage (in fact, not show, a saint)
Had kept his heart and mind secure from taint.
In liberal arts, in healthful manly sports,
In studies fit for councils, camps, and courts,
His moments found their full and best employ,
Nor left one leisure hour for guilty joy.
Since her blue dove-like eyes six springs had seen,
Immured in cloistered shades had Irza been,
From duties done her sole delight deriven,
And her sole care to please the queen of heaven.
None e'er approached her, save the pure and good:

Her promised spouse; that monk who near them stood;
Her viceroy uncle, and some guardian nun
Were all she e'er had seen by moon or sun.
No amorous forms, by wanton art designed,
Had e'er inflamed her blood, or stained her mind:
No hint in books, no coarse or doubtful phrase
E'er bade her curious thought explore the maze
No glowing dream by memory's pencil drawn
Had e'er profaned her sleep, and made her blush at dawn.
With flowers she decked the virgin mother's shrine,
Nor guessed a wonder made that name divine.
The very love, which lent her looks such fire,
Ne'er raised one blameful thought, nor loose desire;
Like streams of gold, which in alembic roll,
The flames she suffered but refined her soul;
Made it more free from stain, more light from dross,
With brighter lustre, and with softer gloss.
That, which she bore her bridegroom, well might claim
A brother's love, and bear a sister's name:
And e'en where now her lips in playful bliss
Sealed on Rosalvo's eyes a balmy kiss,
Love's highest, dearest grace she meant to show,
Nor thought he more could ask, nor she bestow.

III

From Goa's precious sands to Lisbon's shore,
The viceroy's countless wealth that vessel bore:
In heaps there jewels lay of various dyes,
Ingots of gold, and pearls of wondrous size;
And there (two gems worth all that Cortez won)
He placed his angel niece and only son.
Sebastian sought the Moors! With loyal zeal
Rosalvo cased his youthful limbs in steel;
To die or conquer by his sovereign's side
He came; and with him came his destined bride.
E'en now in Lisbon's court for Irza's hair
Virgins the myrtle's nuptial crown prepare,
And Hymen waves his torch from Cintra's towers,
Hails the dull bark, and chides the slow-winged hours.
Seldom in this bad world two hearts we see
So blest, and meriting so blest to be;
Then oh! ye winds, gently your pinions move,
And speed in safety home the bark of love.

Brood, Halcyon, brood: thy sea-spell chaunt again,
And keep the mirror of the enchanted main,
Where his white wing the exulting tropic* dips,
Calm as their hearts, and smiling as their lips.
    The charm prevails! Hushed are the waves and still;
The expanded sails light favouring zephyrs fill,
Wafting with motion scarce perceived; and now
In rapture Irza from the vessel's prow
Gazed on an isle with verdure gay and bright,
Which seemed (so green it shone in solar light)
An emerald set in silver. Long her eyes
Dwelt on its rocks; and 'Oh! dear friend,' she cries,
And clasps Rosalvo's hand,—'admire with me
Yon isle, which rising crowns the silent sea!
How bold those mossy cliffs, which guard the strand,
Like spires, and domes, and towers in fairy-land!
How green the plains! how balsam-fraught the breeze!
How bend with golden fruit the loaded trees;
While, fluttering midst their boughs in joyful notes,
Myriads of birds attune their warbling throats!
Blooms all the ground with flowers! and mark, oh! mark
That giant palm, whose foliage broad and dark
Plays on the sun-clad rock!—Beneath, a cave
Spreads wide its sparry mouth: while loosely wave
A thousand creepers, dyed with thousand stains,
Whose wreaths enrich the trees, and cloathe the plains.
Dear friend, how blest, if passed my life could be
In that fair isle, with God alone and thee,
Far from the world, from man and fiend secure,
No guilt to harm us, and no vice to lure!
Bright round the virgin's shrine would blush and bloom
That world of flowers, which pour such rich perfume;
And sweet yon caves repeat with mellowing swell
Eve's closing hymn, when chimed the vesper-bell.'
    The pilot heard—'Oh! spring of life,' he cried,
'How bright and beauteous seems the world untried!
I too, like you, in youth's romantic bowers
Dreamt not of wasps in fruit, nor thorns in flowers;
And when on banks of sand the sunbeams shone,
I deemed each sparkling flint a precious stone.
Ah! noble lady, learn, that isle so fair,
The fields all roses, and all balm the air,
That isle is one, where every leaf's a spell,

Where no good thing e'er dwelt, nor e'er shall dwell.
No fisher, forced from home by adverse breeze,
Would slake his thirst from yon infernal trees:
No shipwrecked sailor from the following waves
Would seek a shelter in those haunted caves.
There flock the damned! there Satan reigns, and revels!
And thence yon isle is called "The Isle of Devils!"
Nor think, on rumour's faith this tale is given:
Once, hot in youthful blood, when hell nor heaven
Much claimed my thoughts, (the truth with shame I tell;
Holy St Francis, guard thy votary well!)
In quest of water near that isle I drew:
When lo! such monstrous forms appalled my view,
Such shrieks I heard, sounds all so strange and dread,
That from the strand with shuddering haste I fled,
Plyed as for life my oars, nor backward bent my head.
And though since then hath flown full many a year,
Still sinks my heart, still shake my limbs with fear,
Soon as you awful island meets mine eye!
Cross we our breasts! say, "Ave!" and pass by!'

IV

The isle is past. And still in tranquil pride
Bears the rich bark its treasures o'er the tide.
And now the sun, ere yet his lamp he shrouds,
Stains the pure western sky with crimson clouds:
Now from the sea's last verge he sheds his rays,
And sinks triumphant in a golden blaze.
Still o'er the heavens reflected splendours flow,
Which make the world of waters gleam and glow:
Wide and more wide each billow shines more bright,
Till all the empurpled ocean floats in light.
Soon as fair Irza marked the evening's close,
Grave from her seat the young enthusiast rose,
Told o'er her beads, and when the string was said,
'Ave Maria!' sang the enraptured maid;
Her look so humble, so devout her air,
Each worldly wish appeared so lost in prayer,
All felt, no thought could to her mind be near,
That man her form could see, her voice could hear:
Hushed all the ship!—Each sailor checked his glee,
Clasped his hard hands, and bent his trembling knee;
    And each (as rose that soft mysterious strain,

Best help in trouble, and sweet balm in pain)
Gazed on the maid with mingled awe and fear,
Damp on his cheek perceived the unwonted tear,
Then raised to Heaven his eyes in earnest prayer,
And half believed himself already there.
Low too Rosalvo knelt, nor knew, if now
For Mary's grace, or Irza's, rose his vow.
Scarce e'en the monk forbore to kneel; his child
Fondly he viewed, and sweetly, gravely smiled,
And blessed that God, as swelled each melting note,
Who gave such heavenly powers to human throat!

Melodious strains, oh! speed your flight above
On Neptune's wings, and reach the ear of Love!
Oh! spread thy starry robe, celestial queen,
(For much thine aid she needs!) from ills to screen
Thy virgin-votaress!—Silence holds the deep,
And e'en the helmsman's eyes are sealed by sleep:
Yet mark yon gathering clouds!—the moon is fled!—
Mark too that deathlike stillness, deep and dread!
And hark!—from yon black cloud an awful voice
Pours the wild chaunt, and bids the winds rejoice!

SONG OF THE TEMPEST-FIEND

I marked her!—the pennants, how gaily they streamed!—
    How well was she armed for resistance!
The waves that sustained her, how brightly they beamed
In the sun's setting rays, and the sailors all seemed
    To forget the storm-spirit's existence.

But I marked her!—and now from the clouds I descend!
    My spells to the billows I mutter!
I clap my black pinions! my wand I extend,
In darkness the sky and the ocean to blend,
    And the winds mark the charms which I utter.

Now more and more rapid in eddies I whirl,
    In my voice while the thunder-clap rumbles:
And now the white mountainous waves, as they curl,
I joy o'er the deck of the vessel to hurl,
    And laugh, as she tosses and tumbles.

The crew is alarmed; but the tempest prevails,
    No care from my fury delivers!
Ere there's time for their furling the canvass, the sails
From the top to the bottom I split with my nails,
    And they stream in the blast, rent in shivers!

The sky and the ocean, fierce battle they wage;
   The elements all are in action!
No sailor the storm longer hopes to assuage:
What clamours, what hurry, what oaths, and what rage!
   Oh, brave! what despair, what distraction!

Their heart-strings, they ache, while my ravage they view;
   Each knee 'gainst its fellow is knocking!
My eyes, darting lightnings to dazzle the crew,
Burn and blaze; and those lightnings so forked and so blue
   Make the darkness of midnight more shocking.

The morn to that vessel no succour shall bring!
   Now high o'er the main-mast I hover;
Now I plunge from the sky to the deck with a spring,
And I shatter the mast with one flap of my wing;
   It cracks! and it breaks! and goes over!

Hew away, gallant seamen! fatigue never dread;
   You shall all rest to-night from your labours!
The ocean's wide mantle shall o'er you be spread,
The white bones of mariners pillow your head,
   And the whale and the shark be your neighbours.

For I swoop from aloft, and I blaze, and I burn,
   While my spouts the salt billows are drinking:
And I drive 'gainst the vessel, and beat down the stern,
And pour in a flood, which shall never return,
   And all cry—'She's sinking! she's sinking!'—

The barge?—well remembered!—'tis strong, and 'tis large,
   And will live in the billows' commotion;
But now all my spouts from the clouds I discharge,
And down goes the vessel, and down goes the barge!
   Hurrah! I reign lord of the ocean!

How their shrieks rose in chorus!   Now all is at rest;
   The tempest no longer is brewing!
My dreams by the harm newly done will be blest,
So I'll sleep for a while on a thunder-cloud's breast,
   Then rouze to hurl round me fresh ruin.

V

   Hushed is the storm: the heavens no longer frown;
And o'er that spot, where late the bark went down,
All bright and smiling flows the treacherous wave,
Like sunshine playing on a new-made grave.

Full rose the watery moon: it showed a plank,
To which, all deadly pale, with tresses dank,
And robes of white, on which the sea had flung
Loose wreaths of ocean-flowers, unconscious clung
A fair frail form:—'twas Irza!—to the shore
Each following wave the virgin nearer bore;
And now the mountain surge o'erwhelmed the land,
Then flying left her on the wished-for strand.

　　Soon hope and love of life her powers renew;
Swift tow'rds a cliff she speeds, which towers in view,
Nor waits the wave's return; and now again
Safe on the shore, and rescued from the main,
Prostrate she falls, and thanks the Sire of life,
Whose arm hath snatched her from the billowy strife.
That duty done, she rose, and gazed around:
Mossed are the rocks, and flowers bestrew the ground.
Not distant far, a group of fragrant trees
Bend with their golden fruit. The ocean-breeze
Shakes a gigantic palm, which o'er a cave
Its dark green foliage spreads, and wildly wave
Their blooming wreaths, all starred with midnight dews,
A thousand creeping plants of thousand hues.
Then flashed the dreadful truth on Irza's view!
That cave—those trees—that giant palm she knew!
Then from her lips for ever fled the smile:
—'Mother of God!' she shrieked, 'the Demon-Isle!'—

　　Long on a broken crag she knelt, and prayed,
And wearied every saint for strength and aid;
Then speechless, heedless, senseless lay; when, lo!
Strange mutterings near her roused from torpid woe
Her soul to fresh alarms. Her head she reared,
And near her face an hideous face appeared;
But straight 'twas gone!—In trembling haste she rose,
And saw a ring of monstrous dwarfs inclose
Her rugged couch. Not Teniers'* hand could paint
Forms more grotesque to scare the tempted saint,
Than here, as on they pressed in circling throng,
With gnashing teeth seemed for her blood to long,
And grinned, and glared, and gloated! Quicker grew
Her breath! Death hemmed her round! As yet, 'tis true,
Far off they kept; but soon, more daring grown,
More near they crept, oft sharpening on some stone
Their long crookt claws; and still, as on they came,

They screeched and chattered; and their eyes of flame,
Twinkling and goggling, told, what pleasure grim
'Twould give to rack and rend her limb from limb:
—'Heaven take my soul!' she cried,—when, hark! a moan,
So full, so sad, so strange—not shriek—not groan—
Something scarce earthly—breathed above her head—
'Twas heard, and instant every imp was fled.

What was that sound? What pitying saint from high
Had stooped to save her? Now to heaven her eye
Grateful she raised.   Almighty powers!—a form,
Gigantic as the palm, black as the storm,
All shagged with hair, wild, strange in shape and show,
Towered on the loftiest cliff, and gazed below.
On *her* he gazed, and gazed so fixed, so hard,
Like knights of bronze some hero's tomb who guard.
Bright wreaths of scarlet plumes his temples crowned,
And round his ankles, arms, and wrists were wound
Unnumbered glassy strings of crystals bright,
Corals, and shells, and berries red and white.
On *her* he gazed, and floods of sable fires
Rolled his huge eyes, and spoke his fierce desires,
As on his club, a torn-up lime, he leaned.—
'Help, Heaven!' thought Irza, ''tis the master-fiend!'

Not long he paused: he now with one quick bound
Sprang from the cliff, and lighted on the ground.
Back fled the maid in terror; but her fear
Was needless.   Humbly, slowly crept he near,
Then kissed the earth, his club before her laid,
And of his neck her footstool would have made:
But from his touch she shrank.   He raised his head,
And saw her limbs convulsed, her face all dread,
And felt the cause his presence!   Sad and slow
He rose, resumed his club, and turn'd to go.
Reproachful was his look, but still 'twas kind;
He climb'd the rock, but oft he gazed behind;
He reach'd the cave; one look below he threw;
Plaintive again he moan'd, and with slow steps withdrew.

She is alone; she breathes again!—Fly, fly!—
Ah! wretched girl, too late! with frenzied eye,
(Scarce gone the master-fiend) his imps she sees,
Pour from the rocks, and drop from all the trees
With yell, and squeak, and many a horrid sound,
And form a living fence to hedge her round:

—'Now then,' she cried, 'all's over!—oh! farewell,
Farewell, Rosalvo!' On her knee she fell,
And told her beads with trembling hands.   Yet still
On came the throng; and soon, with wanton skill
(Lured by its coral glow and cross of gold),
One snatch'd her chaplet, nor forsook his hold,
Though hard she struggled: while more bold, more fierce
Another seized her arm, and dared to pierce
With his sharp teeth its snow.   The pure blood stream'd
Fast from the wound, and loud the virgin scream'd;
And strait again was heard that sad strange moan,
And instant all the dwarfs again were flown.

   Scarce conscious that she lived, scarce knowing why,
Half grieved, half grateful, Irza raised her eye:
Still on the rock (not dared he down to spring)
Dark and majestic stood the demon-king;
Then lowly knelt, and raised his arm to wave
An orange bough, and court her to his cave.
Lost are her friends; no help, no hope is nigh;
What can she do, and whither can she fly?
To *him* already twice her life she owes,
And but his presence now restrains her foes.
On wings of flame the sun had left the main;
And peeping from the trees, the imps too plain
Shot darts of rage from their green orbs of sight:
She heard their gibberings, and she mark'd their spite;
And, while they eyed her form, their care she saw
To grind their teeth, and whet each cruel claw.
Demons alike, the monarch-demon's breast
Appear'd least fierce; of ills she chose the best,
Sought, where profaned her coral rosary lay,
Then slowly mounted where he show'd the way.

   Cautious he led her tow'rds his lone abode,
And clear'd each stone that might impede her road.
With pain she trod: she reach'd the cave; but there
No more their weight her wearied limbs could bear.
Exhausted, fainting, anguish, terror, thirst,
Fatigue o'erpower'd her frame: her heart must burst,
Her eyes grow dim!   Sunk on the rock she lies,
And sinking, prays she never more may rise.

VI

Long in this deathlike swoon she lay: at length
Exhausted nature show'd forth all its strength,
And call'd her back to life. Her opening eyes
Beheld a grotto vast in depth and size,
Whose high straight sides forbade all hopes of flight:
The fractured roof gave ample space for light,
Through which in gorgeous guise the day-star shone
On many a lucid shell and brilliant stone.
Through pendent spars and crystals as it falls,
Each beam with rainbow hues adorns the walls,
Gilds all the roof, emblazes all the ground,
And scatters light, and warmth, and splendour round.
Gently on pillowing furs reposed her head;
With many a verdant rush her couch was spread;
A gourd with blushing fruits was near her placed,
Whose scent and colour woo'd alike her taste;
And round her strewn there bloom'd unnumber'd flowers;
Charming her sense with aromatic powers.
One only object chill'd her blood with fear:
Far off removed (but still, alas! too near),
Scarce breathing, lest a breath her sleep might break,
There stood the fiend, and watch'd to see her wake.

In sooth, if credit outward show might crave,
Than Irza, ne'er had nymph an humbler slave.
He watched her every glance; her frown he fear'd;
And if his pains to meet her wish appear'd,
All pains seem'd far o'er-paid, all cares appeased,
And so *she* found but pleasure, *he* was pleased.
One power he claim'd, but claim'd that power alone:
Still, when he left her side, a mass of stone
Barr'd up the grotto, nor allow'd her feet
To pass the limits of her bright retreat.
But when in quest of food not forced to stray,
In Irza's sight he wore the livelong day,
And show'd her living springs and noontide shades,
Spice-breathing groves, and flower-enamell'd glades.
For her he still selects the sweetest roots,
The coolest waters, and the loveliest fruits;
To deck her charms the softest furs he brings,
And plucks their plumage from flamingo wings;
Bids blooming shrubs, to shade her, bend in bowers,
And strews her couch with fragrant herbs and flowers;

While many an ivy-twisted grate restrains
The splendid tenants of the etherial plains.
Then, when she sought her lonesome grot at eve,
And waved her hand, and warn'd him take his leave,
Her will was his: he breathed his plaintive moan,
Gazed one last look, then gently roll'd the stone.

　　Perhaps, such constant care and worship paid,
More fit for angel than for mortal maid,
At length had won her, with more grateful mind
To view his gifts, and pay respect so kind;
But, as her giant-gaoler she esteem'd
Some prince of subterraneous fire, she deem'd
His favours snares, his presents only given
To shake her faith, and steal her soul from heaven.
Still then her loathing heart remain'd the same,
Joy'd when he went, and shudder'd when he came;
And when to share his fruits by hunger press'd,
Ever she bless'd them first, and cross'd her breast.

VII

　　Days creep—months roll—no change! no hope! and oh!
Rosalvo lost, what hope can life bestow?
Death, only death, she feels, can end her woes;
Nor doubts death soon will bring that wish'd-for close;
For now her frame, her mind, confess disease;
Painful and faint she moves; her tottering knees
Scarce bear her weight; and oft, by humour moved,
Her sickening soul now loathes what late it loved.
It comes! the moment comes! Her frame is rent
By sharper pangs; her nerves, too strongly bent,
Seem on the point to break; her forehead burns;
Her curdling blood is fire, is ice by turns;
Her heart-strings crack!—'This hour is sure her last!'
Fainting she sinks, and hopes 'that hour is pass'd!'

　　Wake, Irza, wake to grief most strange and deep!
Still must thou live, and only live to weep!
Oh, lift thine aching head, thy languid eyes,
And mark what hideous stranger near thee lies.
'Guard me, all blessed saints!'—A monster child
Press'd her green couch; and, as it grimly smiled,
Its shaggy limbs, and eyes of sable fire,
Betray'd the crime, and claim'd its hellish sire!

　　'Lost! lost! My soul is lost!' the affrighted maid,

(Ah, now a maid no more!) distracted, said,
And wrung her hands. Those words she scarce could say;
Yet *would* have pray'd, but fear'd 'twas sin to pray!
That only veil which ne'er admits a stain,
The veil of ignorance, was rent in twain:
In spite of virtue, cloisters, horror, youth,
She knows, and feels, and shudders at the truth.
That night accursed!—In death-like swoon she slept—
Then near her couch if that dark demon crept—
Oh! where was then her guardian angel's aid?
And would not heavenly Mary save her maid?
Deprived of sense—betray'd by place and time—
Then was she doom'd to share the unconscious crime?
Debased, deflower'd, and stamp'd a wretch for life,
A monster's mother, and a demon's wife?
    Oh! at that thought her soul what passions tear!
How then she beats her breast, how rends her hair,
And bids, with golden ringlets scatter'd round,
Stream all the air, and glitter all the ground!
Sighs, sobs, and shrieks the place of words supply;
And still she mourns to live, and prays to die,
Till heart denies to groan, and eyes to flow;
Then, on her couch of rushes sinking low,
Languid and lost she lies, in silent, senseless woe.
    What lifts her burning head? why opes her eye?
What makes her blood run back? A faint shrill cry!
Too well, alas! that cry was understood:
The monster pined for want, and claim'd its food.
Then in her heart what rival passions strove!
How shrinks disgust, how yearns maternal love!
Now to its life her feelings she prefers;
Now Nature wakes, and makes her own—''Tis hers!'
Loathing its sight, she melts to hear its cries,
And, while she yields the breast, averts her eyes.
    Not so the demon-sire: the child he raised,
He kiss'd it—danced it—nursed it—knelt, and gazed,
Till joyful tears gush'd forth, and dimm'd his sight:
Scarce Irza's self was view'd with more delight.
He held it tow'rds her—horror seem'd to thrill
Her frame. He sigh'd, and clasp'd it closer still.
Once, and but once, his features wrath express'd:
He saw her shudder, as it drain'd her breast:

And, while reproach half mingled with his moan,
Snatch'd it from her's, and press'd it to his own.

VIII

Three months had pass'd; still lived the monster-brat:
Its sire had sought the wood; alone she sat:
She sheds no tears—no tears are left to shed;
Unmoisten'd burn her eyes—her heart seems dead—
Her form seems marble. Lo! from far the sound
Of music steals, and fills the caves around.
She starts!—scarce breathing—trembling;—'Oh! for wings!'—
But hark! for nearer now the minstrel sings.

SONG

I

When summer smiled on Goa's bowers
  They seem'd so fair;
All light the skies, all bloom the flowers,
  All balm the air!
The mock-bird swell'd his amorous lay,
  Soft, sweet, and clear;
And all was beauteous, all was gay,
  For *she* was near.

2

But now the skies in vain are bright
  With Summer's glow;
The pea-dove's call to Love's delight
  Augments my woe;
And blushing roses vainly bloom;
  Their charms are fled,
And all is sadness, all is gloom,
  For *she* is dead!

3

Now o'er thy head, my virgin love,
  Rolls Ocean's wave;
But fond regret, in myrtle grove,
  Hath dug thy grave.
Sweet flowers, around her vacant urn
  Your wreaths I'll twine,
And pray such flowers, ere Spring's return,
  May garland mine!

'He! he!'—That love-lorn dirge—that heavenly tongue—
That air, *she* taught him; 'twas Rosalvo sung!
Rosalvo, whom the waves, which wreck'd their bark,
Had borne, like her, for purpose sad and dark,
To that strange isle; though far remote the beach
From Irza's grot, which Fate ordain'd him reach;
But now at length his curious search explores
These rude and slippery crags and distant shores;
And while he treads his dangerous path, the strains
Which Irza taught him soothe her lover's pains.
    She hears his steps, and hears them soon more near;
And loud she cries—'Rosalvo! Hear! oh, hear!
'Tis Irza calls!' and now more quick, more nigh,
Down the steep rock she hears those footsteps fly.
Again she calls. He comes! He searches round;
He seeks the gate, and soon the gate is found.
Alas! 'tis found in vain! the marble guard
Seem'd rooted as the rock, whose mouth it barr'd.
Yet still, with labouring nerves, to move the stone
He struggles. Now he stops; and, hark! A groan!
But one; then all was hush'd! A sickening chill
Seized Irza's heart, and seem'd her veins to thrill.
Fain had she call'd her youthful bridegroom's name;
Her tongue Fear's numbing fingers seem'd to lame.
Footsteps!—more near they drew:—slow rolled the stone—
The infernal gaoler came, but came alone.
With anxious glance his eye explored the cell;
But when it fix'd on her's, abash'd it fell.
He knelt, and seem'd to fear her frown. He bore
His club. 'Twas splash'd with brains! 'twas wet with gore!
She fear'd—she guess'd—she rush'd—she ran—she flew,—
Nor dared the fiend her frantic course pursue.
'Rosalvo! speak! Rosalvo!'   Shrill, yet sweet,
She wakes the echoes. What obstructs her feet?
'Tis he, the young, the good, the kind, the fair!
As some frail lily, which the passing share[1]
Or wanton boy hath wounded, droops its head,
Its whiteness wither'd, and its fragrance fled,
Low lay the youth, and from his temple's wound
With precious streams bedew'd the ensanguin'd ground.

---

[1] 'Purpureus veluti flos,' etc.—Virgil.*

Then reason fled its seat! She shrieks! she raves!
And fills with hideous yells the ocean caves;
Rends her bright locks, and laughs to see them fly,
And bids them seek Rosalvo in the sky.
To dig his grave she fiercely ploughs the ground,
Loud shrieks his name, nor feels the flints that wound
Her bosom's globes, and stain their snow with gore,
As wild she dashes down, and beats in rage the floor.

 Now fail her strength, her spirits; mute she sits,
Silent and sad; then laughs and sings by fits.
A statue now she seems, or one just dead,
Her looks all gloom, her eyes two balls of lead:
Then simply smiles, and chaunts, with idiot glee,
'Ave Maria! Benedicite!'
Till, Nature's powers revived by rest, again
The fury passions riot in her brain,
And all is rage, revenge, and helpless, hopeless pain.

IX

 Days, weeks, months pass. Time came with slow relief;
But still at length it came. No more her grief
Disturbs her brain: she knows 'that groan was his!'
And fully feels herself the wretch she is.
She rises: towards the grotto's mouth she goes,
Nor dares the fiend her wandering steps oppose.
She seeks the spot on which Rosalvo fell,
On which he died! She knows that spot too well!
But, lo! no corse was there! All smooth and green
A velvet turf o'erstrewn with flowers was seen,
And fenced with roses. 'Oh! whose pious care
Hath deck'd this grave? Hear, gracious Heaven, his prayer,
When most he needs!' While thus in doubt she stands,
She marks the fiend's approach. His ebon hands
Sustain'd a gourd of flowers of various hue;
He pour'd them, kiss'd the turf, and straight withdrew.

 Hither each morn his blooming gifts he bore,
Smooth'd the green sod, and strew'd it o'er and o'er.
Hither, each morn, came Irza; on those flowers
She wept, she pray'd, she sang away her hours.
So mourns the nightingale on poplar spray,[1]

---

[1] 'Qualis populeâ,' etc.—Virgil.*

Her callow brood by shepherds borne away,
Weeps all the night, and from her green retreat
Fills the wide groves with warblings sad as sweet.

X

    And still fresh woes succeed. She feels again
Mysterious pangs, nor doubts her cause of pain.
Too sure, while lost in maniac state she lay,
Her sense, her wits, her feeling all away,
The fiend once more had seized the unguarded hour
To force her weakness, and abuse his power.
Again Lucina* came. That new-born cry,
Shuddering, again she heard; her fearful eye
Wander'd around awhile, nor dared to stay.
'There, there he lies! my child!' With fresh essay
Once more she turn'd. But when at length her sight
Dwelt on its face, her wonder—her delight—
Can ne'er by tongue be told, by fancy guess'd!
Frantic she caught, she kiss'd, and lull'd him on her breast.
    Oh! who can paint how Irza loved that child!
Grieved when he moan'd, and smiled whene'er he smiled!
His dimpled arm soft on the rushes lay;
Through his fine skin the blood was seen to play;
That skin than down of swans more smooth and white;
Nor e'er shone summer sky so blue and bright,
As shone the eyes of that same cherub elf;
In small the model of her beauteous self.
The scant gold locks which gilt his ivory brow,
Were sun-beams gleaming on a globe of snow;
And on his coral lips the red which stood,
Shamed the first rose, whose milk was Paphia's* blood.
By fairy-thefts since nurses were beguiled,
Never stole fairy yet a lovelier child!
In Nature's costlier charms no babe array'd,
At length a mother's fears and throes repaid:
Not when Lucina first in myrtle grove,
To Beauty's kiss presented new-born Love;
And while, with wond'ring eyes, the immortal boy
Imbibed new light, and pour'd ecstatic joy:
He kiss'd and drain'd by turns her fragrant breast,
Till amorous ring-doves coo'd the god to rest.
    Mothers may love as much, but never more,
Nor e'er did mother love so well before,

As Irza loved that child! Her sable lord
Mark'd well that love; and now, to health restored,
He felt her child to home would chain her feet,
Nor roll'd the stone to close her lone retreat.
Still, when he went, he with him bore away
That fav'rite babe, nor fear'd she far would stray.
Arm'd with his club, she now might safely rove
Through verdant vale, or weep in shadowy grove;
For soon the dwarfs were used to bear her sight,
Knew that dread club, nor dared indulge their spite.
Still from afar off looks of rage they cast,
And shrilly squeal'd and clamour'd as she pass'd;
But by their flight when near she came, 'twas seen,
They own'd allegiance, and confess'd their queen.

XI

One morn her savage lord, in quest of food,
Forsook the cave, and sought th' adjacent wood;
And as her darling boy he with him bore,
Irza, unwatch'd, might pace the sounding shore.
Listless and slow she moved, and climb'd with pain
A tow'ring cliff, which beetled o'er the main.
Now three full years had flown, since Irza's eye
Had dwelt on human form, and since reply
From human tongue had blest her ear. 'Tis true,
Throned on a rock, which spread before her view
The sea's wide-stretching plains, she once descried
A gallant vessel plough the neighbouring tide.
By cries to draw it near she long essay'd,
And oft a palm-bough waved in sign for aid:
But all her cries and all her signs were vain;
On sail'd the bark, nor e'er return'd again!
On that same rock she sat, and eyed the wave,
And wish'd she there had found her wat'ry grave!
Fain had she sought one then, plunged from the steep,
And buried all her suff'rings in the deep;
But faith alike and reason bade her shun
That wish, nor break a thread which God had spun.
Hark!—was it fancy?—hark again!—the shores
Echo the sound of fast approaching oars.
Oh! how she gazed!—a barge (by friars 'twas mann'd)
Cut the smooth waves, and sought the rocky strand.
Soon (while his wither'd hands a crosier hold,

All rich with gems, and rough with sculptured gold),
Landing alone, a reverend monk appear'd:—
His jewell'd cross—his flowing silver beard—
'Tis he!—'tis he!'—swift down the steep she flies,
Falls at the stranger's feet, and frantic cries,
Down her pale cheek while tears imploring roll,
'Help, father abbot! save me! save my soul!'
'Twas he indeed! that bark which ne'er return'd,
Well on the cliff her fair wild form discern'd,
But deem'd some island-fiend had spread a snare
To lure them with a form so wild and fair.
Yet oft in Lisbon would those seamen tell,
How angled for their souls the prince of hell;
And warmly paint, their leisure to beguile,
The fallen angel of th' enchanted isle.
At length this wonder reach'd the abbot's ear,
And prompt affection made the wonder clear:—
''Twas Irza! shipwreck'd Irza! none but she
So heav'nly fair, so lonely lost could be!'
Straight he prepares anew that sea to brave,
Which once already seem'd to yawn his grave;
Nor ask, how chanced it that he reach'd the shore:
'Twas through a miracle and nothing more.
Whether on monkish frock as safe rode he,
As night-hags skim in sieves o'er Norway's sea;*
Or like Arion* plough'd the wat'ry plain,
Horsed on some monster of the astonish'd main,
Some shark, some whale, some kraken, some sea-cow—
St Francis saved him, and it boots not how.
And now again the saint his priest survey'd,
From waves and winds imploring heavenly aid;
Resolved for Irza's sake to brave the worst
Which fate could offer on that isle accurst.
      Far off his ship was anchor'd; on that strand
Not India's wealth could make a layman land!
Therefore with none but monks he mann'd his barge,
Which bore of beads and bells a sacred charge;
Whole heaps of relics lent by Cintra's nuns,
And holy water (blest at Rome) by tons!
      His toils were all o'erpaid! he saw again
His fav'rite child, and kindly soothed her pain;
And while her tale he heard, oft dropp'd a tear,
And sign'd his beard-swept breast in awe and fear:

Then bade her speed the friendly bark to gain,
And fly the infernal monarch's green domain;
Nor yield her tyrant time to cast a spell,
And rouse to cross her flight the powers of hell.
　　Then first from Irza's cheek the glow of red,
By hope of rescue raised, grew faint, and fled;
Trembling she nam'd her cherub-boy, confess'd
A mother's fondness fill'd his mother's breast;
Described how fair he look'd, how sweet he smiled,
And fear'd her flight might quite destroy her child.
Then rose the abbot's ire—'Oh, guilty care!'
Frowning, he cried, and shook his hoary hair:
'Fair is the imp! and shall he therefore breathe
To win new subjects for the realms beneath?
The fiends most dangerous are those spirits bright,
Who toil for hell, and show like sons of light;
And still when Satan spreads his subtlest snares,
The baits are azure eyes, the lines are golden hairs.
Name thou the brat no more! To Cintra's walls
Fly, where thy footsteps mild repentance calls.
I'll hear no plaint! kneel not! I'm deaf to prayer!
Swift, brethren, to the barge this maniac bear;
Speed! speed!—no tears!—no struggling!—no delay!
Row, brethren, row, and waft us swift away!'

XII

　　The monks obeyed. Then, then in Irza's soul
What various passions raged, and mock'd control!
Now how she mourn'd, now how she wept for joy,
How loathed the sire, and how adored the boy!
The barge is gain'd; they row. When, lo! from high
Her ear again receives that well-known cry,
That sad, strange moan! she starts, and lifts her eye.
There, on a rock which fenced the strand, once more
She saw her demon-husband stand: he bore
Her beauteous babe; and, while he view'd the barge,
Keen anguish seem'd each feature to enlarge,
And shake each giant limb. With piteous air
His arms he spread, his hands he clasp'd in prayer;
Knelt, wept, and while his eye-balls seem'd to burn,
Oft show'd the child, and woo'd her to return.
His suit the monks disdain; the barge recedes;
More humbly now he kneels, more earnest pleads.

But when he found no tears their courses delay,
And still the boat pursued its watery way;
Then, 'gainst his grief and rage no longer proof,
He gnash'd his teeth, he stamp'd his iron hoof,
Whirl'd the boy wildly round and round his head,
Dash'd it against the rocks, and howling fled.

    Loud shrieks the mother! changed to stone she stands,
And silent lifts to heav'n her clay-cold hands:
Then, sinking down, stretch'd on the deck she lies,
Hid her pale face, and closed her aching eyes.
But hark! why shout the monks?—'Again,' they said,
'Again the demon comes!' with desperate dread
Starts the poor wretch, and lifts her anguish'd head.
Yes! there the infant-murderer stood once more,
But now far different were the looks he wore.
No bending knee, no suppliant glance was seen,
Proud was his port, and stern and fierce his mien.
His blood-stain'd eye-balls glared with vengeful ire;
His spreading nostrils seem'd to snort out fire.
Swiftly from crag to crag he following sprung,
While round his neck his shaggy offspring clung;
And now, like some dark tow'r, erect he stood,
Where the last rock hung frowning o'er the flood:—

    'Look! look!' he seem'd to say, with action wild,
'Look, mother, look! this babe is still your child!
With him as me all social bonds you break,
Scorn'd and detested for his father's sake:
My love, my service only wrought disdain,
And nature fed his heart from yours in vain!
Then go, Ingrate, far o'er the ocean go,
Consign your friend, your child to endless woe!
Renounce us! hate us! pleased, your course pursue,
And break their hearts who lived alone for you!'
His eyes, which flash'd red fire—his arms spread wide,
Her child raised high to heaven—too plain implied,
Such were his thoughts, though nature speech denied.
And now with eager glance the deep he view'd,
And now the barge with savage howl pursued;
Then to his lips his infant wildly press'd,
And fondly, fiercely, clasp'd it to his breast:
Three piteous moans, three hideous yells he gave,
Plunged headlong from the rock, and made the sea his grave.

XIII

Where, screen'd by orange groves and myrtle bowers,
Saint-favour'd Cintra rears her gothic towers;
A nun there dwells, most holy, sad, and fair,
Her only business penance, fasts, and prayer;
Her only joy with flowers the shrines to dress,
Weep with the suff'ring, and relieve distress.
A poor lay-sister she; yet golden rain
Showers from her hand to glad each barren plain:
In other eyes she lights up joy, but ne'er
Those eyes of hers were seen a smile to wear:
From other breasts she plucks the thorn of grief,
But feels, her own admits of no relief.
Where age and sickness count the hours by groans,
Uncall'd, she comes to hear and hush their moans.
There, ever humble, watchful, patient, kind,
No nauseous task, no servile care declined,
O'er the sick couch, all day, all night she hangs,
Till health or death relieves the sufferer's pangs.
No thanks she takes, no praise from man receives,
Her duty done, the rest to God she leaves;
But only when her care redeems a life,
Parting she says—'Pray for a demon's wife!'
With blessings still, whene'er that nun they view,
The young, the aged her sainted steps pursue,
And cry, with bended knee and suppliant air,
'Sister of mercy, name us in thy prayer!'
With beads the night, in gracious acts the day,
So wore her youth, so wears her age away.
Now cease, my lay! thy mournful task is o'er;
Irza, farewell! I wake thy lute no more.

XIV

'Was such her fate? and did her days thus creep
So sad, so slow, till came the long last sleep?
And did for this her hands with roses twine
The Saviour's altars and the Virgin's shrine?
Pure, beauteous, rich, did all these blessings tend,
But from the world in prime of life to send
This gifted maid, in prayer to waste her hours,
And weep a fancied crime in cloister'd bowers?'
    Oh, blind to fate! perhaps that fancied crime

Which bade her quit the world in youthful prime,
Snatch'd her from paths, where beauty, wealth, and fame
Had proved but snares to load her soul with shame,
And spared her pangs from wilful guilt which flow,
The only serious ills that man can know!
Ah! what avails it, since they ne'er can last,
If gay or sad our span of days be past?
Pray, mortals, pray, in sickness or in pain,
Not long nor blest to live, but pure from stain.
A life of pleasure, and a life of woe,
When both are past, the difference who can show?
But all can tell, how wide apart in price
A life of virtue, and a life of vice.

Then still, sad Irza, tread your thorny way,
Since life must end, and merits ne'er decay.
Wounded past hope, still prize the pleasure pure,
To heal those hearts which yet can hope a cure;
Nor doubt, the soul which joys in noble deeds
Shall reap a rich reward when most it needs.
When comes that day to conscious guilt so dread,
Angels unseen shall bathe your burning head:
The prayers of orphans fan with balmy breath,
And widow's blessings drown the threats of death;
Each sigh your pity hush'd shall swelling rise
In loud hosannas when you mount the skies;
And every tear on earth to sorrow given,
Be precious pearls to wreathe your brows in heaven!

May 17

Piansi i riposi di quest' umil vita,
*E sospirai la mia perduta pace!**

I regret the loss of our dead calm and our crawling pace of a knot and a half an hour; for during the last four days we have had nothing but gales and squalls, mountainous waves, the vessel rolling and pitching incessantly, and the sea perpetually pouring in at the windows and down through the hatchway. Into the bargain, we are now sufficiently towards the north to find the weather perishingly cold, and we have neither wood nor coals enough on board to allow a fire for the cabin. But, among all our inconveniences, that which is the most intolerable undoubtedly arises from the sick apothecary. It seems that his complaint is the consequence of dram-drinking, which has affected his liver. Since his coming on board, he has continued to indulge his taste; and growing worse (as might be expected), he has now thought proper to put himself in a state of salivation: the consequence is, that what with the mercury and what with the man, aided by the concomitant effluvia of our cargo of sugar, rum, and coffee, for a combination of villanous smells, Falstaff's buckbasket* was nothing to the cabin of the Sir Godfrey Webster. I could almost fancy myself Slawkenbergius's Don Diego* just returned from the Promontory of Noses, and that I had exchanged my snub for a proboscis; so much do all my other senses appear to be absorbed in that of smelling, and so completely do I seem to myself to be nose all over. As to the poor apothecary, his mercury annoys us without any signs as yet of its benefiting himself. He grows worse daily, and I greatly doubt his ever reaching England.

May 19 (Sunday)

I have not been able to ascertain exactly the negro notions concerning the *Duppy*; indeed, I believe that his character and qualities vary in different parts of the country. At first, I thought that the term Duppy meant neither more nor less than a ghost; but sometimes he is spoken of as 'the Duppy', as if there were but one, and then he seems to answer to the devil. Sometimes he is a kind of malicious spirit, who haunts burying-grounds (like the Arabian gouls), and delights in playing tricks to those who may pass that way. On other occasions, he seems to be a supernatural attendant on the practitioners of Obeah, in the shape of some animal, as familiar imps are supposed to belong to our English witches; and this latter is the part assigned to him in the following 'Nancy-story':—

'Sarah Winyan was scarcely ten years old, when her mother died, and bequeathed to her considerable property. Her father was already dead; and the guardianship of the child devolved upon his sister, who had always resided in the same house, and who was her only surviving relation. Her mother, indeed, had left two sons by a former husband, but they lived at some distance in the wood, and seldom came to see their mother; chiefly from a rooted aversion to this aunt; who, although from interested motives she stooped to flatter her sister-in-law, was haughty, ill-natured, and even suspected of Obeahism, from the occasional visits of an enormous black dog, whom she called Tiger, and whom she never failed to feed and caress with marked distinction. In case of Sarah's death, the aunt, in right of her brother, was the heiress of his property. She was determined to remove this obstacle to her wishes; and after treating her for some time with harshness and even cruelty, she one night took occasion to quarrel with her for some trifling fault, and fairly turned her out of doors. The poor girl seated herself on a stone near the house, and endeavoured to beguile the time by singing—

> Ho–day poor me, O!
> Poor me, Sarah Winyan, O!
> They call me neger, neger!
> They call me Sarah Winyan, O!

But her song was soon interrupted by a loud rushing among the bushes; and the growling which accompanied it announced the approach of the dreaded Tiger. She endeavoured to secure herself against his attacks by climbing a tree: but it seems that Tiger had not been suspected of Obeahism without reason; for he immediately growled out an assurance to the girl, that come down she must and should! Her aunt, he said, had made her over to him by contract, and had turned her out of doors that night for the express purpose of giving him an opportunity of carrying her away. If she would descend from the tree, and follow him willingly to his own den to wait upon him, he engaged to do her no harm; but if she refused to do this, he threatened to gnaw down the tree without loss of time, and tear her into a thousand pieces. His long sharp teeth, which he gnashed occasionally during the above speech, appeared perfectly adequate to the execution of his menaces, and Sarah judged it most prudent to obey his commands. But as she followed Tiger into the wood, she took care to resume her song of

> Ho–day, poor me, O!

in hopes that some one passing near them might hear her name, and come to her rescue. Tiger, however, was aware of this, and positively forbad her singing. However, she contrived every now and then to loiter behind; and when she thought him out of hearing, her

> Ho–day! poor me, O!

began again; although she was compelled to sing in so low a voice, through fear of her four-footed master, that she had but faint hopes of its reaching any ear but her own. Such was, indeed, the event, and Tiger conveyed her to his den without molestation. In the meanwhile, her two half-brothers had heard of their mother's death, and soon arrived at the house to enquire what was become of Sarah. The aunt received them with every appearance of welcome; told them that grief for the loss of her only surviving parent had already carried her niece to the grave, which she showed them in her garden; and acted her part so well, that the youths departed perfectly satisfied of the decease of their sister. But while passing through the wood on their return, they heard some one singing, but in so low a tone that it was impossible to distinguish the words. As this part of the wood was the most unfrequented, they were surprised to find any one concealed there. Curiosity induced them to draw nearer, and they soon could make out the

> Ho-day! poor me, O!
> Poor me, Sarah Winyan, O!

There needed no more to induce them to hasten onwards; and upon advancing deeper into the thicket, they found themselves at the mouth of a large cavern in a rock. A fire was burning within it; and by its light they perceived their sister seated on a heap of stones, and weeping, while she chanted her melancholy ditty in a low voice, and supported on her lap the head of the formidable Tiger. This was a precaution which he always took when inclined to sleep, lest she should escape; and she had taken advantage of his slumbers to resume her song in as low a tone as her fears of waking him would allow. She saw her brothers at the mouth of the cave: the youngest fortunately had a gun with him, and he made signs that Sarah should disengage herself from Tiger if possible. It was long before she could summon up courage enough to make the attempt; but at length, with fear and trembling, and moving with the utmost caution, she managed to slip a log of wood between her knees and the frightful head, and at length drew herself away without waking him. She then crept softly out of the cavern, while the youngest brother crept as softly into it: the monster's head still reposed upon the block of wood; in a moment it was blown into a thousand pieces; and the brothers, afterwards cutting the body into four parts, laid one in each quarter of the wood.'

From that time only were dogs brought into subjection to men; and the inhabitants of Jamaica would never have been able to subdue those ferocious animals, if Tiger had not been killed and quartered by Sarah Winyan's brothers. As to the aunt, she received the punishment which she merited, but I cannot remember what it was exactly. Probably, the brothers killed and quartered *her* as well as her four-footed ally: or, perhaps, she was turned into a wild beast, and supplied the vacancy left by Tiger, as was the case with the celebrated Zingha, queen of Angola;* who, although she embraced Christianity on her death-bed, and died according to the most orthodox forms of the Romish religion, still had conducted herself in such a manner while alive, that shortly after her decease, the kingdom being ravaged by a hyena, her subjects could not be persuaded but that the soul of this most Christian queen had transmigrated into the body of the hyena. Yet this was surely doing the hyena great injustice; for she, at least, had never been in the habit of composing ointments by pounding little children in a mortar with her own hands; an amusement which Zingha had introduced at the court of Angola. It took surprisingly; shortly, no woman thought her toilette completed, unless she had used some of this ointment. Pounding children became all the rage; and ladies who aspired to be the leaders of fashion, pounded their own.

May 20

EPIGRAM—(From the French)

'Whose can that little monster be?
  Its parents really claim one's pity!'
'Madam, that child belongs to me.'—
  'Well, I protest, she's vastly pretty!'

May 21

The weather gets no better, the apothecary gets no worse, and both are as foul and as disagreeable as they can well be. As to the man, it is wonderful that he is still alive, for he has swallowed nothing for the last three weeks except drams and laudanum. He drinks, and he stinks, and he does nothing else earthly or celestial. The quantity of spirits which he pours down his throat incessantly should, of itself, be sufficient to finish him; but he seems to have accustomed himself to drams, as Mithridates used himself to poisons, till his stomach is completely proof against them; or like the Scythian princess, who was fed upon ratsbane pap from her infancy, for the express purpose of one day or other poisoning Alexander in her embraces; and who arrived at such perfection, that although the venom did no harm to her own constitution, she killed a condemned criminal with a single kiss. The consequence was, that hemp fell fifty per cent, and Jack Ketch's nose was put out of joint completely; for the devil a culprit of any pretensions to taste could be found in all Scythia, who could be prevailed upon to be executed except by her royal highness's own lips. I am afraid this story is not strictly historical, and that we should look for it in vain in Quintus Curtius.*

May 23

A gale of wind began to show itself on Monday night; it has continued to blow ever since with increasing violence, and is now become very serious. The captain says that he never experienced weather so severe at this season: this is only my usual luck. Certainly nothing can be more disagreeable than a ship on these occasions. The sea breaks over the vessel every minute, and it is really something awful to see the waves raised into the air by the force of the gale, hovering for a while over the ship, and then coming down upon us swop, to inundate every thing below deck as well as upon it. The wind is piercingly cold; the floors and walls are perpetually streaming. But a fire is quite out of the question; and, indeed, at one time to-day, our eating appeared to be out of the question too; for at four o'clock the cook sent us word, that the sea put the kitchen-fire out as fast as he could light it; that he was almost frozen, having been for the last eight hours up to his waist in water; and that we must make up our minds to get no dinner to-day. However, the steward coaxed him, and encouraged him, and poured spirits down his throat, and at last a dinner of some kind was put upon the table; but it had not been there ten minutes, before a tremendous sea poured itself down the companion stairs and through the hatchway, set every thing on the table afloat, deluged the cabin, ducked most of the company, and drove us all into the other room. I was lucky enough to escape with only a sprinkling; but Mrs Walker was soaked through from head to foot. We can only cross the cabin by creeping along by the sides as if we were so many cats. Walking the deck, even for the sailors, is absolutely out of the question; and the little cabin-boy has so fairly given up the attempt, that he goes crawling about upon all fours. Even our Spanish mastiff, Flora, finds it impossible to keep her four legs upon deck. Every five minutes up they all go, away rolls the dog over and over; and when she gets up again, shakes her ears, and howls in a tone of the most piteous astonishment.

May 24

Though the gale was itself sufficiently serious, its effects at first were ludicrous enough; but yesterday it produced a consequence truly shocking and alarming. Edward Sadler, the second mate, was at breakfast in the steerage: the boatswain had been cutting some beef with a large case-knife, which he had afterwards put down upon the chest on which they were sitting: a sudden heel of the ship threw them all to the other side of the cabin: the knife fell with its haft against the ladder; and poor Edward falling against it, at least three inches of the blade were forced into his right side. The wound was dressed without the loss of a moment; but, from its depth, the jaggedness of the weapon with which it was made, and from a pain which immediately afterwards seized the poor fellow in his chest, the apothecary thinks that his recovery is very improbable: he says that the liver is certainly perforated, and so probably are the lungs. If the latter have escaped, it must have been only by the breadth of a hair. Every one in the ship is distressed beyond measure at this accident, for the young man is a universal favourite. He is but just one and twenty, good-looking, with manners much superior to his station; and so unusually steady, as well as active, that if Providence grants him life, he cannot fail to raise himself in his profession.

May 25

Edward complains no longer of the pain in his chest; he sleeps well, eats enough, has no fever, and every symptom is so favourable, that Dr Ashman encourages us to hope that he has received no material injury. Our ship-carpenter has always appeared to be the sulkiest and surliest of sea-bears: yet, on the day of Edward's accident, he passed every minute that he could command by the side of his sofa, kneeling, and praying, and watching him as if he had been his son; and every now and then wiping away his 'own tears' with the dirtiest of all possible pocket-handkerchiefs. So that what Goldsmith said of Dr Johnson may be applied to this old man: 'He has nothing of a bear but his skin.' After tearing every sail in the ship into shivers, and being as disagreeable as ever it could be, the gale has at length abated. Yesterday it was a storm, and we were going to Ireland, Lisbon, Brest—in short, every where except to England; to-day, it is a dead calm, and we are going nowhere at all.

May 26 (Sunday)

The gale has returned with increased violence, and we are once more at our old trade of dead lights; however, for this time, the wind, at least, is in our favour.

May 28

The wounded mate is so much recovered as to come upon deck for a few hours to-day, and may now be considered as completely out of danger; although Dr Ashman is positive (from his difficulty of breathing at first, and the subsequent pain in his chest) that his lungs must actually have been wounded, however slightly. We are now nearly abreast of Scilly; we fell in with several Scilly boats to-day, from whom we obtained a very acceptable supply of fish, vegetables, and newspapers.

May 29

An African Nancy-story.—'The headman (*i.e.* the king) of a large district in Africa, in one of his tours, visited a young nobleman, to whom he lost a considerable sum at play. On his departure he loaded his host with caresses, and insisted on his coming in person to receive payment at court; but his pretended kindness had not deceived the nurse of the young man. She told him, that the headman was certainly incensed against him for having conquered him at play, and meant to do him some injury; that having been so positively ordered to come to court, he could not avoid obeying; but she advised him to take the river-road, where, at a particular hour, he would find the king's youngest and favourite daughter bathing; and she instructed him how to behave. The youth reached the river, and concealed himself, till he saw the princess enter the stream alone; but when she thought fit to regain the bank, she found herself extremely embarrassed.—"Ho-day! what is become of my clothes? ho-day! who has stolen my clothes? ho-day! if any one will bring me back my clothes, I promise that no harm shall happen to him this day—O!"—This was the cue for which the youth had been instructed to wait. "Here are your clothes, missy!" said he, stepping from his concealment: "a rogue had stolen them, while you were bathing; but I took them from him, and have brought them back."—"Well, young man, I will keep my promise to you. You are going to court, I know; and I know also, that the headman will chop off your head, unless at first sight you can tell him which of his three daughters is the youngest. Now I am she; and in order that you may not mistake, I will take care to make a sign; and then do not you fail to pitch upon me." The young man assured her, that, having once seen her, he never could possibly mistake her for any other, and then set forwards with a lightened heart. The headman received him very graciously, feasted him with magnificence, and told him that he would present him to his three daughters, only that there was a slight rule respecting them to which he must conform. Whoever could not point out which was the youngest, must immediately lose his head. The young man kissed the ground in obedience, the door opened, and in walked three little black dogs. Now, then, the necessity of the precaution taken by the princess was evident; the youth looked at the dogs earnestly; something induced the headman to turn away his eyes for a moment, and in that moment one of the dogs lifted up its fore paw. "This," cried the youth—"this is your youngest daughter;"—and instantly the dogs vanished, and three young women appeared in their stead. The headman was equally surprised and incensed; but concealing his rage, he professed the more pleasure at that discovery; because, in consequence, the law of that country obliged him to give his youngest daughter in marriage to the person who should recognise her; and he charged his future son-in-law to return in a week, when he should receive his bride. But his feigned caresses could no longer deceive the young man: as it was evident that the headman practised

Obeah, he did not dare to disobey him; and knew that to escape by flight would be unavailing. It was, therefore, with melancholy forebodings that he set out for court on the appointed day; and (according to the advice of his old nurse) he failed not to take the road which led by the river. The princess came again to bathe; her clothes again vanished; she had again recourse to her "Ho-day! what is become of my clothes?" and on hearing the same promise of protection, the youth again made his appearance. "Here are your clothes, missy," said he; "the wind had blown them away to a great distance; I found them hanging upon the bushes, and have brought them back to you." Probably the princess thought it rather singular, that whenever her petticoats were missing, the same person should always happen to be in the way to find them: however, as he was remarkably handsome, she kept her thoughts to herself, swallowed the story like so much butter, and assured him of her protection. "My father," said she, "will again ask you which is the youngest daughter; and as he suspects me of having assisted you before, he threatens to chop off *my* head instead of yours, should I disobey him a second time. He will, therefore, watch me too closely to allow of my making any sign to you; but still I will contrive something to distinguish me from my sisters; and do you examine us narrowly till you find it." As she had foretold, the headman no sooner saw his destined son-in-law enter, than he told him that he should immediately receive his bride; but that if he did not immediately point her out, the laws of the kingdom sentenced him to lose his head. Upon which the door opened, and in walked three large black cats, so exactly similar in every respect, that it was utterly impossible to distinguish one from the other. The youth was at length on the point of giving up the attempt in despair, when it struck him, that each of the cats had a slight thread passed round its neck; and that while the threads of two were scarlet, that of the third was blue. "*This* is your youngest daughter"; cried he, snatching up the cat with the blue thread. The headman was utterly at a loss to conceive by what means he had made the discovery; but could not deny the fact, for there stood the princesses in their own shape. He therefore affected to be greatly pleased, gave him his bride, and made a great feast, which was followed by a ball; but in the midst of it the princess whispered her lover to follow her silently into the garden. Here she told him, that an old Obeah woman, who had been her father's nurse, had warned him, that if his youngest daughter should live to see the day after her wedding, he would lose his power and his life together; that she, therefore, was sure of his intending to destroy both herself and her bridegroom that night in their sleep; but that, being aware of all these circumstances, she had watched him so narrowly as to get possession of some of his magical secrets, which might possibly enable her to counteract his cruel designs. She then gathered a rose, picked up a pebble, filled a small phial with water from a rivulet; and thus provided, she and her lover betook themselves to flight upon a couple of the swiftest steeds in her father's stables. It was midnight before the headman missed them: his rage was excessive; and immediately mounting his great horse, Dandy, he set forwards in pursuit of the lovers. Now Dandy galloped at the rate of ten miles a minute. The princess was soon aware of her pursuer: without loss of time she pulled the rose to pieces, scattered the leaves behind her, and had the satisfaction of seeing them instantly grow up into a wood of briars, so strong and so thickly planted, that Dandy vainly attempted to force his way through them. But, alas! this fence was but of a very perishable nature. In the time that it would have taken to wither its parent rose-leaves, the briars withered away; and Dandy was soon able to trample them down, while he continued his pursuit. Now, then, the pebble was thrown in his passage; it burst into forty pieces, and every piece in a minute became a rock as lofty as the Andes. But the Andes themselves would have offered no insurmountable obstacles to Dandy, who bounded from precipice to precipice; and the lovers and the headman could once more clearly distinguish each other by the first beams of the rising sun. The headman roared, and threatened, and brandished a monstrous sabre; Dandy tore up the ground as he ran, neighed louder than thunder, and gained upon the fugitives every moment. Despair left the princess no choice, and she violently dashed her phial upon the ground. Instantly the water which it contained swelled itself into a tremendous torrent, which carried away every thing before it,—rocks, trees, and houses; and "the horse and his rider" were carried away among the rest.— "*Hic finis Priami fatorum!*"* There was an end of the headman and Dandy! The princess then returned to court, where she raised a strong party for herself; seized her two sisters, who were no better than their father, and had assisted him in his witchcraft; and having put them and all their partisans to death by a summary mode of proceeding, she established herself and her husband on the throne as headman and headwoman. It was from this time that *all* the kings of Africa have been uniformly mild and benevolent sovereigns. Till then they were all tyrants, and tyrants they would all still have continued, if this virtuous princess had not changed the face of things by drowning her father, strangling her two sisters, and chopping off the heads of two or three dozen of her nearest and dearest relations.'

It seems to be an indispensable requisite for a Nancy-story, that it should contain a witch, or a duppy, or, in short, some marvellous personage or other. It is a kind of '*pièce à machines*'.* But the creole slaves are very fond of another species of tale, which they call 'Neger-tricks', and which bear the same relation to a Nancy-story which a farce does to a tragedy. The following is a specimen:—

A Neger-trick.—'A man who had two wives divided his provision-grounds into two parts, and proposed that each of the women should cultivate one half. They were ready to do their proper share, but insisted that the husband should at least take his third of the work. However, when they were to set out, the man was taken so ill, that he found it impossible to move; he quite roared with pain, and complained bitterly of a large lump which had formed itself on his cheek during the night. The wives did what they could to relieve him, but in vain; they boiled a negro-pot for him, but he was too ill to swallow a morsel: and at length they were obliged to leave him, and go to take care of the provision-grounds. As soon as they were gone, the husband became perfectly well, emptied the contents of the pot with great appetite, and enjoyed himself in ease and indolence till evening, when he saw his wives returning; and immediately he became worse than ever. One of the women was quite shocked to see the size to which the lump had increased during her absence: she begged to examine it; but although she barely touched it with the tip of her finger as gingerly as possible, it was so tender that the fellow screamed with agony. Unluckily, the other woman's manners were by no means so delicate; and seizing him forcibly by the head to examine it, she undesignedly happened to hit him a great knock on the jaw, and, lo and behold! out flew a large lime, which he had crammed into it. Upon which both his wives fell upon him like two furies; beat him out of the house; and whenever afterwards he begged them to go to the provision-grounds, they told him that he had got no lime in his mouth *then*, and obliged him from that time forwards to do the whole work himself.'

A negro was brought to England; and the first point shown him being the chalky cliffs of Dover, 'O ki!' he said; 'me know now what makes the buckras all so white!'

May 29

We once more saw the 'Lizard', the first point of England; and, indeed, it was full time that we should. Besides that our provisions were nearly exhausted by the length of the voyage, our crew was in a great measure composed of fellows of the most worthless description; and the captain lately discovered that some of them had contrived to break a secret passage into the hold, where they had broached the rum-casks, and had already passed several nights in drinking, with lighted candles: a single spark would have been sufficient to blow us all up to the moon!

June 1 (Saturday)

We took our river pilot on board; and on Wednesday, the 5th, we reached Gravesend. I went on shore at nine in the morning; and here I conclude my Jamaica Journal.

1817

November 5 (Wednesday)

I left London, and embarked for Jamaica on board the same vessel, commanded by the same captain, which conveyed me thither in 1815. We did not reach the Downs till Sunday, the 9th, after experiencing in our passage a severe gale of wind, which broke the bowsprit of a vessel in our sight, but did no mischief to ourselves. On arriving in the Downs, we found all the flags lowered half way down the masts, which is a signal of mourning; and we now learnt, that, in a few hours after giving birth to a still-born son, the Princess Charlotte of Wales had expired at half-past two on Thursday morning.

November 16 (Sunday)

'Peaceful slumbering on the ocean.' Here we are still in the Downs, and no symptoms of a probable removal. Indeed, when we weighed our anchor at Gravesend, it gave us a broad hint that there was no occasion as yet for giving ourselves the trouble; for, before it could be got on board, the cable was suffered to slip, and down again went the anchor, carrying along with it one of the men who happened to be standing upon it at the moment, and who in consequence went plump to the bottom. Luckily, the fellow could swim; so in a few minutes he was on board again, and no harm done.

November 19

We resumed our voyage with fine weather, but wind so perverse, that we did not arrive in sight of Portsmouth till the evening of the 21st. A pilot came on board, and conveyed us into Spithead.

November 22

This morning we quitted Portsmouth, and this evening we returned to it. The Needle rocks were already in sight, when the wind failed completely. There was no getting through the passage, and the dread of a gale would not admit of our remaining in so dangerous a roadstead. So we had nothing for it but to follow Mad Bess's example, and 'return to the place whence we came'.* We are now anchored upon the Motherbank, about two miles from Ryde in the Isle of Wight.

November 30 (Sunday)

Edward, the young man who was so dangerously wounded on our return from my former voyage to Jamaica, is now chief mate of the vessel, and feels no other inconvenience from his accident, except a slight difficulty in raising his left arm above his head.

December 1 (Monday)

Here we are, still riding at anchor, with no better consolation than that of Klopstock's half-devil Abadonna;* the consciousness that others are deeper damned than ourselves. Another ship belonging to the same proprietor left the West India Docks three weeks before us, and here she is still rocking cheek by jowl alongside of us,

> One writ with us in sour misfortune's book.*

December 3

A tolerably fair breeze at length enabled us to set sail once more.

December 24 (Wednesday)

I had often heard talk of 'a hell upon earth', and now I have a perfect idea of 'a hell upon water'. It must be precisely our vessel during the last three weeks. At twelve at noon upon the 4th, we passed Plymouth, and were actually in sight of the Lizard point, when the wind suddenly became completely foul, and drove us back into the Channel. It continued to strengthen gradually but rapidly; and by the time that night arrived, we had a violent gale, which blew incessantly till the middle of Sunday, the 7th, when we were glad to find ourselves once more in sight of Plymouth, and took advantage of a temporary abatement of the wind to seek refuge in the Sound. Here, however, we soon found that we had but little reason to rejoice at the change of our situation. The Sound was already crowded with vessels of all descriptions; and as we arrived so late, the only mooring still unoccupied, placed us so near the rocks on one side, and another vessel astern, that the captain confessed that he should feel considerable anxiety if the gale should return with its former violence. So, of course, about eleven at night, the gale *did* return; not, indeed, with its former violence, but with its violence increased tenfold; and once we were in very imminent danger from our ship's swinging round by a sudden squall, and narrowly escaping coming in contact with the ship astern, which had not, it seems, allowed itself sufficient cable. Luckily, we just missed her; and our cables (for both our anchors were down) being new and good, we rode out the storm without driving, or meeting with any accident whatever. The next day was squally; and in spite of the Breakwater, the rocking of the ship from the violent agitation of the waves by the late stormy weather was almost insupportable. However, on the 9th, the wind took a more favourable turn, though in so slight a degree, that the pilot expressed great doubts whether it would last long to do us any service. But the captain felt his situation in Plymouth Sound so uneasy, that he resolved at least to make the attempt; and so we crept once more into the Channel. In a few hours the breeze strengthened; about midnight we passed the lights upon the Lizard, and the next morning England was at length out of sight. This cessation of ill luck soon proved to be only '*reculer pour mieux sauter*'.* The gale, it seems, had only stopped to take breath: about four in the afternoon of Wednesday, the wind began to rise again; and from that time till the middle of the 23d it blew a complete storm day and night, with only an occasional intermission of two or three hours at a time. Every one in the ship declared that they had never before experienced so obstinate a persecution of severe weather: every rag of sail was obliged to be taken down; the sea was blown up into mountains, and poured itself over the deck repeatedly. The noise was dreadful; and as it lasted incessantly, to sleep was impossible; and I passed ten nights, one after another, without closing my eyes; so that the pain in the nerves of them at length became almost intolerable, and I began to be seriously afraid of going blind. In truth, the captain could not well have pitched upon a set of passengers worse calculated to undergo the trial of a passage so rough. As for myself, my brain is so weak, that the continuation of any violent noise makes me absolutely light-headed;

and a pop-gun going off suddenly is quite sufficient at any time to set every nerve shaking, from the crown of my head to the sole of my foot. Then we had a young lady who was ready to die of sea-sickness, and an old one who was little better through fright; and I had an Italian servant* into the bargain, who was as sick as the young lady, and as frightened as the old one. The poor fellow had never been on board a ship before; and with every crack which the vessel gave, he thought that to be sure, she was splitting right in half. The sailors, too, appeared to be quite knocked up from the unremitting fatigue to which they were subjected by the perseverance of this dreadful weather. Several of them were ill; and one poor fellow actually died, and was committed to the ocean. To make matters still worse, during the first week the wind was as foul as it could blow; and we passed it in running backwards and forwards, without advancing a step towards our object; till at length every drop of my very small stock of patience was exhausted, and I could no longer resist suggesting our returning to port, rather than continue buffeting about in the chops of the Channel, so much to the damage of the ship, and all contained in her. A change of wind, however, gave a complete answer to this proposal. On Thursday it became favourable as to the prosecution of our voyage, but its fury continued unabated till the evening of the 23d. It then gradually died away, and left us becalmed before the island of Madeira; where we are now rolling backwards and forwards, in sight of its capital, Funchal, on the 24th of December, being seven immortal weeks since my departure from Gravesend. The evening sun is now very brilliant, and shines full upon the island, the rocks of which are finely broken; the height of the mountains cause their tops to be lost in the clouds; the sides are covered with plantations of vines and forests of cedars; and the white edifices of Funchal, built upon the very edge of the shore, have a truly picturesque appearance. We are now riding between the island and an isolated group of inaccessible rocks called 'the Deserters';[1] and the effect of the scene altogether is beautiful in the extreme.

[1] The Dezertas.

December 25 (Christmas-day)

A light breeze sprang up in the night, and this morning Madeira was no longer visible.

December 31 (Wednesday)

We are now in the latitudes commonly known by the name of 'the Horse Latitudes'.* During the union of America and Great Britain, great numbers of horses used to be exported from the latter; and the winds in these latitudes are so capricious, squally, and troublesome in every respect,—now a gale, and then a dead calm—now a fair wind, and the next moment a foul one,—that more horses used to die in this portion of the passage than during all the remainder of it. These latitudes from thence obtained their present appellation, and extend from 29° to 25° or 24½°.

1818—January 1 (Thursday)

On this day, on my former voyage, I landed at Black River. Now we are still at some distance from the line, and are told that we cannot expect to reach Jamaica in less than three weeks, even with favourable breezes; and our breezes at present are *not* favourable. Nothing but light winds, or else dead calms; two knots an hour, and obliged to be thankful even for that! A-weel! this is weary work!

January 17 (Saturday)

On Saturday, the 3d, we managed to crawl over the line, and had no sooner got to the other side of it, than we were completely becalmed; and even when we resumed our progress, it was at such a pace that a careless observer might have been pardoned for mistaking our manner of moving for a downright standing still. Day after day produced nothing better for us than baffling winds, so light that we scarcely made two miles an hour, and so variable that the sails could be scarcely set in one direction before it became necessary to shift them to another; while the monotony of our voyage was only broken by an occasional thunder-storm, the catching a stray dolphin now and then, watching a shoal of flying fish, or guessing at the complexion of the corsairs on board some vessel in the offing: for the Caribbean Sea is now dabbed all over like a painter's pallette with corsairs of all colours,—black from St Domingo, brown from Carthagena, white from North America, and pea-green from the Cape de Verd Islands. On the afternoon of the 4th, one of them was at no very great distance from us; she hoisted English colours on seeing ours; but there was little doubt, from her peculiar construction and general appearance, that she was a privateer from Carthagena. She set her head towards us, and seemed to be doing her best to come to a nearer acquaintance; but the same calm which hindered us from bravely running away from her, hindered her also from reaching us, although at nightfall she seemed to have gained upon us. In the night we had a violent thunder-storm, and the next morning she was not to be seen. Still we continued to creep and to crawl, grumbling and growling, till on Sunday, the 11th, the long-looked-for wind came at last. The trade wind began to blow with all its might and main right in the vessel's poop, and sent us forward at the rate of 200 miles a day. We passed between Deseada and Antigua in the night of the 15th; and, on the 16th, the rising sun showed us the island mountain of Montserrat; the sight of which was scarcely less agreeable to our eyes from its romantic beauty, than welcome from its giving us the assurance that our long-winded voyage is at length drawing towards its termination.

January 19

Yesterday morning a miniature shark chose to swallow the bait laid for dolphins, and in consequence soon made his appearance upon deck. It was a very young one, not above three feet long. I ordered a slice of him to be broiled at dinner, but he was by no means so good as a dolphin; but still there was nothing in the taste so unpalatable as to prevent the flesh from being very acceptable in the absence of more delicate food. In the evening, a bird, about the size of a large pigeon, flew on board, and was knocked down by the mate with his hat. It was sulky, and would not be persuaded to eat any thing that was offered, so he was suffered to escape this morning. It was beautifully shaped, with a swallow-tail, wings of an extraordinary spread in comparison with the smallness of the body, a long sharp bill, black and polished like a piece of jet, and eyes remarkably large and brilliant. The head, back, and outside of the wings were of a brownish slate colour, and the rest of his feathers of the most dazzling whiteness. It is called a crab-catcher.

January 24 (Saturday)

Our favourable breeze lasted till Tuesday, the 20th; when, having brought us half way between St Domingo and Jamaica, it died away, and we dragged on at the rate of two or three miles an hour till Thursday afternoon, which placed us at the mouth of Black River. If we had arrived one hour earlier, we could have immediately entered the harbour; but, with our usual good fortune, we were just too late for the daylight. We therefore did not drop anchor till two o'clock on Friday, before the town of Black River; and on Saturday morning, at four o'clock, I embarked in the ship's cutter* for Savannah la Mar. Every one assured us that we could not fail to have a favourable sea-breeze the whole way, and that we should be on land by eight: instead of which, what little wind there was veered round from one point of the compass to the other with the most indefatigable caprice; and we were not on shore till eleven. Here I found Mr T. Hill, who luckily had his phaëton* ready, in which he immediately conveyed me once more to my own estate. The accounts of the general behaviour of my negroes is reasonably good, and they all express themselves satisfied with their situation and their superintendents. Yet, among upwards of three hundred and thirty negroes, and with a greater number of females than men, in spite of all indulgences and inducements, not more than twelve or thirteen children have been added annually to the list of the births. On the other hand, this last season has been generally unhealthy all over the island, and more particularly so in my parish; so that I have lost several negroes, some of them young, strong, and valuable labourers in every respect; and in consequence, my sum total is rather diminished than increased since my last visit. I had been so positively assured that the custom of plunging negro infants, immediately upon their being born, into a tub of cold water, infallibly preserved them from the danger of tetanus, that, on leaving Jamaica, I had ordered this practice to be adopted uniformly. The negro mothers, however, took a prejudice against it into their heads, and have been so obstinate in their opposition, that it was thought inadvisable to attempt the enforcing this regulation. From this and other causes I have lost several infants; but I am told, that on other estates in the neighbourhood they have been still more unfortunate in regard to their children; and one was named to me, on which sixteen were carried off in the course of three days.

January 26 (Monday)

The joy of the negroes on my return was quite sufficiently vociferous, and they were allowed to-day for a holiday. They set themselves to singing and dancing yesterday, in order to lose no time; and to show their gratitude for the indulgence, not one of the five pen-keepers chose to go to their watch last night; the consequence was, that the cattle made their escape, and got into one of my very best cane-pieces. The alarm was given; my own servants and some of the head people had grace enough to run down to the scene of action; but the greatest part remained quietly in the negro-houses, beating the gumby-drum, and singing their joy for my arrival with the whole strength of their lungs, but without thinking it in the least necessary to move so much as a finger-joint in my service. The cattle were at length replaced in their pen, but not till the cane-piece had been ruined irretrievably. Such is negro gratitude, and such my reward for all that I have suffered on ship-board. To be sure, as yet there could not be a more ill-starred expedition than my present one. I only learned, yesterday, that before making the island of Madeira an Algerine corsair was actually in sight, and near enough to discern the turbans of the crew; but we lost each other through the violence of the gale.

January 29

There is a popular negro song, the burden of which is,—

> 'Take him to the Gulley! Take him to the Gulley!
> But bringee back the frock and board.'—
> 'Oh! massa, massa! me no deadee yet!'—
> 'Take him to the Gulley! Take him to the Gulley!'
>   'Carry him along!'

This alludes to a transaction which took place some thirty years ago, on an estate in this neighbourhood, called Spring-Garden; the owner of which (I think the name was Bedward) is quoted as the cruellest proprietor that ever disgraced Jamaica. It was his constant practice, whenever a sick negro was pronounced incurable, to order the poor wretch to be carried to a solitary vale upon his estate, called the Gulley, where he was thrown down, and abandoned to his fate; which fate was generally to be half devoured by the john-crows, before death had put an end to his sufferings. By this proceeding the avaricious owner avoided the expence of maintaining the slave during his last illness; and in order that he might be as little a loser as possible, he always enjoined the negro bearers of the dying man to strip him naked before leaving the Gulley, and not to forget to bring back his frock and the board on which he had been carried down. One poor creature, while in the act of being removed, screamed out most piteously 'that he was not dead yet'; and implored not to be left to perish in the Gulley in a manner so horrible. His cries had no effect upon his master, but operated so forcibly on the less marble hearts of his fellow-slaves, that in the night some of them removed him back to the negro village privately, and nursed him there with so much care, that he recovered, and left the estate unquestioned and undiscovered. Unluckily, one day the master was passing through Kingston, when, on turning the corner of a street suddenly, he found himself face to face with the negro, whom he had supposed long ago to have been picked to the bones in the Gulley of Spring-Garden. He immediately seized him, claimed him as his slave, and ordered his attendants to convey him to his house; but the fellow's cries attracted a crowd round them, before he could be dragged away. He related his melancholy story, and the singular manner in which he had recovered his life and liberty; and the public indignation was so forcibly excited by the shocking tale, that Mr Bedward was glad to save himself from being torn to pieces by a precipitate retreat from Kingston, and never ventured to advance his claim to the negro a second time.

January 30

A man has been tried, at Kingston, for cruel treatment of a Sambo female slave, called Amey. She had no friends to support her cause, nor any other evidence to prove her assertions, than the apparent truth of her statement, and the marks of having been branded in five different places. The result was, that the master received a most severe reprimand for his inhuman conduct, and was sentenced to close confinement for six months, while the slave, in consequence of her sufferings, was restored to the full enjoyment of her freedom.

It appears to me than nothing could afford so much relief to the negroes, under the existing system of Jamaica, as the substituting the labour of animals for that of slaves in agriculture, where-ever such a measure is practicable. On leaving the island, I impressed this wish of mine upon the minds of my agents with all my power; but the only result has been the creating a very considerable additional expense in the purchase of ploughs, oxen, and farming implements; the awkwardness, and still more the obstinacy, of the few negroes, whose services were indispensable, was not to be overcome: they broke plough after plough, and ruined beast after beast, till the attempt was abandoned in despair. However, it was made without the most essential ingredient for success, the superintendence of an English ploughman; and such of the ploughs as were of cast-iron could not be repaired when once broken, and therefore ought not to have been adopted; but I am told, that in several other parts of the island the plough has been introduced, and completely successful. Another of my farming speculations answered no better: this was to improve the breed of cattle in the county, for which purpose Lord Holland and myself sent over four of the finest bulls that could be procured in England. One of them got a trifling hurt in its passage from the vessel to land; but the remaining three were deposited in their respective pens without the least apparent damage. They were taken all possible care of, houses appropriated to shelter them from the sun and rain, and, in short, no means of preserving their health was neglected. Yet, shortly after their arrival in Jamaica, they evidently began to decline; their blood was converted into urine; they paid no sort of attention to the cows, who were confined in the same paddock; and at the end of a fortnight not one was in existence, two having died upon the same day. The injured one, having been bled the most copiously in consequence of its hurt, was that which survived the longest.

January 31

Some days ago, a negro woman, who has lost four children, and has always been a most affectionate mother, brought the fifth, a remarkably fine infant, into the hospital. She complained of its having caught cold, a fever, and so on; but nothing administered was of use, and its manner of breathing made the doctor enquire, whether the child had not had a fall? The mother denied this most positively, and her fondness for the infant admitted no doubt of her veracity. Still the child grew worse and worse; still the question about the fall was repeated, and as constantly denied; until luckily being made in the presence of a new-comer, the latter immediately exclaimed, 'that to her certain knowledge the infant had really had a fall, for that the mother having fastened it behind her back, the knot of the handkerchief had slipped, and the baby had fallen upon the floor.'—'It is false,' answered the mother: 'the child did not fall; for when the knot slipped, I had time to catch it by the foot, and so I saved it from falling, just as its head struck against the ground.' Fear of being blamed as having occasioned the baby's illness through her own carelessness had induced her to adopt this equivocation, and its life had nearly been the sacrifice of her duplicity. A proper mode of treatment was now adopted without loss of time; their beneficial effect was immediately visible, and the poor little negro is now recovering rapidly. But certainly there is no folly and imprudence like unto negro folly and imprudence. One of my best disposed and most sensible Eboes has had a violent fever lately, but was so nearly well as to be put upon a course of bark.* On Wednesday morning a son of his died of dirt-eating,*—a practice which neither severity nor indulgence could induce him to discontinue. The boy was buried that night according to African customs, accompanied with dancing, singing, drinking, eating, and riot of all kinds; and the father, although the kindest-hearted negro on my estate, and remarkably fond of his children, danced and drank to such an excess, that I found him on the following morning in a raging fever, and worse than he was when he first entered the hospital. I had warned him against the consequences of the funeral, reminded him of the dangerous malady from which he was but just recovering, and he had promised solemnly to be upon his guard; and such was the manner in which he performed his promise.

February 1 (Sunday)

During my former visit to Jamaica I had interceded in behalf of a negro belonging to Greenwich estate, named Aberdeen, who had run away repeatedly, but who attributed his misconduct to the decay of his health, which rendered him unable to work as well as formerly, and to the fear of consequent punishment for not having performed the tasks assigned to him. The fellow while he spoke to me had tears running down his cheeks, looked feeble and ill, and indeed seemed to be quite heart-broken. On my speaking to the attorney, he readily promised to enquire into the truth of the man's statement, and to take care that he should be only allotted such labour as his strength might be fully equal to. This morning he came over to see me, and so altered, that I could scarcely believe him to be the same man. He was cleanly dressed, walked with his head erect, and his eyes sparkled, and his mouth grinned from ear to ear, while he told me, that during my absence every thing had gone well with him, nobody had 'put upon him'; he had been tasked no more than suited his strength; as much as he was able to do, he had done willingly, and had never run away. Even his asthma was better in consequence of the depression being removed from his spirits. So, he said, as soon as he heard of my return, he thought it his duty to come over and show himself to me, and tell me that he was well, and contented, and behaving properly; for that 'to be sure, if massa no speak that good word for me to trustee, me no livee now; me good, massa!' Gratitude made him absolutely eloquent: his whole manner, and the strong expression of his countenance, put his sincerity out of all doubt, and I never saw a man seem to feel more truly thankful. All negroes, therefore, are not absolutely without some remembrance of kindness shown them; and indeed I ought not in justice to my own people to allow myself to forget, that when I sent a reward to those who had roused themselves to drive the cattle out of my canes the other night, there was considerable difficulty in persuading them to accept the money: they sent me word, 'that as they were all well treated on the estate, it was their business to take care that no mischief was done to it, and that they did not deserve to be rewarded for having merely done their duty by me.' Nor was it till after they had received repeated orders from me, that their delicacy could be overcome, and themselves persuaded to pocket the affront and the *maccaroni*.

February 2

One of the deadliest poisons used by the negroes (and a great variety is perfectly well known to most of them) is prepared from the root of the cassava. Its juice being expressed and allowed to ferment, a small worm is generated, the substance of which being received into the stomach is of a nature the most pernicious. A small portion of this worm is concealed under one of the thumb-nails, which are suffered to grow long for this purpose; then when the negro has contrived to persuade his intended victim to eat or drink with him, he takes an opportunity, while handing to him a dish or cup, to let the worm fall, which never fails to destroy the person who swallows it. Another means of destruction is to be found (as I am assured) in almost every negro garden throughout the island: it is the arsenic bean, neither useful for food nor ornamental in its appearance; nor can the negroes, when questioned, give any reason for affording it a place in their gardens; yet there it is always to be seen. The alligator's liver also possesses deleterious properties; and the gall is said to be still more dangerous.

February 3

On Friday I was made to observe, in the hospital, a remarkably fine young negro, about twenty-two years of age, stout and strong, and whom every one praised for his numerous good qualities, and particularly for his affection for his mother, and the services which he rendered her. He complained of a little fever, and a slight pain in his side. On Saturday he left the hospital, and intended to go to his provision grounds, among the mountains, on Sunday morning; but, as he complained of a pain in his head, his mother prevented his going, and obliged him to return to the hospital in the evening. On Monday he was seized with fainting fits, lost his speech and power of motion, and this morning I was awaked by the shrieks and lamentations of the poor mother, who, on coming to the hospital to enquire for her son, found, that in spite of all possible care and exertions on the part of his medical attendants, he had just expired. Whether it be the climate not agreeing with their African blood (genuine or inherited), or whether it be from some defect in their general formation, certainly negroes seem to hold their lives upon a very precarious tenure. Nicholas, John Fuller, and others of my best and most favoured workmen, the very servants, too, in my own house, are perpetually falling ill with little fevers, or colds, or pains in the head or limbs. However, the season is universally allowed to have been peculiarly unhealthy for negroes; and, indeed, even for white people, the deaths on board the shipping having been unusually numerous this year. As to the barracks, which are scarcely a couple of miles distant from my estate, there the yellow fever has established itself, and, as I hear, is committing terrible ravages, particularly among the wives of the soldiers.——This morning several negro-mothers, belonging to Friendship and Greenwich,* came to complain to their attorney (who happened to be at my house) that the overseer obliged them to wean their children too soon.* Some of these children were above twenty-two months old, and none under eighteen; but, in order to retain the leisure and other indulgences annexed to the condition of nursing-mothers, the female negroes, by their own good-will, would never wean their offspring at all. Of course their demands were rejected, and they went home in high discontent; one of them, indeed, not scrupling to declare aloud, and with a peculiar emphasis and manner, that if the child should be put into the weaning-house against her will, the attorney would see it dead in less than a week.

February 4

The violent gale of wind which persecuted us with so much pertinacity on our leaving the English Channel is supposed to have been the tail of a tremendous hurricane, which has utterly laid waste Barbados and several other islands. No less than sixteen of the ships which sailed at the same time with us are reported to have perished upon the passage; so that I ought to consider it at least as a negative piece of good luck to have reached Jamaica myself, 'no bones broke, though sore peppered';* but I am still trembling in uncertainty for the fate of the vessel which is bringing out all my Irish supplies, and the non-arrival of which would be a misfortune to me of serious magnitude. The negroes are so obstinate and so wilful in their general character, that if they do not receive the precise articles to which they have been accustomed, and which they expect as their right, no compensation, however ample, can satisfy them. Thus, at every Christmas it would go near to create a rebellion if they did not receive a certain proportion of salt fish; but if, in the intervening months, accident should prevent their receiving their usual allowance of herrings, the giving them salt fish to the amount of double the value would be considered by them as an act of the grossest injustice.

February 5

On Saturday, about eight in the evening, a large centipede dropped from the ceiling upon my dinner-table, and was immediately cut in two exact halves by one of the guests. As it is reported in Jamaica that these reptiles, when thus divided, will re-unite again, or if separated will reproduce their missing members, and continue to live as stoutly as ever, I put both parts into a plate, under a glass cover. On Sunday they continued to move about their prison with considerable agility, although the tail was evidently much more lively and full of motion than the head: perhaps the centipede was a female. On Monday the head was dead, but the tail continued to run about, and evidently endeavoured to make its escape, although it appeared not to know very well how to set about it, nor to be perfectly determined as to which way it wanted to go: it only seemed to have Cymon's reason for wishing to take a walk, and 'would rather go any where, than stay with any body'.* On Wednesday, at twelve o'clock, its vivacity was a little abated, but only a little; the wound was skinned over, and I was waiting anxiously to know whether it would subsist without its numskull till a good old age, or would put forth an entirely spick and span new head and shoulders; when, on going to look at the plate on Thursday morning, lo and behold! the dead head and the living tail had disappeared together. I suppose some of the negro servants had thrown them away through ignorance, but they deny, one and all, having so much as touched the plate, most stoutly; and as a paper case, pierced in several places, had been substituted for the glass cover, some persons are of opinion that the tail made its escape through one of these air-holes, and carried its head away with it in its forceps. Be this as it may, gone they both are, and I am disappointed beyond measure at being deprived of this opportunity of reading the last volume of 'The Life and Adventures of a Centipede's Tail'. I have proclaimed a reward for the bringing me another, but I am told that these reptiles are only found by accident; and that, very possibly, one may not be procured previous to my leaving the island.

February 6

Mr Lutford, the proprietor of a considerable estate in the parish of Clarendon, had frequently accused a particular negro of purloining coffee. About six months ago the slave was sent for, and charged with a fresh offence of the same nature, when he confessed the having taken a small quantity; upon which his master ordered him to fix his eyes on a particular cotton tree, and then, without any further ceremony, shot him through the head. His mistress was the coroner's natural daughter, and the coroner himself was similarly connected with the custos of Clarendon. In consequence of this family compact, no inquest was held, no enquiry was made; the whole business was allowed to be slurred over, and the murder would have remained unpunished if accident had not brought some rumours respecting it to the governor's ear. An investigation was ordered to take place without delay; but Mr Lutford received sufficient warning to get on shipboard, and escape to America; and the displacing of the custos of Clarendon, for neglecting his official duty, was the only means by which the governor could express his abhorrence of the act.

February 8 (Sunday)

My estate is greatly plagued by a negress named Catalina; she is either mad, or has long pretended to be so, never works, and always steals. About a week before my arrival she was found in the trash-house, which she had pitched upon as the very fittest place possible for her kitchen; and there she was sitting, very quietly and comfortably, boiling her pot over an immense fire, and surrounded on all sides by dry canes, inflammable as tinder. This vagary was of too dangerous a nature to allow of her being longer left at liberty, and she was put into the hospital. But her husband was by no means pleased with her detention, as he never failed to appropriate to himself a share of her plunder, and when discovered, the blame of the robbery was laid upon his wife, in a fit of insanity. So, while the general joy at my first arrival drew the hospital attendants from their post, he took the opportunity to carry off his wife, and conceal her. The consequence was, that this morning complaints poured upon me of gardens robbed by Catalina, who had carried off as much as she could, dug up and destroyed the rest, and had shown as little conscience in providing herself with poultry as in helping herself to vegetables. I immediately despatched one of the negro-governors with a party in pursuit of her, who succeeded in lodging her once more in the hospital; where she must remain till I can get her sent to the asylum at Kingston, the only hospital for lunatics in the whole island.

February 12 (Thursday)

On my former visit to Jamaica, I found on my estate a poor woman nearly one hundred years old, and stone blind. She was too infirm to walk; but two young negroes brought her on their backs to the steps of my house, in order, as she said, that she might at least touch massa, although she could not see him. When she had kissed my hand, 'that was enough,' she said; 'now me hab once kiss a massa's hand, me willing to die to-morrow, me no care.' She had a woman appropriated to her service, and was shown the greatest care and attention; however, she did not live many months after my departure. There was also a mulatto, about thirty years of age, named Bob, who had been almost deprived of the use of his limbs by the horrible cocoa-bay, and had never done the least work since he was fifteen. He was so gentle and humble, and so fearful, from the consciousness of his total inability of soliciting my notice, that I could not help pitying the poor fellow; and whenever he came in my way I always sought to encourage him by little presents, and other trifling marks of favour. His thus unexpectedly meeting with distinguishing kindness, where he expected to be treated as a worthless incumbrance, made a strong impression on his mind. Soon after my departure his malady assumed a more active appearance; but during the last stages of its progress the only fear which he expressed was, that he should not live till last Christmas, when my return was expected to a certainty. In the mean while he endeavoured to find out a means of being of some little use to me, although his weak constitution would not allow of his being of much. Some of his relations being in opulent circumstances, they furnished him with a horse, for he was too weak to walk for more than a few minutes at a time; and, mounted upon this, he passed all his time in traversing the estate, watching the corn that it might not be stolen, warning the pen-keepers if any of the cattle had found their way into the cane-pieces, and doing many other such little pieces of service to the property; so that, as the negroes said, 'if he had been a white man he might have been taken for an overseer'. At length Christmas arrived; it was known that I was on the sea; Bob, too, was still alive; but still there was nothing to be heard of me. His perpetual question to all who came to visit him was, How was the wind? and he was constantly praying to the wind and the ocean to bring massa's vessel soon to Savanna la Mar, that he might but see him once more, and thank him, before he died. At length I landed; and when, on the day of my arrival on my estate, I expressed my surprise at the non-appearance of several of the negroes, who had appeared to be most attached to me, and I had expected to find most forward in greeting me, I was told that a messenger had been sent to call them, and that their absence was occasioned by their attendance at poor Bob's funeral. Several of his relations, who nursed him on his death-bed, have assured me, that the last audible words which he uttered were—'Are there still no news of massa?'

February 13

Talk of Lucretia!* commend me to a she-turkey! The hawk of Jamaica is an absolute Don Giovanni;* and he never loses an opportunity of being extremely rude indeed to these feathered fair ones; not even scrupling to use the last violence, and that without the least ceremony, not so much as saying, 'With your leave', or 'By your leave', or using any of the forms which common civility expects upon such occasions. The poor timid things are too much frightened by the sudden attack of this Tarquin with a beak and claws, to make any resistance; but they no sooner recover from their flutter sufficiently to be aware of what has happened, than they feel so extremely shocked, that they always make a point of dying; nor was a female turkey ever known to survive the loss of her honour above three days.

February 14

I think that I really may now venture to hope that my plans for the management of my estate have succeeded beyond even my most sanguine expectations. I have now passed three weeks with my negroes, the doors of my house open all day long, and full liberty allowed to every person to come and speak to me without witnesses or restraint; yet not one man or woman has come to me with a single complaint. On the contrary, all my enquiries have been answered by an assurance, that during the two years of my absence my regulations were adhered to most implicitly, and that, 'except for the pleasure of seeing massa', there was no more difference in treatment than if I had remained upon the estate. Many of them have come to tell me instances of kindness which they have received from one or other of their superintendents; others, to describe some severe fit of illness, in which they must have died but for the care taken of them in the hospital; some, who were weakly and low-spirited on my former visit, to show me how much they are improved in health, and tell me 'how they keep up heart now, because since massa come upon the property nobody put upon them, and all go well'; and some, who had formerly complained of one trifle or other, to take back their complaints, and say, that they wanted no change, and were willing to be employed in any way that might be thought most for the good of the estate; but although I have now at least *seen* every one of them, and have conversed with numbers, I have not yet been able to find one person who had so much as even an imaginary grievance to lay before me. Yet I find, that it has been found necessary to punish with the lash, although only in a very few instances; but then this only took place on the commission of absolute *crimes*, and in cases where its necessity and justice were so universally felt, not only by others, but by the sufferers themselves, that instead of complaining, they seem only to be afraid of their offence coming to my knowledge; to prevent which, they affect to be more satisfied and happy than all the rest, and now when I see a mouth grinning from ear to ear with a more than ordinary expansion of jaw, I never fail to find, on enquiry, that its proprietor is one of those who have been punished during my absence. I then take care to give them an opportunity of making a complaint, if they should have any to make; but no, not a word comes; 'every thing has gone on perfectly well, and just as it ought to have done.' Upon this, I drop a slight hint of the offence in question; and instantly away goes the grin, and down falls the negro to kiss my feet, confess his fault, and 'beg massa forgib, and them never do so bad thing more to fret massa, and them beg massa pardon, hard, quite hard!' But not one of them has denied the justice of his punishment, or complained of undue severity on the part of his superintendents. On the other hand, although the lash has thus been in a manner utterly abolished, except in cases where a much severer punishment would have been inflicted by the police, and although they are aware of this unwillingness to chastise, my trustee acknowledges that during my absence the negroes have been quiet and tractable, and have not only laboured as well as they used to do, but have done much more work than the negroes on an adjoining property, where there are forty more negroes, and where, moreover, a considerable sum is paid for hired assistance. Having now waited three weeks to see how they would conduct themselves, and found no cause of dissatisfaction since the neglect of the watchman to guard the cattle (and which they one and all attributed to their joy at seeing me again), I thought it time to distribute the presents which I had brought with me for them from England. During my absence I had ordered a new and additional hospital to be built, intended entirely for the use of lying-in women, nursing mothers, and cases of a serious nature, for which purpose it is to be provided with every possible comfort; while the old hospital is to be reserved for those who have little or nothing the matter with them, but who obstinately insist upon their being too ill to work, in defiance of the opinion of all their medical attendants. The new hospital is not quite finished; but wishing to connect it as much as possible with pleasurable associations, I took occasion of the distribution of presents to open it for the first time. Accordingly, the negroes were summoned to the new hospital this morning; the rooms were sprinkled with Madeira for good luck; and the toast of 'Health to the new hospital, and shame to the old lazy house!' was drunk by the trustee, the doctoresses, the governors, etc., and received by the whole congregation of negroes with loud cheering; after which, every man received a blue jacket lined with flannel, every woman a flaming red stuff petticoat, and every child a frock of white cotton. They then fell to dancing and singing, and drinking rum and sugar, which they kept up till a much later hour than would be at all approved of by the bench of bishops; for it is now Sunday morning, and they are still dancing and singing louder than ever.

February 15 (Sunday)

To-day divine service was performed at Savanna la Mar for the first time these five weeks. The rector has been indisposed lately with the lumbago: he has no curate; and thus during five whole weeks there was a total cessation of public worship. I had told several of my female acquaintance that it was long since they had been to church; that I was afraid of their forgetting 'all about and about it', and that if there should be no service for a week longer I should think it my duty to come and hear them say their Catechism myself. Luckily the rector recovered, and saved me the trouble of hearing them; but the long privation of public prayer did not seem to have created any very great demand for the article, as I have seldom witnessed a more meagre congregation. It was literally 'two or three gathered together',* and it seemed as if five or six would be too many, and forfeit the promise. I cannot discover that the negroes have any external forms of worship, nor any priests in Jamaica, unless their Obeah men should be considered as such; but still I cannot think that they ought to be considered as totally devoid of all natural religion. There is no phrase so common on their lips as 'God bless you!' and 'God preserve you!' and 'God will bless you wherever you go!' Phrases which they pronounce with every appearance of sincerity, and as if they came from the very bottom of their hearts. 'God-A'mity! God-A'mity!' is their constant exclamation in pain and in sorrow; and with this perpetual recurrence to the Supreme Being, it must be difficult to insist upon their being atheists. But they have even got a step further than the belief in a God; they also allow the existence of an evil principle. One of them complained to me the other day, that when he went to the field his companions had told him 'that he might go to hell, for he was not worthy to work with them'; and one of his adversaries in return accused him of being so lazy, 'that instead of being a slave upon Cornwall estate, he was only fit to be the slave of the devil'. Then surely they could not be afraid of duppies (or ghosts) without some idea of a future state; and indeed nothing is more firmly impressed upon the mind of the Africans, than that after death they shall go back to Africa, and pass an eternity in revelling and feasting with their ancestors. The proprietor of a neighbouring estate lately used all his influence to persuade his foster-sister to be christened; but it was all in vain: she had imbibed strong African prejudices from her mother, and frankly declared that she found nothing in the Christian system so alluring to her taste as the post-obit balls and banquets promised by the religion of Africa. I confess, that this prejudice appears to me to be so strongly rooted, that in spite of the curates expected from the hands of the bishop of London,* I am sadly afraid, that 'the pulpit drum ecclesiastic'* will find it a hard matter to overpower the gumby; and that the joys of the Christian paradise will be seen to kick the beam, when they are weighed against the pleasures of eating fat hog, drinking raw rum, and dancing for centuries to the jam-jam and kitty-katty. In the negro festivals in this life, the chief point lies in making as much noise as possible, and the Africans and Creoles dispute it with the greatest pertinacity. I am just informed that at the dance last night the Eboes obtained a decided triumph, for they roared and screamed and shouted and thumped their drums with so much effect, that the Creoles were fairly rendered deaf with the noise of their rivals, and dumb with their own, and obliged to leave off singing altogether.

February 16

On my arrival I found that idle rogue Nato, as usual, an inmate of the hospital, where he regularly passes at least nine months out of the twelve. He was with infinite difficulty persuaded, at the end of a fortnight, to employ himself about the carriage-horses for a couple of days; but on the third he returned to the hospital, although the medical attendants, one and all, declared nothing to be the matter with him, and the doctors even refused to insert his name in the sick list. Still he persisted in declaring himself to be too ill to do a single stroke of work: so on Thursday I put him into one of the sick rooms by himself, and desired him to get well with the doors locked, which he would find to the full as easy as with the doors open; at the same time assuring him, that he should never come out, till he should be sufficiently recovered to cut canes in the field. He held good all Friday; but Saturday being a holy-day, he declared himself to be in a perfect state of health, and desired to be released. However, I was determined to make him suffer a little for his lying and obstinacy, and would not suffer the doors to be opened for him till this morning, when he quitted the hospital, saluted on all sides by loud huzzas in congratulation of his amended health, and which followed him during his whole progress to the cane-piece. I was informed that a lad, named Epsom, who used to be perpetually running away, had been stationary for the last two years. So on Wednesday last, as he happened to come in my way, I gave him all proper commendation for having got rid of his bad habits; and to make the praise better worth his having, I added a maccarony: he was gratified in the extreme, thanked me a thousand times, promised most solemnly never to behave ill again, and ran away that very night. However, he returned on Saturday morning, and was brought to me all rags, tears, and penitence, wondering 'how he could have had such *bad manners* as to make massa fret'.

February 17

Some of the free people of colour possess slaves, cattle, and other property left them by their fathers, and are in good circumstances; but few of them are industrious enough to increase their possessions by any honest exertions of their own. As to the free blacks, they are almost uniformly lazy and improvident, most of them half-starved, and only anxious to live from hand to mouth. Some lounge about the highways with pedlar-boxes, stocked with various worthless baubles; others keep miserable stalls provided with rancid butter, damaged salt-pork, and other such articles: and these they are always willing to exchange for stolen rum and sugar, which they secretly tempt the negroes to pilfer from their proprietors; but few of them ever make the exertion of earning their livelihood creditably. Even those who profess to be tailors, carpenters, or coopers, are for the most part careless, drunken, and dissipated, and never take pains sufficient to attain any dexterity in their trade. As to a free negro hiring himself out for plantation labour, no instance of such a thing was ever known in Jamaica, and probably no price, however great, would be considered by them as a sufficient temptation.

February 18

The Africans and Creoles certainly do hate each other with a cordiality which would have appeared highly gratifying to Dr Johnson in his 'Love of Good Haters'. Yesterday, in the field, a girl who had taken some slight offence at something said to her by a young boy, immediately struck him with the bill, with which she was cutting canes. Luckily, his loose wrapper saved him from the blow; and, on his running away, she threw the bill after him in his flight with all the fury and malice of a fiend. This same vixen, during my former visit, had been punished for fixing her teeth in the hand of one of the other girls, and nearly biting her thumb off; and on hearing of this fresh instance of devilism, I asked her mother, 'how she came to have so bad a daughter, when all her sons were so mild and good?'—'Oh, massa,' answered she, 'the girl's father was a Guinea-man.'

February 19

Neptune came this morning to request that the name of his son, Oscar, might be changed for that of Julius, which (it seems) had been that of his own father. The child, he said, had always been weakly, and he was persuaded, that its ill-health proceeded from his deceased grandfather's being displeased, because it had not been called after him. The other day, too, a woman, who had a child sick in the hospital, begged me to change its name for any other which might please me best: she cared not what; but she was sure that it would never do well, so long as it should be called Lucia. Perhaps this prejudice respecting the power of names produces in some measure their unwillingness to be christened. They find no change produced in them, except the alteration of their name, and hence they conclude that this name contains in it some secret power; while, on the other hand, they conceive that the ghosts of their ancestors cannot fail to be offended at their abandoning an appellation, either hereditary in the family, or given by themselves. It is another negro-prejudice that the eructation of the breath of a sucking child has something in it venomous; and frequently nursing mothers, on showing the doctor a swelled breast, will very gravely and positively attribute it to the infant's having broken wind while hanging at the nipple.

February 20

I asked one of my negro servants this morning whether old Luke was a relation of his. 'Yes,' he said——'Is he your uncle, or your cousin?'—'No, massa.'—'What then?'—'He and my father were shipmates, massa.'

February 23

The law-charges in Jamaica have lately been regulated by the House of Assembly; and by all accounts (except that of the lawyers) it was full time that something should be done on the subject. A case was mentioned to me this morning of an estate litigated between several parties. At length a decision was given: the estate was sold for 16,000*l.*; but the lawyer's claim must always be the first discharged, and as this amounted to more than 16,000*l.* the lawyer found himself in possession of the estate. This was the fable of Æsop's oyster* put in action with a vengeance.

February 25

A negro, named Adam, has long been the terror of my whole estate. He was accused of being an Obeah-man, and persons notorious for the practice of Obeah had been found concealed from justice in his house, who were afterwards convicted and transported. He was strongly suspected of having poisoned more than twelve negroes, men and women; and having been displaced by my former trustee from being principal governor, in revenge he put poison into his water jar. Luckily he was observed by one of the house servants, who impeached him, and prevented the intended mischief. For this offence he ought to have been given up to justice; but being brother of the trustee's mistress she found means to get him off, after undergoing a long confinement in the stocks. I found him, on my arrival, living in a state of utter excommunication; I tried what reasoning with him could effect, reconciled him to his companions, treated him with marked kindness, and he promised solemnly to behave well during my absence. However, instead of attributing my lenity to a wish to reform him, his pride and confidence in his own talents and powers of deception made him attribute the indulgence shown him to his having obtained an influence over my mind. This he determined to employ to his own purposes upon my return; so he set about forming a conspiracy against Sully, the present chief governor, and boasted on various estates in the neighbourhood that on my arrival he would take care to get Sully broke, and himself substituted in his place. In the mean while he quarrelled and fought to the right and to the left; and on my arrival I found the whole estate in an uproar about Adam. No less than three charges of assault, with intent to kill, were preferred against him. In a fit of jealousy he had endeavoured to strangle Marlborough with the thong of a whip, and had nearly effected his purpose before he could be dragged away: he had knocked Nato down in some trifling dispute, and while the man was senseless had thrown him into the river to drown him; and having taken offence at a poor weak creature called Old Rachael, on meeting her by accident he struck her to the ground, beat her with a supple-jack, stamped upon her belly, and begged her to be assured of his intention (as he eloquently worded it) 'to kick her guts out'. The breeding mothers also accused him of having been the cause of the poisoning a particular spring, from which they were in the habit of fetching water for their children, as Adam on that morning had been seen near the spring without having any business there, and he had been heard to caution his little daughter against drinking water from it that day, although he stoutly denied both circumstances. Into the bargain, my head blacksmith being perfectly well at five o'clock, was found by his son dead in his bed at eight; and it was known that he had lately had a dispute with Adam, who on that day had made it up with him, and had invited him to drink, although it was not certain that his offer had been accepted. He had, moreover, threatened the lives of many of the best negroes. Two of the cooks declared, that he had severally directed them to dress Sully's food apart, and had given them powders to mix with it. The first to whom he applied refused positively; the second he treated with liquor, and when she had drunk, he gave her the poison, with instructions how to use it. Being a timid creature, she did not dare to object, so threw away the powder privately, and pretended that it had been administered; but finding no effect produced by it, Adam gave her a second powder, at the same time bidding her remember the liquor which she had swallowed, and which he assured her would effect her own des-truction through the force of Obeah, unless she prevented it by sacrificing his enemy in her stead. The poor creature still threw away the powder, but the strength of imagination brought upon her a serious malady, and it was not till after several weeks that she re-covered from the effects of her fears. The terror thus produced was universal throughout the estate, and Sully and several other princi-pal negroes requested me to remove them to my property in St Thomas's, as their lives were not safe while breathing the same air with Adam. However, it appeared a more salutary measure to remove Adam himself; but all the poisoning charges either went no further than strong suspicion, or (any more than the assaults) were not liable by the laws of Jamaica to be punished, except by flogging or tem-porary imprisonment, which would only have returned him to the estate with increased resentment against those to whom he should ascribe his sufferings, however deserved. However, on searching his house, a musket with a plentiful accompaniment of powder and ball was found concealed, as also a considerable quantity of materials for the practice of Obeah: the possession of either of the above articles (if the musket is without the consent of the proprietor) authorises the magistrates to pronounce a sentence of transportation. In consequence of this discovery, Adam was immediately committed to gaol; a slave court was summoned, and to-day a sentence of transportation from the island was pronounced, after a trial of three hours. As to the man's guilt, of that the jury entertained no doubt after the first half hour's evidence; and the only difficulty was to restrain the verdict to transportation. We produced nothing which could possibly affect the man's life; for although perhaps no offender ever better deserved hanging; yet I confess my being weak-minded enough to entertain doubts whether hanging or other capital punishment ought to be inflicted for any offence whatever: I am at least certain, that if offenders waited till they were hanged by me, they would remain unhanged till they were all so many old Parrs.* However, although I did my best to prevent Adam from being hanged, it was no easy matter to prevent his hanging himself. The Obeah ceremonies always commence with what is called, by the negroes, 'the Myal dance'.* This is intended to remove any doubt of the chief Obeah-man's supernatural powers; and in the course of it, he undertakes to show his art by killing one of the persons present, whom he pitches upon for that purpose. He sprinkles various powders over the devoted victim, blows upon him, and dances round him, obliges him to drink a liquor prepared for the occasion, and finally the sorcerer and his assistants seize him and whirl him rapidly round and round till the man loses his senses, and falls on the ground to all appearance and the belief of the spectators a perfect corpse. The chief Myal-man then utters loud shrieks, rushes out of the house with wild and frantic gestures, and conceals himself in some neighbouring wood. At the end of two or three hours he returns with a large bundle of herbs, from some of which he squeezes the juice into the mouth of the dead person; with others he anoints his eyes and stains the tips of his fingers, accompanying the ceremony with a great variety of grotesque actions, and chanting all the while something between a song and a howl, while the assistants hand in hand dance slowly round them in a circle, stamping the ground loudly with their feet to keep time with his chant. A considerable time elapses before the desired effect is produced, but at length the corpse gradually recovers animation, rises from the ground perfectly recovered, and the Myal dance concludes. After this proof of his power, those who wish to be revenged upon their enemies apply to the sorcerer for some of the same powder, which produced apparent death upon their companion, and as they never employ the means used for his recovery, of course the powder once administered never fails to be lastingly fatal. It must be superfluous to mention that the Myal-man on this second occasion substitutes a poison for a narcotic. Now, among other suspicious articles found in Adam's hut, there was a string of beads of various sizes, shapes, and colours, arranged in a form peculiar to the performance of the Obeah-man in the Myal dance. Their use was so well known, that Adam on his trial did not even attempt to deny that they could serve for no purpose but the practice of Obeah; but he endeavoured to refute their being his own property, and with this view he began to narrate the means by which he had become possessed of them. He said that they belonged to Fox (a negro who was lately transported), from whom he had taken them at a Myal dance held on the estate of Dean's Valley; but as the assistants at one of these dances are by law condemned to death equally with the principal performer, the court had the humanity to interrupt his confession of having been present on such an occasion, and thus saved him from criminating himself so deeply as to render a capital punishment inevitable. I understand that he was quite unabashed and at his ease the whole time; upon hearing his sentence, he only said very coolly, 'Well! I ca'n't help it!' turned himself round, and walked out of court. That nothing might be wanting, this fellow had even a decided talent for hypocrisy. When on my arrival he gave me a letter filled with the grossest lies respecting the trustee, and every creditable negro on the estate, he took care to sign it by the name which he had lately received in baptism; and in his defence at the bar to prove his probity of character and purity of manners, he informed the court that for some time past he had been learning to read, for the sole purpose of learning the Lord's Prayer. The nickname by which he was generally known among the negroes in this part of the country, was Buonaparte, and he always appeared to exult in the appellation. Once condemned, the marshal is bound under a heavy penalty to see him shipped from off the island before the expiration of six weeks, and probably he will be sent to Cuba. He is a fine-looking man between thirty and forty, square built, and of great bodily strength, and his countenance equally expresses intelligence and malignity. The sum allowed me for him is one hundred pounds currency, which is scarcely a third of his worth as a labourer, but which is the highest value which a jury is permitted to mention.

March 1 (Sunday)

Last night the negroes of Friendship took it into their ingenious heads to pay me a compliment of an extremely inconvenient nature. They thought, that it would be highly proper to treat me with a nightly serenade just by way of showing their *enjoyment* on my return; and accordingly a large body of them arrived at my doors about midnight, dressed out in their best clothes, and accompanied with drums, rattles, and their whole orchestra of abominable instruments, determined to pass the whole night in singing and dancing under my windows. Luckily, my negro-governors heard what was going forwards, and knowing my taste a little better than my visiters, they hastened to assure them of my being in bed and asleep, and with much difficulty persuaded them to remove into my village. Here they contented themselves with making a noise for the greatest part of the night; and the next morning, after coming up to see me at breakfast, they went away quietly. One of them only remained to enquire particularly after Lady H——, as her mother had been her nurse, and she was very particular in her enquiries as to her health, her children, their ages and names. When she went away, I gave her a plentiful provision of bread, butter, plantains, and cold ham from the breakfast table; part of which she sat down to eat, intending, as she said, to carry the rest to her piccaninny at home. But in half an hour after she made her appearance again, saying she was come to take leave of me, and hoped I would give her a *bit* to buy tobacco. I gave her a maccaroni, which occasioned a great squall of delight. Oh! since I had given her so much, she would not buy tobacco but a fowl; and then, when I returned, she would bring me a chicken from it for my dinner; that is, if she could keep the other negroes from stealing it from her, a piece of extraordinary good luck of which she seemed to entertain but slender hopes. At length off she set; but she had scarcely gone above ten yards from the house, when she turned back, and was soon at my writing-table once more, with a 'Well! here me come to massa again!' So then she said, that she had meant to eat part of the provisions which I had given her, and carry home the rest to her boy; but that really it was so good, she could not help going on eating and eating, till she had eaten the whole, and now she wanted another bit of cold ham to carry home to her child, and then she should go away perfectly contented. I ordered Cubina to give her a great hunch of it, and Mrs Phillis at length took her departure for good and all.

March 4 (Wednesday)

I set out to visit my estate in St Thomas's in the East, called Hordley. It is at the very furthest extremity of the island, and never was there a journey like unto my journey. Something disagreeable happened at every step; my accidents commenced before I had accomplished ten miles from my own house; for in passing along a narrow shelf of rock, which overhangs the sea near Blue-fields, a pair of young blood-horses in my carriage took fright at the roaring of the waves which dashed violently against them, and twice nearly overturned me. On the second occasion one of them actually fell down into the water, while the off-wheel of the curricle flew up into the air, and thus it remained suspended, balancing backwards and forwards, like Mahomet's coffin.* Luckily, time was allowed the horse to recover his legs, down came the wheel once more on terra firma, and on we went again. We slept at Cashew (an estate near Lacovia), and the next morning at daylight proceeded to climb the Bogr, a mountain so difficult, that every one had pronounced the attempt to be hopeless with horses so young as mine; but those horses were my only ones, and therefore I was obliged to make the trial. The road is bordered by tremendous precipices for about twelve miles; the path is so narrow, that a servant must always be sent on before to make any carts which may be descending stop in recesses hollowed out for this express purpose; and the cartmen are obliged to sound their shells repeatedly, in order to give each other timely warning. The chief danger, however, proceeds from the steepness of the road, which in some places will not permit the waggons to stop, however well their conductors may be inclined; then down they come drawn by twelve or fourteen, or sometimes sixteen oxen, sweeping every thing before them, and any carriage unlucky enough to find itself in their course must infallibly be dashed over the precipice. To-day, it really appeared as if all the estates in the island had agreed to send their produce by this particular road; the shells formed a complete chorus, and sounded incessantly during our whole passage of the mountain; and at one time there was a very numerous accumulation of carts and oxen in consequence of my carriage coming to a complete stop. As we were ascending,—'It is very well,' said a gentleman who was travelling with me, (Mr Hill) 'that we did not come by this road three months sooner. I remember about that time travelling it on horseback, and an enormous tree had fallen over the path, which made me say to myself as I passed under it, "Now, how would a chaise with a canopy get along here? The tree hangs so low that the carriage never could pass, and it would certainly have to go all the way home again." Of course, the obstacle must now be removed; but if I remember right, this must have been the very spot ... and as I hope to live, yonder is the very tree still!'—And so it proved; although three months had elapsed, the impediment had been suffered to remain in unmolested possession of the road, and to pass my carriage under it proved an absolute impossibility. After much discussion, and many fruitless attempts, we at length succeeded in unscrewing the wheels, lifting off the body, which we carried along, and then built the curricle up again on the opposite side of the tree. However, by one means or other (after leaving a knocked-up saddle-horse at a coffee plantation, to the owner of which I was a perfect stranger, but who very obligingly offered to take charge of the animal) we found ourselves at the bottom of the mountain; but the fatal tree, and the delay occasioned by taking unavoidable shelter from tremendous storms of rain, had lost us so much time, that night surprised us when we were still eight miles distant from our destined inn. The night was dark as night could be; no moon, no stars, nor any light except the flashing of myriads of fire-flies, which, flapping in the faces of the young horses, frightened them, and made them rear. The road, too, was full of water-trenches, precipices, and deep and dangerous holes. As to the ground, it was quite invisible, and we had no means of proceeding with any chance of safety except by making some of the servants lead the horses, while others went before us to explore the way, while they cried out at every moment,—'Take care; a little to the left, or you will slip into that water-trench—a little to the right, or you will tumble over that precipice.'—Into the bargain there was neither inn nor gentleman's house within reach; and thus we proceeded crawling along at a foot's pace for five eternal miles, when we at length stopped to beg a shelter for the night at a small estate called Porous. By this time it was midnight; all the family was gone to bed; the gates were all locked; and before we could obtain admittance a full hour elapsed, during which I sat in an open carriage, perspiration streaming down from my head to my feet through vexation, impatience and fatigue, while the night-dew fell heavy and the night-breeze blew keen; which (as I had frequently been assured) was the very best recipe possible for getting a Jamaica fever. On such I counted both for myself and my white servant, when I at length laid myself down in a bed at Porous; but to my equal surprise and satisfaction we both rose the next morning without feeling the slightest inconvenience from our risks of the preceding day, and in the evening of Friday, the 5th, I reached Miss Cole's hotel at the Spanish Town. One of my young horses, however, was so completely knocked up by the fatigue of crossing the mountain, that I could get no further than Kingston (only fourteen miles) this next day. In consequence of the delay, I was enabled to visit the Kingston theatre;* the exterior is rather picturesque; within it has no particular recommendations; the scenery and dresses were shabby, the actors wretched, and the stage ill lighted; the performance was for the benefit of the chief actress, who had but little reason to be satisfied with the number of her audience; and I may reckon it among my other misfortunes on this ill-starred expedition, that it was my destiny to sit out the tragedy of 'Adelgitha',* whom the author meant only to be killed in the last act, but whom the actors murdered in all five. The heroine was the only one who spoke tolerably, but she was old enough and fat enough for the Widow Cheshire;* Guiscard did not know ten words of his part; the tyrant was really comical enough; and Lothair was played by a young Jamaica Jew about fifteen years of age, and who is dignified here with the name of 'the Creole Roscius'.* His voice was just breaking, which made him 'pipe and whistle in the sound', his action was awkward, and altogether he was but a sorry specimen of theatrical talent: however, his *forte* is said to lie in broad farce, which perhaps may account for his being no better in tragedy. On Sunday, the 8th, I resumed my journey, but my horses were so completely knocked up, that I was obliged to hire an additional pair to convey me to Miss

Hetley's inn on the other side of the Yallacks River, which is nine-teen miles from Kingston. This river, as well as that of Morant (which I passed about ten miles further) both in breadth and strength sets all bridges at defiance, and in the rainy season it is sometimes impassable for several weeks. On this occasion there was but little water in either, and I arrived without difficulty at Port Morant, where I found horses sent by my trustee to convey me to Hordley. The road led up to the mountains, and was one of the steepest, roughest, and most fatiguing that I ever travelled, in spite of its picturesque beauties. At length I reached my estate, jaded and wearied to death; here I expected to find a perfect paradise, and I found a perfect hell. Report had assured me, that Hordley was the best managed estate in the island, and as far as the soil was concerned, report appeared to have said true; but my trustee had also assured me, that my negroes were the most contented and best disposed, and here there was a lamentable incorrectness in the account. I found them in a perfect uproar; complaints of all kinds stunned me from all quarters: all the blacks accused all the whites, and all the whites accused all the blacks, and as far as I could make out, both parties were extremely in the right. There was no attachment to the soil to be found *here*; the negroes declared, one and all, that if I went away and left them to groan under the same system of oppression without appeal or hope of redress, they would follow my carriage and establish themselves at Cornwall. I had soon discovered enough to be certain, that although they told me plenty of falsehoods, many of their complaints were but too well founded; and yet how to protect them for the future or satisfy them for the present was no easy matter to decide. Trust-ing to these fallacious reports of the Arcadian state of happiness upon Hordley, I supposed, that I should have nothing to do there but grant a few indulgences, and establish the regulations already adopted with success on Cornwall; distribute a little money, and allow a couple of play-days for dancing; and under this persuasion I had made it quite impossible for me to remain above a week at Hordley, which I conceived to be fully sufficient for the above purpose. As to grievances to be redressed, I was totally unprepared for any such necessity; yet now they poured in upon me incessantly, each more serious than the former; and before twenty-four hours were elapsed I had been assured, that in order to produce any sort of tranquillity upon the estate, I must begin by displacing the trustee, the physician, the four white book-keepers, and the four black governors, all of whom I was modestly required to remove and provide better substitutes in the space of five days and a morning. What with the general clamour, the assertions and denials, the tears and the passion, the odious falsehoods, and the still more odious truths, and (worst of all to me) my own vexation and disappointment at finding things so different from my expectations, at first nearly turned my brain; and I felt strongly tempted to set off as fast as I could, and leave all these black devils and white ones to tear one another to pieces, an amusement in which they appeared to be perfectly ready to indulge themselves. It was, however, considerable relief to me to find, upon examination, that no act of personal ill-treatment was alleged against the trustee himself, who was allowed to be sufficiently humane in his own nature, and was only complained of for allowing the negroes to be maltreated by the book-keepers, and other inferior agents, with absolute impunity. Being an excellent planter, he confined his attention entirely to the cultivation of the soil, and when the negroes came to complain of some act of cruelty or oppression committed by the book-keepers or the black governors, he refused to listen to them, and left their complaints unenquired into, and consequently unredressed. The result was, that the negroes were worse off, than if he had been a cruel man himself; for his cruelty would have given them only one tyrant, whereas his indolence left them at the mercy of eight. Still they said, that they would be well contented to have him continue their trustee, provided that I would appoint some protector, to whom they might appeal in cases of injustice and ill-usage. The trustee declaring himself well satisfied that some such appointment should take place, a neighbouring gentleman (whose humanity to his own negroes had established him in high favour with mine) was selected for this purpose. I next ordered one of the book-keepers (of the atrocious brutality of whose conduct the trustee himself upon examination allowed that there could be no doubt) to quit the estate in two hours under pain of prosecution; away went the man, and when I arose the next morning, another book-keeper had taken himself off of his own accord, and that in so much haste that he left all his clothes behind him. My next step was to displace the chief black governor, a man deservedly odious to the negroes, and whom a gross and insolent lie told to myself enabled me to punish without seeming to displace him in compliance with their

complaints against him; and these sources of discontent being removed, I read to them my regulations for allowing them new holidays, additional allowances of salt-fish, rum, and sugar, with a variety
of other indulgences and measures taken for protection, etc. All
which, assisted by a couple of dances and distribution of money on
the day of my departure had so good an effect upon their tempers,
that I left them in as good humour apparently, as I found them in
bad. But to leave them was no such easy matter; the weather had been
bad from the moment of my commencing my journey, but from the
moment of my reaching Hordley, it became abominable. The rain
poured down in cataracts incessantly; the old crazy house stands on
the top of a hill, and the north wind howled round it night and day,
shaking it from top to bottom, and threatening to become a hurricane. The storm was provided with a very suitable accompaniment
of thunder and lightning; and to complete the business, down came
the mountain torrents, and swelled Plantain Garden River to such a
degree, that it broke down the dam-head, stopped the mill, and all
work was at a stand-still for two days and nights. But the worst of all
was that this same river lay between me and Kingston; bridge there
was none, and it soon became utterly impassable. Thus it continued
for four days; on the fifth (the day which I had appointed for my
departure, and on which I gave the negroes a parting holiday) the
water appeared to be somewhat abated at a ford about four miles
distant; for as to crossing at my own, that was quite out of the question for a week at least. A negro was despatched on horseback to
ascertain the height of the water; his report was very unfavourable.
However, as at worst I could but return, and had no better means of
employing my time, I resolved to make the experiment. About forty
of the youngest and strongest negroes left their dancing and drinking, and ran on foot to see me safe over the water. The few hours
which had elapsed since my messenger's examination, had operated
very favourably towards the reduction of the water, although it was
still very high. But a servant going before to ascertain the least dangerous passage, and the negroes rushing all into the river to break
the force of the stream, and support the carriage on both sides, we
were enabled to struggle to the opposite bank, and were landed in
safety with loud cheering from my sable attendants, who then left
me, many with tears running down their cheeks, and all with thanks
for the protection which I had shown them, and earnest entreaties

that I would come to visit them another time. Whether my visit will have been productive of essential service to them must remain a doubt; the trustee at least promised me most solemnly that my regulations for their happiness and security should be obeyed, and that the slave-laws (of which I had detected beyond a doubt some very flagrant violations) should be carried into effect for the future with the most scrupulous exactness. If he breaks his promise, and I discover it, I have pledged myself most solemnly to remove him, however great may be his merits as a planter; if he contrives to keep me in ignorance of his proceedings (which, however, from the precautions which I have now taken, I trust, will be no easy matter), and the state of the negroes should continue after my departure to be what it was before my arrival, then I can only console myself with thinking, that the guilt is his, not mine; and that it is on *his* head that the curse of the sufferers and the vengeance of heaven will fall, not on my own. I have been told that this estate of mine is one of the most beautiful in the island. It may be so for anything that I can tell of the matter. The badness of the weather and the disquietude of my mind during the whole of my short stay, made every thing look gloomy and hideous; and when I once found myself again beyond my own limits, I felt my spirits lighter by a hundred weight. Of all the points which had displeased me at Hordley, none had made me more angry for the time, than the lie told me by the chief governor, which occasioned my displacing him. This fellow, who for the credit of our family (no doubt) had got himself christened by the name of John Lewis, had the impudence to walk into my parlour just as I was preparing to go to bed, and inform me, that he could not get the business of the estate done. Why not? He could get nobody to come to the night-work at the mill, which he supposed was the consequence of my indulging the negroes so much. Indeed! and where were the people who ought to come to their night-work? in the negro village? No; they were in the hospital, and refused to come out to work. Upon which I blazed up like a barrel of gunpowder, and volleying out in a breath all the curses that I ever heard in my life, I asked him, whether any person really had been insolent enough to select a whole night party from the sick people in the hospital, not one of whom ought to stir out of it till well? There stood the fellow, trembling and stammering, and unable to get out an answer, while I stamped up and down the piazza, storming and swearing, banging all the doors till

the house seemed ready to tumble about our ears, and doing my best
to out-herod Herod,* till at last I ordered the man to begone that
instant, and get the work done properly. He did not wait to be told
twice, and was off in a twinkling. In a quarter of an hour I sent for
him again, and enquired whether he had succeeded in getting the
proper people to work at the mill? Upon which he had the assurance
to answer, that all the people were there, and that it was not of their
not being at the mill that he had meant to complain. Of what was it
then? 'Of their not being in the field.' When? 'Yesterday. He could
not get the negroes to come to work, and so there had been none
done all day.' And who refused to come? 'All the people.' But who?
'All.' But who, who, who?—their names, their names, their names?
'He could not remember them all.' Name one—well?—speak then,
speak! 'There was Beck.' And who else? 'There was Sally, who used
to be called Whanica.' And who else? 'There was . . . there was
Beck.' But who else? 'Beck . . . and Sally' . . . But who else? who
else? 'Little Edward had gone out of the hospital, and had not come
to work.' Well! Beck and Sally, and little Edward; who else? 'Beck,
and little Edward, and Sally.' But who else: I say, who else? 'He could
not remember any body else.' Then to be sure I was in such an imperial passion, as would have done honour to 'her majesty the queen
Dolallolla'.* Why, you most impudent of all impudent fellows that
ever told a lie, have you really presumed to disturb me at this time
of night, prevent my going to bed, tell me that you can't get the business done, and that none of the people would come to work, and
make such a disturbance, and all because two old women and a little
boy missed coming into the field yesterday! Down dropped the fellow
in a moment upon his marrow bones: 'Oh, me good massa,' cried he
(and out came the truth, which I knew well enough before he told
me), 'me no come of my own head; me *ordered* to come; but me never
tell massa lie more, so me pray him forgib me!' But his obeying any
person on my own estate in preference to me, and suffering himself
to be converted into an instrument of my annoyance, was not to be
easily overlooked; so I turned him out of the house with a flea in his
ear as big as a camel; and the next morning degraded him to the rank
of a common field negro. The trustee pleaded hard for his being permitted to return to the waggons, from whence he had been taken,
and where he would be useful. But I was obdurate. Then came his
wife to beg for him, and then his mother, and then his cousin, and

then his cousin's cousin: still I was firm; till on the day of my departure, the new chief governor came to me in the name of the whole
estate, and begged me to allow John Lewis to return to the command
of the waggons, 'for that all the negroes said, that it would be *too sad
a thing* for them to see a man who had held the highest place among
them, degraded quite to be a common field negro'. There was something in this appeal which argued so good a feeling, that I did not
think it right to resist any longer; so I hinted that if the trustee should
ask it again as a favour to himself, I might perhaps relent; and the
proper application being thus made, John Lewis was allowed to quit
the field, but with a positive injunction against his ever being
employed again in any office of authority over the negroes. I found
baptism in high vogue upon Hordley, but I am sorry to say, that I
could not discover much effect produced upon their minds by having
been made Christians, except in one particular: whenever one of
them told me a monstrous lie (and they told me whole dozens), he
never failed to conclude his story by saying—'And now, massa, you
know, I've been christened; and if you do not believe what I say, I'm
ready to *buss the book* to the truth of it.' The whole advantages to be
derived by negroes from becoming Christians, seemed to consist with
them in two points; being a superior species of magic itself, it preserved them from black Obeah; and by enabling them to take an oath
upon the Bible to the truth of any lie which it might suit them to
tell, they believed that it would give them the power of humbugging
the white people with perfect ease and convenience. They had
observed the importance attached by the whites to such an attesta-
tion, and the conviction which it always appeared to carry with it; as
to the crime or penalty of perjury, of that they were totally ignorant,
or at least indifferent; therefore they were perfectly ready to 'buss
the book', which they considered as a piece of buckra superstition,
mighty useful to the negroes, and valued taking their oath upon the
Bible to a lie, no more than Mrs Mincing did the oath which she took
in the Blue Garret 'upon an odd volume of Messalina's Poems'.*
Although I set out from Hordley at two o'clock, it was past seven
before I reached an estate called 'The Retreat', which was only twelve
miles off, so abominable was the road. Here I stopped for the night,
which I passed at supper with the musquitoes,—'not where I ate, but
where I was eaten'.* Morant River had been swelled by the late heavy
rains to a tremendous height, and its numerous quicksands render

the passage in such a state extremely dangerous. However, a negro having been sent early to explore it, and having returned with a favourable report, we proceeded to encounter it. A Hordley negro, well acquainted with these perilous rivers, had accompanied me for the express purpose of pointing out the most practicable fords; but for some time his efforts to find a safe one were unavailing, his horse at the end of a minute or two plunging into a quicksand or some deep hole, among the waters thrown up from which he totally disappeared for a moment, and then was seen to struggle out again with such an effort and leap, as were quite beyond the capability of any carriage's attempting. However, at the end of half an hour he was fortunate to find a place, where he could cross (up to his horse's belly in the water, to be sure), but at least without tumbling into holes and quicksands; and here we set out, conscious that our whole chance of reaching the opposite shore consisted in keeping precisely the path which he had gone already, and determined to stick as close as possible to his horse's tail. But no sooner were we fairly in the water, than my young horses found themselves unable to resist the strength and rapidity of the torrent, which was rolling down huge stones as big as rocks from the mountain; and to my utter consternation, I perceived the curricle carried down the stream, and the distance from my guide (who, by swimming his horse, had reached the destined landing-place in safety) growing wider and wider with every moment. We were now driving at all hazards; every moment I expected to see a horse or a wheel sink down into some deep hole, the chaise overturned, and ourselves either swallowed up in a quicksand, or dashed to pieces against the stones, which were rolling around us. I never remember to have felt myself so completely convinced of approaching destruction, and I roared out with all my might and main:—'We are carried away! all is over!' although, to be sure, I might as well have held my tongue, seeing that all my roaring could not do the least possible good. However, my horses, although too weak to resist the current, were fortunately strong enough to keep their legs; while they drifted down the stream, they struggled along in an oblique direction, which gradually (though but slowly) brought us nearer to the opposite shore; and after several minutes passed in most painful anxiety, a desperate plunge out of the water enabled them to *jump* the carriage upon terra firma on the same side with my guide, although at a considerable distance from the spot where he had landed. The Yallack's

River was less dangerous; but even this too had been sufficiently swelled to make the crossing it no easy matter; so that what with one obstacle and another, when I reached Kingston at six o'clock with my bones and my vehicle unbroken, I was almost as much surprised as satisfied. I dined with the curate of Kingston (Rev. G. Hill), where I met the admiral upon this station, Sir Home Popham,* and a large party. At Kingston I was obliged to send back a horse, which had been lent me in aid of my own; another had been dropped at 'the Retreat'; a third could get no farther than the mountains; and my companion's three horses had found themselves unable even to reach Spanish Town, and I had thus been obliged to leave them and theirs behind upon the road. On the morning of our departure from Cornwall, when my Italian servant saw the quantity of horses, mules, servants, and carriages collected for the journey, he clapped his hands together in exultation, and exclaimed,—'They will certainly take us for the king of England!' But now when after leaving one horse in one place and another horse in another, on the morning of Monday the 16th, he beheld my whole caravan reduced to one pair of chaise horses and a couple of miserable mules, he cast a rueful look upon my diminished cavalry and sighed to himself,—'I verily believe, we shall return home on foot after all!' I reached Spanish Town in time to dine with the chief justice (Mr Jackson), and intended to remain two or three days longer; but the fatality, which had persecuted me from the very commencement of this abominable journey, was not exhausted yet. On Tuesday morning, my landlady just hinted, that 'she thought it right to let me know, that to be sure there *was* a gentleman unwell in the house; but she supposed, that I should not care about it: however, if I particularly disliked the neighbourhood of a sick person, she would procure me lodgings.' I asked, 'What was the complaint?' 'Oh! he was a little sick, that was all.' To which I only could answer, that, 'in that case I hoped he would get better'; and thought no more about it. However, when I went to visit the governor, I found, that this 'little sickness' of my landlady's was neither more nor less than the yellow fever; of which the gentleman in question was now dying, of which a lady had died only two days before, and of which another European, newly arrived, had fallen ill in this very same hotel only a fortnight before, and had died, after throwing himself out of an upper window in a fit of delirium. Under all these circumstances, I thought it to the full as prudent not to prolong my residence in Spanish Town; and accordingly, on Wednesday the 18th, I resumed my journey homewards. I travelled the north side of the island, which was the road used by me on my return two years ago. I have nothing to add to my former account of it, except that there need not be better inns anywhere than the Wellington hotel at Rio Bueno, and Judy James's at Montego Bay, which latter is now, in my opinion, by far the prettiest town in Jamaica. Indeed, all the inns upon this road are excellent, with the solitary exception of the Black-heath Tavern, which I stopped at by a mistake instead of that of Montague. At this most miserable of all inns that ever entrapped an unwary traveller, there was literally nothing to be procured for love or money: no corn for the horses; no wine without sending six miles for a bottle; no food but a miserable starved fowl, so tough that the very negroes could not eat it; and a couple of eggs, one of which was addled: there was but one pair of sheets in the whole house, and neither candles, nor oranges, nor pepper, nor vinegar, nor bread, nor even so much as sugar, white or brown. Yams there were, which prevented my servants from going to bed quite empty, and I contented myself with the far-fetched bottle of wine and the solitary egg, which I eat by the light of a lamp filled with stinking oil. The one pair of sheets I seized upon to my own share, and my servants made themselves as good beds as they could upon the floor with great coats and travelling mantles. It was on Wednesday night, that after the fatigue of crossing Mount Diablo, 'myself I unfatigued'* in this delectable retreat, which seemed to have been established upon principles diametrically opposite to those of Shenstone's. On Thursday I slept at Rio Bueno, on Friday at Montego Bay, passed Saturday at Anchovy estate (Mr Plummer's), and was very glad, on Sunday the 22d, to find myself once more quietly established at Cornwall, fully determined to leave it no more, till I leave it on my return to England. The lady, who had died so lately at Kingston, had arrived not long before in a vessel, both the crew and passengers of which landed (to all appearance) in perfect health after a favourable passage from England. Of course, they soon dispersed in different directions; yet almost all of them were attacked nearly at the same period by the fever, which seemed to have a particular commission to search out such persons as had arrived by that particular ship, at however remote a distance they might be from each other.

March 29 (Sunday)

This morning (without either fault or accident) a young, strong, healthy woman miscarried of an eight months' child; and this is the third time that she has met with a similar misfortune. No other symptom of child-bearing has been given in the course of this year, nor are there above eight women upon the breeding list out of more than one hundred and fifty females. Yet they are all well clothed and well fed, contented in mind, even by their own account, over-worked at no time, and when upon the breeding list are exempted from labour of every kind. In spite of all this, and their being treated with all possible care and indulgence, rewarded for bringing children, and therefore anxious themselves to have them, how they manage it so ill I know not, but somehow or other certainly the children do not come.

March 31

During the whole three weeks of my absence, only two negroes have been complained of for committing fault. The first was a domestic quarrel between two Africans; Hazard stole Frank's calabash of sugar, which Frank had previously stolen out of my boiling-house. So Frank broke Hazard's head, which in my opinion settled the matter so properly, that I declined spoiling it by any interference of my own. The other complaint was more serious. Toby, being ordered to load the cart with canes, answered 'I wo'nt'—and Toby was as good as his word; in consequence of which the mill stopped for want of canes, and the boiling-house stopped for want of liquor. I found on my return that for this offence Toby had received six lashes, which Toby did not mind three straws. But as his fault amounted to an act of downright rebellion, I thought that it ought not by any means to be passed over so lightly, and that Toby ought to be *made* to mind. I took no notice for some days; but the Easter holidays had been deferred till my return, and only began here on Friday last. On that day, as soon as the head governor had blown the shell, and dismissed the negroes till Monday morning, he requested the pleasure of Mr Toby's company to the hospital, where he locked him up in a room by himself. All Saturday and Sunday the estate rang with laughing, dancing, singing, and huzzaing. Salt-fish was given away in the morning; the children played at ninepins for jackets and petticoats in the evening; rum and sugar was denied to no one. The gumbys thundered; the kitty-katties clattered; all was noise and festivity; and all this while, 'qualis mœrens Philomela',* sat solitary Toby gazing at his four white walls! Toby had not minded the lashes; but the loss of his amusement, and the disgrace of his exclusion from the fête operated on his mind so forcibly, that when on the Monday morning his door was unlocked, and the chief governor called him to his work, not a word would he deign to utter; let who would speak, there he sat motionless, silent, and sulky. However, upon my going down to him myself, his voice thought proper to return, and he began at once to complain of his seclusion and justify his conduct. But he no sooner opened his lips than the whole hospital opened theirs to censure his folly, asking him how he could presume to justify himself when he knew that he had done wrong? and advising him to humble himself and beg my pardon; and their clamours were so loud and so general (Mrs Sappho, his wife, being one of the loudest, who not only 'gave it him on both sides of his ears', but enforced her arguments by a knock on the pate now and then), that they fairly drove the evil spirit out of him; he confessed his fault with great penitence, engaged solemnly never to commit such another, and set off to his work full of gratitude for my granting him forgiveness. I am more and more convinced every day, that the best and easiest mode of governing negroes (and governed by some mode or other they must be) is not by the detestable lash, but by confinement, solitary or otherwise; they cannot bear it, and the memory of it seems to make a lasting impression upon their minds; while the lash makes none but upon their skins, and lasts no longer than the mark. The order at my hospital is, that no negro should be denied admittance; even if no symptoms of illness appear, he is allowed one day to rest, and take physic, if he choose it. On the second morning, if the physician declares the man to be shamming, and the plea of illness is still alleged against going to work, then the negro is locked up in a room with others similarly circumstanced, where care is taken to supply him with food, water, physic, etc., and no restraint is imposed except that of not going out. Here he is suffered to remain unmolested as long as he pleases, and he is only allowed to leave the hospital upon his own declaration that he is well enough to go to work; when the door is opened, and he walks away unreproached and unpunished, however evident his deception may have been. Before I adopted this regulation, the number of patients used to vary from thirty to forty-five, not more than a dozen of whom perhaps had anything the matter with them: the number at this moment is but fourteen, and all are sores, burns, or complaints the reality of which speaks for itself. Some few persevering tricksters will still submit to be locked up for a day or two; but their patience never fails to be wearied out by the fourth morning, and I have not yet met with an instance of a patient who had once been locked up with a fictitious illness, returning to the hospital except with a real one. In general, they offer to take a day's rest and physic, promising to go out to work the next day, and on these occasions they have uniformly kept their word. Indeed, my hospital is now in such good order, that the physician told the trustee the other day that 'mine gave him less trouble than any hospital in the parish'. My boilers, too, who used to make sugar the colour of mahogany, are now making excellent; and certainly, if appearances may be trusted, and things will but last, I may flatter myself with the complete success of my system of management, as far as the time elapsed is sufficient to warrant an opinion. I only wish from my soul that I were but half as certain of the good treatment and good behaviour of the negroes at Hordley.

April 1 (Wednesday)

Jug-Betty having had two leathern purses full of silver coin stolen out of her trunk, her cousin Punch told her to have patience till Sunday, and he thought that by that time he should be able to find it for her. Upon which she very naturally suspected her cousin Punch of having stolen the money himself, and brought him to day to make her charge against him. However, he stuck firmly to a denial, and as several days had been suffered to elapse since the theft, there could be no doubt of his having concealed the money, and therefore no utility in searching his person or his house. I found great fault with the persons in authority for not having taken such a measure without a moment's delay; but the trustee informed me that it frequently produced very serious consequences, many instances having occurred of the disgrace of their house being searched having offended negroes so much to the heart, as to occasion their committing suicide: so that it was a proceeding which was seldom ventured upon without urgent necessity. It was now too late to take it, at all events; the man confessed, indeed, that he had quitted his work, and gone down to the negro-village on the day of the robbery, which rendered his guilt highly probable, but he could be brought to confess no more; and as to his saying that he thought he could find the money by Sunday, he explained *that* into an intention of 'going to consult a brown woman at the bay, who was a fortune-teller, and who when any thing was stolen, could always point out the thief by *cutting the cards*'. This was all that we could extract from him, and we were obliged to dismiss him. However, the fright of his examination was not without good consequences: one of the stolen purses had belonged to a sister of Jug-Betty's, not long deceased; and on her return home, *this* purse (with its contents untouched) was found lying on the sister's grave in her garden. Perhaps, the thief had taken it without knowing the owner; and on finding that it had belonged to a dead person, he had surrendered it through apprehension of being haunted by her *duppy*.

April 5 (Sunday)

Clearing their grounds by fire is a very expeditious proceeding, consequently in much practice among the negroes; but in this tindery country it is extremely dangerous, and forbidden by the law. As I returned home to-day from church, I observed a large smoke at no great distance, and Cubina told me, he supposed that the negroes of the neighbouring estate of Amity were clearing their grounds. 'Then they are doing a very wrong thing,' said I; 'I hope they will fire nothing else but their grounds, for with so strong a breeze a great deal of mischief might be done.' However, in half an hour it proved that the smoke in question arose from my own negro-grounds, that the fire had spread itself, and I could see from my window the flames and smoke pouring themselves upwards in large volumes, while the crackling of the dry bushes and brush-wood was something perfectly terrific. The alarm was instantly given, and whites and blacks all hurried to the scene of action. Luckily, the breeze set the contrary way from the plantations; a morass interposed itself between the blazing ground and one of my best cane-pieces: the flames were suffered to burn till they reached the brink of the water, and then the negroes managed to extinguish them without much difficulty. Thus we escaped without injury, but I own I was heartily frightened.

April 8

This morning I was awaked by a violent coughing in the hospital; and as soon as I heard any of the servants moving, I despatched a negro to ask, 'whether any body was bad in the hospital?' He returned and told me, 'No, massa; nobody bad there; for Alick is better, and Nelson is dead.' Nelson was one of my best labourers, and had come into the hospital for a glandular swelling. Early this morning he was seized with a violent fit of coughing, burst a large artery, and was immediately suffocated in his blood! This is the sixth death in the course of the first three months of the year, and we have not as yet a single birth for a set-off. Say what one will to the negroes, and treat them as well as one can, obstinate devils, they will die!

April 9

I had mentioned to Mr Shand my having found a woman at Hordley, who had been crippled for life, in consequence of her having been kicked in the womb by one of the book-keepers. He writes to me on this subject:— 'I trust that conduct so savage occurs rarely in *any* country. I can only say, that in my long experience nothing of the kind has ever fallen under my observation.' Mr S. then ought to consider *me* as having been in high luck. I have not passed six months in Jamaica, and I have already found on one of my estates a woman who had been kicked in the womb by a white book-keeper, by which she was crippled herself, and on another of my estates another woman who had been kicked in the womb by another white book-keeper, by which he had crippled the child. The name of the first man and woman were Lory and Jeannette; those of the second were Fullwood and Martia: and thus, as my two estates are at the two extremities of the island, I am entitled to say, from my own knowledge (*i.e.* speaking *literally*, observe), that 'white book-keepers kick black women in the belly *from one end of Jamaica to the other*'.

April 15 (Wednesday)

About noon to-day a well-disposed healthy lad of seventeen years of age was employed in unhaltering the first pair of oxen of one of the waggons, in doing which he entangled his right leg in the rope. At that moment the oxen set off full gallop, and dragged the boy along with them round the whole inclosure, before the other negroes could succeed in stopping them. However, when the prisoner was extricated, although his flesh appeared to have been terribly lacerated, no bones were broken, and he was even able to walk to the hospital without support. He was blooded instantly, and two physicians were sent for by express. At two o'clock he was still in perfect possession of his senses, and only complained of the soreness of his wounds: but in half an hour after he became apoplectic; sank into a state of utter insensibility, during which a dreadful rattling in his throat was the only sign of still existing life, and before six in the evening all was over with him!

April 17

Pickle had accused his brother-in-law, Edward the Eboe, of having given him a pleurisy by the practice of Obeah. During my last visit I had convinced him that the charge was unjust (or at least he had declared himself to be convinced), and about six weeks ago they came together to assure me, that ever since they had lived upon the best terms possible. Unluckily, Pickle's wife miscarried lately, and for the third time; previously to which Edward had said, that his wife would remain sole heiress of the father's property. This was enough to set the suspicious brains of these foolish people at work; and to-day Pickle and his father-in-law, old Damon, came to assure me, that in order to prevent a child coming to claim its share of the grandfather's property, Edward had practised Obeah to make his sister-in-law miscarry; the only proof of which adduced was the above expression, and the woman's having miscarried 'just according to Edward's very words!' To reason with such very absurd persons was out of the case. I found too, that the two sisters were quarrelling perpetually, and always on the point of tearing each other's eyes out. Therefore, as domestic peace 'in a house so disunited' was out of the question, I ordered the two families to separate instantly, and to live at the two extremities of the negro village; at the same time forbidding all intercourse between them whatsoever: a plan, which was received with approbation by all parties; and Edward moved his property out of the old man's house into another without loss of time. Among other charges of Obeah, Pickle declared, that his house having been robbed, Edward had told him that Nato was the offender; and in order to prove it beyond the power of doubt, he had made him look at something round, 'just like massa's watch', out of which he had taken a sentee (a something) which looked like an egg; this he gave to Pickle, at the same time instructing him to throw it at night against the door of Nato's house; which he had no sooner done and broken the egg, than the very next day Nato's wife Philippa 'began to bawl, and halloo, and went mad'. Now that Philippa had bawled and hallooed enough was certainly true; but it was also true that she had confessed her madness to have been a trick for the purpose of exciting my compassion, and inducing me to feed her from my own table. Yet was this simple fellow persuaded that he had made her go mad by the help of his broken egg, and his old fool of a father-in-law was goose enough to encourage him in the persuasion.

April 19 (Sunday)

'And massa,' said Bridget, the doctoress, this morning, 'my old mother a lilly *so-so* to-day; and him tank massa much for the good supper massa send last night; and him like it so well.—Laud! massa, the old lady was just thinking what him could yam (eat) and him no fancy nothing; and him could no yam salt, and him just wishing for something fresh, when at that very moment Cubina come to him from massa with a stewed pig's head so fresh: it seemed just as if massa had got it from the Almighty's hands himself.'

April 22

Naturalists and physicians, philosophers and philanthropists, may argue and decide as they please; but certainly, as far as mere observation admits of my judging, there does seem to be a very great difference between the brain of a black person and a white one. I should think that Voltaire would call a negro's reason 'une raison très particulière'. Somehow or other, they never can manage to do anything *quite* as it should be done. If they correct themselves in one respect to-day they are sure of making a blunder in some other manner to-morrow. Cubina is now twenty-five, and has all his life been employed about the stable; he goes out with my carriage twice every day; yet he has never yet been able to succeed in putting on the harness properly. Before we get to one of the plantation gates we are certain of being obliged to stop, and put something or other to rights: and I once remember having laboured for more than half an hour to make him understand that the Christmas holidays came at Christmas; when asked the question, he always hesitated, and answered, at hap-hazard, 'July' or 'October'. Yet, Cubina is far superior in intellect to most of the negroes who have fallen under my observation. The girl too, whose business it is to open the house each morning, has in vain been desired to unclose all the jalousies: she never fails to leave three or four closed, and when she is scolded for doing so, she takes care to open those three the next morning, and leaves three shut on the opposite side. Indeed, the attempt to make them correct a fault is quite fruitless: they never can do the same thing a second time in the same manner; and if the cook having succeeded in dressing a dish well is desired to dress just such another, she is certain of doing something which makes it quite different. One day I desired, that there might be always a piece of salt meat at dinner, in order that I might be certain of always having enough to send to the sick in the hospital. In consequence, there was nothing at dinner but salt meat. I complained that there was not a single fresh dish, and the next day, there was nothing but fresh. Sometimes there is scarcely anything served up, and the cook seems to have forgotten the dinner altogether: she is told of it; and the next day she slaughters without mercy pigs, sheep, fowls, ducks, turkeys, and everything that she can lay her murderous hands upon, till the table absolutely groans under the load of her labours. For above a month Cubina and I had perpetual quarrels about the cats being shut into the gallery at nights, where they threw down plates, glasses, and crockery of all kinds, and made such a clatter that to get a wink of sleep was quite out of the question. Cubina, before he went to rest, hunted under all the beds and sofas, and laid about him with a long whip for half an hour together; but in half an hour after his departure the cats were at work again. He was then told, that although he had turned them out, he must certainly have left some window open: he promised to pay particular attention to this point, but that night the uproar was worse than ever; yet he protested that he had carefully turned out all the cats, locked all the doors, and shut all the windows. He was told, that if he had really turned out all the cats, the cats must have got in again, and therefore that he must have left some one window open at least.

'No,' he said, 'he had not left one; but a pane in one of the windows had been broken two months before, and it was there that the cats got in whenever they pleased.' Yet he had continued to turn the cats out of the door with the greatest care, although he was perfectly conscious that they could always walk in again at the window in five minutes after. But the most curious of Cubina's modes of proceeding is, when it is necessary for him to attack the pigeon-house. He steals up the ladder as slily and as softly as foot can fall; he opens the door, and steals in his head with the utmost caution; on which, to his never-failing surprise and disappointment, all the pigeons make their escape through the open holes; he has now no resource but entering the dove-cot, and remaining there with unwearied patience for the accidental return of the birds, which nine times out of ten does not take place till too late for dinner, and Cubina returns empty-handed. Having observed this proceeding constantly repeated during a fortnight, I took pity upon his embarrassment, and ordered two wooden sliders to be fitted to the holes. Cubina was delighted with this exquisite invention, and failed not the next morning to close all the holes on the right with one of the sliders; he then stepped boldly into the dove-cot, when to his utter confusion the pigeons flew away through the holes on the left. Here then he discovered where the fault lay, so he lost no time in closing the remaining aperture with the second slider, and the pigeons were thus prevented from returning at all. Cubina waited long with exemplary patience, but without success, so he abandoned the new invention in despair, made no farther use of the sliders, and continues to steal up the ladder as he did before. A few days ago, Nicholas, a mulatto carpenter, was ordered to make a box for the conveyance of four jars of sweetmeats, of which he took previous measure; yet first he made a box so small that it would scarcely hold a single jar, and then another so large that it would have held twenty; and when at length he produced one of a proper size, he brought it nailed up for travelling (although it was completely empty), and nailed up so effectually too, that on being directed to open it that the jars might be packed, he split the cover to pieces in the attempt to take it off. Yet, among all my negroes, Nicholas and Cubina are not equalled for adroitness and intelligence by more then twenty. Judge then what must be the remaining three hundred!

April 23

In my medical capacity, like a true quack I sometimes perform cures so unexpected, that I stand like Katterfelto, 'with my hair standing on end at my own wonders'.* Last night, Alexander, the second governor, who has been seriously ill for some days, sent me word, that he was suffering cruelly from a pain in his head, and could get no sleep. I knew not how to relieve him; but having frequently observed a violent passion for perfumes in the house negroes, for want of something else I gave the doctoress some oil of lavender, and told her to rub two or three drops upon his nostrils. This morning, he told me that 'to be sure what I had sent him was a grand medicine indeed', for it had no sooner touched his nose than he felt something cold run up to his forehead, over his head, and all the way down his neck to the back-bone; instantly, the headach left him, he fell fast asleep, nor had the pain returned in the morning. But I am afraid, that even this wonderful oil would fail of curing a complaint which was made to me a few days ago. A poor old creature, named Quasheba,* made her appearance at my breakfast table, and told me, 'that she was almost eighty, had been rather weakly for some time past, and somehow she did not feel as she was by any means right'. 'Had she seen the doctor? Did she want physic?' 'No, she had taken too much physic already, and the doctor would do her no good; she did not want to see the doctor.' 'But what then was her complaint?' 'Oh! she had no particular complaint; only she was old and weakly, and did not find herself by any means so well as she used to be, and so she came just to tell massa, and see what he could do to make her quite right again, that was all.' In short, she *only* wanted me to make her young again!

April 24

Mr Forbes is dead. When I was last in Jamaica, he had just been poisoned with corrosive sublimate by a female slave, who was executed in consequence. He never was well afterwards; but as he lived intemperately, the whole blame of his death must not be laid upon the poison.

April 30

A free mulatto of the name of Rolph had frequently been mentioned to me by different magistrates, as remarkable for the numerous complaints brought against him for cruel treatment of his negroes. He was described to me as the son of a white ploughman, who at his death left his son six or seven slaves, with whom he resides in the heart of the mountains, where the remoteness of the situation secures him from observation or control. His slaves, indeed, every now and then contrive to escape, and come down to Savannah la Mar to lodge their complaints; but the magistrates, hitherto, had never been able to get a legal hold upon him. However, a few days ago, he entered the house of a Mrs Edgins, when she was from home, and behaving in an outrageous manner to her slaves, he was desired by the head-man to go away. Highly incensed, he answered, 'that if the fellow dared to speak another word, it should be the last that he should ever utter'. The negro dared to make a rejoinder; upon which Rolph aimed a blow at him with a stick, which missed his intended victim, but struck another slave who was interposing to prevent a scuffle, and killed him upon the spot. The murder was committed in the presence of several negroes; but negroes are not allowed to give evidence, and as no free person was present, there are not only doubts whether the murderer will be punished, but whether he can even be put upon his trial.

May 1 (Friday)

This morning I signed the manumission of Nicholas Cameron, the best of my mulatto carpenters. He had been so often on the very point of getting his liberty, and still the cup was dashed from his lips, that I had promised to set him free, whenever he could procure an able negro as his substitute; although being a good workman, a single negro was by no means an adequate price in exchange. On my arrival this year I found that he had agreed to pay 150*l.* for a female negro, and the woman was approved of by my trustee. But on enquiry it appeared that she had a child, from which she was unwilling to separate, and that her owner refused to sell the child, except at a most unreasonable price. Here then was an insurmountable objection to my accepting her, and Nicholas was told to his great mortification, that he must look out for another substitute. The woman, on her part, was determined to belong to Cornwall estate and no other: so she told her owner, that if he attempted to sell her elsewhere she would make away with herself, and on his ordering her to prepare for a removal to a neighbouring proprietor's, she disappeared, and concealed herself so well, that for some time she was believed to have put her threats of suicide into execution. The idea of losing his 150*l.* frightened her master so completely, that he declared himself ready to let me have the child at a fair price, as well as the mother, if she ever should be found; and her friends having conveyed this assurance to her, she thought proper to emerge from her hiding-place, and the bargain was arranged finally. The titles, however, were not yet made out, and as the time of my departure for Hordley was arrived, these were ordered to be got ready against my return, when the negroes were to be delivered over to me, and Nicholas was to be set free. In the meanwhile, the child was sent by her mistress (a free mulatto) to hide some stolen ducks upon a distant property, and on her return blabbed out the errand: in consequence the mistress was committed to prison for theft; and no sooner was she released, than she revenged herself upon the poor girl by giving her thirty lashes with the cattle-whip, inflicted with all the severity of vindictive malice. This treatment of a child of such tender years reduced her to such a state, as made the magistrates think it right to send her for protection to the workhouse, until the conduct of the mistress should have been enquired into. In the meanwhile, as the result of the enquiry might be the setting the girl at liberty, the joint title for her and her mother could not be made out, and thus poor Nicholas's manumission was at a stand-still again. The magistrates at length decided, that although the chastisement had been severe, yet (according to the medical report) it was not such as to authorise the sending the mistress to be tried at the assizes. She was accordingly dismissed from farther investigation, and the girl was once more considered as belonging to me, as soon as the title could be made out. But the fatality which had so often prevented Nicholas from obtaining his freedom, was not weary yet. On the very morning, when he was to sign the title, a person whose signature was indispensable, was thrown out of his chaise, the wheel of which passed over his head, and he was rendered incapable of transacting business for several weeks. Yesterday, the titles were at length brought to me complete, and this morning put Nicholas in possession of the object, in the pursuit of which he has experienced such repeated disappointments. The conduct of the poor child's mulatto mistress in this case was most unpardonable, and is only one of numerous instances of a similar description, which have been mentioned to me. Indeed, I have every reason to believe, that nothing can be uniformly more wretched, than the life of the slaves of free people of colour in Jamaica; nor would any thing contribute more to the relief of the black population, than the prohibiting by law any mulatto to become the owner of a slave for the future. Why should not rich people of colour be served by poor people of colour, hiring them as domestics? It seldom happens that mulattoes are in possession of plantations; but when a white man dies, who happens to possess twenty negroes, he will divide them among his brown family, leaving (we may say) five to each of his four children. These are too few to be employed in plantation work; they are, therefore, ordered to maintain their owner by some means or other, and which means are frequently not the most honest, the most frequent being the travelling about as higglers, and exchanging the trumpery contents of their packs and boxes with plantation negroes for stolen rum and sugar. I confess I cannot see why, on such bequest being made, the law should not order the negroes to be sold, and the produce of the sale paid to the mulatto heirs, but absolutely prohibiting the mulattoes from becoming proprietors of the negroes themselves. Every man of humanity must wish that slavery, even in its best and most mitigated form, had never found a legal sanction, and must regret that its system is now so incorporated with the welfare of Great Britain as well as of Jamaica, as to make its extirpation an absolute impossibility, without the certainty of producing worse mischiefs than the one which we annihilate. But certainly there can be no sort of occasion for continuing in the colonies the existence of *domestic slavery*, which neither contributes to the security of the colonies themselves, nor to the opulence of the mother-country, the revenue of which derived from colonial duties would suffer no defalcation whatever, even if neither whites nor blacks in the West Indies were suffered to employ slaves, except in plantation labour.

May 2

I gave my negroes a farewell holiday, on which occasion each grown person received a present of half-a-dollar, and every child a maccaroni. In return, they endeavoured to express their sorrow for my departure, by eating and drinking, dancing and singing, with more vehemence and perseverance than on any former occasion. As in all probability many years will elapse without my making them another visit, if indeed I should ever return at all, I have at least exerted myself while here to do everything which appeared likely to contribute to their welfare and security during my absence. In particular, my attorney has made out a list of all such offences as are most usually committed on plantations, to which proportionate punishments have been affixed by myself. From this code of internal regulations the overseer is not to be allowed to deviate, and the attorney has pledged himself in the most solemn manner to adhere strictly to the system laid down for him. By this scheme, the negroes will no longer be punished according to the momentary caprice of their superintendent, but by known and fixed laws, the one no more than the other, and without respect to partiality or prejudice. Hitherto, in everything which had not been previously determined by the public law, with a penalty attached to the breach of it, the negro has been left entirely at the mercy of the overseer, who if he was a humane man punished him slightly, and if a tyrant, heavily; nay, very often the quantity of punishment depended upon the time of day when the offence was made known. If accused in the morning, when the overseer was in cold blood and in good humour, a night's confinement in the stocks might be deemed sufficient; whereas if the charge was brought when the superior had taken his full proportion of grog or sangaree,* the very same offence would be visited with thirty-nine lashes. I have, moreover, taken care to settle all disputes respecting property, having caused all negroes having claims upon others to bring them before my tribunal previous to my departure, and determined that from that time forth no such claims should be enquired into, but considered as definitively settled by my authority. It would have done the Lord Chancellor's heart good to see how many suits I determined in the course of a week, and with what expedition I made a clear court of chancery. But perhaps the most astonishing part of the whole business was, that after judgment was pronounced, the losers as well as the gainers declared themselves perfectly satisfied with the justice of the sentence. I must acknowledge, however, that the negro principle that 'massa can do no wrong', was of some little assistance to me on this occasion. 'Oh! quite just, me good, massa! what massa say, quite just! me no say nothing more; me good, massa!' Then they thanked me 'for massa's goodness in giving them so long talk!' and went away to tell all the others 'how just massa had been in taking away what they wanted to keep, or not giving them what they asked for'. It must be owned that this is not the usual mode of proceeding after the loss of a chancery suit in England. But to do the negroes mere justice, I must say, that I could not have wished to find a more tractable set of people on almost every occasion. Some lazy and obstinate persons, of course, there must inevitably be in so great a number; but in general I found them excellently disposed, and being once thoroughly convinced of my real good-will towards them, they were willing to take it for granted, that my regulations must be right and beneficial, even in cases where they were in opposition to individual interests and popular prejudices. My attorney had mentioned to me several points, which he thought it advisable to have altered, but which he had vainly endeavoured to accomplish. Thus the negroes were in the practice of bequeathing their houses and grounds, by which means some of them were become owners of several houses and numerous gardens in the village, while others with large families were either inadequately provided for, or not provided for at all. I made it public, that from henceforth no negro should possess more than one house, with a sufficient portion of ground for his family, and on the following Sunday the overseer by my order looked over the village, took from those who had too much to give to those who had too little, and made an entire new distribution according to the most strict Agrarian law. Those who lost by this measure, came the next day to complain to me; when I avowed its having been done by my order, and explained the propriety of the proceeding; after which they declared themselves contented, and I never heard another murmur on the subject. Again, mothers being allowed certain indulgences while suckling, persist in it for two years and upwards, to the great detriment both of themselves and their children: complaint of this being made to me, I sent for the mothers, and told them that every child must be sent to the weaning-house on the first day of the fifteenth month, but that their indulgences should be

continued to the mothers for two months longer, although the
children would be no longer with them. All who had children of that
age immediately gave them up; the rest promised to do so, when they
should be old enough; and they all thanked me for the continuance
of their indulgences, which they considered as a boon newly granted
them. On my return from Hordley, I was told that the negroes suffered their pigs to infest the works and grounds in the immediate
vicinity of the house in such numbers, that they were become a
perfect nuisance; nor could any remonstrance prevail on them to
confine the animals within the village. An order was in consequence
issued on a Saturday, that the first four pigs found rambling at large
after two days should be put to death without mercy; and accordingly on Monday morning, at the negro breakfast hour, the head
governor made his appearance before the house, armed cap-a-pee,
with a lance in his hand, and an enormous cutlass by his side. The
news of this tremendous apparition spread through the estate like
wildfire. Instantly all was in an uproar; the negroes came pouring
down from all quarters; in an instant the whole air was rent with
noises of all kinds and creatures; men, women, and children shouting and bellowing, geese cackling, dogs barking, turkeys gobbling;
and, look where you would, there was a negro running along as fast
as he could, and dragging a pig along with him by one of the hind
legs, while the pigs were all astonishment at this sudden attack, and
called upon heaven and earth for commiseration and protection,—

> With many a doleful grunt and piteous squeak,
> Poor pigs! as if their pretty hearts would break!*

From thenceforth not a pig except my own was to be seen about the
place; yet instead of complaining of this restraint, several of the
negroes came to assure me, that I might depend on the animals not
being suffered to stray beyond the village for the future, and to thank
me for having given them the warning two days before. What other
negroes may be, I will not pretend to guess; but I am certain that
there cannot be more tractable or better disposed persons (take them
for all in all) than my negroes of Cornwall. I only wish, that in my
future dealings with white persons, whether *in* Jamaica or out of it,
I could but meet with half so much gratitude, affection, and good-
will.

APPENDIX I

Taken from [Margaret Baron-Wilson], *The Life and Correspondence of M. G. Lewis . . . with many pieces in prose and verse, never before published*, 2 vols. (London: Henry Colburn, 1839), ii. 271–86. Baron-Wilson's biography, which also reproduces a number of letters, poems and other pieces, is a somewhat higgledy-piggledy compilation, with many errors, but it remains a prime source of information about Lewis. This letter is to an unknown correspondent. Though Lewis characteristically used the same material in the *Journal* as in his letters, this lively account of the story-teller Goosee-Shoo-shoo, a cross between Mother Goose and Goody Two-Shoes, was omitted.

Cornwall, Jamaica, March 1815

MY DEAR——,

> Far removed, but not forgotten—
> Though absent, still to memory dear.

Oh, for Heaven's sake! do now, be *pretty*—*think* pretty—*write* pretty—I *can't* be pretty, all I try; and really you can't but perceive I am taking uncommon pains. However, you must have at any rate discovered, that I am uncommonly good-humoured: doubtless, because I'm writing to *you*; and as I cannot be 'pretty' in my own person and pen, I'll try to be so by proxy, by telling you a 'pretty' story. In the mean time, here am I, in a bower of beauty, (always including myself you know, in the irresistible combination)—here I sit, all among orange-blossoms, lime-trees, mangoes, mocking-birds, palm-trees,—and all that can render life delicious: every now and then, taking sly peeps in Memory's dear looking-glass, at many an old friend, in their snug European domiciles. Stay though, be hanged if I hadn't nearly forgot the little old woman and her pretty little old story.

I am going to tell you about *Goosee Shoo-shoo!* that is not exactly her name though; but a *sobriquet pour badiner*,[1] bestowed by myself, for a reason I shall tell you by and by: however, she has ever since been called so by all on my estate. I won't keep you much longer in

---

[1] A teasingly affectionate nickname.

suspense, than just to remind you, that the negroes are exceedingly partial to a species of—Now what shall I call it? fairy tale? No, not—*exactly*: more resembling our quaint old *nursery* tales (so cherished for that reason), and that we all, more or less, remember: such as, 'Jack the Giant-killer', 'Cinderella', 'Little Red Riding-hood', etc. They call these wonderful relations, '*Nancy Stories*'. And, by the by, I shall endeavour to collect some of these choice *morceaux*,[1] for a sort of journal I have *in petto*,[2] and which, indeed, I have already begun; meaning it for publication on my return to England.

Now there happens to be on my estate here, a certain (I was just going to say *fair*) lady, who appears wonderfully adroit in her profession; (and I may with great propriety term it so) as she trots about with her marvellous budget,[3] reminding one forcibly, though in more humble grade, of the Eastern story-tellers of certain renowned 'Hunch-backs', 'Wonderful Lamps', etc. etc. When first this most amusing dame came in my way, and I was told of her acquirements, I remember I laughingly observed to a gentleman with me 'That, sir, is our *Goody Two-shoes*.' Something in the sound caught the general fancy, it seems; for ever since she has every where been called by the negroes, '*Goosee Shoo-shoo*'; so now you know the why and because of the matter.

A glass of rum, or a roll of *backy*, is sure to unpack Goosee Shoo-shoo's budget; and the other day I made her recite one of her pet stories; which she did, with her little sable audience squatted round her. You must not be surprised at this; it is quite the custom here; it is impossible to be much alone: and like the Portuguese servants, they squat down in your presence, grin at your jokes, pass remarks, etc., yet still considering themselves as slaves. All this seems strange at first, but it is the custom. I do wish you could see Goosee Shoo-shoo; she is so truly picturesque in her short cloak, her dapper red petticoat, and the strip of white callico so exquisitely rolled about her head, from beneath which, her shrewd black eyes twinkle towards the proffered rum, so expressively; then the short pipe, stuck in the corner of her mouth; and the scarlet string of palm-berries round

[1] Morsels.
[2] In miniature.
[3] A pouch, bag, wallet, usually of leather, and, by extension, as Lewis seems to intend, its contents, here a story hoard.

her shining black throat. Oh! really, old Goosee Shoo-shoo is, decidedly, a most irresistible little woman.

However, to my story—my *pretty*, *pretty* story. All I can remember in the true *gusto* of Shoo-shoo's precise words, you shall have 'neat as imported'. Where I am a little at a loss, you must e'en be content to have the thread of the story taken up by Mat, in the best manner he is able. So pray take it as you can get it; ay, and thank me too, I beg, for reserving this choice bit of originality for your special entertainment.

Goosee Shoo-shoo's true and marvellous history of a 'lilly nigger-man born vidout ed'

'Vonce on time, my piccaninnies' (the *piccaninny* nearest to her, and grinning with extension from ear to ear, being a fellow above six feet, proportionably stout, and apparently between thirty and forty years of age), 'vonce on time dere live voman under cotton-tree, ab lilly son, born vidout ed. So ven she see her son ab got no ed, the voman say, Vat I do now? my son ab no ed; and I 'fraid him look particular, and ebbery body take notice: beside, him no talk—him no hear—him no see—him no yammee (eat)—so what I do now? Tink I know what I do. I get lilly bird sit upon him shoulder; pick up yamee for my son, put in him stomach; so den him do berry well without ed.'

Now it seems this good lady, whose son was so inconveniently situated, possibly from not being able immediately to meet with a 'lilly bird' willing to oblige, by acceding to a request which considering the very peculiar situation of affairs, was by no means unreasonable, suddenly bethought her of an owl, who dwelt hard by, and whose wisdom and gravity were sufficiently renowned, to have accommodated many a head; particularly those that, like his own, though wise in themselves, were never known to make other heads a bit the wiser on that account. To this sage personage, then, goes the embarrassed lady of the cotton-tree. The owl was at home (such being the usual term for seeing company); his head also being in its usual place, it is to be hoped there was something in it: not that this is a consequence to be invariably insisted upon—it might, indeed, be exacting too much in some cases. The distressed dame opens the business, according to Shoo-shoo, in the following affecting ditty:

' "Ho day! hey day! What I do? what I say?
De sun him peep goldee, de berries hang red;
But poor lilly nigger, him neber a ed.

' "How day, massa!"
' "How day, nigger woman," say de owl: "what you want wid me?" '
'So den, my piccaninnies, de woman no like say her son born
widout ed, 'cause she tink he no belieb *dat*; so she say,
' "Oh, massa! my son run along upon de grass, ab lilly misforten—
him ed tumble off, and roll into ribber.—Berry sorry, massa!"
' "Vell," say de owl, "I must tink lilly bit." '

And truly this was a matter not to be decided upon in a hurry, or
without due consideration; for it must be remembered that the owl
had a head, and what is the use of having a head if one does not make
use of it? Besides, I ought here to observe, that Shoo-shoo had, as
she proceeded, informed her auditors that the poor woman's son had,
beside the disadvantage of being without a head, been so unfortunate as to lose his heart; and that to one of those most beautiful
princesses, who usually grace these interesting narrations, and are
always so incomparable whenever they evince an inclination to be
beautiful and presume to be princesses. Having explained thus far, I
shall permit Shoo-shoo to proceed in her own words.

'So den, my picccaninnies, de owl, after him tink lilly bit more, he
say, Pull you *tree* feaders from my tail, and go your way wid your son
to vere de brook-water run shinee; and mind you blow de tree feaders
in face of de first ting you meet, and takee what follow.'

Away trots the dame, straight forwards to the running brook, with
her headless son, just in time to catch an ass at dinner-time. The exi-
gence of the case wouldn't admit of much ceremony; so puff went
the three mysterious feathers in the face of the unsuspecting donkey;
who, without inquiring further into the nature of this abrupt salutation, returned so low a bow, that he left his head at her feet. It must
be evident, that to say the accommodating owl was *no conjuror*, would
be nothing short of defamation of character. The good woman did
not hesitate to avail herself of this turn of luck: she, doubtless, knew
very well there are cases that will not admit of one's being over particular; so, without more ado, she popped the ass's head upon the
shoulders of her distressed son. It fitted to a nicety, and, as they say
in London of a pair of sale shoes, 'just as if made to order'. Now

whether the dame knew any thing about that good old proverb—'two heads better than one', is uncertain: it is clear, however, she was of opinion that *any* head was better than *none at all*: besides, her son being bent upon a wooing expedition, it was obvious that a head of some sort was absolutely necessary, if only to preserve appearances. By the by, how the bereaved donkey managed in the interim without his head, as Shoo-shoo did not think it requisite to explain, why should I presume to meddle? Get on without a head! And why not, I should like to know? Is there any thing so very singular—so very unusual—so very—Pooh! pooh! 'tis really a delicate topic. So now to Shoo-shoo's further account.

'Vell, my piccaninnies, so, ven nigger man ab him ed, *like ebery body else*, him mamma put upon him lilly red coat, and sword by him side; pipe in him mout, and lilly bottel arquedente[1] in him hand; and he go courtee-courtee, 'cause him look so killing den, my piccaninnies!'

How the princess received a beau of such singular recommendations, does not immediately appear: for, according to our story-teller, it turned out, that the head-borrowing gentleman had unluckily obtained more of the nature thereunto appertaining, than was quite convenient or consistent with the delicate nature of his errand; and that, notwithstanding the head he presented being considered no ways peculiar or uncommon, there must doubtless have been *somewhat in the tones of his voice*, as *pleading* his tender suit, that prejudiced minds were unable duly to appreciate: since the luckless nigger-beau was fain to depart amid roars of laughter, together with the awkward accompaniment of sundry cracking whips, signifying the general opinion far more plainly than agreeably; and the poor 'lilly nigger-man', having his ass's head knocked off in the scuffle, ran home to his mother, headless as ever. So again (according to Shoo-shoo) goes the lady of the cotton-tree to her friend and counsellor, the owl, to plead her—

'"Ho day! hey day! What I do? what I say?
De sun him peep goldee, de berries hang red;
But poor lilly nigger him neber a head.

'"How day, massa!"
'"How day, nigger-voman!" say de owl; "what you want wid me?"

---

[1] From the Spanish *aguardiente* (brandy, liquor).

'So den, my piccaninnies, de voman no like for say her son born vidout ed, 'cause she tink he no belieb *dat*; so dis time she say,

'"Oh, massa! my son berry mush hungry von day; so ven him yam-yammee, he make lilly mistake—swallow him own ed in him hurry. Berry sorry, massa."

'So den de owl him think lilly bit agen.'

A plain proof how well he merited his usual appellation of 'The Bird of Wisdom'; since he was evidently aware of the old sayings, 'Look before you leap', 'Turn round three times', 'Think *seven* times', etc. In short, it is clear that the owl was at any rate a bird wise enough to think before he spoke: whether, when he spoke, it was to the purpose, or whether he spoke at all, I confess myself on this, as regarding some other incidents of the story, a little sceptical. I have, however, the authority of Shoo-shoo that he *did* speak, and much to the purpose: that is, to the important and most desirable purpose of clapping a new head upon the shoulders of the luckless little nigger-man. For this time, he replied, (according to Shoo-shoo)—'Takee dose tree lilly egg, and go you way to de palm-tree yonder, vere de pine-nut hanging so red; and mind you trow dem in de face of de fust ting dat you see dere; and takee what follow.'

Away trots the dame again, with her son; and this being a new pro-ceeding, it was accompanied by new hopes. They arrive just in time to find a monstrous hog, snoring at the foot of the palm-tree. The old lady was unwilling to disturb him, so splash go the three eggs full upon the closed eyes of the grunting reveller, who, like most people blinded by rage, and whatever may be flung in their eyes, bounced off in such a passion, as to leave his head behind him. The new head fitted quite as neatly as the former: and really, on the whole, looking as well as many that pass in a crowd. Away again hastes the lover, with his cargo of hopes—fears—his 'lilly red coat', his pipe and bottle of arquedente. It is impossible to say what flattering result had been wrought by our hero's novel pretentions to a lady's favour, had he not unluckily again proved himself a victim to the uncon-querable propensity of the head he had borrowed, by thrusting his snout unceremoniously into every nice dish preparing in the royal kitchen; so that the enraged cook was at last fain to throw out certain unpleasant hints, not only of *basting* him well with the ladle, but also employing the *spit*, and thereby introducing him to the royal banquet, a subject ready *roasted*. Such notions so terribly alarmed the poor little nigger-man, that, leaving his pig's head to stop cookey's tongue, it seems, he ran home to his mammy headless as ever.

It was really most commendable—the unwearied perseverance of the restless dame to obtain that somewhat convenient article, a head, for her luckless son: as again (according to our story-teller) was the old ditty chanted to the patient owl of—

Ho-day! hey-day, etc. etc.,

followed by the usual salutation—

'How day, massa?' To which responded the civil reply, 'How day, nigger-woman? what you want vid me?'

Now, being her *third* visit upon this momentous affair, and third times being, I believe, by established rule, ever fraught with luck (good or ill, as the case may warrant), the lady of the cotton-tree was certainly justified in expecting something definitive, and accordingly determined this time to disclose the true state of the case. Allowing Shoo-shoo therefore to proceed in her own manner:

' "Oh, massa," say de voman, "my son ab no ed, him *nebber* ab ed *at all*. Him born *widout ed.—Berry sorry*, massa." So den de owl him say Vy you no say dis afore nigger-voman? For de owl him know all de time nigger-vomam say two tumping lie, my piccaninnies; and dat why her son ab trubbel so great you see. So den de owl forgib ven she say de trute; and him say, "Let you son go see him lubbee—him soon find him ed." '

Tolerably awake that, for a dozing owl, I think! So it seems the poor nigger beau, finding, I suppose, such ill success with borrowed heads, thought that he would this time try his luck by presenting himself at least in his own proper person; trusting to at least finding a head to match to his own satisfaction, and that of other people. Thus reasoning, he set out 'a wooing to go' for the third time: not being lucky enough, however, to find a head before his arrival, of course he was obliged to present himself without one; and such sights not being common in that dawning era, the fair princess accordingly screamed, tore her hair, kicked, cried, and every thing else that fair ladies do when exceedingly frightened. His majesty her papa also, being by it seems, took occasion to express his extreme consternation, and stamped and swore in such grand *duo* with his screaming daughter, that it became a nice point to determine which was likely to give in first. The old gentleman, however, like many old

gentlemen, reflecting perhaps that if he could get his daughter off
his hands, a head, whether it stood in the way or not, should not at
any rate put him *out* of his way, began at length to argue in favour
of the strange suitor, in a style, which if not immediately convincing, certainly was by no means deficient in point of energy: as proved
by Shoo-shoo, who thus continued:

'So den, my piccaninnies, de princess she say, "Oh la, fader, me
no marry dat man—him hab got no ed!" So den him majesty look
berry grand, all in a tundering passion, and him say, like jentelman,
"Curse your imperance, miss! vat you mean by dat? You no marry
de man? you *sall* marry de man! An for him ed, I soon make him
ed—lookee, now, I make for him ed, berry soon."

'So den, my piccaninnies, him majesty say "bring de vip for
floggee", and directly two ear came all so quick, my piccaninies, two
bootiful big broad ear, so black, so shinee, lay upon him shoulder, all
ready for stick gold ring. "A-ha!" say him majesty, "taut I soon find
for him ear! Now lookee how I make for him mout. Ho dere! bring
me good drop arquedente." So den, my piccaninnies, him mout come
all so quick, so wide, so grinee. "Oh, ho!" say him majesty, "taut I
soon find for him mout! So now for him eye Ho dere! who see
dis tumping piece of gold?" Den, my piccaninnies, dere come all
sudden, two sush eye! so den him majesty put de tumping piece
of gold in nigger-man's hand; and directly ebery body holler, "Oh,
what bootiful ed! what bootiful nose! so broad, so flat, so black, so
shinee! Nebber was sush ed—sush fine ed! Nigger-man for ebber!
hooray."

'So ven de princess hear dis, she tink she marry him arter all; and
dey lib berry appy, an ab plenty rum an backy, de rest of dere day.'

As Goosee Shoo-shoo seemed to think this the best possible
winding up of her story, I took care the cunning old lass should have
her due share of the above highly-prized articles. Their importance,
in her estimation, might perhaps rather supersede the expected
moral of the tale; therefore, in justice to my favourite, I must really
be allowed to observe for her, that people who may have the misfortune to be born without heads, may be assured that telling lies will
prove the very worst cement for preserving heads of any description,
in a proper and becoming situation. Neither should the obvious truth
be allowed to pass without comment, that though an ass may occasionally be tolerated till he opens his mouth, any officious snout

poking where it has no business, is sure to get any *body* thereunto
appertaining soon sent about its own. I trust you give me some credit
for being duly observant—thus to extract something wise from the
head of an ass, and to gather sweet instruction from a pig's nose. At
any rate, let me hope that this specimen of negro *facetiæ* will not fail
to make you laugh heartily: the very best recipe, believe me, for
inward ailments.

APPENDIX II

From [Margaret Baron-Wilson], *The Life and Correspondence of M. G. Lewis* . . . , ii. 214–26, where it is described as a 'fragment of a kind of diary found among Lewis's papers' which 'seems to be written by him during his last visit to Jamaica'. The fragmentary nature of the story draws attention to the problems of communication between slave and slave-holder. It also gives a pleasant idea of Lewis sitting peacefully among the slaves and reading to them, and a quite different experience at night, which might have been very frightening indeed, except that Lewis seems to have been entirely without fear. It certainly shows his absolute trust in and affection for the slaves.

The negroes Quawboo and Jumma retain their place in my favour; nevertheless these two men have lately combined to perplex me— more particularly the former. I have not failed on questioning either of them, ever to receive the same answer, alluding to his *friend* and *adviser*; yet they appear influenced in a very opposite degree, Quawboo seeming irresolute and sad, still expressing his anxiety to 'ab talk vid him friend'; Jumma, on the contrary, is ever cheerful and at ease, assuring me of the pleasure he derives from such communication. Were it not for this circumstance, I should be tempted to imagine that they differed upon some parts of the doctrine I promulgated. However, they both continue unremitting in their attendance.

Affairs are certainly not improved, and in no wise cleared up, which implicate also, it grieves me to add, my favourite Quawboo most unpleasantly. I was yesterday reading among them according to custom, when he appeared to be more than usually affected by my exhortations, particularly when I spoke of the friendly admonishings or accusing voice of conscience; his agitation attracted general notice, causing me to interrogate him afterwards more closely than ever. 'Him friend', was still the vague reply,—those near looked round immediately for Jumma. However, he had already left the place. I asked him if there existed any cause of dispute; still, still that vague reply, followed by 'Dere be *friend*, false friend, dat say bad for nigger sometime, massa.'

'Well, well,' I replied, 'I will inquire further, and you shall be reconciled.'

Again was I perplexed by the bewildered look of this man, as he slowly replied,

'Massa, no speak of Jumma, massa; he'—

I was at this moment so suddenly called away as to be unable to hear the rest. The occasion proved to be one of vexation. An old negro complained to me of a loss he sustained; the particulars of which, as he proceeded, plainly accused Quawboo. Great was my concern and disappointment in my favourite on hearing this charge. I assured the old man of immediate reparation, as well as punishment of the offender, and he left me to the ponderings of my chagrin. The agitation of Quawboo, without doubt, was explained; yet these mysterious expressions, alluding to his 'friend, his false friend',—of whom did he speak? Surely not of Jumma, the ever-cheerful, the simple, light-hearted Jumma.

New suspicions unite with the past; yet the mystery of Quawboo's expression remains the same. I had summoned both the friends to my presence. Quawboo was the first to whom I spoke; he listened to the charge without manifesting surprise, thus tacitly admitting its truth; still an open confession was my aim, together with the elucidation of his continual mysterious allusions, which if not pointing at Jumma, seemed, though vaguely, to implicate some yet undiscovered individual. How disheartening is all this, when I recal my indefatigable endeavours to instil the principles of honesty and uprightness in these poor uncultivated minds!

'Ah, massa!' burst forth the agitated negro, 'me very wicked—me fraid—me no more hear massa talk out of big good book.'

'Nay, Quawboo,' I answered mildly, 'if you are in fault, you will require to hear the good book more than ever: do not suppose that you are turned from its counsels—that is your own work. Come, you just now called me your kind master, and so I ever wish to prove myself; but, Quawboo, if you were to build a wall of mud or any rubbish before my door, so as (by degrees, however slow) to shut me from your sight, the act is yours: while I remain the same indulgent master, I trust that you will not continue to pile this mud wall till you lose sight, not only of your indulgent master, but of the right road altogether. Do you understand me, Quawboo?'

'Iss, massa, iss. Oh! me tell all,' and he fell on his knees: 'me very wicked, and me do bad, but *he—he* teachee me bad.'

'He!' I exclaimed; 'who, man, who?'

'Vy, massa, dat rascal, my *false* friend.'

'Your friend, Quawboo! surely not Jumma?'

Quawboo regarded me a moment with such a bewildered stare, that I became more puzzled than ever. He did not immediately reply, while that appeared brewing in his mind, which evidently occasioned some powerful conflict. After gradually sinking into a sullenness, as peculiar and inexplicable as his previous agitation, he approached nearer, and with firm demeanour, looking me steadfastly in the face, said:

'Massa, me tell you de troot.'

'That's a good fellow,' I replied encouragingly, 'I was sure you would.'

'Iss, massa, tink dat best after all—berry good, berry much fine, as you ab say so oft.'

Here the fellow grinned with an expression of familiarity, I might say impudence, I had never witnessed in him before.

'Massa,' he quietly continued, 'Jumma berry bad man, and—massa, Jumma steal old Mumbee yam.'

I was astonished at this abrupt and unqualified assertion of Quawboo's, and felt even yet more grieved.

'How!' I exclaimed, 'Jumma, the merry, light-hearted Jumma! And can you prove it? for, indeed, old Mumbee did not hesitate very plainly to accuse *you*. However, I must inquire further into this business; meanwhile I shall question Jumma; and you, Quawboo, must remain secured. I am much concerned for you both on this occasion, and can imagine how grievous it must be to you, Quawboo, to turn the accusation upon your intimate friend and companion.'

Quawboo's lip quivered on hearing my last words, while something of his former expression of countenance returned. In a very few moments, however, he exhibited the same sullen air, as leaving the room he slowly and firmly repeated, 'Massa, *Jumma* steal old Mumbee yam.' Upon inquiry, I find that Jumma is just now employed at too great a distance; I must therefore be content, to defer the projected examination until to-morrow.

The mystery appertaining to Quawboo and his *friend* has at length been elucidated, though by an occurrence appearing to threaten the most disastrous result. I have also received a slight bodily injury, but my mind has been relieved, through a most gratifying medium, though in a manner that has caused among some of us even a little degree of mirth. The negro Quawboo remained a close prisoner all that day, while I, perplexed by the singularity of his conduct, willingly acceded to the proposal of those about me to examine the men severally, not so much from a desire of ascertaining the fact who had pilfered from the old man, as to elicit somewhat of his frequent allusions to his coadjutors or 'friends', as he chose to call them (for he now spoke of two), though he evidently considered one of them as undeserving of the appellation,—the sulky negro's detached sentences and broken English, still pointing to these two mysterious individuals; one of whom he appeared to consider as his leader, whose counsels he repented having despised, and the other a 'curse rascal' (as he termed him), who threatened to betray matters, and to whom Quawboo constantly referred his recent evil fortune. I was forcibly impressed by these accounts, which, though somewhat confused, were so similar to the replies I had myself received from the delinquent. Yet I could not apprehend any immediate serious result from one or two of the refractory, that needed, perhaps, but a timely check to recal them to their duty. Consoled by these reflections, which I imparted to those about me, we severally retired to repose; and though, according to the custom of dwellings here, the sultry air is admissible to my apartment, that renders further security than the long Venetian blind insupportable, I did not deem it requisite to prepare for any danger from without. I knew that he who alone had awakened suspicion was secured, and felt it impossible any could advert to the ever-laughing, gaily-singing Jumma, whose return was besides expected on the morrow, when I conjectured, from his naturally ingenuous temper all would be explained. With such thoughts, aided by the habitual hour of repose, I soon lost all recollection in a peaceful slumber. It was near midnight,—when I woke with a kind of feverish start, and a flashing remembrance of the events of the day. All was quiet, and though the night lamp twinkled faintly, I could distinguish most of the objects in my apartment. I was not only literally awake, but painfully so, for such, indeed, was the state of wakefulness at that hour. I closed my eyes as it were with an effort, and tried to fancy myself drowsy. Suddenly a gentle *vampire-like* breeze swayed my light jalousie; yet I scarce heeded the soft-measured whisper, but as serving to lull my restless nerves to the much coveted repose. Such was my wearied hope, when a faint crashing sound at a little distance greeted my ear, tending by no means to calm my irritability. I raised myself to listen—all was again silent; yet I was too thoroughly awake to pass over this circumstance. I stepped softly to the window, and remained some little time breathing the warm languid air, yet to hear nothing more but the monotonous hum of the numerous insects. Presently, however, a few faint moans became distinguishable; they soon ceased, and some strange wild bird flew shrieking past; its receding cry sounding like that which I had just heard. Under the impression that this was indeed the fact, I regained my couch; yet still but to doze and start, and wish for the bright morning, as my wasting lamp alternately shot up a glaring flame, or dimly cast grotesque shadows from the surrounding objects; while a succession of crowding fancies continued to suggest stealthy footsteps and half-suppressed breathings approaching nearer every moment. Continuing to gaze intently, I was at length convinced that a tall shadow passed slowly between the struggling flame and the transparent draperies of my couch; and by a sudden brilliant coruscation, I at length plainly beheld a hand and swarthy arm introduced between the hangings! I did not wait to observe what weapon it brandished, but springing upon the floor grasped tightly the throat of a human being, at the same moment that the extinguished lamp left us both in darkness. The person I had seized so firmly seemed attempting to utter something, but in vain; and in the fierce struggle I fell, striking my head with some violence against a marble pillar. I well remember the sickening return of consciousness as I lay unable to move or summon assistance, yet perfectly aware of the presence of some unseen intruder, who with evidently painful respiration seemed creeping slowly to the spot where I lay. The wound near my temple flowed copiously, and I again became insensible. When I recovered, I perceived that day was just breaking, and that I had been placed on a small sofa near the window. Some one was bending over me, and assiduously bathing my wound. I raised my eyes—they encountered the sable features of the negro Quawboo, expressive of the deepest concern.

'Ungrateful wretch!' I feebly uttered. 'Is it then you?'

Tears flowed from his eyes, as he sobbed out, 'Oh! wake, massa!— no go for die yet—Quawboo die vid grief den—he no come for hurt you ven him come de night so.'

'Merciful heaven! explain, then! Explain every thing this instant. Why come at so strange an hour? and what could be your intention? It was with you, then, that I struggled—was it not?'

'Iss, massa,' he replied; 'me come softly, see if massa awake.'

'But why—why come at all? and why not speak?'

'Massa queese so tight.'

'And how did you escape from confinement?'

'Me break hole, and—'

'So that, then, was the crash I heard?'

'Iss, massa—couldn't help holler lilly bit.'

I remembered the moaning I had heard, as I continued steadfastly to regard the countenance of the negro before me, which exhibited all the simplicity of truth and nature, combined with that of sincere penitence.

'Quawboo,' said I, 'you must now explain a great deal more, that appears to me to threaten serious consequences. In the first place, I suppose you will not now deny the old man's charge, though you were tempted to cast the blame on your friend Jumma.'

(Quawboo blubbering.) 'Iss, massa, I do dat—berry sorra—ope massa forgib dis time—for my friend say—'

'How! do you still accuse Jumma in any way?'

'No, massa, no: dat anoder wicked ting I do—tell lie—lay wickedness on poor Jumma. Oh, dear! oh dear! lay good big lump *on mud wall*, den massa, oh! oh! dat make me come peak to massa in night—cause me no rest—heart so heaby!'

'But, Quawboo, I must know to whom you have so often alluded as being your *friend* and *director*, whose counsel you repent not having taken. Tell me, then, who is he? How do you call him?'

'Got A'mighty, massa!'

Excellent as was the lesson of the man's reply, I could not help still regarding him with a lurking suspicion of some artful evasion.

'Quawboo,' said I, gravely, 'I cannot but commend your assertion of a truth I myself so frequently labour to inculcate: but in order to obtain a clear explanation of your late impressions, I will now ask you another question: who is that *other* of whom you have also spoken, whom you seem to think will betray your interests? How do you call *him*?'

'Him? Oh! him de dibbel, please massa,' answered Quawboo, with the triumphant air of an elated schoolboy. There was a simplicity about the poor negro that dissipated all lingering doubts of his sincerity; and notwithstanding weariness and slight bodily pain that I now felt, I could have laughed outright, from the combined causes of sudden relief from further apprehension.

'My good fellow,' said I, extending my hand, 'I really believe you: so now tell me of your progress with these opposing counsellors, and how you came to speak of the bad one as your *friend*. How was that, Quawboo?'

'Him *seem* friend, massa, cause him say berry much pleasure sometime, but him only say dat for get nigger in scrape. But den sometime me tink me hear *oder* voice, but den the false friend say, "Nebber mind, Quawboo, you like dat—*do* dat—*take* dat; nigger no found out." Ah! massa, dat ven I take old Mumbee yam. De good friend seem say, "Fie, nigger! I grieve for you." Den I no happy; and ven massa peak of Jumma, de *false* friend say, "Aha! dat good for you, Quawboo; say Jumma steal, and nobody nebber know." But I ab feel so grieve, dat if massa ab no lock me up at de moment, I ab peak all de trute—But, oh! massa, forgib dis time, and Quawboo nebber more mind *false* friend, but only him *true* friend, long ab him live.'

I shook hands with the delighted negro in token of forgiveness; and I really think the poor fellow's simple illustration of the voice of conscience striving with temptation, was precisely what he felt, and that the victory which, in this instance, he has gained, will make a lasting impression on his character.

EXPLANATORY NOTES

The notes are intended to provide historical and social details regarding Jamaica and slavery, excluding what is already in the Introduction, as well as to identify Lewis's many casual literary references. For having tracked down many of the latter, I am in debt to Mona Wilson, the only other editor of the *Journal* (Boston and New York: Houghton Mifflin; London: Routledge, 1929), as anyone coming after her must be. My other chief sources are the following:

Compact Edition of the Oxford English Dictionary (Oxford: Oxford University Press, 1971).

Dictionary of Caribbean English Usage, ed. Richard Allsopp (Oxford: Oxford University Press, 1996).

Dictionary of Jamaican English, ed. F. G. Cassidy and R. B. Le Page (Cambridge: Cambridge University Press, 1967).

New Grove Dictionary of Music and Musicians, ed. Stanley Sadie (London: Macmillan; Washington: Grove's Dictionaries of Music, 1980).

Oxford Classical Dictionary, ed. Simon Hornblower and Antony Spawforth, 3rd edn. (Oxford: Oxford University Press, 1996).

Oxford Companion to Ships and the Sea, ed. Peter Kemp (Oxford: Oxford University Press, 1976).

Oxford Companion to the Theatre, ed. Phyllis Hartnoll, 4th edn. (Oxford: Oxford University Press, 1983).

1 *Epigraph*: Lord Byron, *The Complete Poetical Works*, ed. Jerome J. McGann and Barry Weller (Oxford: Clarendon Press, 1991), vi. 13. The full text reads (on 'Monk' Lewis): '"I'd give the lands of Deloraine— | Dark Musgrave were alive again!" | *that is* | I would give many a Sugar Cane | Monk Lewis were alive again!' This epigram was not included in previous collections of Byron's poetry. The editors point out that, by parodying two lines from Scott's 'Lay of the Last Minstrel' (canto v, st. 29), Byron adverts to Lewis's major influence on Scott's poetry.

5 *'Nunc alio patriam quæro sub sole jacentem'*, *Virgil*: 'Now I seek a homeland lying beneath another sun': adapted from *Georgics*, ii. 512.

'black melancholy': Alexander Pope, 'Eloisa to Abelard', 165.

Miss O'Neil: Eliza O'Neill (1791–1872) was an Irish actress who had a highly successful five-year career before she retired in 1819 to marry Mr (later Sir) William Becher. At her Covent Garden debut, she had been greeted as a second Sarah Siddons.

'Elwina': the female lead in Hannah More's *Percy*, first performed at Covent Garden in December 1777. More (1745–1833) was a prolific and well-known writer, although her plays, of which *Percy* was probably the

most highly regarded, are now forgotten. Lewis is recollecting a line from Act V.

6 *crane-necked carriages*: the two main types of coach were distinguished by the design of the undercarriage. A crane-necked carriage had two parallel iron bars, curved in such a way as to allow the front wheels to pass beneath them, thus enabling it to turn even in a narrow street, unlike the carriage connected by a perch (a single straight or slightly bent bar), which was, however, lighter.

7 *brig*: a two-masted vessel, square-rigged, widely used for short and coastal trading voyages.

8 *in the true German style*: an allusion to the cult of male friendship prevailing in late eighteenth-century German life and letters (though without twentieth-century hints of homo-eroticism).

9 *Chops of the Channel*: a common term for the entry of the English Channel into the Atlantic.

10 *'Confusion worse confounded'*: John Milton, *Paradise Lost*, ii. 996.

'or convien morire': 'Now it's best to die.' The phrase Lewis probably had in mind is from Lodovico Ariosto's *Orlando Furioso* (1516; 1532), XXIV. cv. 8. Mandricardo's horse has stepped nobly in front of his master and taken the blow intended for him. The horse's head is split. Simultaneously the narrator says 'onde convien che muoia', translated most accurately as 'and so he dies perforce'.

Don Ferolo Whiskerandos: a character in R. B. Sheridan's *The Critic*. The quotations are a recollection of III. i.

11 *'Nulla quies . . . nullâque silentia parte.'*: 'No quiet within and nowhere silence', Ovid, *Metamorphoses*, xii. 48. The parenthetical *outus* is a playful macaronic antonym for the Latin *intus*.

Tantalus: Tantalus abused his privilege of dining with the gods either by betraying something he had overheard, or by stealing and giving to mortals nectar and ambrosia, or (most commonly) by killing and cooking his own son, Pelops, to see whether the gods would detect the forbidden food. His punishment was to hang on the branch of a tree over a lake, the fruit and water that would appease his hunger and thirst eternally out of reach.

Tooke: Andrew Tooke (1673–1732), master of Charterhouse, had translated and revised *Pantheum Mithicum*, by François Antoine Pomey, as a book for school use. Entitled *The Pantheon, representing the fabulous histories of the Heathen Gods and most illustrious heroes*, it was first published in 1698, and by 1824 was into a 35th edition.

12 *'Manibus date . . . flores!'*: 'Offer lilies with full hands! I shall scatter purple flowers': Virgil, *Aeneid*, vi. 883–4.

13 *the Guelphs and the Ghibellines*: the two great opposing factions in medieval Italian politics. The Guelphs supported the popes against the emperors, the Ghibellines the emperors against the popes.

18 *'peradventure were sleeping, or on a journey'*: allusion to a poem by Edward Thurlow, second Baron Thurlow (1781–1829), 'Hermilda in Palestine', canto I, xxxvii, published in 1812.

Lord Howe: The Glorious First of June was the title given to the first major encounter between the British and French fleets in the Revolutionary War (1793–1801). The commander, Richard, Earl Howe (1726–99), with twenty-five line-of-battle ships, met Admiral Villaret de Joyeuse with twenty-six, took six ships and sank a seventh. The British hailed this as a great victory; the French also considered it a success, since the convoy of grain ships their fleet was protecting reached its destination safely.

19 *Ouragans*: French for 'hurricane'. The French, Spanish, and English versions of this word all derive from *hurakan*, the word used by the Arawaks, who first populated the Carribean islands.

'in my mind's eye, Horatio': Shakespeare, *Hamlet*, I. ii.

Οσσομενος Πατερ' εσθλον ενι φρησιν*!*: 'Imagining his noble father in his mind': *Odyssey* i. 115.

20 *'The Sorrows of Werter'*: *The Sorrows of Young Werther* (*Die Leiden des jungen Werthers*), 1774, by Johann Wolfgang von Goethe, is a short semi-autobiographical epistolary novel, in which the hero commits suicide. It had been a sensational success. Writing to his mother in July 1792, from Weimar, Lewis tells her he has just been introduced to Goethe: 'so that you must not be [s]urprized if I should shoot myself one of these fine Mornings'. (Louis F. Peck, *A Life of Matthew S. Lewis* (Cambridge, Mass.: Harvard University Press, 1961), 190.)

'The Adventures of a Louse': Mona Wilson suggests the following identification: *The History of a French Louse, or the Spy of a New Species in France and England, containing a Description of the most Remarkable Personages in these Kingdoms, giving a Key to the chief events of the year 1779, and those which are to happen in 1780*; translated from the 4th edition of the revised and corrected Paris copy, 1780 (*Journal*, 1929).

'The Recess': *The Recess, or a Tale of Other Times* (1783–5) was a historical novel and best-seller by Sophia Lee (1750–1824), novelist and dramatist. She was a friend of Ann Radcliffe and had a younger sister, Harriet, also a writer.

'Valentine and Orson': a famous early French romance, which first appeared in English *c.*1550.

'Roslin Castle': the village of Roslin (or Rosslyn), on the banks of the Esk south of Edinburgh, is famous for its castle and chapel. The extensive ruins of the fourteenth-century castle were particularly popular with early nineteenth-century tourists.

21 *'of opinion . . . might haply inhabit'*: Shakespeare, *Twelfth Night*, IV. ii.

22 *Lady Townley*: a character in Colley Cibber's *The Provok'd Husband; or, a journey to London*, first produced at Drury Lane in 1728. Vanbrugh had

left behind nearly four acts of a play entitled 'A Journey to London', which Cibber completed.

22 *Phæacians*: the Phæacians, who dwelt on the island of Scheria (Corfu), had magical ships which needed no crew, travelled swiftly as birds, and recognized all the ports.

24 *'still vexed Bermoothes'*: Shakespeare, *The Tempest*, I. ii.

25 *'Che faro senz' Eurydice'*: 'What shall I do without Eurydice?', the famous aria from Christoph Willibald Gluck's opera *Orfeo ed Euridice* (1762).

'He sigh'd . . . and swallow'd again': adapted from John Dryden, 'Alexander's Feast', 119–20.

'Amor despues de la Muerte': Pedro Calderón de la Barca (1600–81), the most celebrated Spanish dramatist of his time, was in high favour with German critics of the Romantic period. *Amar después de la muerte* (To love beyond death) was one of his history plays.

26 *Pende . . . l'altra vita*: 'one true-love knot their lives together ties'; Fairfax translation of Torquato Tasso's *Gerusalemme Liberata* (1580–1). The phrase 'amanti e sposi' (lovers and spouses) occurs in I. lvi. 6, while these lines occur at I. lvii. 3–4.

Edward: Edward Sadler, the second mate, was badly injured on the return voyage, but by the time of Lewis's second voyage had recovered and been promoted chief mate (pp. 189 ff.; 197).

'The Six Princesses of Babylon': identified by Mona Wilson as *The Adventures of the Six Princesses of Babylon in their Travels to the Temple of Virtue*, by Lucy Peacock, a Bookseller in Oxford Street, London, 1786.

27 *'upon an odd volume of Messalina's poems'*: William Congreve, *The Way of the World*, V. Obviously a favourite joke, this turns up again in the *Journal*, and also in a letter (*Peck, Life of Matthew G. Lewis*, 192). Messalina was a notorious Roman empress; Mincing was obviously mispronouncing 'Miscellany'.

Sir Dudley North: Sir Dudley North (1641–91), according to Macaulay 'one of the ablest men of his time', was a leading merchant in the Turkey Company, and made his fortune in commerce before turning to politics. His younger brother, Roger (1653–1734), wrote his life and that of his other brothers: Francis North, Lord Guilford, and Revd Dr John North. Originally published separately, these are best known in the collected edition, which also includes Roger's autobiography: *Lives of the Norths* (1826).

La Perouse: Jean François de Galaup, comte de La Pérouse (1741–88), naval captain and navigator, in 1785 took command of a French government expedition to search for the North-west Passage from the Pacific side. He disappeared at sea in 1788.

28 *'peep through the blanket of the dark'*: Shakespeare, *Macbeth*, I. v.

'firmament of living sapphires': adapted from *Paradise Lost*, iv. 604–5.

29 *Gozzi's farce*: *Turandot* (1761) by Carlo Gozzi, Italian dramatist. Truffaldino is the chief eunuch of Turandot's seraglio. *Turandot*, one of Gozzi's 'fiabe' or fairy-tale plays, is the basis for the libretto of Puccini's well-known opera.

'*hide their diminished heads*': *Paradise Lost*, iv. 35.

'*in Africa the torrid*' '*of temper somewhat mulish*': from John Hookham Frere, 'Elegy on the Death of Jean Bon St André', a comic poem first published in the *Anti-Jacobin*, a weekly paper which ran from 1797 to 1798.

30 '*that bourne*': Shakespeare, *Hamlet*, III. i.

prizes: enemy vessels captured at sea by a ship of war (and also applied to contraband cargo taken from a merchant ship). Under British law at this time, the value of the goods and contents belonged to the captors; the booty was divided into eighths, of which three went to the captain, one to the commander-in-chief, one to the officers, one to the warrant officers, and two to the crew.

Yorick . . . newly recovered sword: a reference to Laurence Sterne's *A Sentimental Journey through France and Italy* (1768). Chapter: The Sword, Rennes. The anecdote related by Yorick, the narrator, has a West Indian connection, the commerce through which the impoverished Marquis regained his fortune and his sword was conducted in Martinique.

32 *Deseada*: the name by which the small island of Désirade was also known.

'*apricis natio gratissima mergis—*': 'A nation most pleasing to sun-loving seagulls': a playful adaptation of Virgil, *Aeneid*, v. 128. Virgil has 'statio': a station (i.e. a haunt).

St Christopher's and St Eustatia: names used interchangeably for St Kitts and St Eustatius, two of the Leeward Islands.

Columbus: in fact, Columbus achieved landfall on Guanahani (now San Salvador), a small island in the Bahamas, on 12 October 1492.

33 '*made all the world look gay*': adapted from Pope, *The Rape of the Lock*, ii. 52.

Caraccas: a group of six small uninhabited islands off the coast of Venezuela, near Cumaná. The heyday of piracy in the Caribbean was the late seventeenth and early eighteenth centuries, but the danger of pirates was still considerable.

'*Sabean odours from the spicy shores*': adapted from, *Paradise Lost*, iv. 162.

34 *Whose groans . . . impel the rain*: adapted from Scott, *The Lay of the Last Minstrel*, v. ii.

'*Hinc illæ lachrymæ!*': (classical Latin *lacrumae* or *lacrimae*). 'Hence those tears', i.e. 'So that's why he's crying!' Terence, *Andria*, 126; quoted by Cicero, *Pro Caelio*, 61, and perhaps proverbial.

Piccaroon: pirate.

35 *pinnace*: a ship's boat, rowed with eight, sometimes sixteen, oars; the larger boats could raise a mast and set a sloop rig when required.

36 *John-Canoe*: (junkanoo). The word derives from African sources, as does the festival itself, which seems likely to be of Yoruba origin, although it has assimilated European traditions of mumming, morris dancing, etc. These Christmas and New Year festivities, loud, lengthy, and highly theatrical, frequently provided the occasion for satirical and subversive comment through songs, comedy, and role-playing, and sometimes even a cover for organizing rebellion. The leader of the troop of dancers usually wore a elaborate head-dress such as Lewis describes (though never a canoe), and sometimes—closer to its African origins—a horned mask. About John-Canoe's opponent, John-Crayfish, whom Lewis mentions (p. 39) nothing is known.

Magno telluris . . . arenâ: 'Disembarking with a great love for land, the Trojans gain the desired sandy shore': Virgil, *Aeneid*, i. 171–2.

37 *Admiral of the Red . . . Admiral of the Blue*: until 1864, the English fleet was divided into three squadrons: in order of ranking, the red, the white, and the blue. Errol Hill, however, argues persuasively that the rival factions are much better explained as the Reds representing the Red-coats (the army), and the Blues the Blue-jackets (navy). See *The Jamaican Stage, 1655–1900: Profile of a Colonial Theatre* (Amherst, Mass.: University of Massachusetts Press, 1992), 239.

'Brown Girls': Lewis's phrasing is perhaps ambiguous: here as elsewhere 'brown' signifies mixed race.

39 *Astley's*: Astley's Amphitheatre, in London, was well known for circuses, burlettas, and pantomimes. After a fire in 1803, it was rebuilt and opened with an equestrian spectacle, of the kind for which it became especially famous. It was Astley's who provided the horses for Lewis's *Timour the Tartar*.

Douglas and Glenalvon: *Douglas* (1756), by the Revd John Home (1722–1808), was a much revived romantic tragedy. The quarrel takes place in IV. i.

'The Fair Penitent': based on Massinger and Field's *The Fatal Dowry*, *The Fair Penitent* (1703) was one of the three so-called 'she-tragedies' which earned its author, Nicholas Rowe (1674–1718) recognition as a leading dramatist of Queen Anne's time. Calista and Lothario are both characters in the play, the latter now proverbial as 'gay Lothario'.

Mr Coates: Robert Coates (1772–1848) was a wealthy eccentric from the West Indies who rented the Theatre Royal in Bath in 1810 so that he could play Romeo. Impervious to ridicule, he enjoyed a brief vogue for that very reason. He played Lothario at a benefit performance in 1811. Soon afterwards he lapsed into poverty and obscurity.

Catalani: Angelica Catalani (1780–1849) was a much-admired Italian soprano, beautiful in person as well as voice, who made her debut in

London in 1806 at the King's Theatre in M. A. Portugal's *Semiramide*. Such was her popularity that for singing twice a week during the 1808 season (2 January–2 August) she commanded the immense sum of £5,250, plus two benefit performances. She remained in London until 1814.

40 *'to fright the realms of Chaos and old Night'*: adapted from *Paradise Lost*, i. 43.

Mr Wilberforce: after a 'conversion' in 1784 which determined him to lead a strictly religious life, William Wilberforce (1759–1833), philanthropist, MP, devoted himself to the emancipation of slaves. He had been elected to Parliament as member for Hull in 1780, and in 1787 took on parliamentary leadership of the abolition movement. It was another twenty years before the Act to abolish the slave trade was passed, and Wilberforce died without seeing emancipation, although he had never slackened in his determination. As late as 1824 he wrote *Appeal to the Religion, Justice, and Humanity of the Inhabitants of the British Empire on behalf of the Negro Slaves in the West Indies*.

41 *'Son of the Morning'*: Isaiah 14: 12.

Lot's wives: Lot's wife was turned into a pillar of salt as a punishment for curiosity. Genesis 19: 26.

curricle and pair . . . gig: the curricle and gig were both light two-wheeled vehicles, but the first was drawn by a pair, the second by one horse only. The curricle was smart and fast, a young man's choice.

42 *'What's in a name?'*: Shakespeare, *Romeo and Juliet*, II. i.

43 *crop time*: according to all authorities this was, in fact, the busiest time of the year on a sugar plantation.

Creole: this term is often misunderstood outside the West Indies as a racial term, implying partial African ancestry. In fact it denotes only born (or made, or produced) in the West Indies. In this reference to Psyche, it is not clear whether Lewis is alluding to a black/white ancestry as well as to Jamaican birth. Later he shows himself well aware that Creole slaves and African slaves were seen—and often saw themselves—as two separate groups. He refers to rivalry and dislike between them. Africans were considered more likely to resist and rebel.

44 *exposed to the dews*: one of the five signs of an unhealthy country listed by James Lind in 1788 was the sudden chilling of the air at sunset; exposure to the associated dews and vapours was thought to cause disease. See B. W. Higman, *Slave Population and Economy in Jamaica, 1807–1834* (Cambridge: Cambridge University Press, 1976), 129.

45 *'a buxom air, embalmed with odours'*: adapted from *Paradise Lost*, ii. 842–3.

E bruna-si; ma il bruno il bel non toglie: 'Black was this queen as jet, yet on her eyes | sweet loveliness, in black attired, lies'; Fairfax translation of Tasso's *Gerusalemme Liberata*, XII. xxi. 8.

46 *Yarico*: the story of Inkle and Yarico, now hardly known but hugely popular in the eighteenth century, appeared in a variety of European languages and literary genres: forty-five separate versions have been identified by Lawrence Price. (For a full discussion see Peter Hulme, *Colonial Encounters: Europe and the Native Caribbean, 1492–1797* (London and New York: Methuen, 1986), ch 6.) After being shipwrecked, Inkle, an Englishman, is cared for by Yarico, a native girl. They fall in love, but after they are rescued Inkle sells Yarico into slavery. Since Lewis later mentions Colman in conjunction with Yarico (p. 98), the version in his mind may be the musical play, *Inkle and Yarico*, by George Colman the younger (1762–1836), first produced at the Haymarket in 1787; both Lewis and Colman were members of the Catamaran club.

Grassini: Josephina Grassini (1773–1850) was a powerful Italian contralto, of striking beauty and with a natural talent for dramatic roles. Her first appearance in London was at the King's Theatre in 1804, as Cora in Gaetano Andreozzi's opera *La vergine del sole*. She spent three seasons in London, during which her greatest success was as Proserpine in Winter's *Il ratto di Proserpina*, in which Mrs Billington, another great favourite of Lewis's, played Ceres.

47 *fire-shell*: the customary way of announcing the passing of time, alerts, alarms, etc. was by the blowing of conch shells, which sounded loud as trumpets. Conch shells (*Strombus gigas*) were the fabled shell trumpets of the Tritons.

50 *fidus Achates*: faithful Achates, i.e. bosom companion, as Achates was to Aeneas in Virgil's *Aeneid*.

52 '*Saltare elegantius, quam necesse est probæ, et cui cariora semper omnia, quam decus et pudicitia fuit.*': '[Able] to dance more elegantly than a good woman needs to; one to whom everything was always dearer than decency and modesty'; adapted from Sallust, *Catiline*, xxv. 2.

Doctor Pedro in petticoats: a reference to *Don Quixote de la Mancha* (1605; 1615) by Miguel de Cervantes, which Lewis has been reading on the voyage.

54 *in the straw*: pregnant.

55 *higglers*: itinerant pedlars, trading or selling small commodities they carried in packs.

59 *Je ne vois que des yeux toujours prêts à sourire*: 'I see only eyes always ready to smile'.

Lucretias: Lucretia, the wife of Tarquinius Collatinus, was raped by Sextus. She killed herself because of the dishonour, heroic in her adherence to the code of female chastity.

63 *it expired*: the symptoms of clenched teeth and the rigidity fit indicate that this was, in modern medical terms, *tetanus neonatorum*, which has disappeared from most of the Caribbean except Haiti. It is contracted

through the umbilical cord, through practices connected with severing and tying where the tetanus spore is present, most commonly as a result of the application of animal dung to the umbilicus. Lewis very typically blames the mother. (Richard Ratzan: private e-mail message, 24 May 1997.)

nine days: this was the customary length of time before a baby was considered really viable. On the estate of Old Montpelier, the mothers whose children had survived for nine days received 13*s*. 4*d*. from the attorney. In 1816, one commentator recommended abolishing the practice of *not* recording in the plantation books the births of any children who did not survive until the ninth day. See Higman, *Slave Population and Economy in Jamaica*, 48–9.

65 *'seasoning'*: the 'seasoning period' was the period during which the slaves became acclimatized, generally assumed to last about three years. As many as one-quarter of recent arrivals died (or committed suicide) during that time, dysentery being a major cause. See Lowell Joseph Ragatz, *The Fall of the Planter Class in the British Caribbean, 1763–1833* (New York: Octagon Books, 1963 (1928)), 87.

Lethe: river in the underworld to be crossed at death. In Virgil's *Aeneid*, Bk. 6, Aeneas visits the underworld, where his father Anchises explains that drinking from Lethe's waters abolishes anxiety along with memory.

66 *'shuffled off this mortal coil'*: Shakespeare, *Hamlet*, III. i.

Caucasus horrens: Virgil, *Aeneid*, iv. 366–7 (horrens | Caucasus). 'Rugged Caucasus [sired you]' (Dido to Aeneas).

'London Tavern': a famous tavern on Bishopsgate Street, rebuilt after a fire in 1765 and finally demolished in 1876.

'Ciborum ambitiosa fames, et lautæ gloria mensæ': 'ostentatious hunger for food and glory in a lavish table': Lucan, *Bellum Civile*, iv. 375–6.

67 *Dragon of Wantley*: a humorous ballad, probably dating from the seventeenth century, satirizing the old verse romances. It was included in Thomas Percy's popular three-volume collection, *Reliques of Ancient English Poetry* (1765), which Lewis knew well since it was the source of several items in a collection of ballads he had edited, *Tales of Wonder* (1801).

Queen Atygatis of Scythia: Atargatis, a Syrian (rather than Scythian) goddess, was a giver of fertility, represented as half-woman, half-fish. Doves were sacred to her as well as fish: one myth records that, having fallen into a lake, she was saved by a fish; another that she was changed into a fish, while her daughter Semiramis became a dove.

too many lampreys: lampreys were a favourite dish of medieval epicures. Henry I (1100–35) died at Rouen of an illness supposedly brought on by eating too many after a day's hunting. D. L. Macdonald has identified the story of Frederick the Great as being from Honoré Gabriel Riqueti, comte de Mirabeau's *Memoirs of the Courts of Berlin and St Petersburg*, anonymous translation (New York, 1910), 40. See 'The Isle of Devils: The Jamaican Journal of M. G. Lewis', in Timothy Fulford and Peter Kitson (eds.), *Romanticism and Colonialism* (Cambridge: Cambridge University Press, 1998), 194.

67 *'All for eel-pye, or this world well lost!'*: adapted from the title of John Dryden's heroic tragedy, *All For Love, or the World Well Lost* (1677).

68 *Sigismunda*: a reference to Dryden's poem, 'Sigismonda and Guiscardo, from Boccace' in *Fables Ancient and Modern* (1700). Sigismonda enjoyed her experience of marriage so much that when her husband died she wished to marry again.

mulatto . . . sambo . . . quadroon . . . mustee . . . musteefino: many writers expended considerable effort on the taxonomy of colour but there was no absolute agreement about these fine distinctions. Mulatto was often used simply to indicate mixed race.

Long . . . asserts: Edward Long, *History of Jamaica* (1774) ii. 335–6, says of the intermarriage of mulattos: 'such matches have generally been defective and barren', and declares that as regards the bearing of children, 'I never heard of such an instance'. Lewis's own assumption that mulattos are 'weak and effeminate' is, of course, equally untenable. The notion was also applied to species other than the human. See p. 121.

70 *Marcia . . . 'fair, oh! how divinely fair!'*: Joseph Addison's *Cato* (1713), I. iv. *Cato* is the best-known example of pseudo-classical tragedy of its time, during which it was very popular. Juba is a 'tawny' Numidian, in love with Cato's daughter, Marcia. Sempronius's complaint comes at the end of Act III.

71 *cane-pieces*: cane-fields.

73 *shagreen*: a species of untanned leather, with a rough granular surface, often dyed green.

Horace Beckford's: the Beckfords' enormous fortune had been built entirely upon the profits from estates held in Jamaica since the mid-seventeenth century.

74 *Lord Holland*: see Introduction, p. xv ff.

76 *A little flattery does well sometimes!*: *The Tragical History of King Richard III*, Bell's Acting Edition (1774), iii. 37. This is an allusion to a line in III. ii, which does not occur in any standard edition of Shakespeare.

Buckra: or backra, from the West African word for 'he who rules'; a common generic term used by slaves to denote whites. See Michael Craton, *Testing the Chains: Resistance to Slavery in the British West Indies* (Ithaca, NY, and London: Cornell University Press, 1982), 341.

79 *The pleasing punishment which women bear*: Shakespeare, *Comedy of Errors*, I. i.

80 *very good effect*: rewarding mothers for success in child-bearing and rearing was often recommended. Lewis was only one of many slave-holders to adopt such practice: Sir William Young made a present of 'five

yards of fine cotton . . . of the gayest pattern', on his estate in St Vincent; Mr Cuthbert of Jamaica gave two dollars to every mother whose infant survived. See Ragatz, *Fall of the Planter Class*, 35.

82 *my husband*: in West African culture, naming someone a close relative was proper etiquette, a traditional mark of respect, as Lewis would later discover, although here he attributes it to flattery. See 'my son', etc. (pp. 145, 158). To have been a 'shipmate' from Africa automatically conferred a familial relationship (p. 219).

83 *a second Vulcan*: Jupiter gave Venus, the goddess of love and beauty, in marriage to Vulcan, the god of fire. Discovering her infidelity with Mars, Vulcan forged a bronze net to trap them both, refusing to release either until the valuable marriage gifts he had made were restored to him. Neptune, who had fallen in love with Venus, agreed to pay, and thus Venus was released. She later renewed her virginity in the sea.

durant: a woollen fabric noted for its long-lasting qualities.

the minister of Savannah la Mar: this is the first of a number of references to Dr Edmund Pope, LLD, Rector of the parish of Westmoreland 1815–20. He seems to have been conscientious in his duties, except when prevented by lumbago (p. 215).

Cacus: Cacus was a monstrous three-headed shepherd who belched flame from each mouth. Hercules battered his face to a pulp.

84 *causa doloris*: Virgil, *Aeneid*, ix. 216 (and probably elsewhere): 'the cause of the pain'.

87 *Miss Whaunica*: the title 'Miss' usually indicated a mulatto (i.e. white father). 'Whaunica' is perhaps a local variant of 'Juanita'.

89 *Dr Bell's plan*: when Andrew Bell (1753–1832) became superintendent of an Orphan Asylum in Madras in 1789, he established a system of teaching, later widely used in England and Wales, in which senior pupils instructed junior ones. It was extremely useful in educating the poor, since it operated with a bare minimum of facilities. Joseph Lancaster was associated with the development of a similar system.

90 *cocoa-bay*: leprosy, also referred to in Jamaica as joint evil, or king's evil. See Higman, *Slave Population and Economy in Jamaica*, 109.

91 *black doctor*: the 'black doctor' turns up on many plantation lists. Lewis's anecdote is an interesting comment on the accepted crossover of medical skills between European and African.

93 *corrosive sublimate*: mercuric chloride, or bichloride of mercury.

95 *'Almanach des Gourmands'*: a pun on the well-known *Almanach de Gotha*, begun in 1764 and published annually, which recorded in a pocket volume all kinds of political and statistical information.

96 *'Fairy Tale'. . . couple of serpents*: 'Les Fées' in Charles Perrault's *Histoires ou Contes du Temps Passé avec des Moralités* (1697).

'I was adored once!': Shakespeare, *Twelfth Night*, II. iii.

98 *kittereen*: a kind of one-horse chaise with an umbrella or raised awning over the seat.

Yarico: see note to p. 46.

the island of Old Providence: now Isla de Providencia, this island has belonged to Colombia since 1822. In the mid-seventeenth century the Spaniards had fortified it and used it as a penal settlement.

99 *Gil Blas*: (1715; 1735) the masterpiece of Alain-René Lesage (1668–1747), a lively, picaresque narrative, translated by Tobias Smollett in 1749. The reference to Captain Rolando is in I. iii ff.; to travelling to Lirias in X. i ff.

100 *Rodney . . . Bacon*: the monument to Admiral Rodney (1719–92), by John Bacon, had been set up in 1793 on the north side of the square to commemorate Rodney's victory over the French off Dominica in 1782. The monument cost a great deal, but Bacon was an indifferent sculptor; Lewis is no doubt right to concentrate upon the qualities of the pedestal.

Chief Justice: John Lewis (1750–1820), brother of Monk Lewis's father, served as Chief Justice of Jamaica 1810–16.

101 *Admiral Benbow*: John Benbow (1653–1702) was commander-in-chief in the West Indies during the War of the Austrian Succession. He died as a result of injuries received in an action against the French squadron, but not before court-martialling six of his captains for deliberately failing to support him: two were shot, two cashiered, and two suspended. He was buried at Port Royal in St Andrew's church, Kingston.

103 *Attorney-General*: Thomas Witter Jackson was Attorney-General 1810–18.

Mr Hill: James Hill had been principal tenor at Bath and Bristol for two years before he went to Covent Garden in 1798. He stayed in London until 1805–6, and then, after some disagreement, disappeared into the provinces. In 1816, he and his wife joined a company headed by William Adamson in Jamaica (see note to p. 227), where he died in 1817.

'The Haunted Tower': a three-act comic opera, first performed at Drury Lane in November 1789. The author, James Cobb, wrote other comic operas, farces, and melodramatic dumbshows.

theatre is neat enough: the Spanish Town theatre had been built by private subscription in 1776, then commandeered for a barracks between 1792 and 1799. It was eventually returned to its original use after having been restored about late 1814. See Hill, *Jamaican Stage*, 21.

governor: the Governor of Jamaica 1813–21 was William, Duke of Manchester.

106 *directs . . . her fame*: adapted from the poem 'Advice to a Lady', written in 1731 by George Lyttelton (1709–73).

the Jamaica company: see note to p. 227.

never breed: see note to p. 68.

107 *the horrors of St Domingo*: the revolution of 1791, in French-held Saint-Domingue (Haiti), only ninety miles from Jamaica, was the most

successful example of slave resistance ever. Led by the black General Toussaint L'Ouverture, it caused panic among planters all over the Caribbean. White French colonists were obliged to flee, numbers of them taking refuge in Jamaica.

108 *Sir Charles Price*: (1708–72) one of the five greatest Jamaican magnates, a land speculator on a grand scale, and Speaker of the Jamaica Assembly 1745–63, Price was unusual in being resident rather than absentee. Lewis's tale is probably apocryphal, although a cane-piece rat, *Mus saccharivorus*, eighteen inches long, was identified by the naturalist Philip Henry Gosse in 1851 (see headnote of Glossary), and may have been eradicated by the small Indian mongooses, imported in 1872 from Calcutta to Jamaica and correlated with the extirpation or extinction of reptile populations in the West Indies. A large rat is still called a Charley Price rat in Jamaica.

109 *Goldsmith*: Oliver Goldsmith, *An History of the Earth and Animated Nature*, 8 vols. (London, 1774), vi. 376–9.

114 *'Miss Peg, who faints at the sound of an organ'*: both Pope and Swift attributed the *History of John Bull*, which appeared in successive parts, to John Arbuthnot (1667–1735). This reference is to the well-known third pamphlet, which deals with religious sectarianism: *John Bull still in his senses: being the Third Part of Law is a Bottomless Pit* (Edinburgh: James Watson, 1712), ch. 2. Miss Peg faints because she abhors the idea of music as part of divine worship.

Apelles: the greatest of ancient painters of the fourth century BC, the favourite painter of Alexander the Great. His most famous picture was of Aphrodite emerging from the sea.

115 *Belinda's great great grandsire*: Pope, 'The Rape of the Lock', v. 90.

wafers: small disks of gum, which, when moistened, were used for sealing letters, etc.

118 *Duchess of York*: Lewis treasured his friendship with Frederica, Duchess of York (1767–1820), a daughter of the King of Prussia. She had made him the gift of a spaniel, and visited him at his house at Barnes, where he had held a party in her honour; they had discussed the slave trade and Mr Wilberforce.

121 *Zanga*: D. L. Macdonald has identified Zanga as the Moorish villain of Edward Young's tragedy *The Revenge* (1764). Macdonald also points out that the postscript to *The Castle Spectre* tries to argue that Lewis's own character, Hassan, the African, was not a copy of Zanga. For a discussion of the character of Hassan, see D. L. Macdonald, *Romanticism and Colonialism*, 190.

their quantity of white: whites were superstitious about colours. 'In 1823 Roughley claimed that it was "an old custom or superstition" in Jamaica to favour red, black or brindle working stock; good, strong beasts of brilliant, varied hues were put to the butcher's knife while weak, meagre ones of the favoured colours were put under the yoke' (Higman, *Slave Population and Economy in Jamaica*, 2).

125 *bilboes*: a long bar of iron, locked to the floor, with sliding shackles which confined the ankles.

127 *'the yaws'*: a disfiguring skin disease common among slaves, yaws was both infectious and contagious. It was marked by ulcers and later infected the bone.

128 *maccarony*: a quarter dollar, which Lewis values at fifteen pence, i.e. one shilling and three pence (p. 145).

132 *extreme laziness*: Lewis is falling back on the stereotype. It is interesting to compare Philip Henry Gosse's later account of the extraction of a jigger from his foot by one of his black servants, whom he commends for being 'quick at discovering, and skilful at extracting' jiggers.

another disease: probably syphilis.

133 *Reporter of the African Institution*: see Introduction, p. xvi.

134 *Bitter-Wood and Assafœtida*: Bitterwood was a decoction prepared from the Jamaican Quassia tree (*Picraena excelsa*), also known as Bitter Ash, Bitter Wood. The name is said to derive from Kwasi, an African slave who used Quassia bark as a fever remedy about 1730. Asafœtida is a resinous substance with a very nasty smell, derived from plants of the family *Ferula*. It was used as an anti-spasmodic, but also rolled into pellets and worn for protection.

135 *Custos*: or magistrate. Twelve members of the Jamaica Assembly, which was dominated by planters, were chosen to serve on the Governor's advisory council. In their parishes (which numbered twenty-one in Lewis's time), they served as magistrates of the petty session courts and as chief magistrates (pl. custodes). Laws had been passed for the protection of slaves, but since enforcement was in the hands of the planters, it was frequently haphazard and half-hearted.

at least to be heard: slaves' testimony was not valid in law.

137 *Pylades*: the loyal friend of Orestes, son of Agamemnon, from boyhood.

Balcarras: Alexander Lindsay, 6th Earl of Balcarres (1752–1825), Governor of Jamaica, 1794–1801, and a well-known if not notorious figure in the history of Jamaica. To assist in putting down the rebellion of the Maroons in 1795, he had sent for one hundred bloodhounds from Cuba, with forty-three keepers, to track down the runaways. The use of these large and ferocious animals, which tore and mangled the hunted, provoked an outcry. The rebel slaves who were caught were transported to Nova Scotia, then a British province. When General Nugent took over from Balcarras as Governor, Lady Nugent commented on Balcarras's slovenly personal habits and the 'dirt and discomfort' of his dwelling. See Lady [Maria] Nugent, *Lady Nugent's Journal of her residence in Jamaica from 1801 to 1805*, ed. Philip Wright (Kingston, Jamaica: Institute of Jamaica, 1966), 11, 15, 17.

143 *'Et il se tira d'affaire . . . Il mourut'*: 'He extricated himself from the situation very neatly. On the day they were going to present him with the first copy, do you know what he did? He died.' Bernard le Bovier de Fontanelle (1657–1757) was a polymath, whose speciality was the popular interpretation of science. His exposition of the Copernican solar system, *Entretiens sur la pluralité des mondes* (1686) in the form of a series of dialogues between the author and a woman friend, was highly influential.

Achelous: a river-god who did battle with Hercules.

144 *Accompong Maroons*: Accompongs town was one of the negro-towns, where dwelt the descendants of those maroons who had negotiated grants of land, etc., from the British after successful resistance, most notably in 1739, when Cudjoe was leader, and Accompong one of his lieutenants. The maroons had later signed a treaty which obliged them to capture runaways or fight rebels on request.

145 *Duchess of York*: see note to p. 118.

'rent hell's concave': adapted from *Paradise Lost*, i. 542.

147 *pen*: the equivalent of an English breeding-farm, where horses, mules, or oxen were raised. See Higman, *Slave Population and Economy in Jamaica*, 30 ff.

149 *trade-winds*: ships arrived from Britain between October and May, and departed between April and August. During the hurricane months (August, September, October), ships and cargoes sailing for Britain paid double insurance.

St Andrews: or San Andrés, the name of a small island and its chief town in the western Caribbean, now belonging to Colombia.

prove to be pie-crust: the proverb is that promises, like pie-crust, are made to be broken.

152 *rogue in scarlet*: a reference to the well-known attractiveness of soldiers in their dashing red coats.

153 *a freeman*: in 1772 Lord Mansfield had handed down a famous ruling that any slave became immediately free upon setting foot on English soil.

155 *Nancy stories*: see Introduction, p. xxvi.

157 *yam-yamme*: eat. See p. 243.

159 *May 8*: in the first edition the month for this entry, and the following eleven entries, reads April. This has been corrected to May in all cases.

160 *Isle of Devils*: as Lewis makes clear in his previous comment, 'The Isle of Devils' had been written months earlier, on the voyage out. It was also printed separately from and prior to the *Journal* (see Note on the Text).

Tempest, Act 3: like many other quotations in the *Journal* this one is not exact. This may be understood as a tribute to Lewis's capacious memory rather than a measure of his carelessness.

160 *Halcyon*: the legend of the kingfisher's nest relates to the Halcyon days (the seven days before and the seven days after the winter solstice), when Aeolus forbids the winds to disturb the waters, so that his daughter Alcyone, who had been transformed into a kingfisher, may raise her brood safely.

Las Guerras Civiles de Granada: a famous Spanish work in eight volumes, by Gines Perez de Hita, which mixed actual events with romantic incidents. It was published 1601–19 and frequently reprinted, often in two separate parts. The English translation, *Las Guerras Civiles; or the Civil Wars of Granada* is by Thomas Rodd (London, 1801). Lewis may also be alluding in the poem to Dryden's two-part heroic tragedy, *The Conquest of Granada* (1670–1), for which *Las Guerras Civiles* had also been a source.

161 *Cynthia*: the Cynthian goddess, i.e. Artemis or Diana, hence the moon.

164 *tropic*: tropic-bird.

168 *Teniers*: David Teniers, father (1582–1649), and the more famous son whom he taught, also David (1610–90), Flemish painters. The early works of the younger Teniers show the influence of Bruegel.

175 '*Purpureus veluti flos,*' *etc.—Virgil*: *Aeneid*, ix. 435. 'As [when] a purple flower . . .'

176 '*Qualis populeâ, etc.—Virgil*: 'qualis populeâ [maerens Philomela sub umbrâ]. Virgil, *Georgics*, iv. 511. 'Just as the nightingale, mourning beneath the poplar's shade, [laments her lost offspring] . . .'

177 *Lucina*: the goddess of childbirth.

Paphia: Aphrodite, who in one legend landed at Paphos in Cyprus.

179 *night-hags . . . Norway's sea*: a reminiscence of the witches in *Macbeth*, I. iii.

Arion: Orion, son of Neptune.

183 *Piansi i riposi di quest' umil vita, | E sospirai la mia perduta pace!*: 'I lamented the [lost] tranquillity of that humble life and I longed for the peace I had lost!' or, in the Fairfax translation, 'I gan my loss of lusty years complain, | and wished I had enjoyed the country's peace'. Tasso, *Gerusalemme Liberata*, VII. xiii. 5–6.

184 *Falstaff's buckbasket*: Shakespeare, *Merry Wives of Windsor*, Acts III and V. A buckbasket held dirty linen.

Slawkenbergius's Don Diego: Laurence Sterne, *The Life and Opinions of Tristram Shandy* (1759–67), Bk. IV.

187 *Zingha, queen of Angola*: Jean Louis Castilhon (1720–*c*.1793), *Zingha, reine d'Angola: histoire africaine* (Paris: Lacombe, 1769).

188 *Quintus Curtius*: Quintus Curtius Rufus (fl. *c*. AD 50), Roman rhetorician and historian, was author of a ten-volume history of Alexander the Great.

193 *Hic finis Priami fatorum!*: Virgil, *Aeneid*, ii. 554. 'This was the end of Priam's fortunes.' The Virgilian text reads 'haec' though *finis* is usually masculine.

194 *'pièce à machines'*: a play with stage effects.

197 *'return to the place whence we came'*: part of a line from a song by Henry Purcell, 'Bess of Bedlam', also known as 'From Silent Shades'; words by Purcell himself or an unknown lyricist. (Susan Murley: private e-mail message, 27 March 1998.)

Klopstock's half-devil Abadonna: Abadonna is a repentant devil in the second canto of *Der Messias*, by the German poet Friedrich Gottlieb Klopstock (1724–1803). When Satan announces his plan to kill the Messiah, Abadonna objects.

One writ with us in sour misfortune's book: adapted from Shakespeare, *Romeo and Juliet*, V. iii.

198 *'reculer pour mieux sauter'*: to step back in order to jump forward better, i.e. a temporary respite.

199 *an Italian servant*: 'Tita', Giovanni Battista Falcieri, engaged during Lewis's continental tour between visits to Jamaica, accompanied Lewis on his second visit and was with him when he died. He was subsequently employed by Byron.

200 *Horse Latitudes*: the term 'dead horse' was used by seamen to refer to the period of work on board ship for which they had been paid for in advance, and the horse latitudes—about two months' sail out of England—to refer to that area of the ocean where those advances would have been worked off.

202 *cutter*: a clinker-built ship's boat, rowed with eight to fourteen oars and rigged with two masts.

phaëton: an open carriage, with one or two seats facing forward, originally with two, later four wheels, usually drawn by a pair of horses.

206 *bark*: also Jesuits' or Peruvian bark, the bark of various species of the cinchona tree, from which quinine is procured. It was formerly ground into powder and taken to reduce fever.

dirt-eating: or geophagy, was said to prevail in wet rather than dry parishes in Jamaica. It has generally been associated with ankylostomiasis (hookworm disease), but iron deficiency is an equally plausible explanation. See Higman, *Slave Population and Economy in Jamaica*, 114.

209 *Friendship and Greenwich*: this was the plantation near Cornwall, owned by the Hollands through the will of Lady Holland's grandfather, Florentius Vassall.

wean . . . too soon: Lewis's complaint is related to contemporary notions of the healthiness of early weaning; present medical opinion tends to support the mothers' view. While Lewis regularly gave the mothers credit for feeling, he gave them none for sense.

'no bones broke though sore peppered': a line adapted from the comedy by Samuel Jackson Pratt (1749–1814), *Hail Fellow! Well Met!, in five acts; as it was for some years performed with universal applause on the continent* (1805), II. ii.

210 *'would rather go any where, than stay with any body'*: adapted from I. i of David Garrick's *Cymon: a dramatic romance*, first performed in 1767.

213 *Lucretia*: see note to p. 59.

Don Giovanni: the Spanish libertine, Don Juan, as he appears in Mozart's opera (1787).

216 *'two or three gathered together'*: Matthew 18: 20.

curates expected from the hands of the bishop of London: the task of these curates would be specifically to instruct the slaves, and monies had been voted by the Jamaica Assembly in 1816 to pay their salaries. See Mary Turner, *Slaves and Missionaries: The Disintegration of Jamaican Slave Society, 1787–1834* (Urbana, Ill.: University of Illinois Press, 1982), 20–1.

'the pulpit drum ecclesiastic': Samuel Butler, *Hudibras* (1662), I. i. 11. Presbyterian clergy were said to have preached Britain into the Civil War. Hence, in pounding their pulpits with their fists, they were said to beat their ecclesiastical drums.

220 *Æsop's oyster*: (or clam or mussel). The fable tells how one crow, unable to break an oyster's shell, is advised by a second to drop it from a great height, whereupon strategy succeeds, and the second crow makes off with the food.

222 *old Parrs*: Thomas Parr became proverbial because of his great age. Supposedly born in 1483, at his death in 1635 he was buried in Westminster Abbey. A view of his cottage was reproduced in the *Gentleman's Magazine* of March 1814.

'the Myal dance': as here described, the Myal–dance is part of Obeah, although Myalism is generally described as a religious movement of African origin, beginning in Jamaica in the eighteenth century, one of whose chief purposes was to combat Obeah. But many of the practices were identical: enlisting the aid of the spirits of the dead, the use of drumming and dancing to induce spirit-possession, and rites and ceremonies including sacrifice of fowls, often performed under a silk-cotton tree. The distinction between Obeah and Myal must often have been more imaginary than real. The Myal–dance is that by which members were initiated, by being apparently rendered dead and then revived.

225 *like Mahomet's coffin*: a proverbial saying, which D. L. Macdonald explains as 'the bizarre rumour, that Mohammed's body had been encased in an iron coffin and suspended in mid-air by means of powerful magnets fixed to the roof of the great mosque in Mecca'. See *Romanticism and Colonialism*, 195.

227 *Kingston theatre*: a theatre had been operating in Kingston since the mid-eighteenth century. The Theatre on the Parade (where there has now been a theatre continuously ever since) opened in 1775, and had been renovated in early 1815. The seating, for 700, was segregated. A new manager had been appointed in 1814, William Adamson, leader of a troupe from Barbados, which included Mrs Elizabeth Shaw, to whose performance as

'chief actress' Lewis refers. Lewis's dislike of the production may have given him a jaundiced view: the theatre in Kingston was at this time prospering, although subject to the usual green-room squabbles (p. 106). See Hill, *Jamaican Stage*, 26–7, 32–3, 132–3.

'Adelgitha': Lewis's own play, *Adelgitha; or, The Fruits of a Single Error. A Tragedy, in Five Acts*, 1806; first performed at Drury Lane, 30 April 1807.

Widow Cheshire: Mrs Cheshire was a character in John O'Keeffe's *The Agreeable Surprise, a comic opera in two acts*, with music by Samuel Arnold, first performed in 1781.

'the Creole Roscius': Roscius was the most famous Roman actor, a legend even before his death in 62 BC. The actor here referred to is John Castello, who remained a popular performer in Jamaica for many years. See Hill, *Jamaican Stage*, 132 ff.

232 *out-herod Herod*: Shakespeare, *Hamlet*, III. ii. The biblical Herod, a stock figure in popular Elizabethan drama, was noted for being played with an excess of sound and fury.

Dolallolla: in Henry Fielding's burlesque *The Tragedy of Tragedies, or, Life and Death of Tom Thumb the Great* (1731), the queen Dollalolla had a voice 'like twenty screech-owls' (I. v). Fielding wrote many plays early in his career.

233 *Messalina's Poems*: see note to p. 27.

'not where I ate, but where I was eaten': adapted from Shakespeare, *Hamlet*, IV. iii.

235 *Sir Home Popham*: Sir Home Riggs Popham (1762–1820), after a somewhat chequered career, had been promoted rear-admiral in 1814. He was Naval Commander-in-Chief at Jamaica, 1817–20. Popham's major contribution to the Navy was an improved system of signalling.

236 *'myself I unfatigued'*: imitation of well-known phrase from Henry Carey's burlesque, *The Tragedy of Chrononhotonthologos: being the most Tragical Tragedy, that ever was Tragediz'd by any company of tragedians* (1734).

238 *'qualis mœrens Philomela'*: (classical Latin *maerens*). See note to p. 176.

246 *'with my hair standing on end at my own wonders'*: adapted from William Cowper, *The Task*, Bk. IV, 'The Winter Evening', 86. Katterfelto, said originally to have been a Prussian soldier, was a quack and conjuror famous in London 1792–3. He advertised himself by sending round two black servants wearing green and red livery who blew trumpets and gave out handbills; the wonders he announced included use of the microscope and electrical experiments during which black cats gave off sparks. His fame and prosperity were short-lived, and before his death in 1799 he was imprisoned in Shrewsbury as a vagrant and impostor.

Quasheba: one Ashanti custom was to name a child according to sex and the day of the week on which he or she was born. Quasheba would have been born on a Sunday.

250   *sangaree*: from Spanish sangria, a drink composed of lemon juice and red
      wine.

252   *With many a doleful grunt . . . as if their pretty hearts would break!*: a rec-
      ollection of lines from John Dryden's *Fables Ancient and Modern* (1700):
      'The Cock and the Fox; or The Tale of the Nun's Priest, from Chaucer',
      732–3.

GLOSSARY

LEWIS'S REFERENCES TO PLANT AND
ANIMAL LIFE IN JAMAICA

From time to time, Lewis turns his attention to the flora and fauna of Jamaica, recording whatever interests him, principally anything that can be eaten. He details the slaves' preferences and diet, and tries most fare the island has to offer, including alligator with onion sauce and a stew made of cane-piece cat. But the mangrove tree, with its strange stilt roots, is merely mentioned in passing (p. 36), only a little space is given to the rich variety of birds, even less to insects, and none to butterflies. Even so, those interested in the natural history of the region invariably quote from the *Journal*, as did Philip Henry Gosse (1810–88), who resided for eighteen months in the mid-1840s at Bluefields (mentioned twice by Lewis (pp. 98, 225) and only about fifteen miles from Cornwall estate) and wrote a well-respected account of what he had found. My main sources here are the following:

Adams, C. D., *Flowering Plants of Jamaica*, with contributions by G. R. Proctor, R. W. Read, *et al.* (Mona, Jamaica: University of the West Indies Press, 1972).

Dictionary of Caribbean English Usage, ed. Richard Allsopp (Oxford: Oxford University Press, 1996).

Dictionary of Jamaican English, ed. F. G. Cassidy and R. B. Le Page (Cambridge: Cambridge University Press, 1967).

Gosse, Philip Henry, assisted by Richard Hill, *A Naturalist's Sojourn in Jamaica* (London: Longman, Brown, Green, and Longmans, 1851).

Schwartz, Albert, and Henderson, Robert W., *Amphibians and Reptiles of the West Indies* (Gainesville, Fla.: University of Florida Press, 1991).

abba or abbay palm, the African oil palm, *Elaeis guineensis*, whose small reddish fruits have an outer covering which yields oil

achie or akee, named *Blighia sapida* in recognition of Bligh's achievement (*see* bread-fruit), bears a pear-shaped red, or yellow-tinged red fruit. It had been introduced from West Africa about 1778

alligator the native crocodile of Jamaica, *Crocodylus acutus*

arsenic bean an impossibility, but presumably some seed was poisonous enough to deserve the name

black crabs the purple or black land crab, *Gecarcinus ruricola*, which visits the sea only once a year to spawn, is common in Jamaica. Together with the mountain mullet and the ring-tail dove, it was one of the three proverbial delicacies of the island

black snake *Alsophis ater*, the most common Jamaican snake in Gosse's time. A tree-climber about 850 mm. long, its ground colour is black or dark olive. It is diurnal, ground-dwelling, and an active forager whose diet includes the lizard *Celestus*. Like all Jamaican snakes, not venomous

bread nut *Brosimum alicastrum*, a tall hardwood-timber tree whose leaves make excellent animal fodder

bread-fruit in 1793, 347 bread-fruit plants, *Artocarpus altilis*, had been distributed on the arrival of HMS *Providence*, and Captain William Bligh had been granted 1,000 guineas for his services in delivering them. The name of the bread-fruit tree was often confused with that of the bread nut

broad-leaf *Terminalia latifolia*, a great timber tree, with leaves like those of the horse chestnut, though much larger, and edible nuts

calabashes the football-sized fruit of the calabash gourd tree, *Crescentia cujete*, dried, halved, scraped out, and used as containers or dippers

calalue a generic name for edible spinach greens, including the species *Amarantus* and the leaves of the coccos plant

cane-piece cat a euphemism (of which Lewis was probably unaware) for the cane-piece rat when served as food. The cane-piece rat was a common field rat which subsisted almost entirely on sugar-cane. See further note to p. 108

cassava Lewis identifies three types (p. 130): sweet, bitter, and sweet-and-bitter. The many varieties of cassava, all of whose roots are commonly used as food, belong to the family *Manihot*, and are divided into sweet and bitter. All contain some poison. Sweet cassava is not poisonous before processing, but its crop yield is much lower than that of the bitter species. Bitter cassava roots contain prussic acid in quantities which must be expressed before the root is eaten, typically by grating, squeezing, and washing

coccos *see* coco[a]

cocoa poyers either a misprint or Lewis's error for 'coco-taya', another kind of coco, probably *Xanthosoma sagittifolium*

cocoa-nuts *see* coco[a]

coco[a] three separate usages should be distinguished: (1) **cocoa-bay**, a name for leprosy; (2) **cocoa-nut [palm]**, the coconut, *Cocos nucifera*; (3) **coccos** or coco plant, *Colocasia esculenta*, with its wide-spreading leaves, also commonly called **cocoa-finger**, from the shape of the tuber. Both leaves (called calalue) and tubers are edible

cotton tree the silk cotton or Ceiba, *Ceiba pentandra*, perhaps Jamaica's

largest and—with cacti, creepers, wild pines, and lianas growing on it—
most spectacular tree. Gosse, who records heights of 150 feet and
a stump 40 feet in diameter, calls it 'the giant of the lowlands'. It was
an object of reverence to the slaves, who associated it with the sacred
Akata tree of Ashanti religion. Dug-out canoes were made from single
logs

crab-catcher a name most commonly applied to herons or bitterns,
family *Ardeidae*, but also generally to fisher birds

deep-water silk family *Lutjanidae*—snappers. Probably the silk snapper,
Lutjanus vivanus, which is found at depths of 70–240 m. To a length of
240 cm., it is excellent eating

doctor fish family *Acanthuridae*—surgeonfish. The fish carries on each
side of the base of the tail fin a knife-like spine, which ordinarily lies
flat but can be flipped out when the fish is threatened

galli-wasp the common name of at least two of the seven species of
lizard which have now been identified in Jamaica, including *Celestus
occiduus* (now presumed extinct) and *Celestus crusculus*. Dreaded because
their bite was considered fatal, they are in fact quite harmless

god-dammies small brownish-black river fish, the reason for whose
name we can only guess. They are commonly stringed, dried, and salted
before frying crisp

granadillo or granadilla. Borne on the vine of the tropical species of the
passion-flower, *Passiflora quadrangularis*, the granadilla is a heavy
yellowish-green, melon-shaped fruit with a nearly liquid pulp inside,
popular in making iced drinks and punches

grape or cluster fruit grapefruit, *Citrus paradisi*

great yellow snake the yellow boa, *Epicrates subflavus*, about 2,000 mm.
in length, with irregular black bandings. Gosse said it was frequently
found in houses, seeking rats. Like all Jamaican snakes, not venomous

groupas or groupers, family *Serranidae*—sea basses. There are over 400
species in this very large family, and they are adept at changing colour,
making identification difficult

grunts family *Pomadasyidae*, one of the species *Haemulon*, named
'grunts' because of the noise they make when taken from the water.
They grind together the teeth located in the throat, and the adjacent air
bladder magnifies the sound. Although rarely exceeding a kilo in weight,
they are popular food fishes

hoccoco-pickang red and yellow-flowered, the **wild Ipecacuanha,
John-to-Heal**, also known as red-head or red-top, *Asclepias curassav-
ica*, is much valued in herbal medicine

hog's meat or hogweed, is a term applied to all species of *Boerhavia*,
chiefly trailing or climbing plants, which were gathered to feed hogs

hog-fish *Lachnolaemus maximus*, family *Labridae*—wrasses, a cigar-shaped fish to about 3 feet long. The elongated snout which gives it its name develops in large adult fish

Jamaica nightingale *Mimus polyglottos*, the very common northern mockingbird, one of a small family of New World birds who make up in song for what they lack in colourful plumage. It is the 'master-musician' according to Gosse

Jew-fish or June fish, dew-fish, *Epinephelus itajara*, family *Serranidae*, is the giant sea bass of the western Atlantic. It is a brownish fish, up to 8 feet long and 500 lbs. in weight. The name is also applied to a large river fish, about 300 lbs. Both are good eating

John-Crow the turkey vulture, *Cathartes aura*. The head is red in adult birds, dark in immatures

Lima bean although Lewis disliked the taste of this variety of *Phaseolus lunatus*, a kidney-shaped bean like the broad bean, many liked it

locust tree West Indian locust, *Hymenaea courbaril*, or Stinking Toe, a timber tree, with hard, straight-grained wood, much favoured in furniture-making, boat-building, and for pilings. It should be distinguished from the locust plants Lewis was carrying for Lord Holland (see Introduction, p. xvii)

logwood *Haematoxylum campechianum*, a small tree which had been introduced into Jamaica from Honduras about 1715. The red heart of logwood was exported for use in dye-making, and thus common cargo on a return voyage: the *Sir Godfrey Webster* had just been carrying it (p. 19). Very similar to the English hawthorn, and giving an English look to the landscape, by the mid-1840s Gosse notes logwood taking over many spots in the west of the island

manati or manatee, or dugong, or sea cow, *Trichechus manatus*, a slow-moving aquatic, vegetarian mammal which inhabits shallow coastal waters. Up to 3 m. long, it has a large rounded body, a short head with a square muzzle, front flippers but no hind limbs, and a tail ending in a flat, oval fluke

mango *Mangifera indica*, had been introduced in 1782

mangrove the red mangrove, *Rhizophora mangle*, grows in salt water, throwing out curving 'prop' or 'stilt' roots which grow down from the stem and root in the sand or mud. It is common on muddy seashores, especially on the south coast. Often the black mangrove, *Avicennia germinans*, grows behind it

men-of-war birds now more commonly called frigate-birds, *Fregata magnificens*, large black or black-and-white sea birds with deeply forked tails and sharp narrowly angled wings of a 2 m. span. They are noted for high soaring, and for thieving on the wing

mountain mullet the torpedo-shaped grey freshwater mullet, *Mugil* *curema*, together with the black crab and the ring-tail dove, one of the three proverbial delicacies of Jamaica

mud fish a generic name for many fish which hide in the mud

ochra or okra, *Hibiscus esculentus*, grown chiefly for its edible green pods, also has medicinal uses

peppers in the gardens around their dwellings on the plantations, slaves grew many varieties of the family *Capsicum*. **Pepperpot** was the name of a favourite Jamaican stew

plantain of the same family as the **banana**, *Musaceae*, the plantain is much larger, matures hard and green, and is cooked as a vegetable

prickly-yellow or the club of Hercules, *Fagara martinicensis*, 'horrid with bristling spines', as Gosse remarks, is a valuable timber tree

provision grounds usually at some distance from the plantation, often in the mountains, the slaves' provision grounds were cleared from the forest by slash-and-burn. Initially unsightly, they rapidly became neat and beautiful under cultivation. Lewis does not mention having visited any site; Gosse did, noting, as well as the plants Lewis names, pumpkins, melons, some sugar canes, a few bushes of the castor-oil plant, a carefully weeded patch of arrowroot and ginger, and two or three cotton bushes

quail the Bobwhite quail, *Colinus virginianus*, family *Phasianidae*, had been introduced from North America about 1747, and flourished until the mid-nineteenth century, but only a few were surviving by the end of the century, and it is now extinct

rifle ant Gosse passes on his collaborator, Richard Hill's story of the raffle-ant, or Tom Raffles ant (of which Lewis's word is a corruption). The ant had supposedly been imported from Cuba in 1762, for the purpose of attacking the young of the cane rat, by Thomas Raffles, a planter. The ant known by this name was identified in 1891 as *Prenolepsis fulva*, extremely unlikely to perform any such function

ring-tail dove *Columba caribaea*, one of twelve species of the family *Columbidae* to be found in Jamaica, two of which were introduced. Together with the mountain mullet and the black crab, the ring-tail was one of the three proverbial delicacies of Jamaica

sea turtle a number of species of sea turtle, order *Testudines*, occur in the Caribbean, including the green turtle and the hawksbill

sensitive plant or shame weed, *Mimosa pudica*, a common prickly creeping plant, whose leaves close at a touch. It had to be cut out by hand labour, and sheep were used to feed it down

shaddock one of the many varieties of citrus which had been introduced for fruit, fragrant flowers, timber, and shade. Gosse describes the shaddock, *Citrus grandis*, as hung with their golden fruits 'as large as a child's head'. They were called **forbidden fruit**, as were some other citrus fruits, presumably as an extension of the Latin classification of grape-fruit, *Citrus paradisi*. Lewis took quantities with him on the second voyage home, offering them with typical kindliness to those feeling unwell

snappers snappers are the large family *Lutjanidae* (seventeen genera and about 185 species) which repeatedly 'snap' their jaws shut after removal from hook or net, thus sometimes catching the unwary. Of many different colours and sizes, snappers are highly prized as food

soldier crabs *Coenobita Diogenes* or *Paquarias insignis*, a species of hermit crab, inhabiting the shells of larger molluscs for protection. Gosse said they were very common and often found a long way from the sea

sugar cane *Saccharum officinarum*, had been brought to the West Indies about 1520

sweet-wood several varieties of tree are given this name. Since Lewis mentions it in connection with the rafters for slave dwellings, his reference is probably to the timber sweet-wood, *Nectandra sanguinea*, whose wood is hard and esteemed for domestic use

tamarind *Tamarindus indica*, introduced shortly before 1647, was a spreading tree of great girth with hard brown pods containing edible pulp

tropic birds Lewis describes the white-tailed tropic bird, *Phaethon lepturus*, fully, although his specimen seems to have lost one of its customary two tail feathers

trumpet tree *Cecropia peltata*, a tall forest tree, palm-like in appearance with a slender jointed stem rising 40–50 feet, surmounted by a cluster of gigantic leaves like those of a horse chestnut, radiating horizontally

Vassal's grass which bears Lady Holland's family name, Vassall, remains unidentified

whangra the sesame, *Sesamum indicum*, the plant and seeds of which were used in Obeah practices

whip snake probably *Typhlops jamaicensis*, which is distinctively bi-coloured in the way Lewis's description suggests, and fairly common. Like all Jamaican snakes, not venomous

wild pines so-called because of their similarity to the pineapple, to whose family *Bromeliaceae* they belong. They are rarely perennial shrubs, usually epiphytic (growing parasitically on trees, rocks, etc.), and brilliantly coloured in crimson, purple, and yellow

yam-poys family *Dioscorea*—yams, probably *Dioscorea trifida*, a small, delicious variety, purple outside and white within

ANTHONY TROLLOPE

An Autobiography

Ayala's Angel

Barchester Towers

The Belton Estate

The Bertrams

Can You Forgive Her?

The Claverings

Cousin Henry

Doctor Thorne

Doctor Wortle's School

The Duke's Children

Early Short Stories

The Eustace Diamonds

An Eye for an Eye

Framley Parsonage

He Knew He Was Right

Lady Anna

The Last Chronicle of Barset

Later Short Stories

Miss Mackenzie

Mr Scarborough's Family

Orley Farm

Phineas Finn

Phineas Redux

The Prime Minister

Rachel Ray

The Small House at Allington

La Vendée

The Warden

The Way We Live Now

THE OXFORD SHERLOCK HOLMES

ARTHUR CONAN DOYLE

The Adventures of Sherlock Holmes

The Case-Book of Sherlock Holmes

His Last Bow

The Hound of the Baskervilles

The Memoirs of Sherlock Holmes

The Return of Sherlock Holmes

The Valley of Fear

Sherlock Holmes Stories

The Sign of the Four

A Study in Scarlet

SERGEI AKSAKOV — **A Russian Gentleman**

ANTON CHEKHOV — **Early Stories**
Five Plays
The Princess and Other Stories
The Russian Master and Other Stories
The Steppe and Other Stories
Twelve Plays
Ward Number Six and Other Stories
A Woman's Kingdom and Other Stories

FYODOR DOSTOEVSKY — **An Accidental Family**
Crime and Punishment
Devils
A Gentle Creature and Other Stories
The Idiot
The Karamazov Brothers
Memoirs from the House of the Dead
Notes from the Underground and
The Gambler

NIKOLAI GOGOL — **Village Evenings Near Dikanka and**
Mirgorod
Plays and Petersburg

ALEXANDER HERZEN — **Childhood, Youth, and Exile**

MIKHAIL LERMONTOV — **A Hero of our Time**

ALEXANDER PUSHKIN — **Eugene Onegin**
The Queen of Spades and Other Stories

LEO TOLSTOY — **Anna Karenina**
The Kreutzer Sonata and Other Stories
The Raid and Other Stories
Resurrection
War and Peace

IVAN TURGENEV — **Fathers and Sons**
First Love and Other Stories
A Month in the Country

The
Oxford
World's
Classics
Website

www.worldsclassics.co.uk

- Information about new titles
- Explore the full range of Oxford World's Classics
- Links to other literary sites and the main OUP webpage
- Imaginative competitions, with bookish prizes
- Peruse *Compass*, the Oxford World's Classics magazine
- Articles by editors
- Extracts from Introductions
- A forum for discussion and feedback on the series
- Special information for teachers and lecturers

www.worldsclassics.co.uk

American Literature

British and Irish Literature

Children's Literature

Classics and Ancient Literature

Colonial Literature

Eastern Literature

European Literature

History

Medieval Literature

Oxford English Drama

Poetry

Philosophy

Politics

Religion

The Oxford Shakespeare

A complete list of Oxford Paperbacks, including Oxford World's Classics, OPUS, Past Masters, Oxford Authors, Oxford Shakespeare, Oxford Drama, and Oxford Paperback Reference, is available in the UK from the Academic Division Publicity Department, Oxford University Press, Great Clarendon Street, Oxford OX2 6DP.

In the USA, complete lists are available from the Paperbacks Marketing Manager, Oxford University Press, 198 Madison Avenue, New York, NY 10016.

Oxford Paperbacks are available from all good bookshops. In case of difficulty, customers in the UK can order direct from Oxford University Press Bookshop, Freepost, 116 High Street, Oxford OX1 4BR, enclosing full payment. Please add 10 per cent of published price for postage and packing.